IT'S A BIG WORLD, CHARLIE BROWN

BY CHARLES M. SCHULZ

Ballantine Books * New York

A Ballantine Book
Published by The Ballantine Publishing Group
Copyright © 2001 by United Feature Syndicate, Inc.

www.randomhouse.com/BB/
www.snoopy.com

A Library of Congress card number is available from the publisher upon request.

ISBN 0-345-44270-9

Cover design by Paige Braddock, Charles M. Schulz Creative Associates

Manufactured in the United States of America

First Edition: September 2001

10 9 8 7 6 5 4 3 2 1

It's a Big World, Charlie Brown

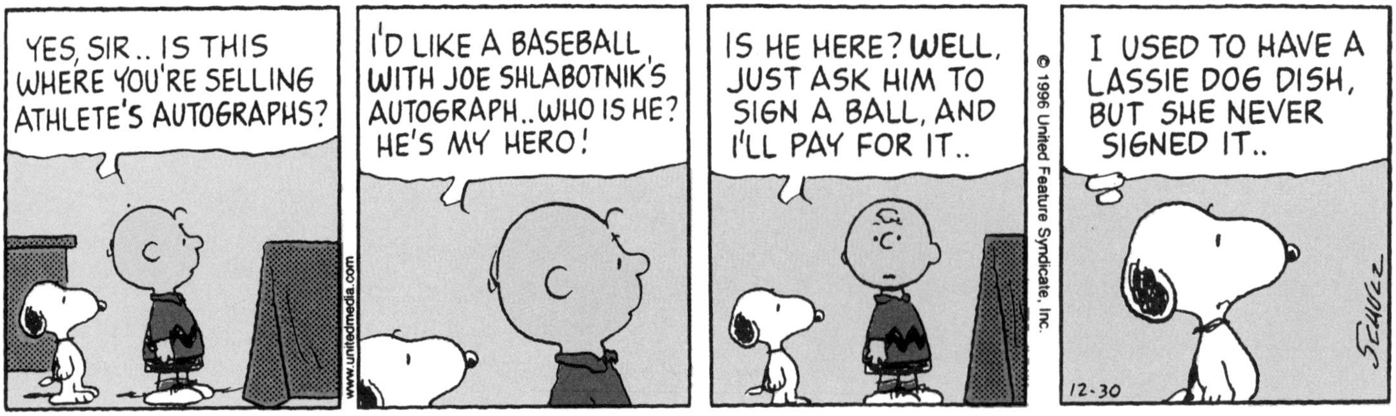
YES, SIR.. IS THIS WHERE YOU'RE SELLING ATHLETE'S AUTOGRAPHS?
I'D LIKE A BASEBALL WITH JOE SHLABOTNIK'S AUTOGRAPH.. WHO IS HE? HE'S MY HERO!
IS HE HERE? WELL, JUST ASK HIM TO SIGN A BALL, AND I'LL PAY FOR IT..
I USED TO HAVE A LASSIE DOG DISH, BUT SHE NEVER SIGNED IT..
www.unitedmedia.com
© 1996 United Feature Syndicate, Inc.
12-30

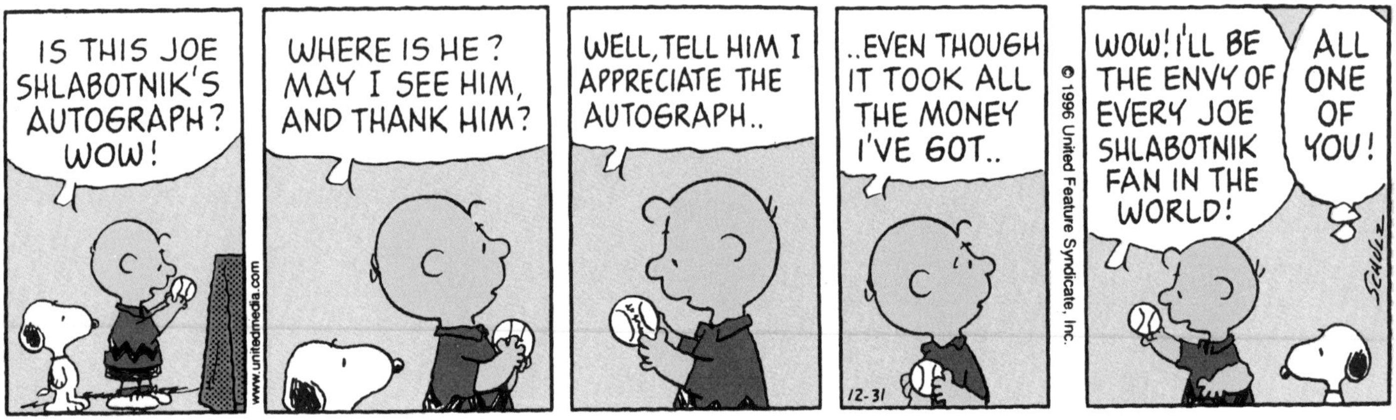
IS THIS JOE SHLABOTNIK'S AUTOGRAPH? WOW!
WHERE IS HE? MAY I SEE HIM, AND THANK HIM?
WELL, TELL HIM I APPRECIATE THE AUTOGRAPH..
..EVEN THOUGH IT TOOK ALL THE MONEY I'VE GOT..
WOW! I'LL BE THE ENVY OF EVERY JOE SHLABOTNIK FAN IN THE WORLD!
ALL ONE OF YOU!
www.unitedmedia.com
© 1996 United Feature Syndicate, Inc.
12-31

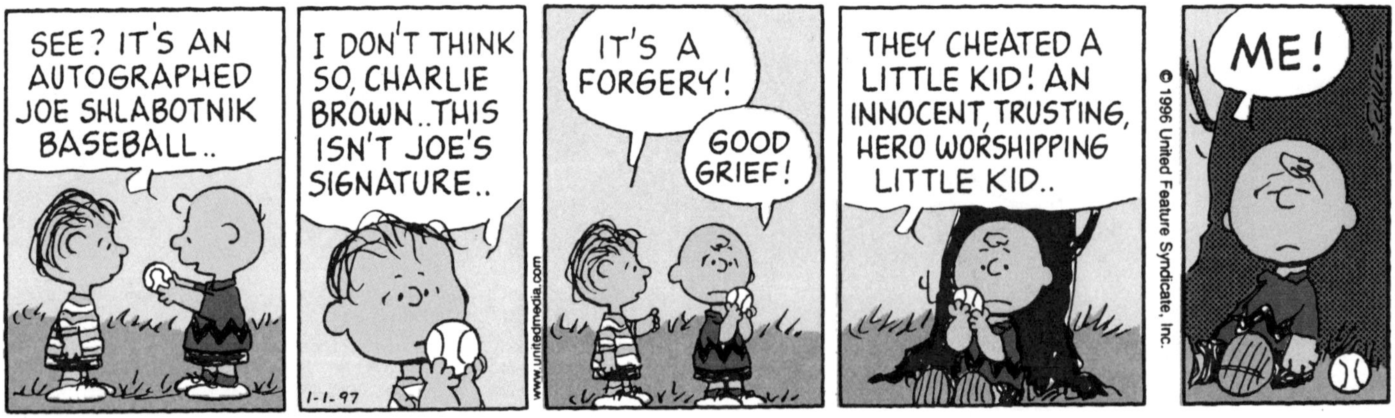
SEE? IT'S AN AUTOGRAPHED JOE SHLABOTNIK BASEBALL..
I DON'T THINK SO, CHARLIE BROWN..THIS ISN'T JOE'S SIGNATURE..
IT'S A FORGERY!
GOOD GRIEF!
THEY CHEATED A LITTLE KID! AN INNOCENT, TRUSTING, HERO WORSHIPPING LITTLE KID..
ME!
www.unitedmedia.com
© 1996 United Feature Syndicate, Inc.
1-1-97

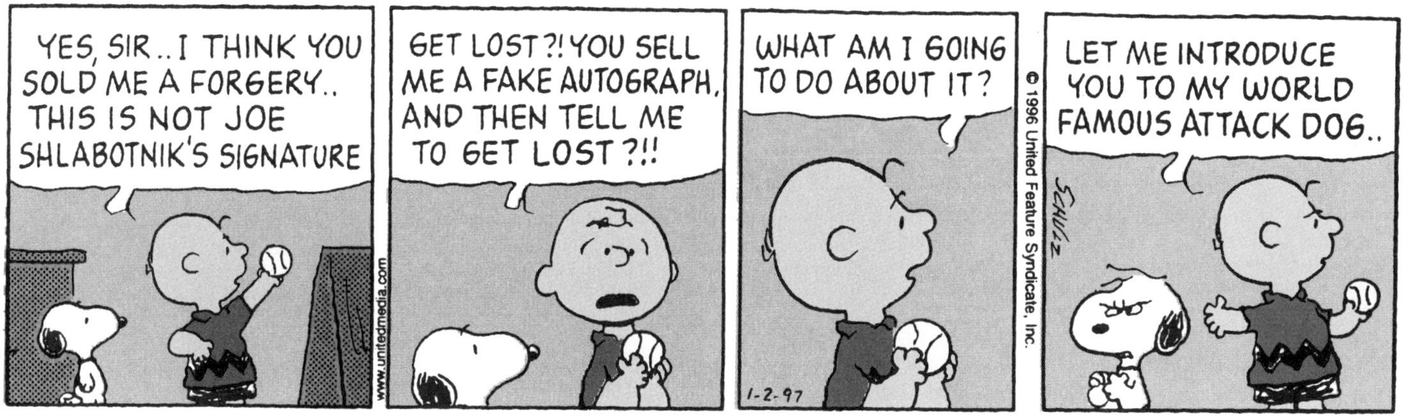
YES, SIR.. I THINK YOU SOLD ME A FORGERY.. THIS IS NOT JOE SHLABOTNIK'S SIGNATURE
GET LOST?! YOU SELL ME A FAKE AUTOGRAPH, AND THEN TELL ME TO GET LOST?!!
WHAT AM I GOING TO DO ABOUT IT?
LET ME INTRODUCE YOU TO MY WORLD FAMOUS ATTACK DOG..
www.unitedmedia.com
1-2-97
© 1996 United Feature Syndicate, Inc.

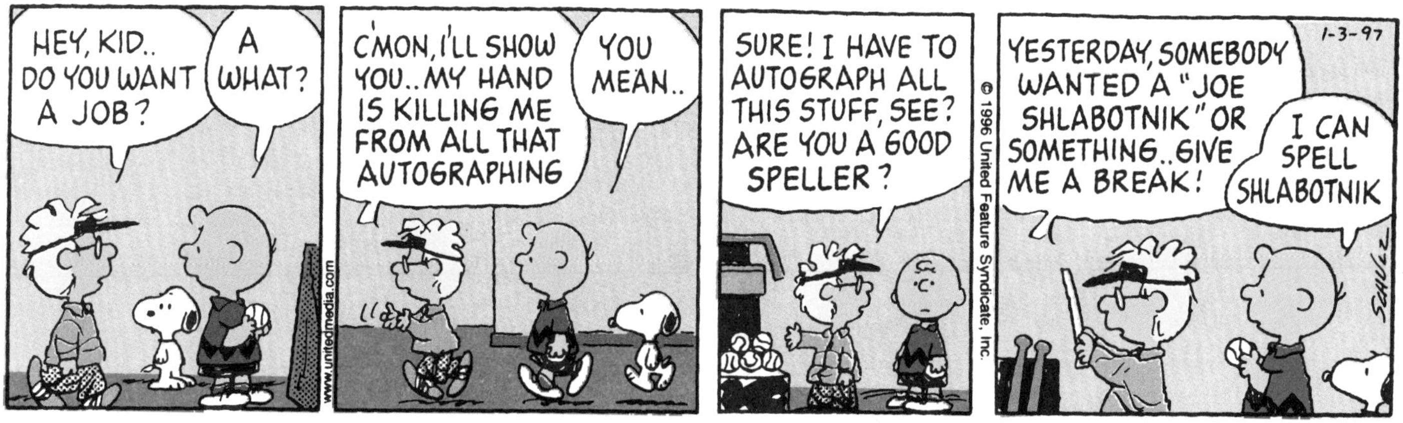
HEY, KID.. DO YOU WANT A JOB?
A WHAT?
C'MON, I'LL SHOW YOU.. MY HAND IS KILLING ME FROM ALL THAT AUTOGRAPHING
YOU MEAN..
SURE! I HAVE TO AUTOGRAPH ALL THIS STUFF, SEE? ARE YOU A GOOD SPELLER?
YESTERDAY, SOMEBODY WANTED A "JOE SHLABOTNIK" OR SOMETHING.. GIVE ME A BREAK!
I CAN SPELL SHLABOTNIK
www.unitedmedia.com
© 1996 United Feature Syndicate, Inc.
1-3-97

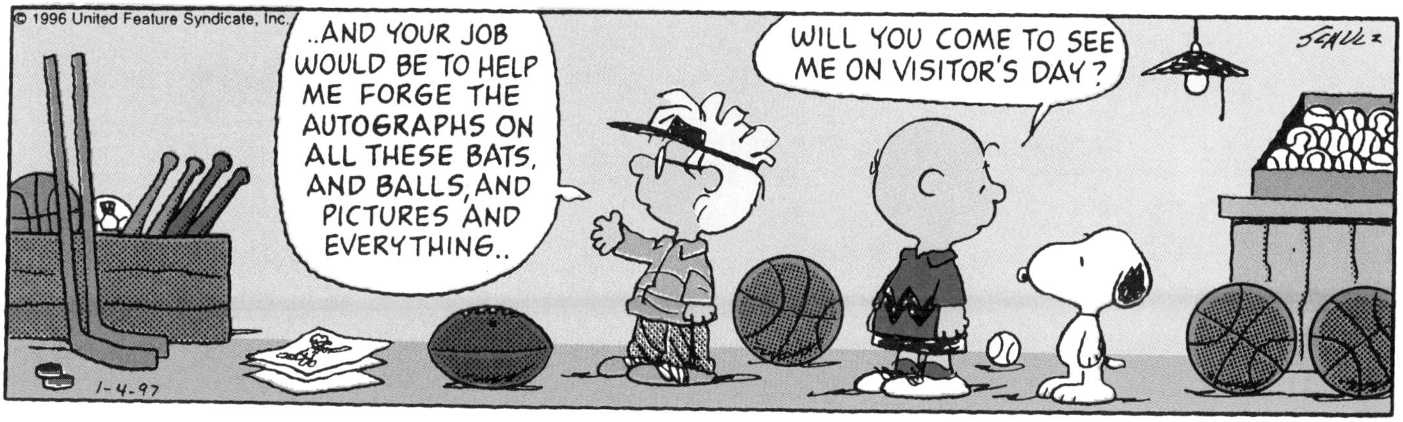
© 1996 United Feature Syndicate, Inc.
..AND YOUR JOB WOULD BE TO HELP ME FORGE THE AUTOGRAPHS ON ALL THESE BATS, AND BALLS, AND PICTURES AND EVERYTHING..
WILL YOU COME TO SEE ME ON VISITOR'S DAY?
1-4-97

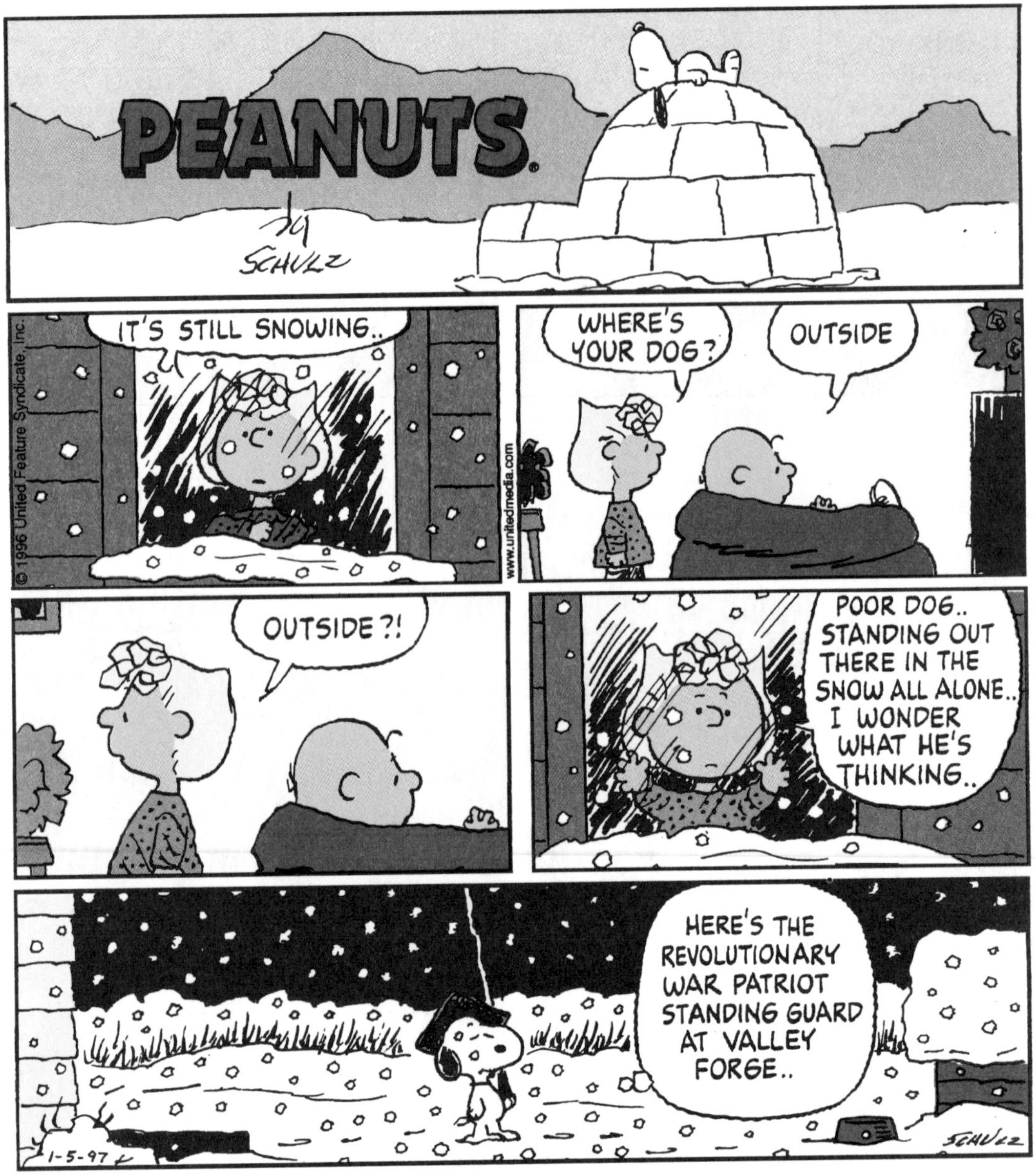
PEANUTS
SCHULZ
© 1996 United Feature Syndicate, Inc.
IT'S STILL SNOWING..
www.unitedmedia.com
WHERE'S YOUR DOG?
OUTSIDE
OUTSIDE?!
POOR DOG.. STANDING OUT THERE IN THE SNOW ALL ALONE.. I WONDER WHAT HE'S THINKING..
HERE'S THE REVOLUTIONARY WAR PATRIOT STANDING GUARD AT VALLEY FORGE..
1-5-97
SCHULZ

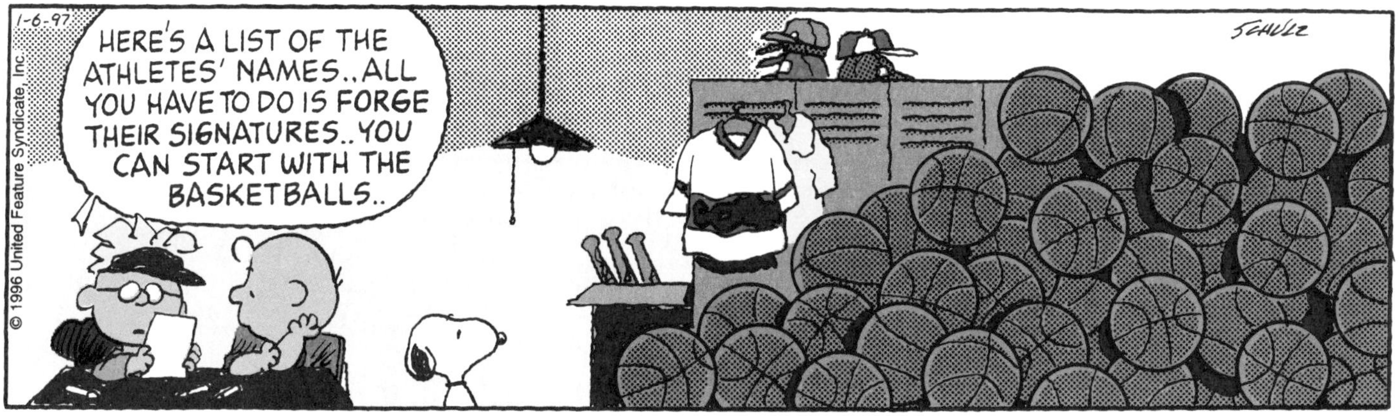
HERE'S A LIST OF THE ATHLETES' NAMES..ALL YOU HAVE TO DO IS FORGE THEIR SIGNATURES..YOU CAN START WITH THE BASKETBALLS..

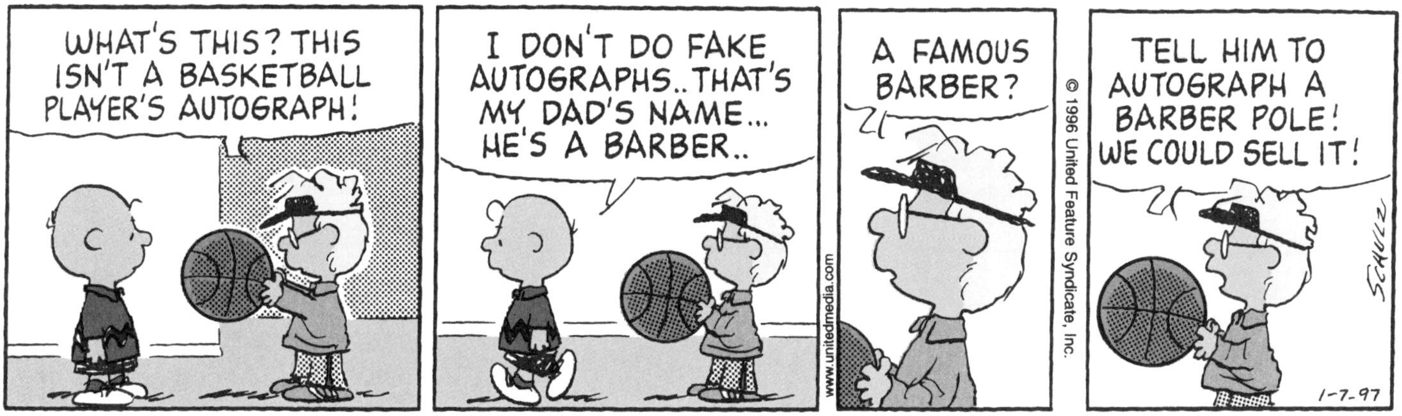
WHAT'S THIS? THIS ISN'T A BASKETBALL PLAYER'S AUTOGRAPH!
I DON'T DO FAKE AUTOGRAPHS..THAT'S MY DAD'S NAME... HE'S A BARBER..
A FAMOUS BARBER?
TELL HIM TO AUTOGRAPH A BARBER POLE! WE COULD SELL IT!

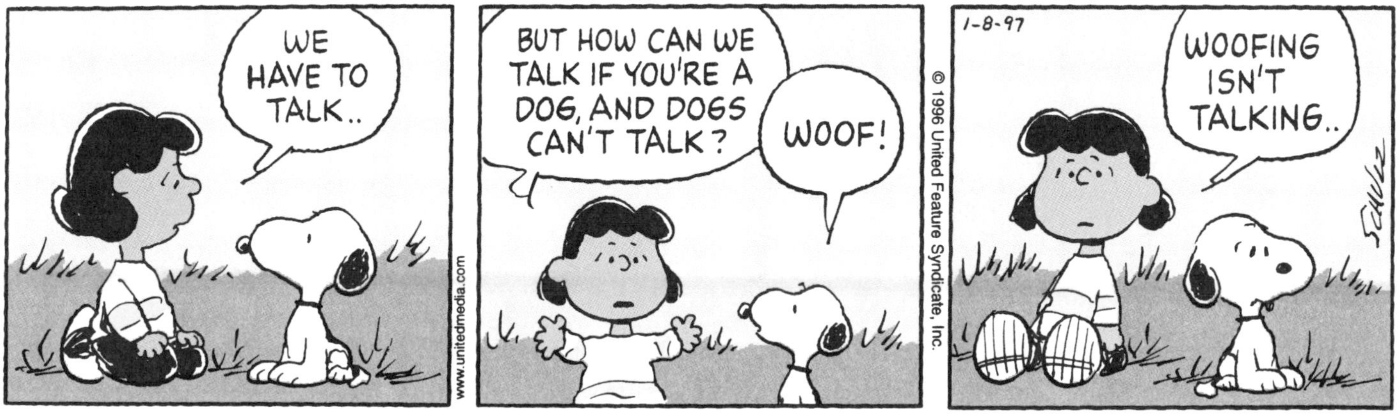
WE HAVE TO TALK..
BUT HOW CAN WE TALK IF YOU'RE A DOG, AND DOGS CAN'T TALK?
WOOF!
WOOFING ISN'T TALKING..

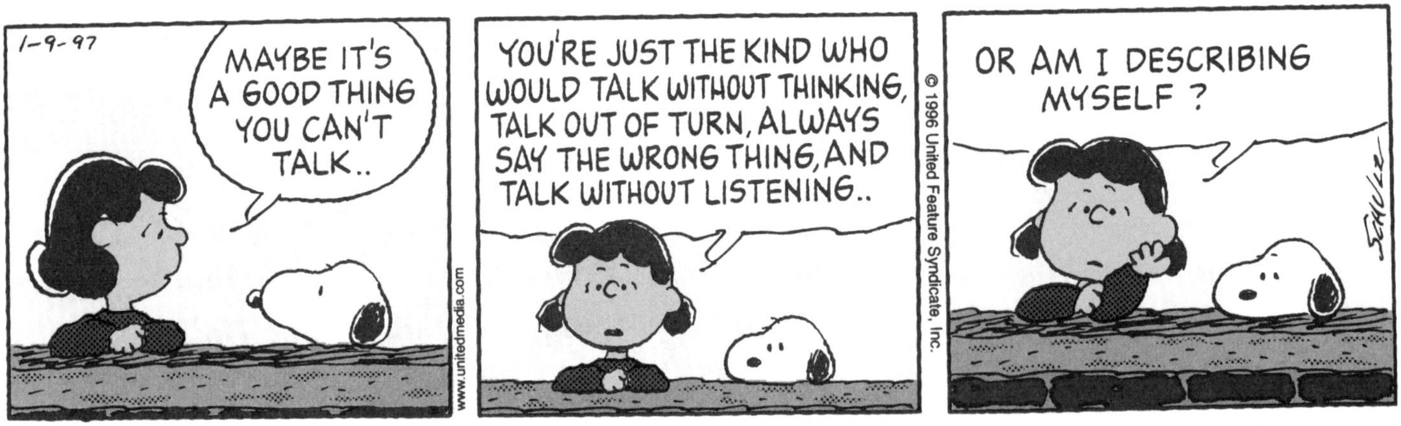
1-9-97
MAYBE IT'S A GOOD THING YOU CAN'T TALK..
YOU'RE JUST THE KIND WHO WOULD TALK WITHOUT THINKING, TALK OUT OF TURN, ALWAYS SAY THE WRONG THING, AND TALK WITHOUT LISTENING..
OR AM I DESCRIBING MYSELF ?
www.unitedmedia.com
© 1996 United Feature Syndicate, Inc.
SCHULZ

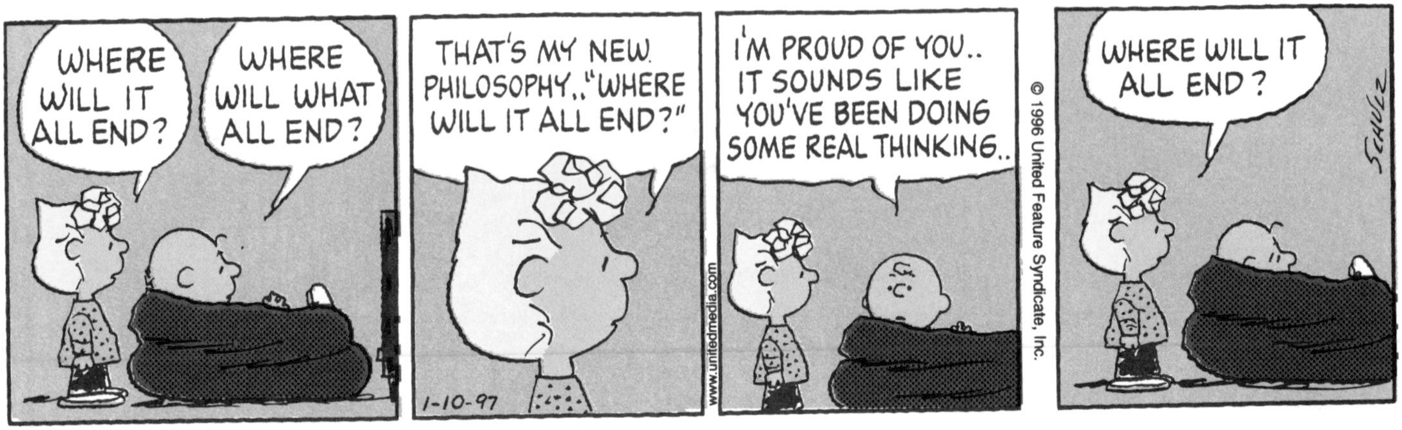
WHERE WILL IT ALL END?
WHERE WILL WHAT ALL END?
THAT'S MY NEW PHILOSOPHY.. "WHERE WILL IT ALL END?"
1-10-97
I'M PROUD OF YOU.. IT SOUNDS LIKE YOU'VE BEEN DOING SOME REAL THINKING..
WHERE WILL IT ALL END?
www.unitedmedia.com
© 1996 United Feature Syndicate, Inc.
SCHULZ

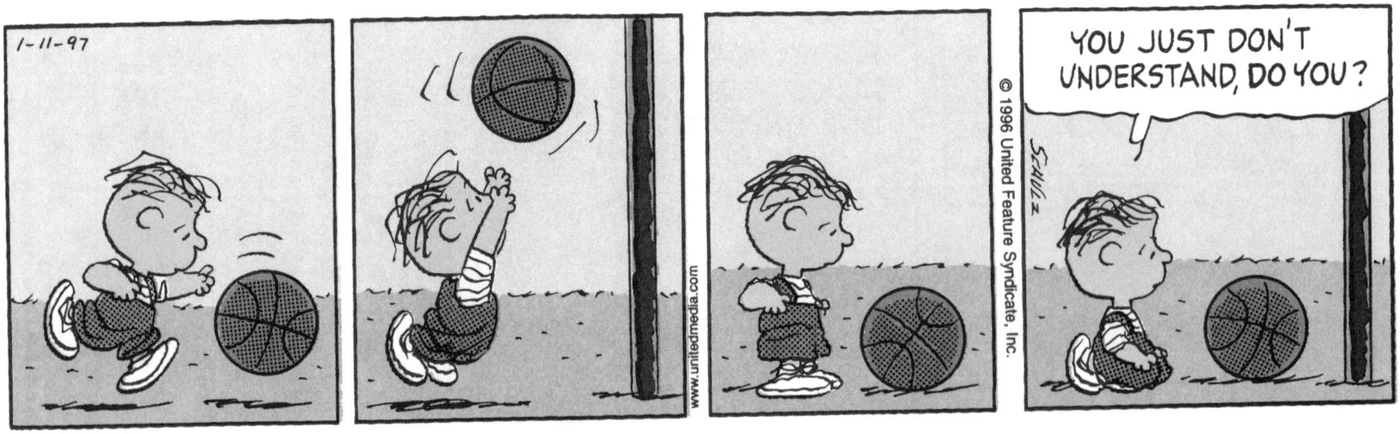
1-11-97
YOU JUST DON'T UNDERSTAND, DO YOU?
www.unitedmedia.com
© 1996 United Feature Syndicate, Inc.
SCHULZ

PEANUTS by SCHULZ

"DEAR MOM, I'VE NEVER BEEN SO COLD IN MY LIFE"

HERE'S THE WORLD FAMOUS REVOLUTIONARY WAR PATRIOT STANDING GUARD AT VALLEY FORGE..

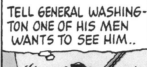

TELL GENERAL WASHINGTON ONE OF HIS MEN WANTS TO SEE HIM..

YES, SIR.. I HAVE A LITTLE SUGGESTION..

YOU MAY OR MAY NOT HAVE NOTICED THAT THERE'S A LOT OF SNOW HERE..

© 1997 United Feature Syndicate, Inc.

1-12

MY IDEA IS WE BUILD A SKATING RINK OUT THERE..WE COULD ORGANIZE A HOCKEY TEAM..

MAYBE EVEN START SOME KIND OF A FIGURE SKATING CLUB..

WE COULD EVEN INVITE SOME OF THE CHICKS FROM TOWN FOR A SKATING PARTY..

I DIDN'T GET A CHANCE TO TELL HIM HE COULD DRIVE THE ZAMBONI..

www.unitedmedia.com

SCHULZ

9

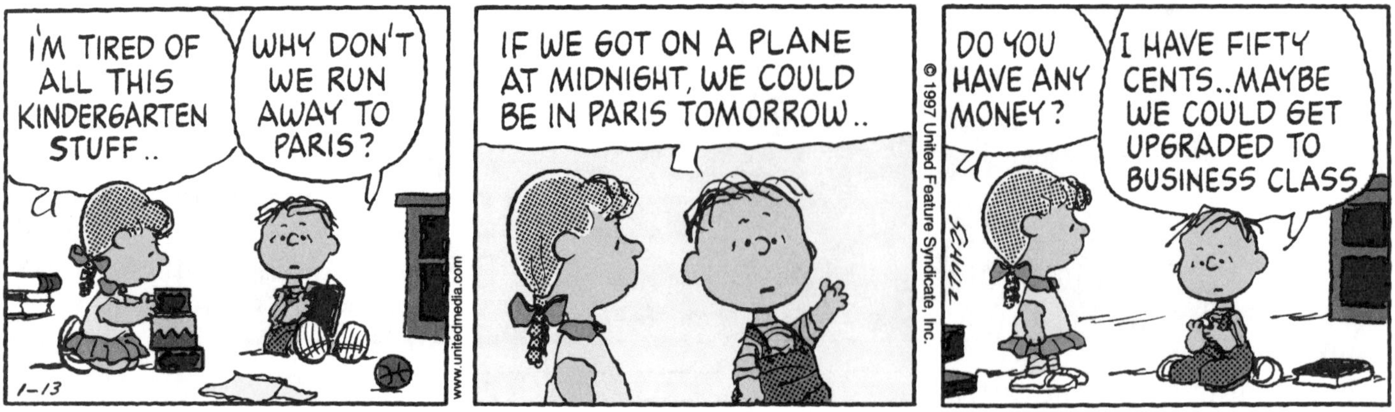
I'M TIRED OF ALL THIS KINDERGARTEN STUFF..
WHY DON'T WE RUN AWAY TO PARIS?
1-13
www.unitedmedia.com
IF WE GOT ON A PLANE AT MIDNIGHT, WE COULD BE IN PARIS TOMORROW..
© 1997 United Feature Syndicate, Inc.
DO YOU HAVE ANY MONEY?
I HAVE FIFTY CENTS..MAYBE WE COULD GET UPGRADED TO BUSINESS CLASS
SCHULZ

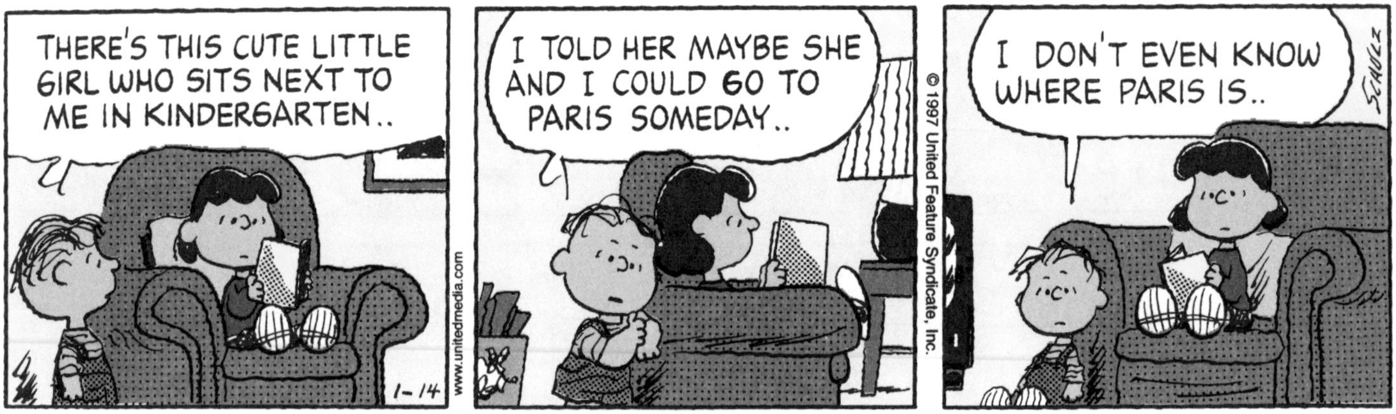
THERE'S THIS CUTE LITTLE GIRL WHO SITS NEXT TO ME IN KINDERGARTEN..
1-14
www.unitedmedia.com
I TOLD HER MAYBE SHE AND I COULD GO TO PARIS SOMEDAY..
© 1997 United Feature Syndicate, Inc.
I DON'T EVEN KNOW WHERE PARIS IS..
SCHULZ

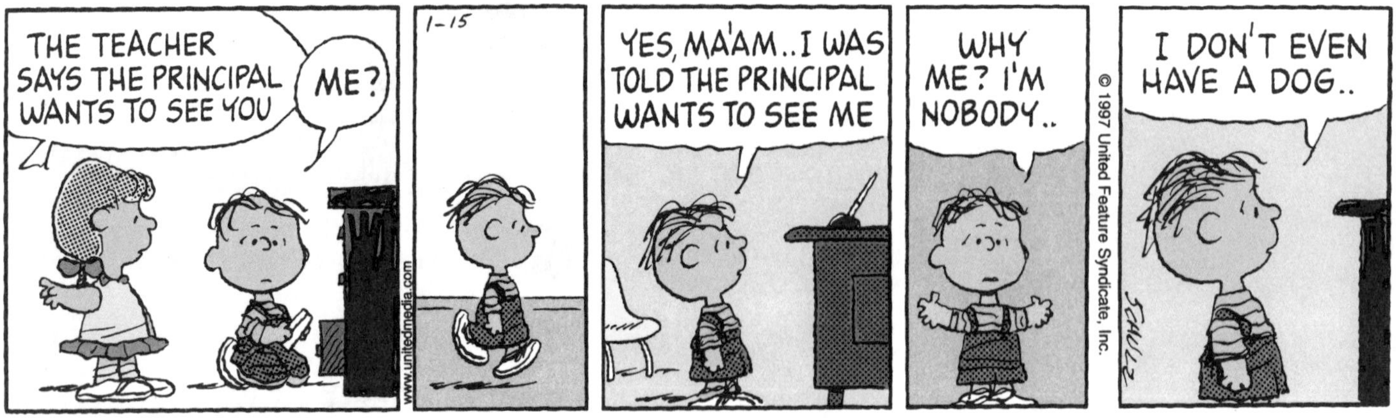
THE TEACHER SAYS THE PRINCIPAL WANTS TO SEE YOU
ME?
www.unitedmedia.com
1-15
YES, MA'AM..I WAS TOLD THE PRINCIPAL WANTS TO SEE ME
WHY ME? I'M NOBODY..
© 1997 United Feature Syndicate, Inc.
I DON'T EVEN HAVE A DOG..
SCHULZ

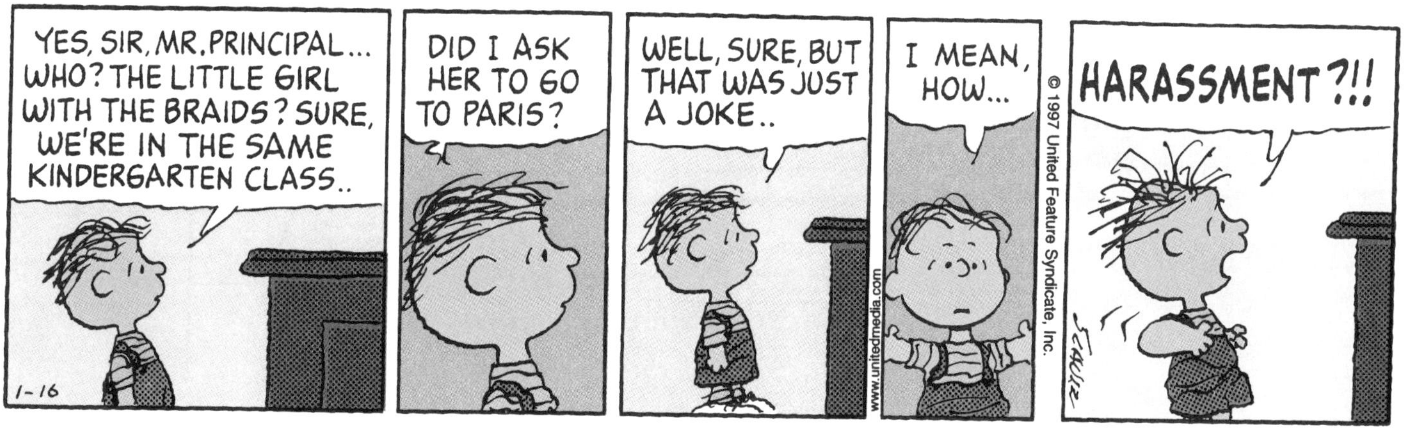
YES, SIR, MR. PRINCIPAL... WHO? THE LITTLE GIRL WITH THE BRAIDS? SURE, WE'RE IN THE SAME KINDERGARTEN CLASS..
1-16
DID I ASK HER TO GO TO PARIS?
WELL, SURE, BUT THAT WAS JUST A JOKE..
www.unitedmedia.com
I MEAN, HOW...
© 1997 United Feature Syndicate, Inc.
HARASSMENT?!!
SCHULZ

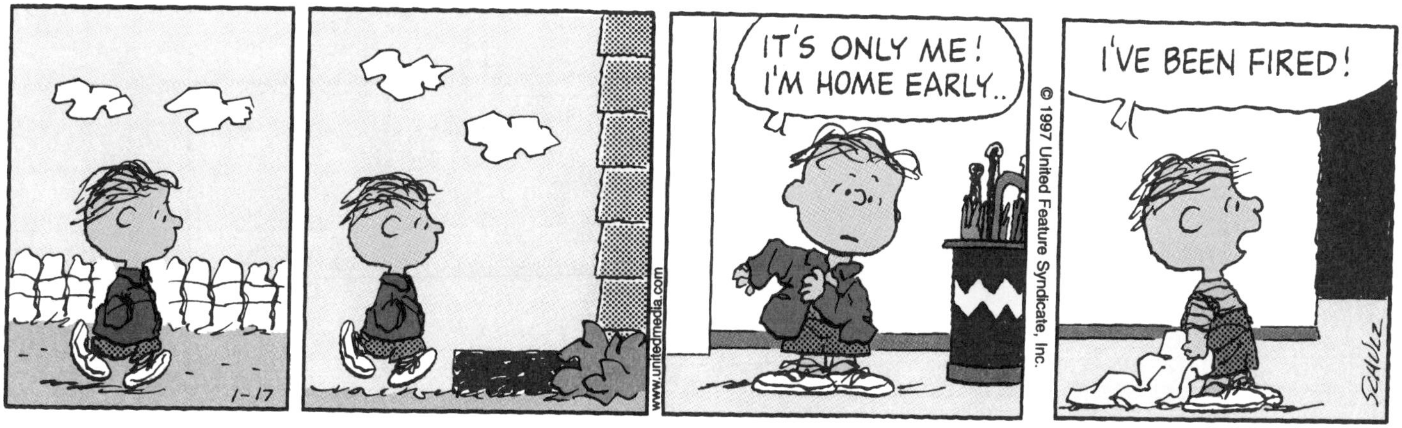
1-17
www.unitedmedia.com
IT'S ONLY ME! I'M HOME EARLY..
© 1997 United Feature Syndicate, Inc.
I'VE BEEN FIRED!
SCHULZ

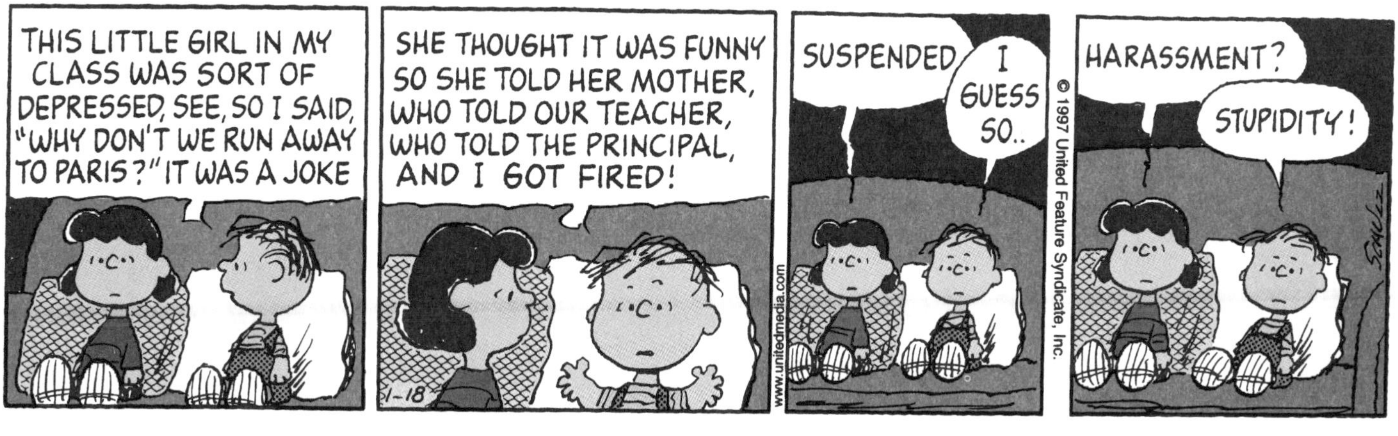
THIS LITTLE GIRL IN MY CLASS WAS SORT OF DEPRESSED, SEE, SO I SAID, "WHY DON'T WE RUN AWAY TO PARIS?" IT WAS A JOKE
SHE THOUGHT IT WAS FUNNY SO SHE TOLD HER MOTHER, WHO TOLD OUR TEACHER, WHO TOLD THE PRINCIPAL, AND I GOT FIRED!
1-18
www.unitedmedia.com
SUSPENDED
I GUESS SO..
© 1997 United Feature Syndicate, Inc.
HARASSMENT?
STUPIDITY!
SCHULZ

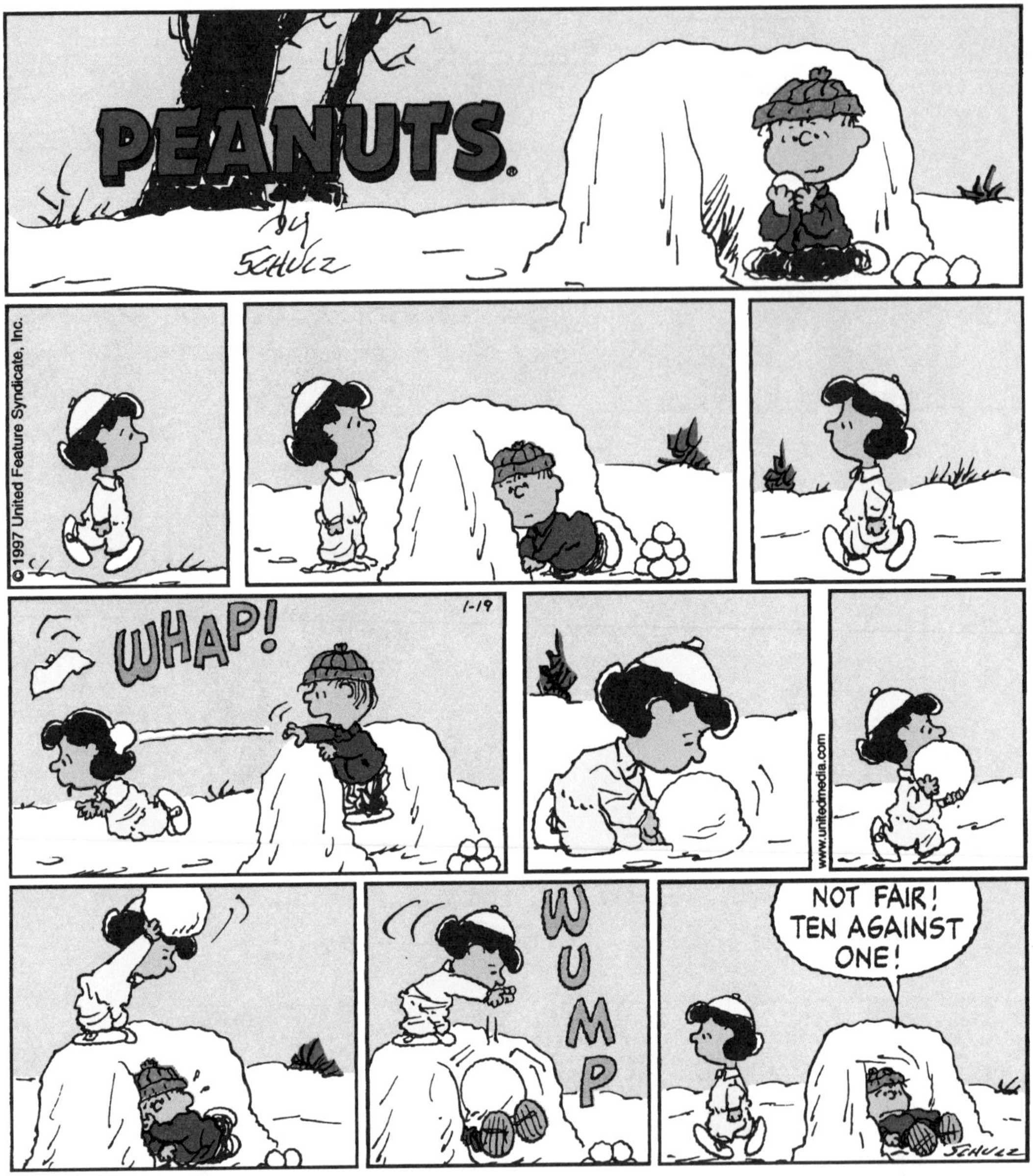
PEANUTS
by SCHULZ
© 1997 United Feature Syndicate, Inc.
1-19
WHAP!
www.unitedmedia.com
WUMP
NOT FAIR! TEN AGAINST ONE!
SCHULZ

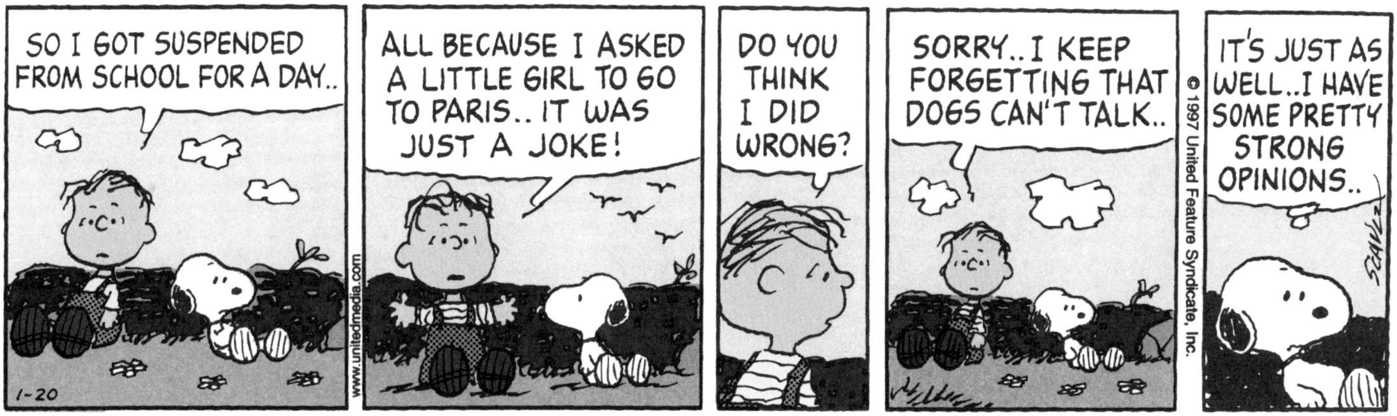
SO I GOT SUSPENDED FROM SCHOOL FOR A DAY..
1-20
www.unitedmedia.com
ALL BECAUSE I ASKED A LITTLE GIRL TO GO TO PARIS.. IT WAS JUST A JOKE!
DO YOU THINK I DID WRONG?
SORRY.. I KEEP FORGETTING THAT DOGS CAN'T TALK..
© 1997 United Feature Syndicate, Inc.
IT'S JUST AS WELL.. I HAVE SOME PRETTY STRONG OPINIONS..
SCHULZ

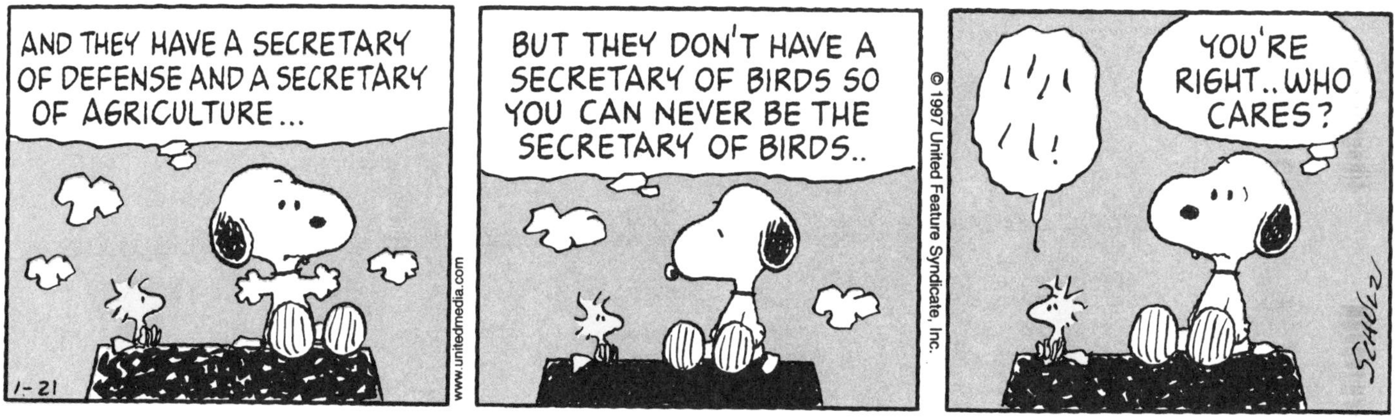
AND THEY HAVE A SECRETARY OF DEFENSE AND A SECRETARY OF AGRICULTURE...
1-21
www.unitedmedia.com
BUT THEY DON'T HAVE A SECRETARY OF BIRDS SO YOU CAN NEVER BE THE SECRETARY OF BIRDS..
© 1997 United Feature Syndicate, Inc.
YOU'RE RIGHT.. WHO CARES?
SCHULZ

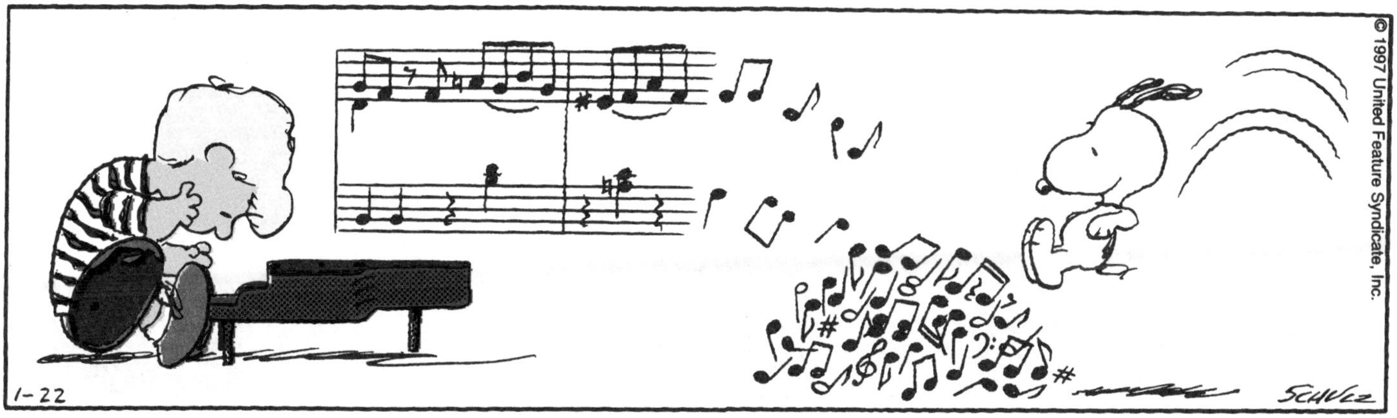
© 1997 United Feature Syndicate, Inc.
1-22
SCHULZ

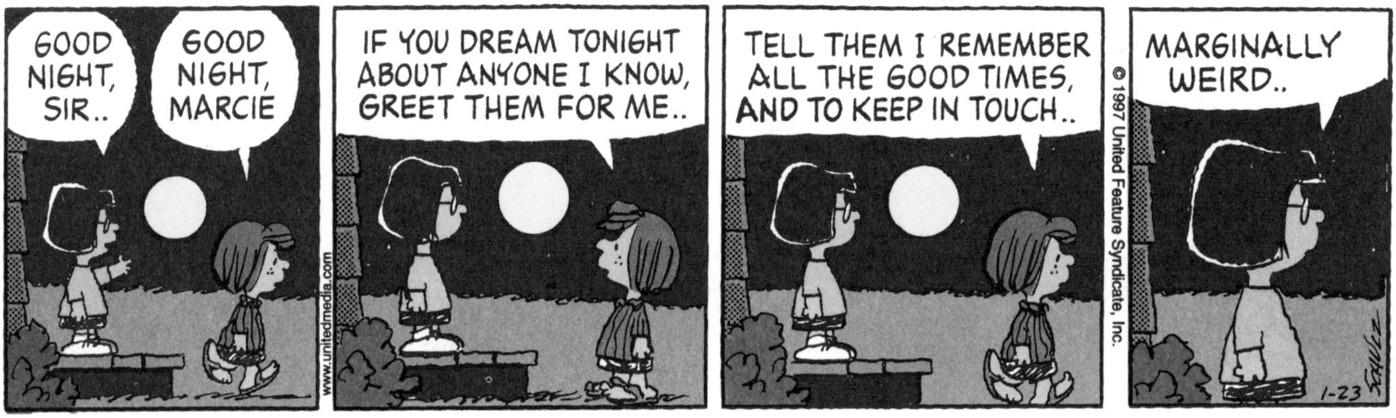
GOOD NIGHT, SIR..
GOOD NIGHT, MARCIE
IF YOU DREAM TONIGHT ABOUT ANYONE I KNOW, GREET THEM FOR ME..
TELL THEM I REMEMBER ALL THE GOOD TIMES, AND TO KEEP IN TOUCH..
MARGINALLY WEIRD..
www.unitedmedia.com
© 1997 United Feature Syndicate, Inc.
1-23

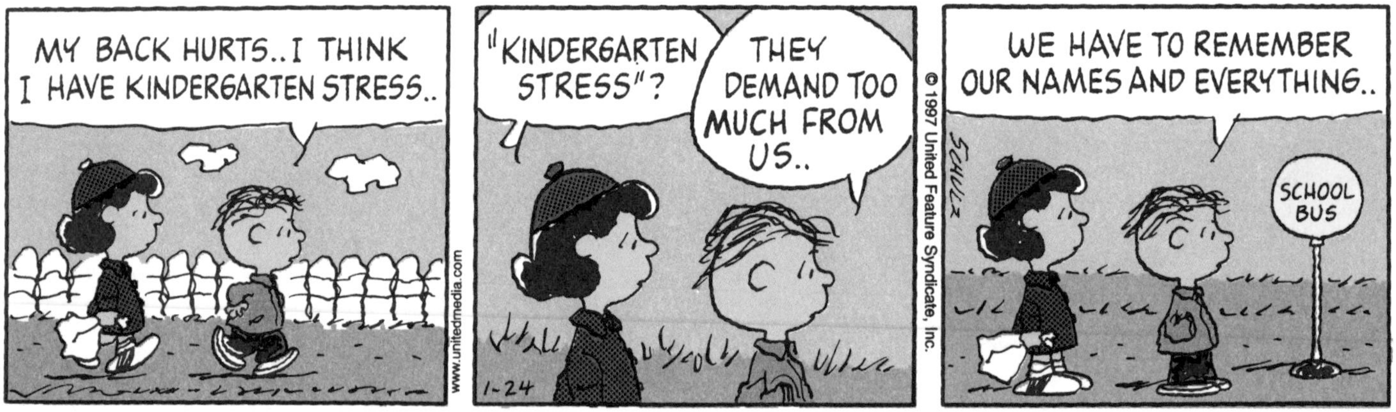
MY BACK HURTS..I THINK I HAVE KINDERGARTEN STRESS..
"KINDERGARTEN STRESS"?
THEY DEMAND TOO MUCH FROM US..
WE HAVE TO REMEMBER OUR NAMES AND EVERYTHING..
SCHOOL BUS
www.unitedmedia.com
© 1997 United Feature Syndicate, Inc.
1-24

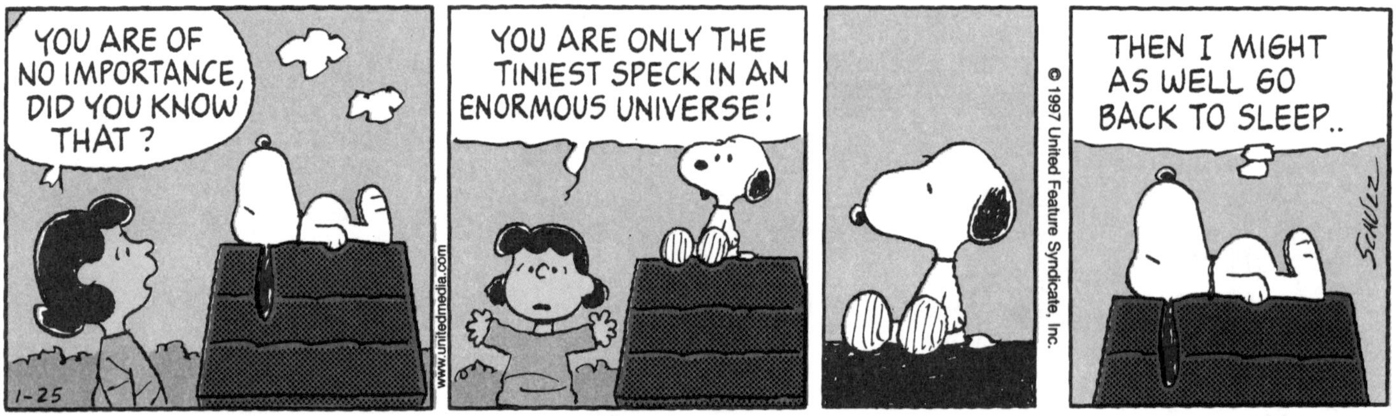
YOU ARE OF NO IMPORTANCE, DID YOU KNOW THAT?
YOU ARE ONLY THE TINIEST SPECK IN AN ENORMOUS UNIVERSE!
THEN I MIGHT AS WELL GO BACK TO SLEEP..
www.unitedmedia.com
© 1997 United Feature Syndicate, Inc.
1-25

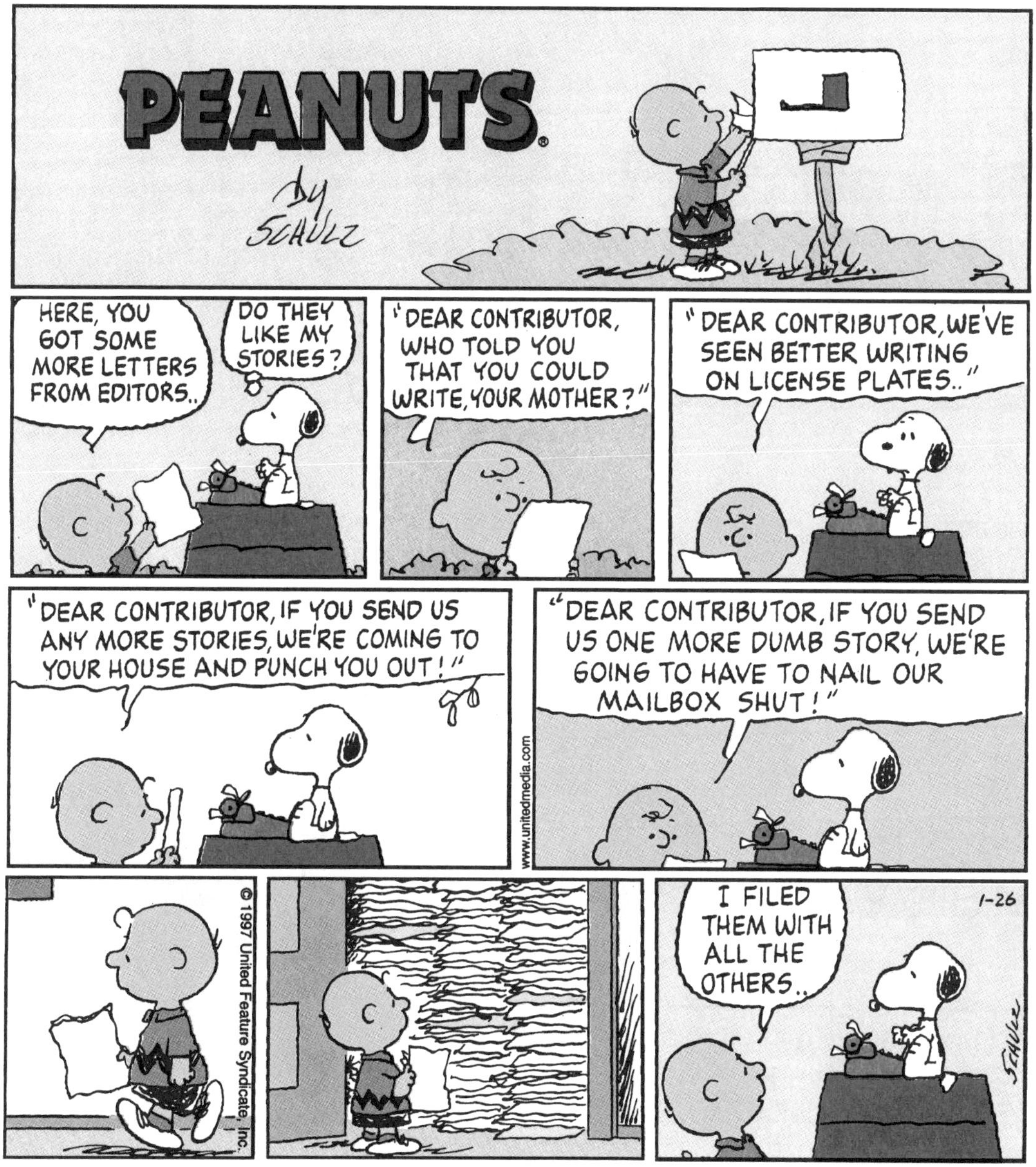
PEANUTS
by SCHULZ
HERE, YOU GOT SOME MORE LETTERS FROM EDITORS..
DO THEY LIKE MY STORIES?
"DEAR CONTRIBUTOR, WHO TOLD YOU THAT YOU COULD WRITE, YOUR MOTHER?"
"DEAR CONTRIBUTOR, WE'VE SEEN BETTER WRITING ON LICENSE PLATES.."
"DEAR CONTRIBUTOR, IF YOU SEND US ANY MORE STORIES, WE'RE COMING TO YOUR HOUSE AND PUNCH YOU OUT!"
www.unitedmedia.com
"DEAR CONTRIBUTOR, IF YOU SEND US ONE MORE DUMB STORY, WE'RE GOING TO HAVE TO NAIL OUR MAILBOX SHUT!"
© 1997 United Feature Syndicate, Inc.
1-26
I FILED THEM WITH ALL THE OTHERS..
SCHULZ

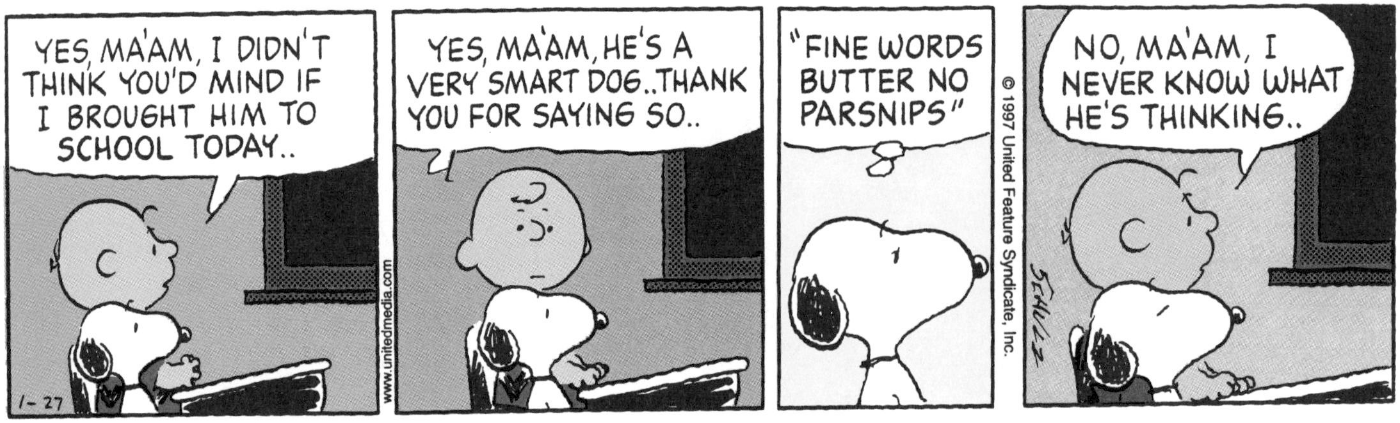
YES, MA'AM, I DIDN'T THINK YOU'D MIND IF I BROUGHT HIM TO SCHOOL TODAY..
1-27
www.unitedmedia.com
YES, MA'AM, HE'S A VERY SMART DOG..THANK YOU FOR SAYING SO..
"FINE WORDS BUTTER NO PARSNIPS"
© 1997 United Feature Syndicate, Inc.
NO, MA'AM, I NEVER KNOW WHAT HE'S THINKING..

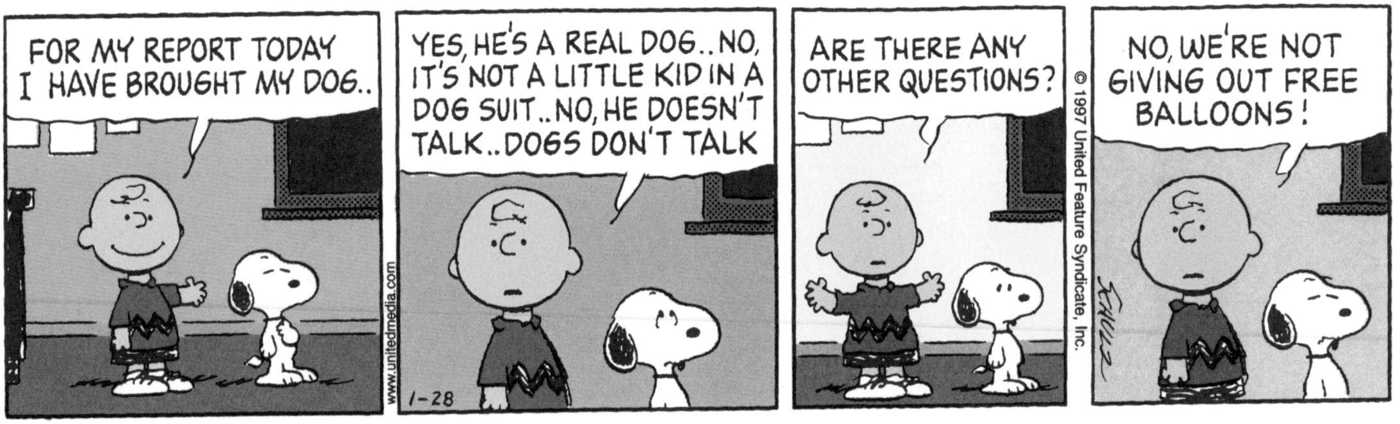
FOR MY REPORT TODAY I HAVE BROUGHT MY DOG..
www.unitedmedia.com
YES, HE'S A REAL DOG..NO, IT'S NOT A LITTLE KID IN A DOG SUIT..NO, HE DOESN'T TALK..DOGS DON'T TALK
1-28
ARE THERE ANY OTHER QUESTIONS?
© 1997 United Feature Syndicate, Inc.
NO, WE'RE NOT GIVING OUT FREE BALLOONS!

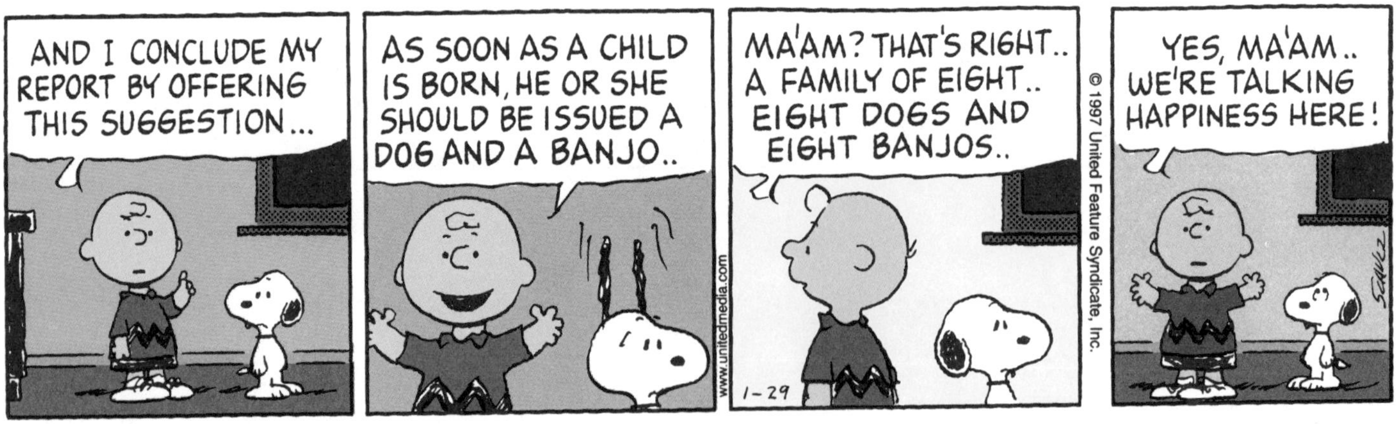
AND I CONCLUDE MY REPORT BY OFFERING THIS SUGGESTION...
AS SOON AS A CHILD IS BORN, HE OR SHE SHOULD BE ISSUED A DOG AND A BANJO..
www.unitedmedia.com
MA'AM? THAT'S RIGHT.. A FAMILY OF EIGHT.. EIGHT DOGS AND EIGHT BANJOS..
1-29
© 1997 United Feature Syndicate, Inc.
YES, MA'AM.. WE'RE TALKING HAPPINESS HERE!

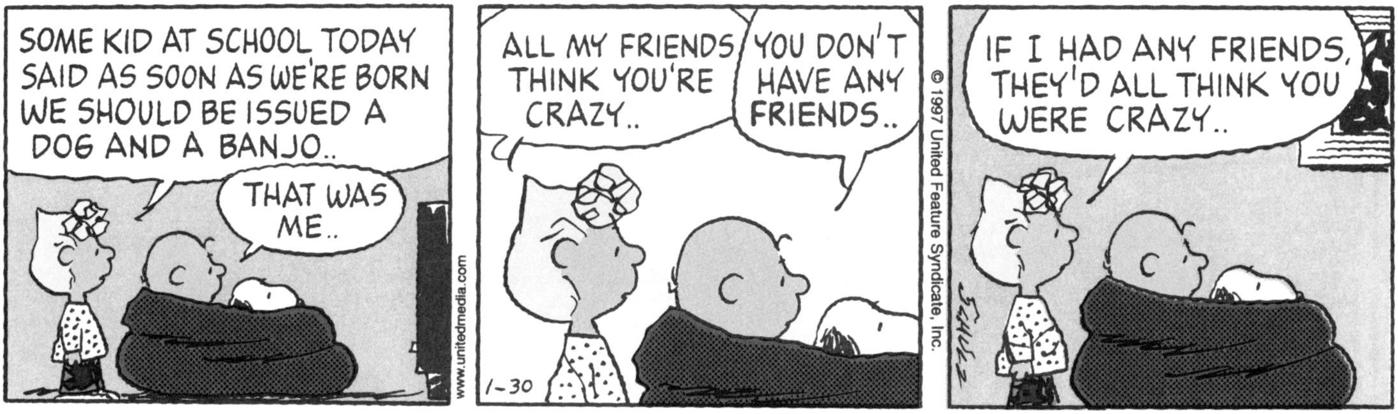
SOME KID AT SCHOOL TODAY SAID AS SOON AS WE'RE BORN WE SHOULD BE ISSUED A DOG AND A BANJO..
THAT WAS ME..
ALL MY FRIENDS THINK YOU'RE CRAZY..
YOU DON'T HAVE ANY FRIENDS..
IF I HAD ANY FRIENDS, THEY'D ALL THINK YOU WERE CRAZY..
www.unitedmedia.com
1-30
© 1997 United Feature Syndicate, Inc.
SCHULZ

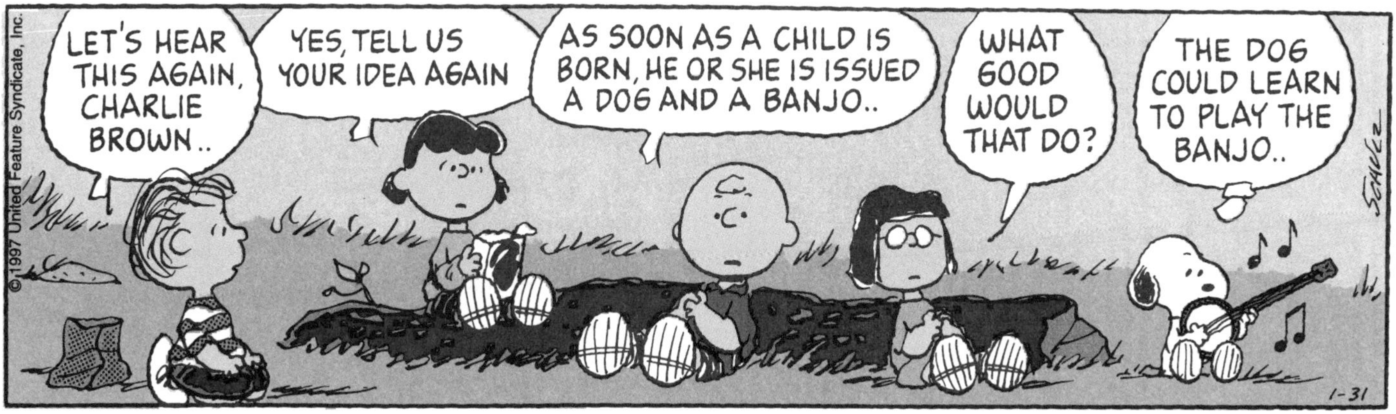
LET'S HEAR THIS AGAIN, CHARLIE BROWN..
YES, TELL US YOUR IDEA AGAIN
AS SOON AS A CHILD IS BORN, HE OR SHE IS ISSUED A DOG AND A BANJO..
WHAT GOOD WOULD THAT DO?
THE DOG COULD LEARN TO PLAY THE BANJO..
© 1997 United Feature Syndicate, Inc.
SCHULZ
1-31

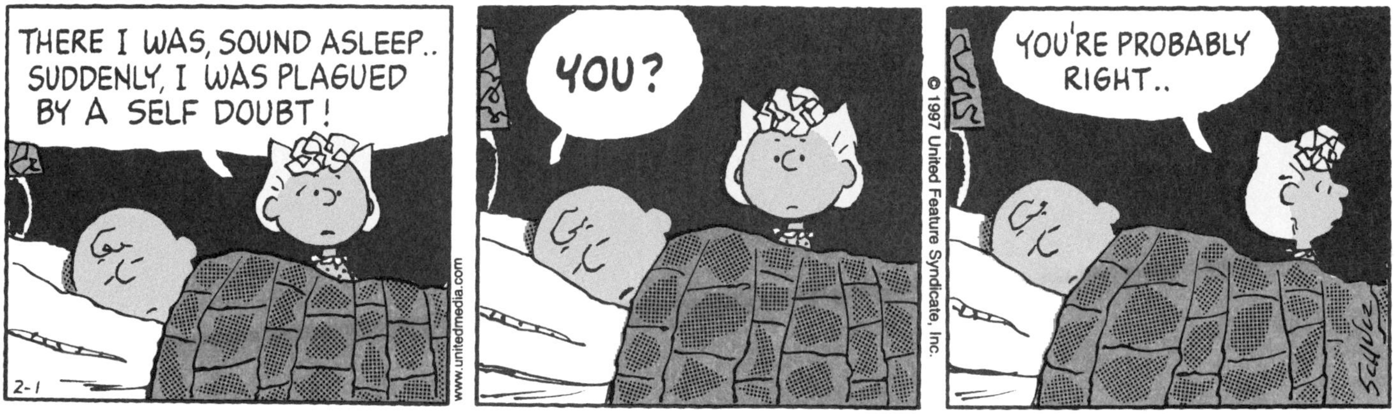
THERE I WAS, SOUND ASLEEP.. SUDDENLY, I WAS PLAGUED BY A SELF DOUBT!
YOU?
YOU'RE PROBABLY RIGHT..
2-1
www.unitedmedia.com
© 1997 United Feature Syndicate, Inc.
SCHULZ

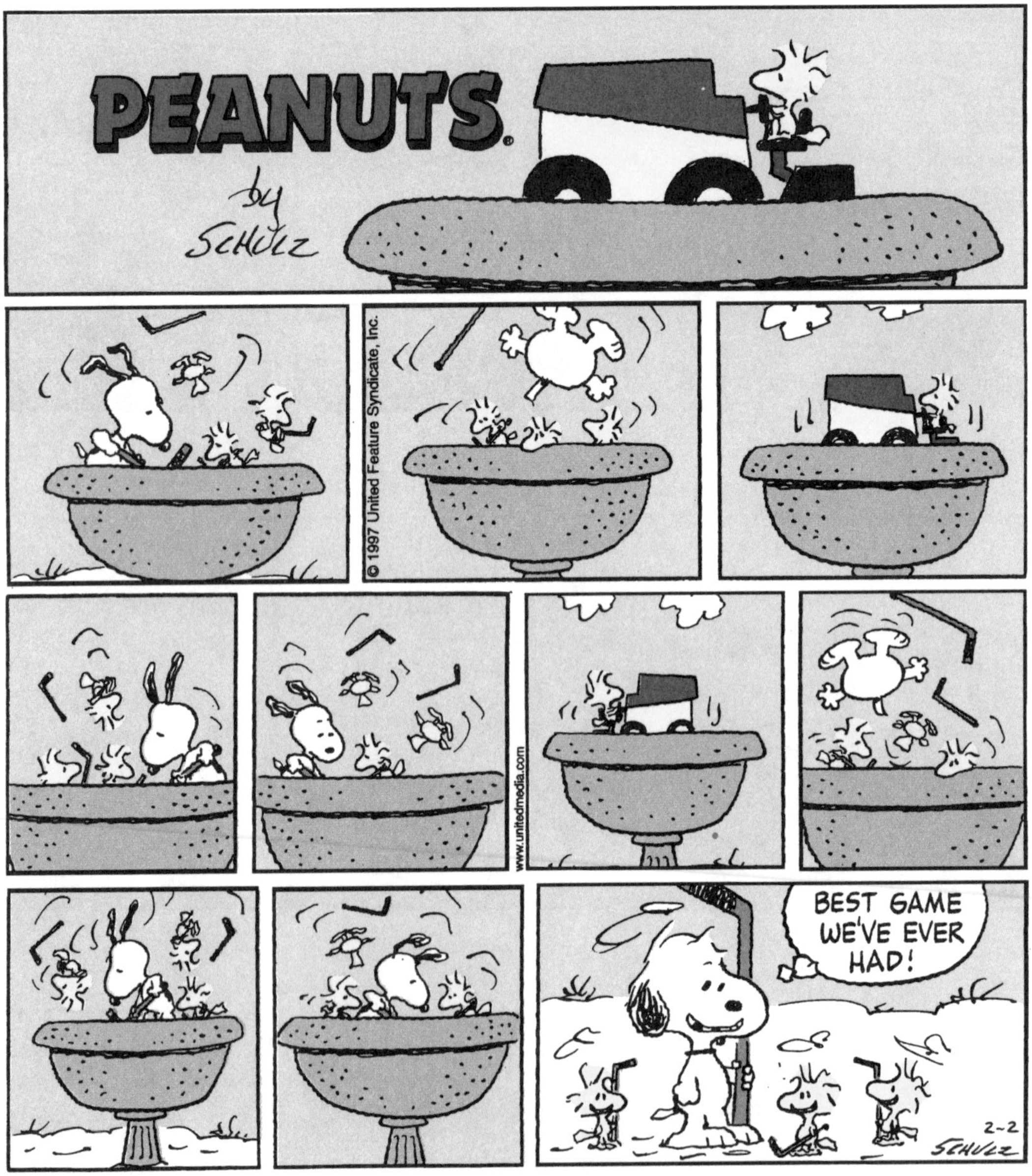
PEANUTS
by SCHULZ
© 1997 United Feature Syndicate, Inc.
www.unitedmedia.com
BEST GAME WE'VE EVER HAD!
2-2
SCHULZ

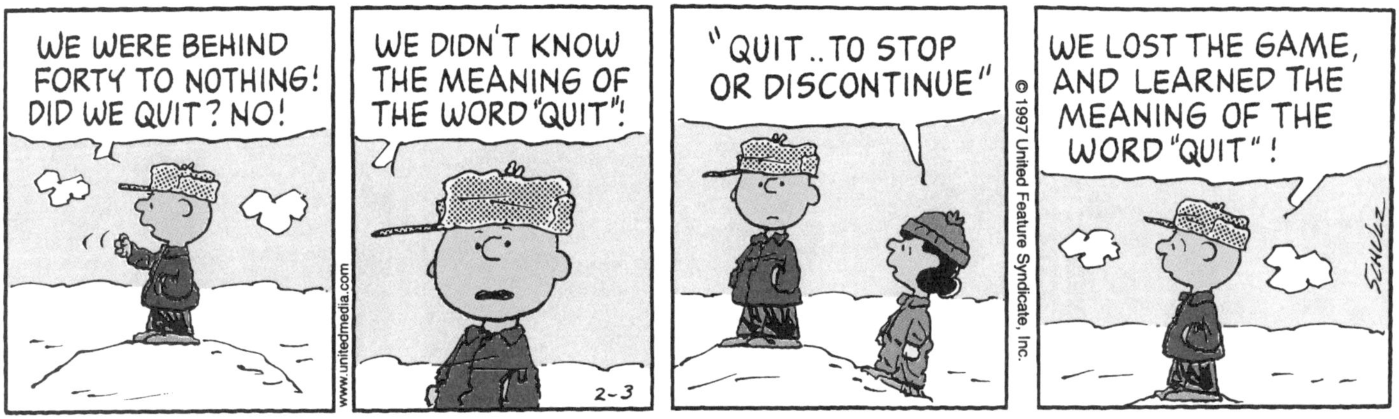
WE WERE BEHIND FORTY TO NOTHING! DID WE QUIT? NO!
www.unitedmedia.com
WE DIDN'T KNOW THE MEANING OF THE WORD "QUIT"!
2-3
"QUIT.. TO STOP OR DISCONTINUE"
© 1997 United Feature Syndicate, Inc.
WE LOST THE GAME, AND LEARNED THE MEANING OF THE WORD "QUIT"!
SCHULZ

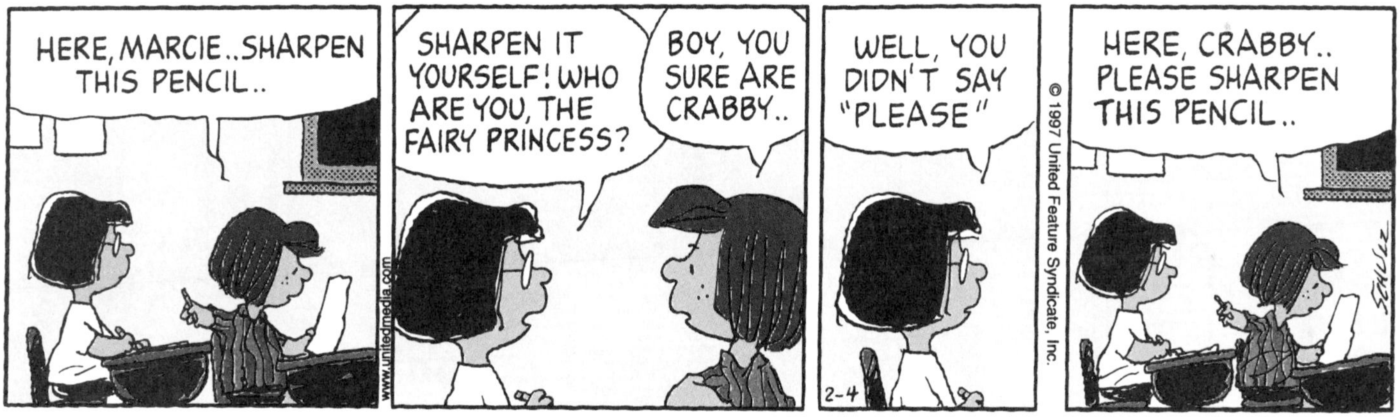
HERE, MARCIE.. SHARPEN THIS PENCIL..
www.unitedmedia.com
SHARPEN IT YOURSELF! WHO ARE YOU, THE FAIRY PRINCESS?
BOY, YOU SURE ARE CRABBY..
WELL, YOU DIDN'T SAY "PLEASE"
2-4
© 1997 United Feature Syndicate, Inc.
HERE, CRABBY.. PLEASE SHARPEN THIS PENCIL..
SCHULZ

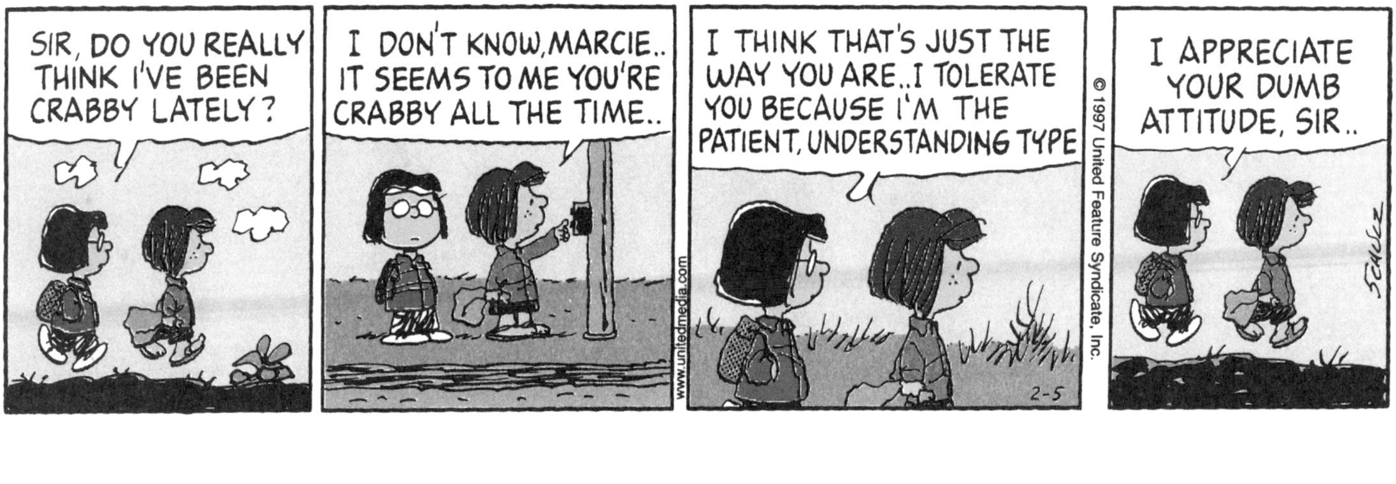
SIR, DO YOU REALLY THINK I'VE BEEN CRABBY LATELY?
I DON'T KNOW, MARCIE.. IT SEEMS TO ME YOU'RE CRABBY ALL THE TIME..
www.unitedmedia.com
I THINK THAT'S JUST THE WAY YOU ARE.. I TOLERATE YOU BECAUSE I'M THE PATIENT, UNDERSTANDING TYPE
2-5
© 1997 United Feature Syndicate, Inc.
I APPRECIATE YOUR DUMB ATTITUDE, SIR..
SCHULZ

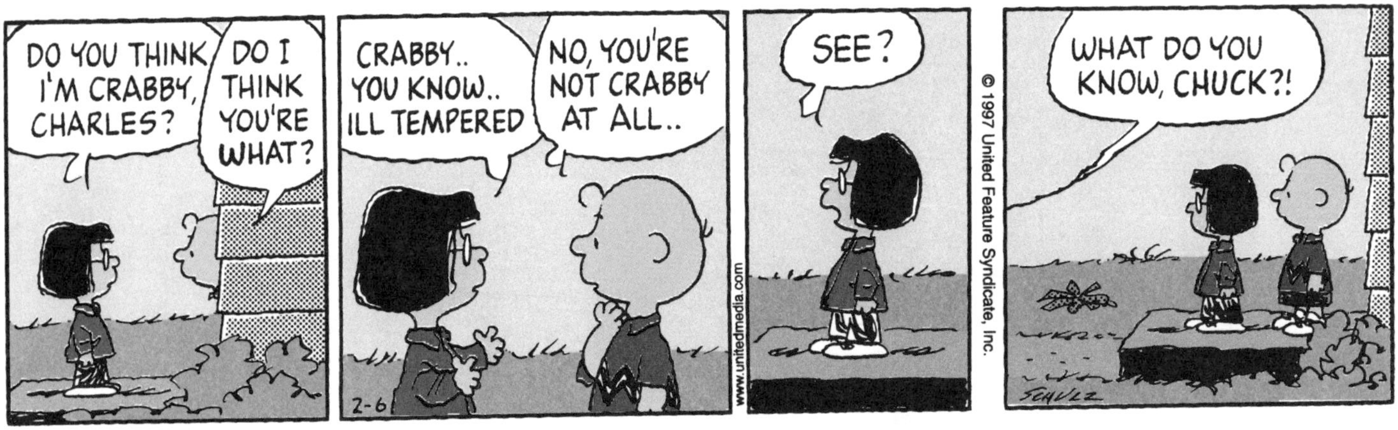
DO YOU THINK I'M CRABBY, CHARLES?
DO I THINK YOU'RE WHAT?
CRABBY.. YOU KNOW.. ILL TEMPERED
NO, YOU'RE NOT CRABBY AT ALL..
SEE?
WHAT DO YOU KNOW, CHUCK?!
2-6
www.unitedmedia.com
© 1997 United Feature Syndicate, Inc.
SCHULZ

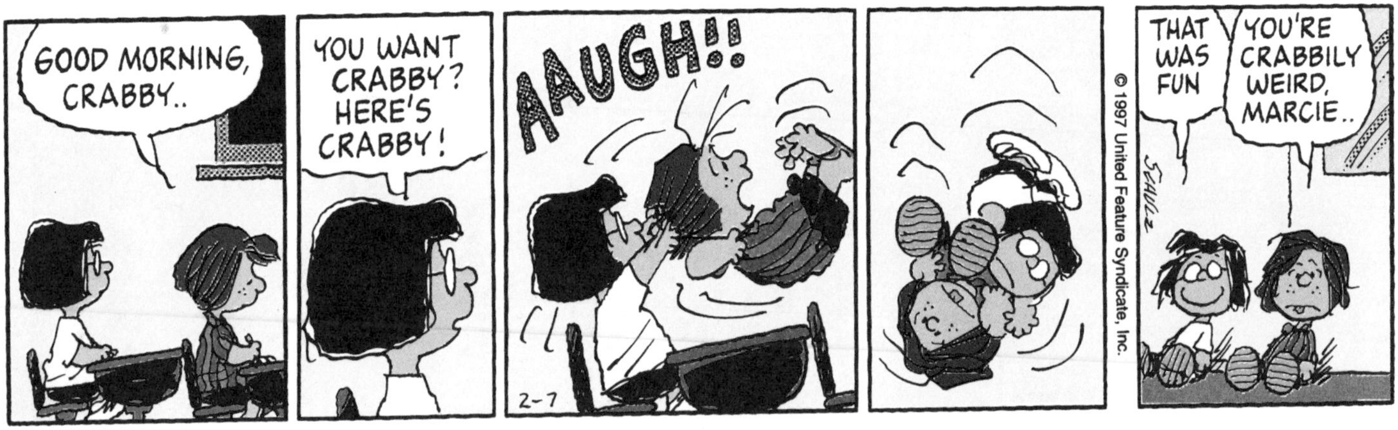
GOOD MORNING, CRABBY..
YOU WANT CRABBY? HERE'S CRABBY!
AAUGH!!
2-7
THAT WAS FUN
YOU'RE CRABBILY WEIRD, MARCIE..
© 1997 United Feature Syndicate, Inc.
SCHULZ

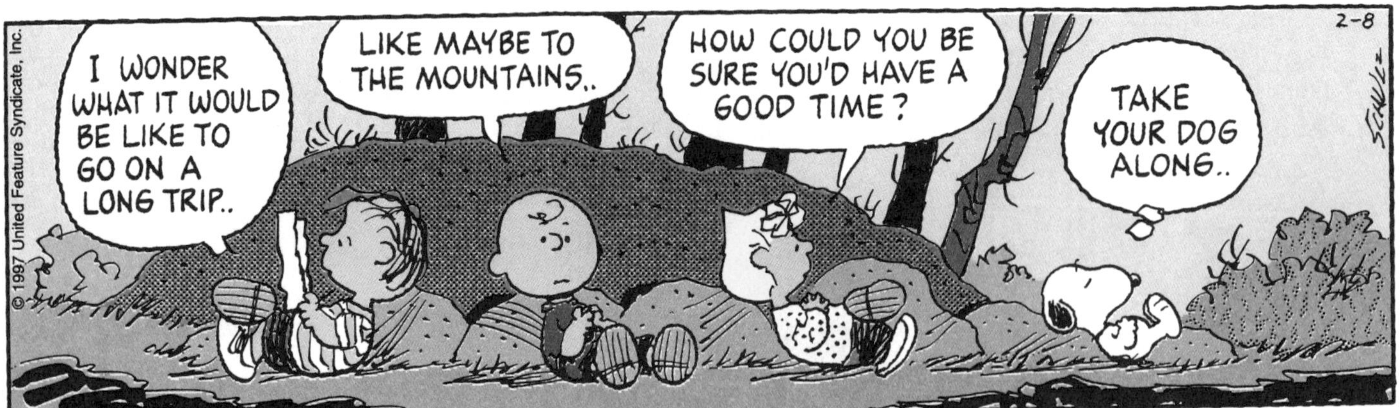
I WONDER WHAT IT WOULD BE LIKE TO GO ON A LONG TRIP..
LIKE MAYBE TO THE MOUNTAINS..
HOW COULD YOU BE SURE YOU'D HAVE A GOOD TIME?
TAKE YOUR DOG ALONG..
2-8
© 1997 United Feature Syndicate, Inc.
SCHULZ

PEANUTS
by SCHULZ
YES, MA'AM..
MY REPORT TODAY ASKS THE QUESTION, "WHERE WILL IT ALL END?"
WE ALL NEED A PHILOSOPHY.. MY OLD PHILOSOPHY WAS, "WHATEVER, WHO CARES? AND HOW SHOULD I KNOW?"
CAN A PHILOSOPHY CARRY US THROUGH TROUBLED TIMES?
© 1997 United Feature Syndicate, Inc.
www.unitedmedia.com
WHAT HAPPENS WHEN OUR PHILOSOPHY FAILS?
2-9
WE TURN TO THAT MOST ANCIENT OF DESPERATE CRIES..
"MOM!"
SCHULZ
HAVE YOU EVER HAD TWENTY-EIGHT STUDENTS AND A TEACHER LOOK AT YOU LIKE YOU'VE LOST YOUR MIND?

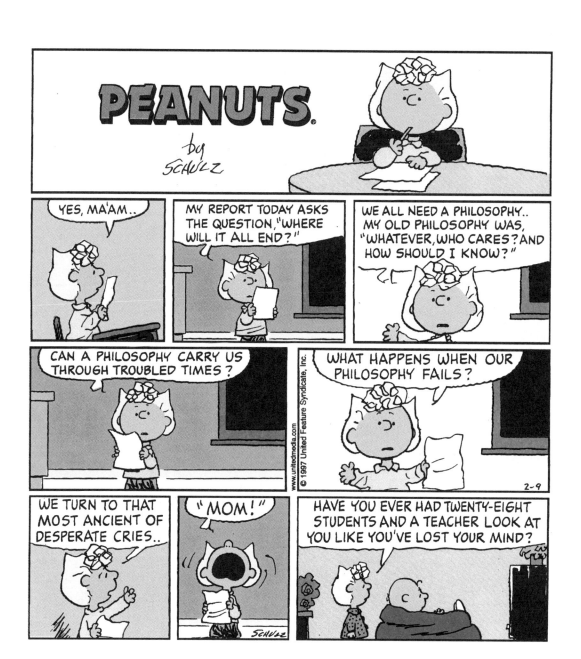

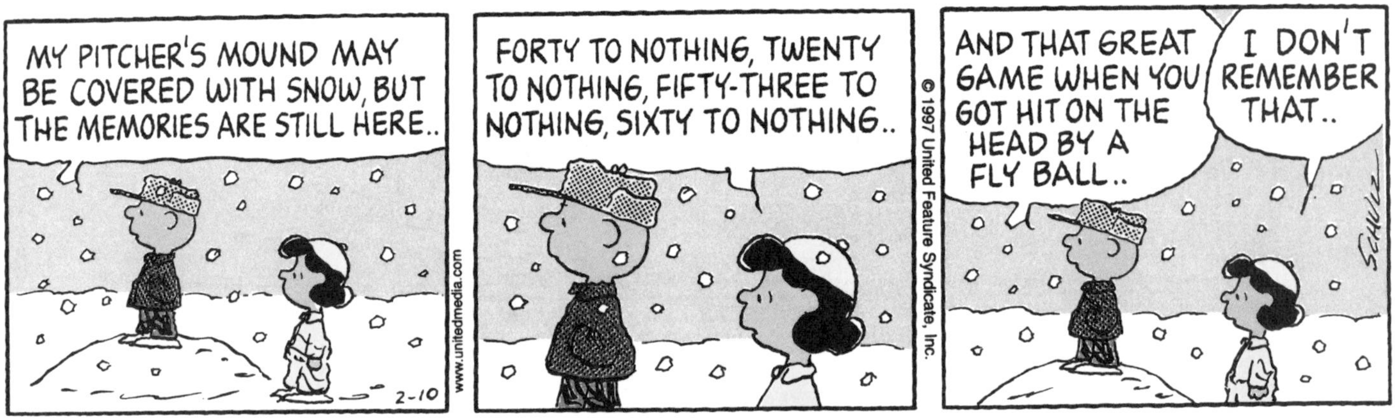
MY PITCHER'S MOUND MAY BE COVERED WITH SNOW, BUT THE MEMORIES ARE STILL HERE..
2-10
www.unitedmedia.com
FORTY TO NOTHING, TWENTY TO NOTHING, FIFTY-THREE TO NOTHING, SIXTY TO NOTHING..
© 1997 United Feature Syndicate, Inc.
AND THAT GREAT GAME WHEN YOU GOT HIT ON THE HEAD BY A FLY BALL..
I DON'T REMEMBER THAT..
SCHULZ

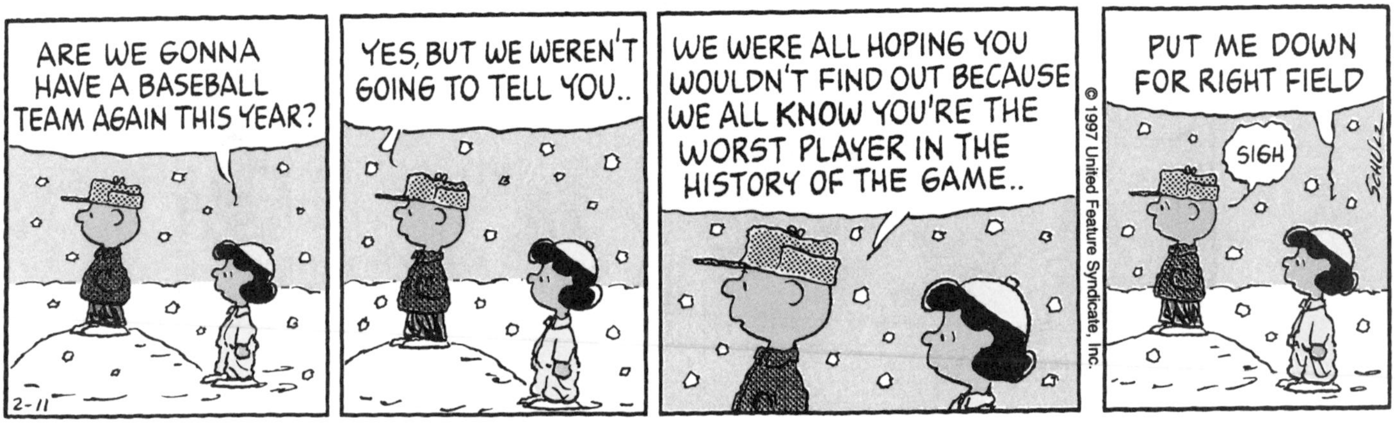
ARE WE GONNA HAVE A BASEBALL TEAM AGAIN THIS YEAR?
2-11
YES, BUT WE WEREN'T GOING TO TELL YOU..
WE WERE ALL HOPING YOU WOULDN'T FIND OUT BECAUSE WE ALL KNOW YOU'RE THE WORST PLAYER IN THE HISTORY OF THE GAME..
© 1997 United Feature Syndicate, Inc.
PUT ME DOWN FOR RIGHT FIELD
SIGH
SCHULZ

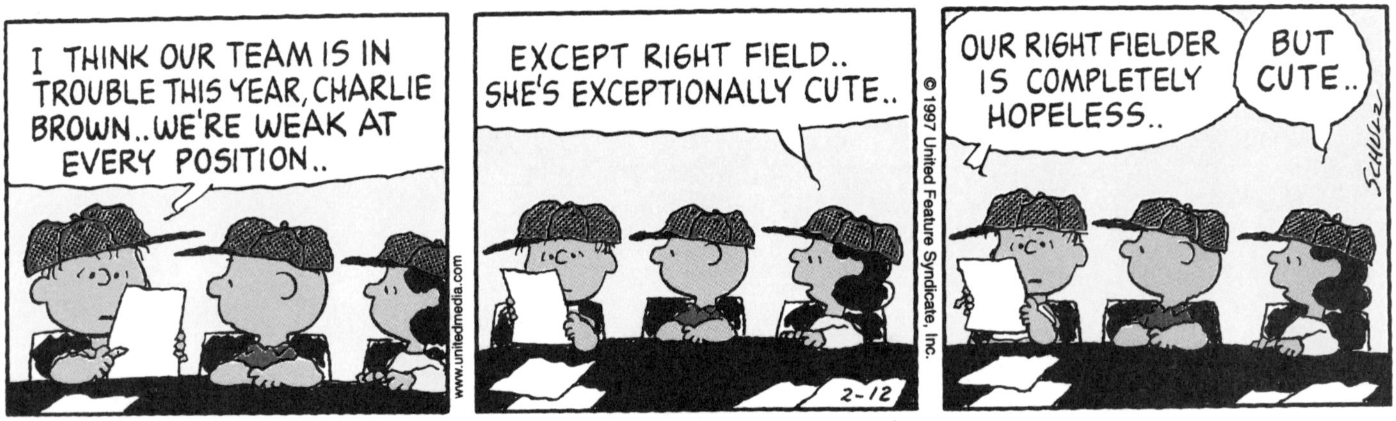
I THINK OUR TEAM IS IN TROUBLE THIS YEAR, CHARLIE BROWN.. WE'RE WEAK AT EVERY POSITION..
www.unitedmedia.com
EXCEPT RIGHT FIELD.. SHE'S EXCEPTIONALLY CUTE..
2-12
© 1997 United Feature Syndicate, Inc.
OUR RIGHT FIELDER IS COMPLETELY HOPELESS..
BUT CUTE..
SCHULZ

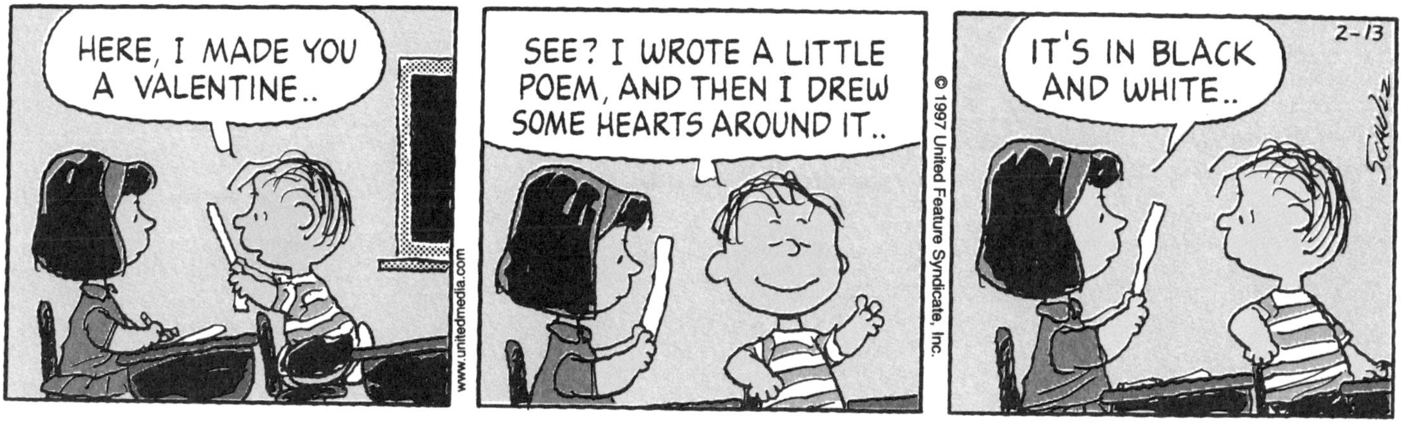
HERE, I MADE YOU A VALENTINE..
www.unitedmedia.com
SEE? I WROTE A LITTLE POEM, AND THEN I DREW SOME HEARTS AROUND IT..
© 1997 United Feature Syndicate, Inc.
2-13
IT'S IN BLACK AND WHITE..
SCHULZ

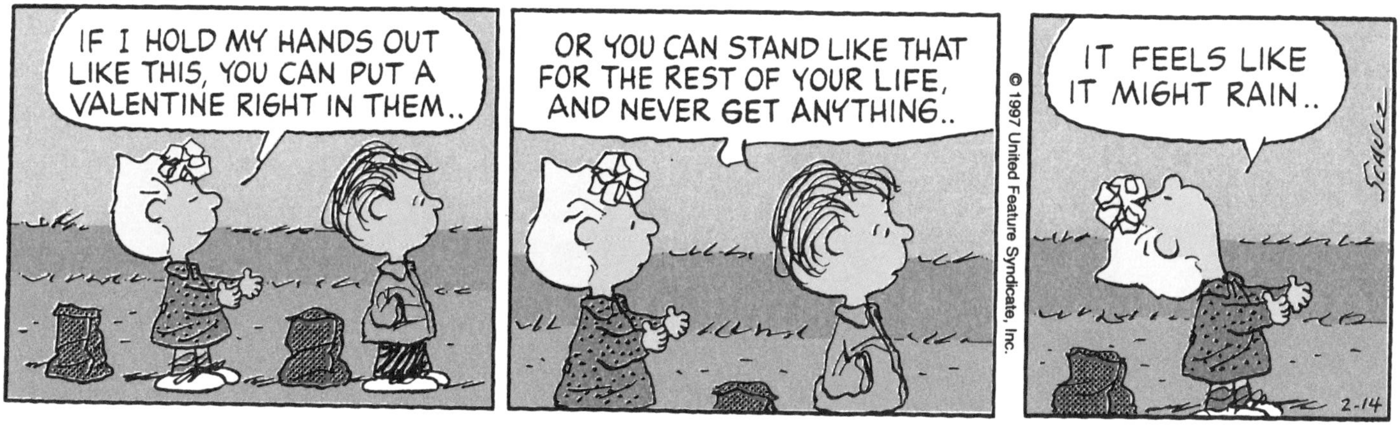
IF I HOLD MY HANDS OUT LIKE THIS, YOU CAN PUT A VALENTINE RIGHT IN THEM..
OR YOU CAN STAND LIKE THAT FOR THE REST OF YOUR LIFE, AND NEVER GET ANYTHING..
© 1997 United Feature Syndicate, Inc.
IT FEELS LIKE IT MIGHT RAIN..
SCHULZ
2-14

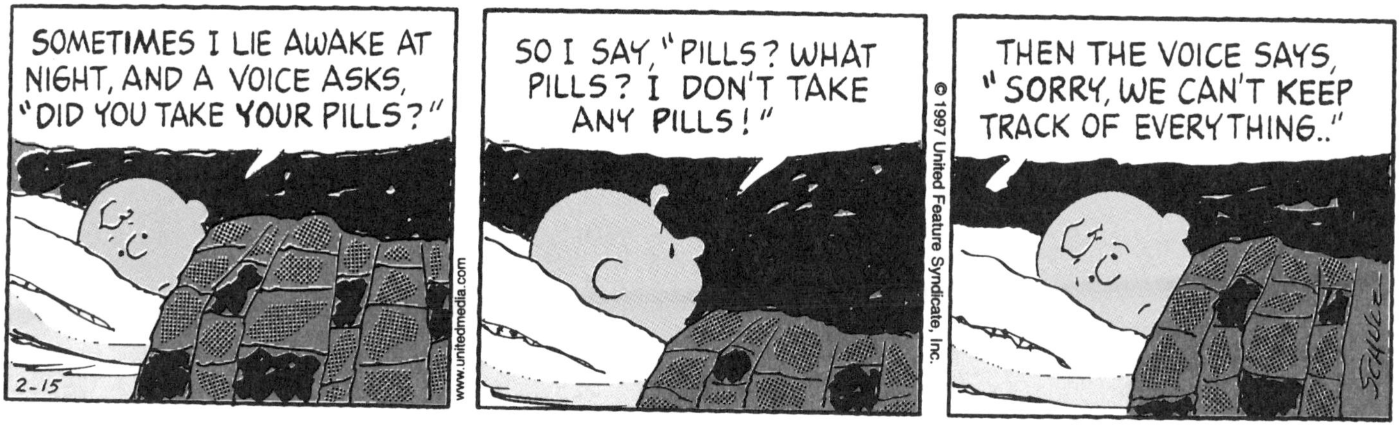
SOMETIMES I LIE AWAKE AT NIGHT, AND A VOICE ASKS, "DID YOU TAKE YOUR PILLS?"
2-15
www.unitedmedia.com
SO I SAY, "PILLS? WHAT PILLS? I DON'T TAKE ANY PILLS!"
© 1997 United Feature Syndicate, Inc.
THEN THE VOICE SAYS, "SORRY, WE CAN'T KEEP TRACK OF EVERYTHING.."
SCHULZ

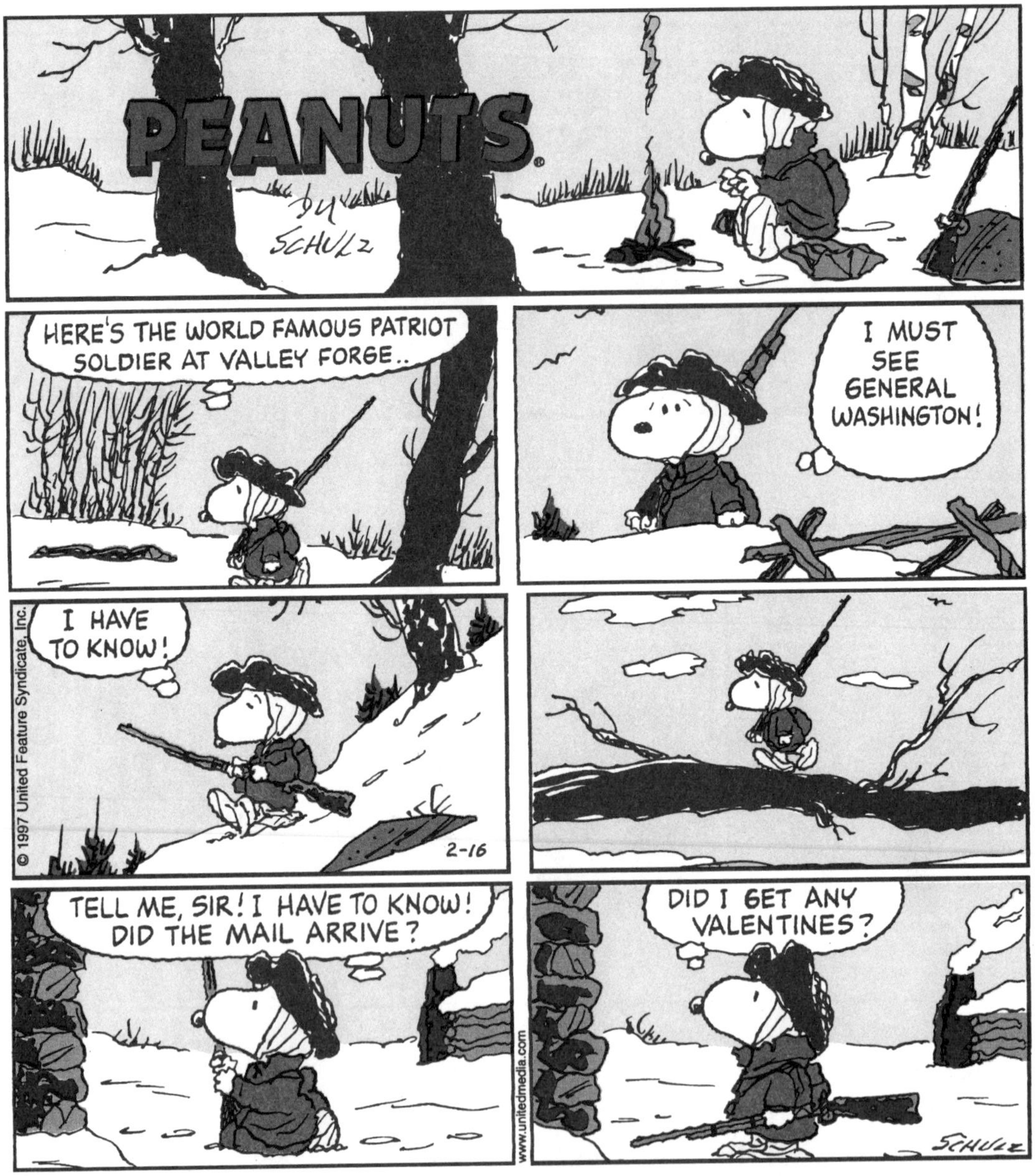
PEANUTS
SCHULZ
HERE'S THE WORLD FAMOUS PATRIOT SOLDIER AT VALLEY FORGE..
I MUST SEE GENERAL WASHINGTON!
I HAVE TO KNOW!
© 1997 United Feature Syndicate, Inc.
2-16
TELL ME, SIR! I HAVE TO KNOW! DID THE MAIL ARRIVE?
www.unitedmedia.com
DID I GET ANY VALENTINES?
SCHULZ

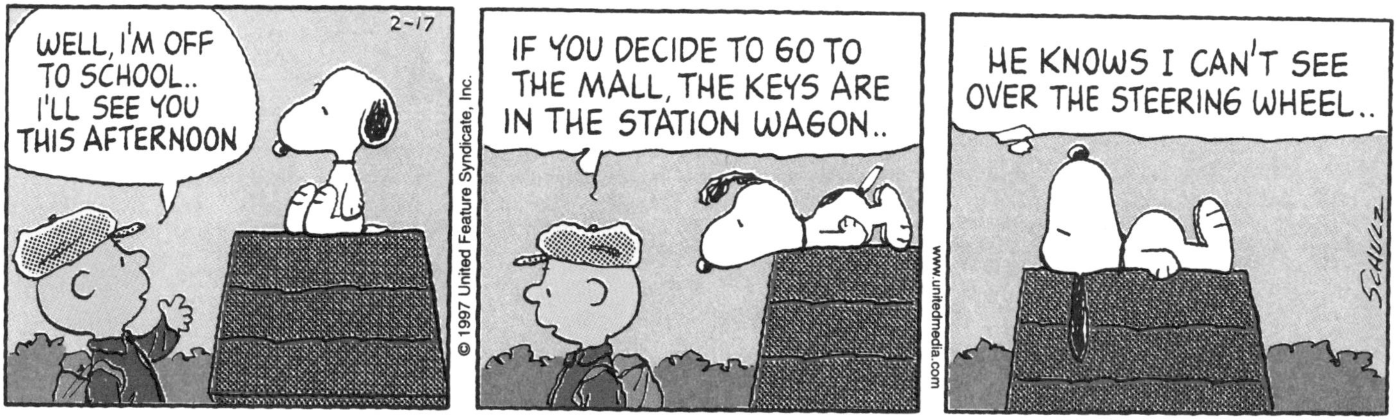
2-17
WELL, I'M OFF TO SCHOOL.. I'LL SEE YOU THIS AFTERNOON
© 1997 United Feature Syndicate, Inc.
IF YOU DECIDE TO GO TO THE MALL, THE KEYS ARE IN THE STATION WAGON..
www.unitedmedia.com
HE KNOWS I CAN'T SEE OVER THE STEERING WHEEL..
SCHULZ

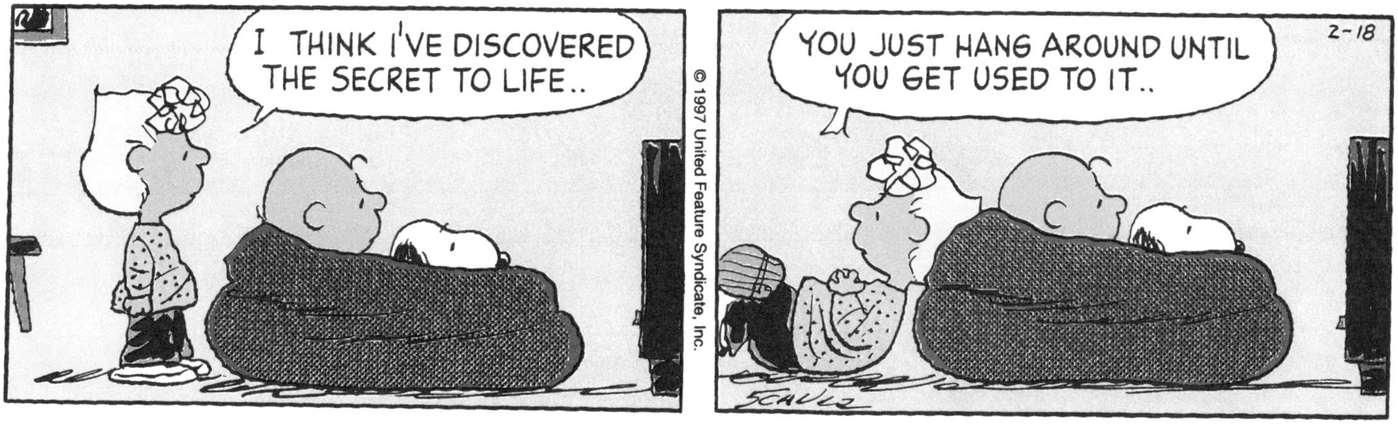
I THINK I'VE DISCOVERED THE SECRET TO LIFE..
© 1997 United Feature Syndicate, Inc.
2-18
YOU JUST HANG AROUND UNTIL YOU GET USED TO IT..
SCHULZ

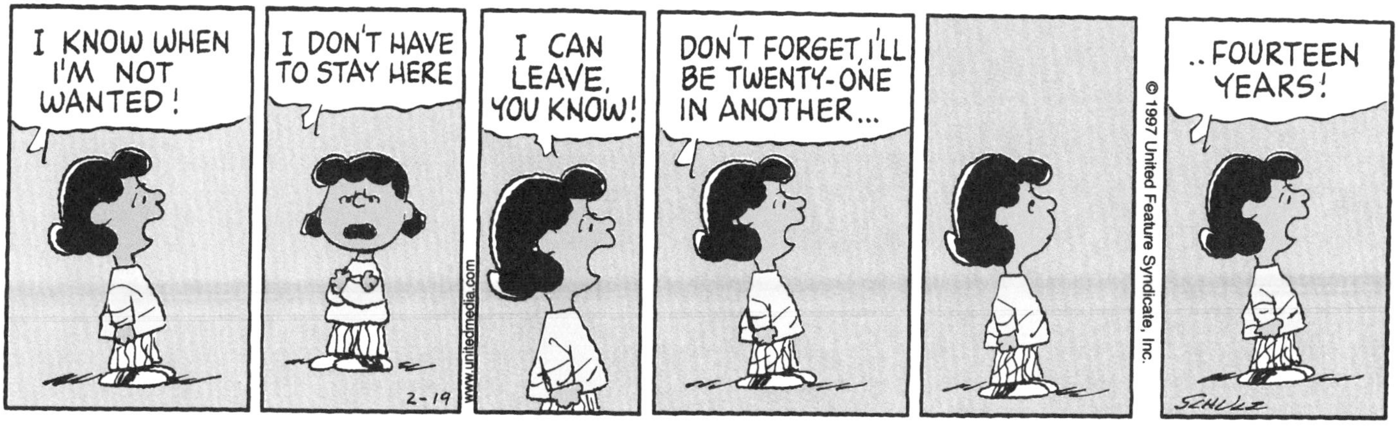
I KNOW WHEN I'M NOT WANTED!
I DON'T HAVE TO STAY HERE
2-19
www.unitedmedia.com
I CAN LEAVE, YOU KNOW!
DON'T FORGET, I'LL BE TWENTY-ONE IN ANOTHER...
© 1997 United Feature Syndicate, Inc.
..FOURTEEN YEARS!
SCHULZ

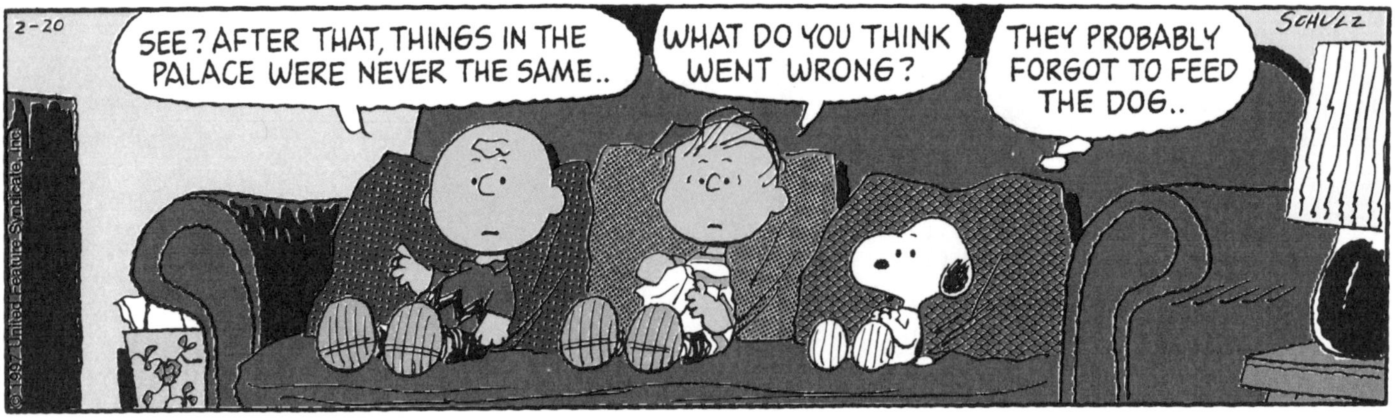
2-20
SEE? AFTER THAT, THINGS IN THE PALACE WERE NEVER THE SAME..
WHAT DO YOU THINK WENT WRONG?
THEY PROBABLY FORGOT TO FEED THE DOG..
SCHULZ
© 1997 United Feature Syndicate, Inc.

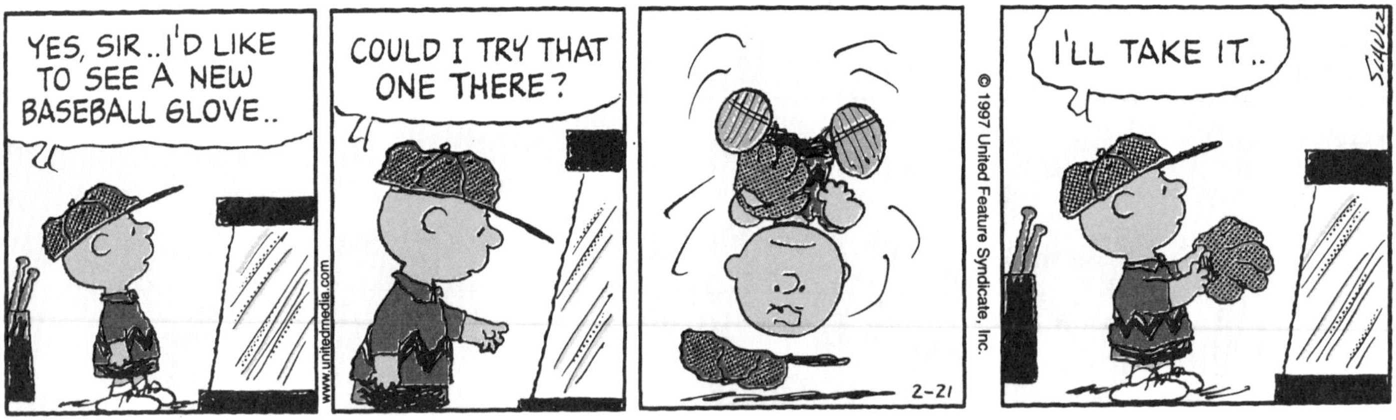
YES, SIR.. I'D LIKE TO SEE A NEW BASEBALL GLOVE..
www.unitedmedia.com
COULD I TRY THAT ONE THERE?
2-21
© 1997 United Feature Syndicate, Inc.
I'LL TAKE IT..
SCHULZ

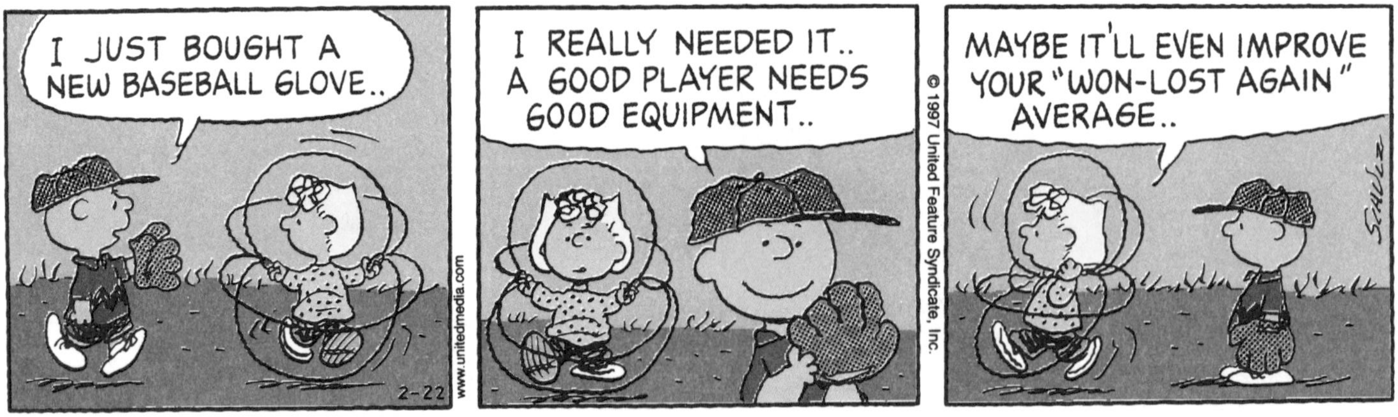
I JUST BOUGHT A NEW BASEBALL GLOVE..
2-22
www.unitedmedia.com
I REALLY NEEDED IT.. A GOOD PLAYER NEEDS GOOD EQUIPMENT..
© 1997 United Feature Syndicate, Inc.
MAYBE IT'LL EVEN IMPROVE YOUR "WON-LOST AGAIN" AVERAGE..
SCHULZ

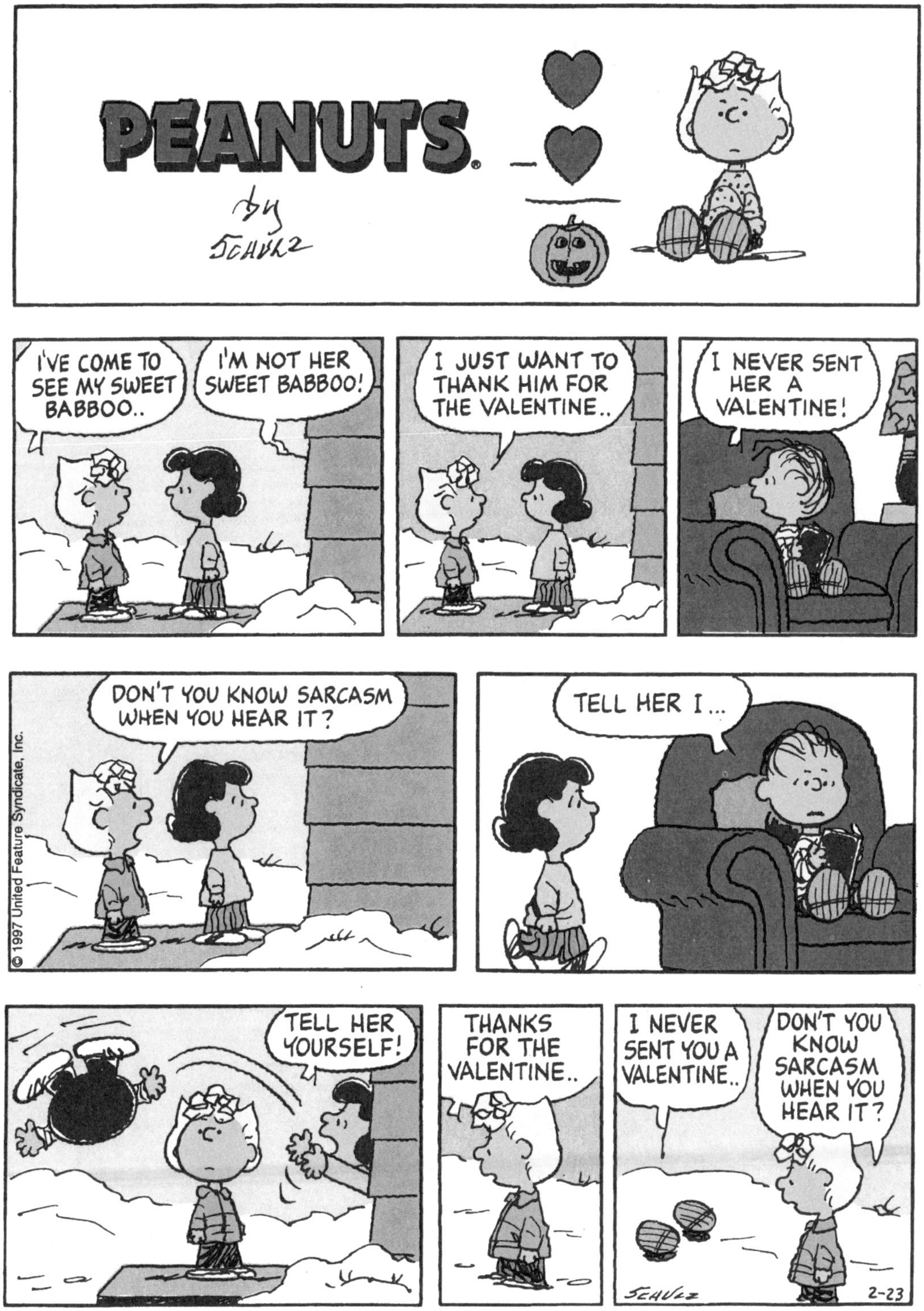
PEANUTS®
by Schulz
I'VE COME TO SEE MY SWEET BABBOO..
I'M NOT HER SWEET BABBOO!
I JUST WANT TO THANK HIM FOR THE VALENTINE..
I NEVER SENT HER A VALENTINE!
DON'T YOU KNOW SARCASM WHEN YOU HEAR IT?
© 1997 United Feature Syndicate, Inc.
TELL HER I...
TELL HER YOURSELF!
THANKS FOR THE VALENTINE..
I NEVER SENT YOU A VALENTINE..
DON'T YOU KNOW SARCASM WHEN YOU HEAR IT?
SCHULZ
2-23

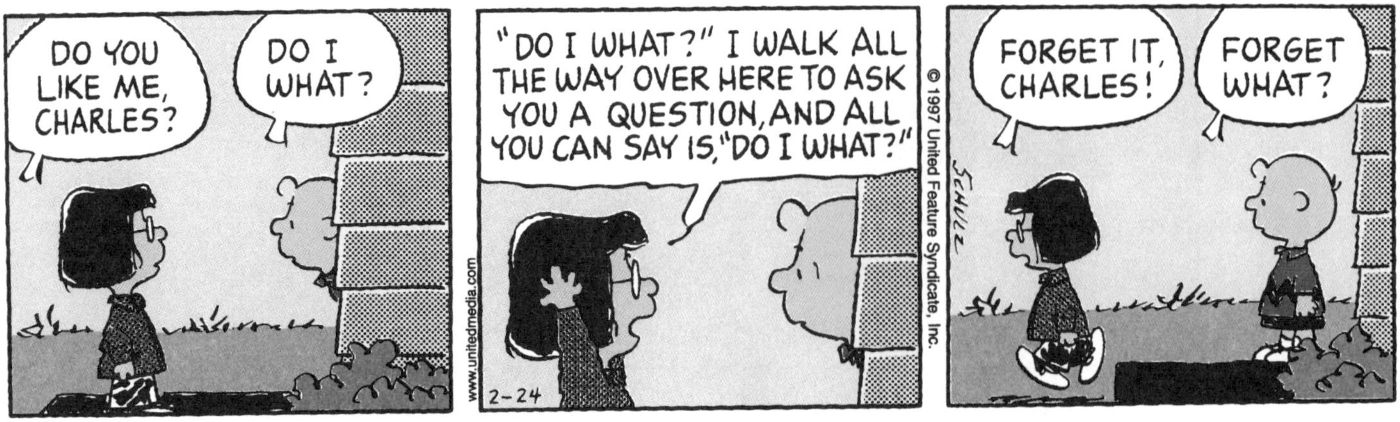
DO YOU LIKE ME, CHARLES?
DO I WHAT?
"DO I WHAT?" I WALK ALL THE WAY OVER HERE TO ASK YOU A QUESTION, AND ALL YOU CAN SAY IS, "DO I WHAT?"
www.unitedmedia.com
2-24
© 1997 United Feature Syndicate, Inc.
FORGET IT, CHARLES!
FORGET WHAT?
SCHULZ

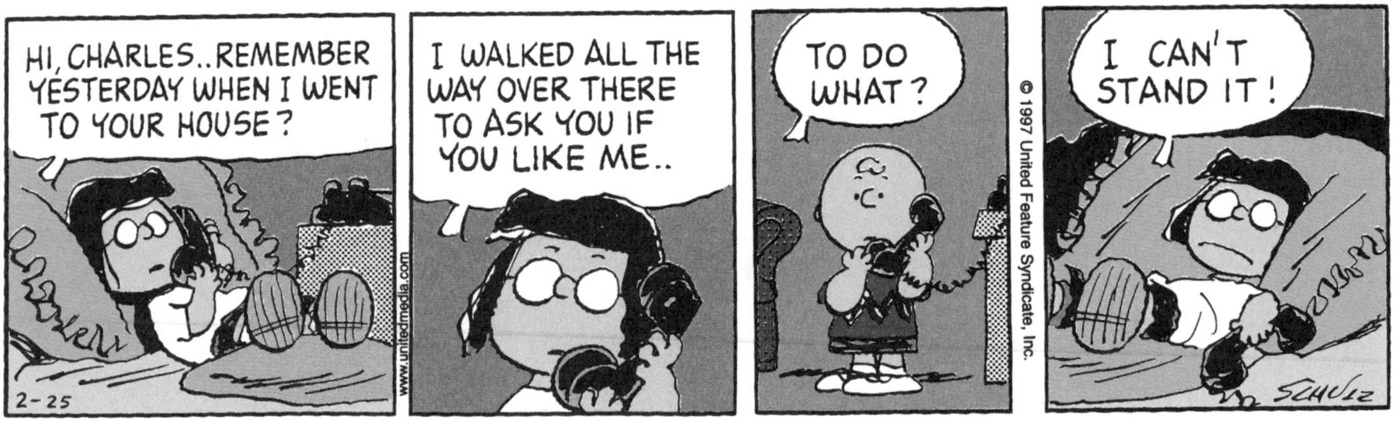
HI, CHARLES..REMEMBER YESTERDAY WHEN I WENT TO YOUR HOUSE?
2-25
www.unitedmedia.com
I WALKED ALL THE WAY OVER THERE TO ASK YOU IF YOU LIKE ME..
TO DO WHAT?
© 1997 United Feature Syndicate, Inc.
I CAN'T STAND IT!
SCHULZ

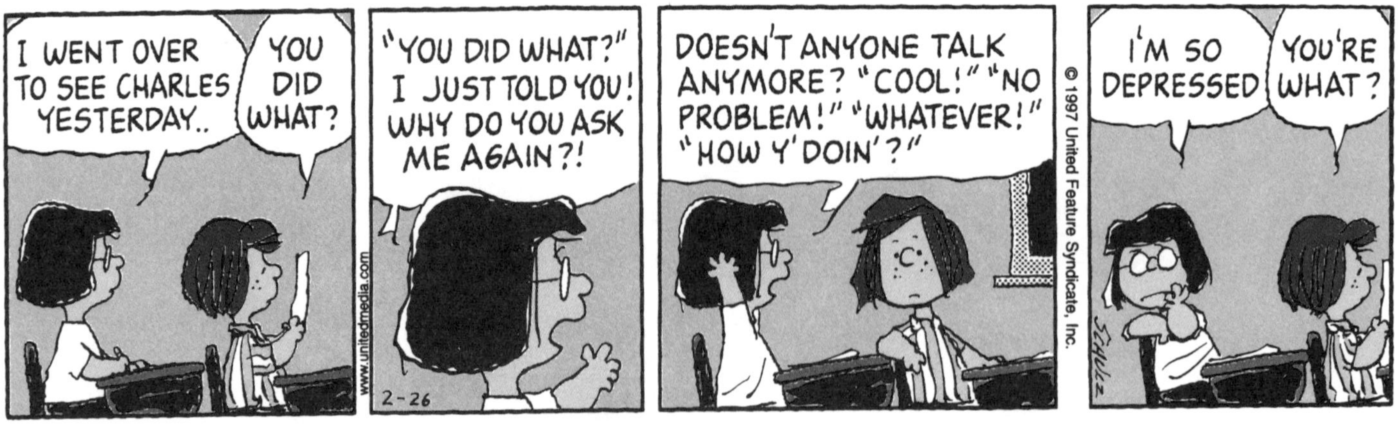
I WENT OVER TO SEE CHARLES YESTERDAY..
YOU DID WHAT?
www.unitedmedia.com
"YOU DID WHAT?" I JUST TOLD YOU! WHY DO YOU ASK ME AGAIN?!
2-26
DOESN'T ANYONE TALK ANYMORE? "COOL!" "NO PROBLEM!" "WHATEVER!" "HOW Y'DOIN'?"
© 1997 United Feature Syndicate, Inc.
I'M SO DEPRESSED
YOU'RE WHAT?
SCHULZ

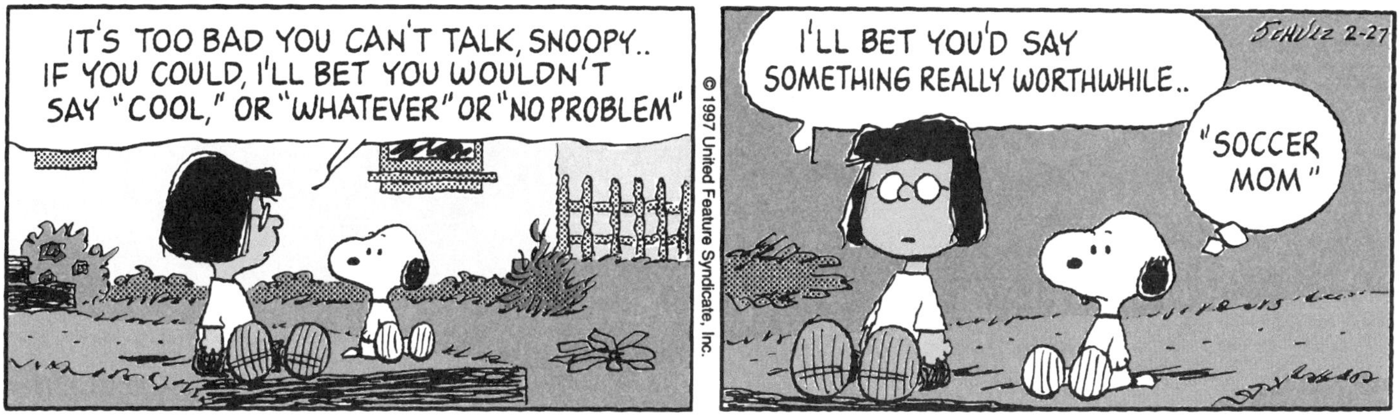
IT'S TOO BAD YOU CAN'T TALK, SNOOPY.. IF YOU COULD, I'LL BET YOU WOULDN'T SAY "COOL," OR "WHATEVER" OR "NO PROBLEM"
© 1997 United Feature Syndicate, Inc.
SCHULZ 2-27
I'LL BET YOU'D SAY SOMETHING REALLY WORTHWHILE..
"SOCCER MOM"

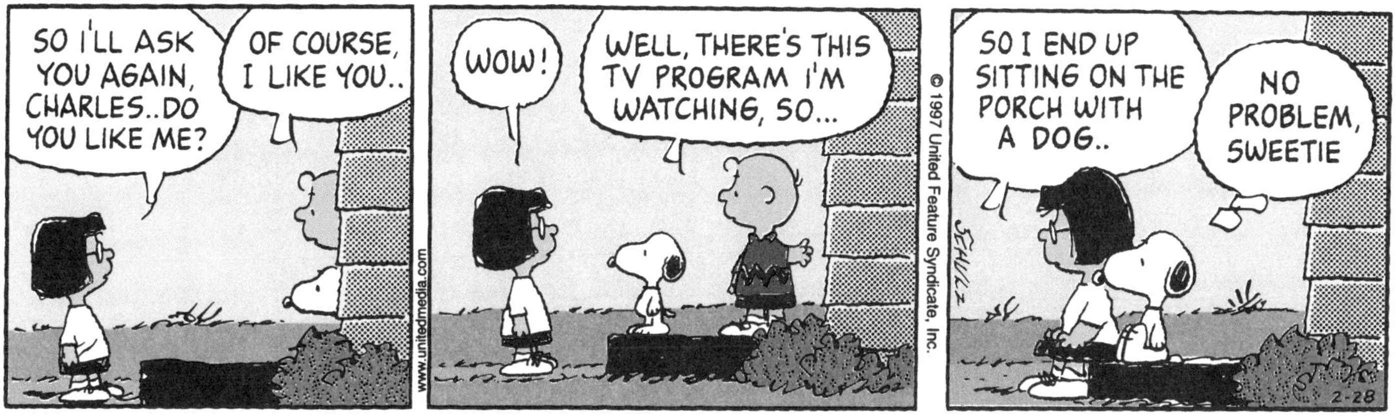
SO I'LL ASK YOU AGAIN, CHARLES..DO YOU LIKE ME?
OF COURSE, I LIKE YOU..
www.unitedmedia.com
WOW!
WELL, THERE'S THIS TV PROGRAM I'M WATCHING, SO...
© 1997 United Feature Syndicate, Inc.
SCHULZ
SO I END UP SITTING ON THE PORCH WITH A DOG..
NO PROBLEM, SWEETIE
2-28

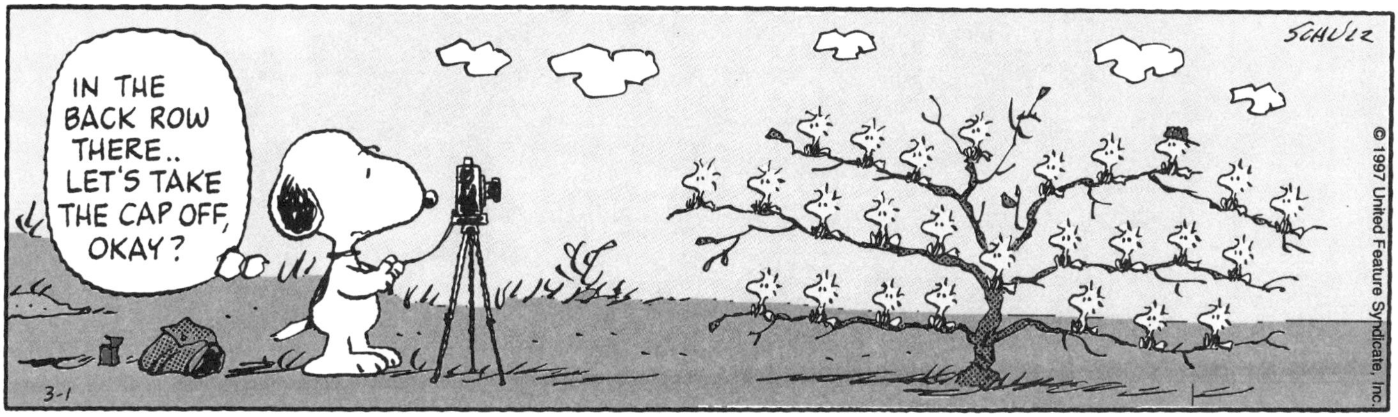
SCHULZ
IN THE BACK ROW THERE.. LET'S TAKE THE CAP OFF, OKAY?
© 1997 United Feature Syndicate, Inc.
3-1

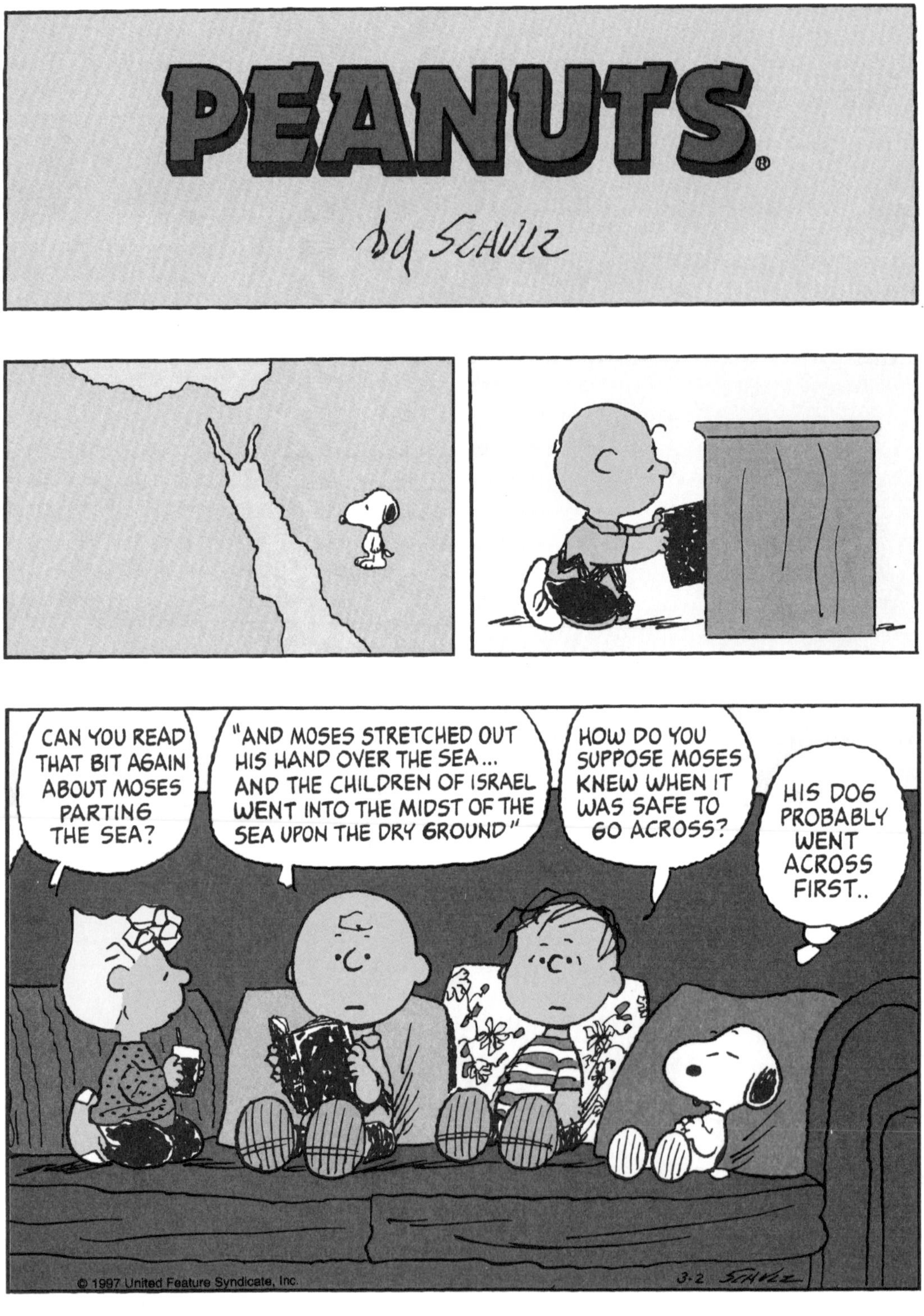
PEANUTS®
by SCHULZ
CAN YOU READ THAT BIT AGAIN ABOUT MOSES PARTING THE SEA?
"AND MOSES STRETCHED OUT HIS HAND OVER THE SEA... AND THE CHILDREN OF ISRAEL WENT INTO THE MIDST OF THE SEA UPON THE DRY GROUND"
HOW DO YOU SUPPOSE MOSES KNEW WHEN IT WAS SAFE TO GO ACROSS?
HIS DOG PROBABLY WENT ACROSS FIRST..
© 1997 United Feature Syndicate, Inc.
3-2 SCHULZ

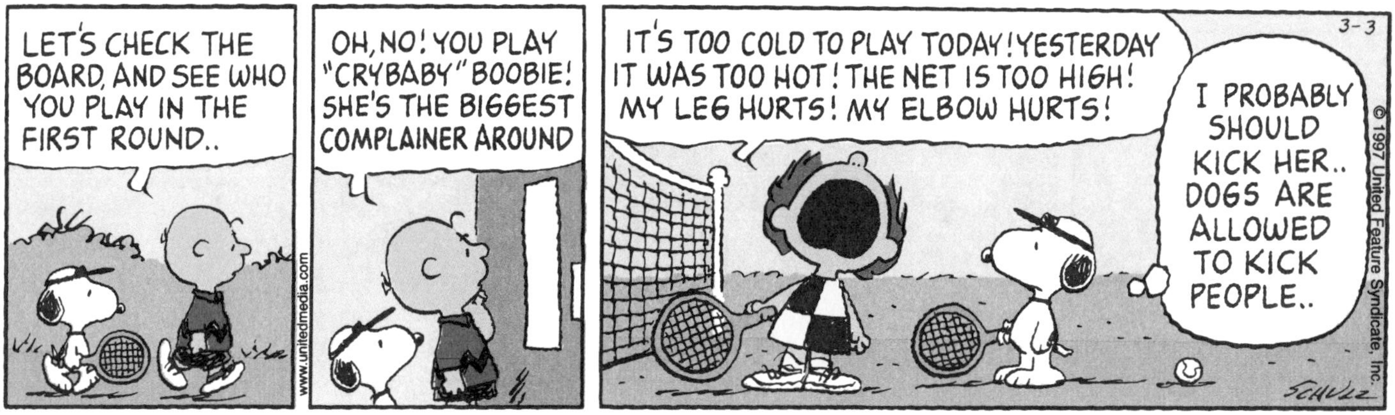
LET'S CHECK THE BOARD, AND SEE WHO YOU PLAY IN THE FIRST ROUND..
OH, NO! YOU PLAY "CRYBABY" BOOBIE! SHE'S THE BIGGEST COMPLAINER AROUND
IT'S TOO COLD TO PLAY TODAY! YESTERDAY IT WAS TOO HOT! THE NET IS TOO HIGH! MY LEG HURTS! MY ELBOW HURTS!
I PROBABLY SHOULD KICK HER.. DOGS ARE ALLOWED TO KICK PEOPLE..
3-3
© 1997 United Feature Syndicate, Inc.
www.unitedmedia.com
SCHULZ

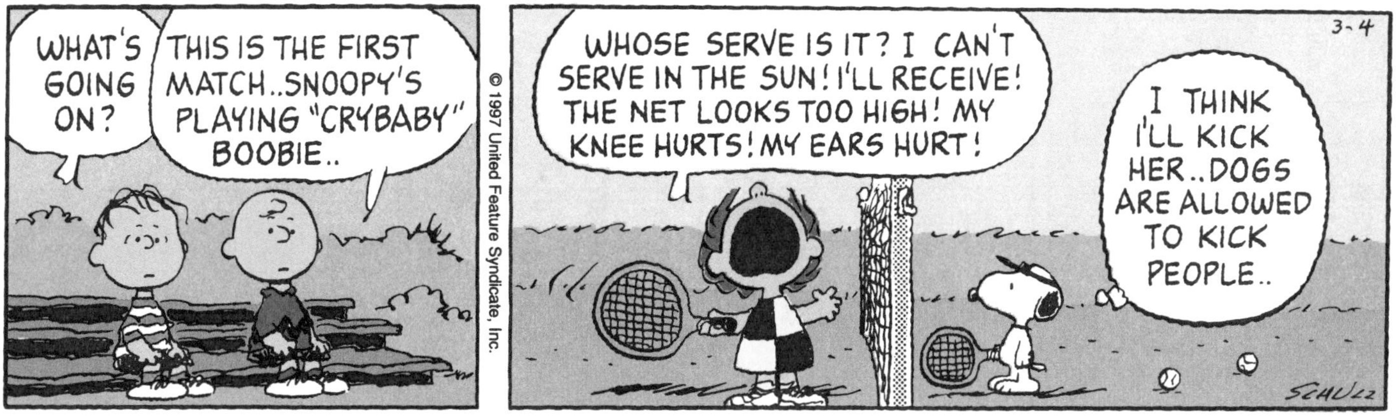
WHAT'S GOING ON?
THIS IS THE FIRST MATCH..SNOOPY'S PLAYING "CRYBABY" BOOBIE..
WHOSE SERVE IS IT? I CAN'T SERVE IN THE SUN! I'LL RECEIVE! THE NET LOOKS TOO HIGH! MY KNEE HURTS! MY EARS HURT!
I THINK I'LL KICK HER..DOGS ARE ALLOWED TO KICK PEOPLE..
3-4
© 1997 United Feature Syndicate, Inc.
SCHULZ

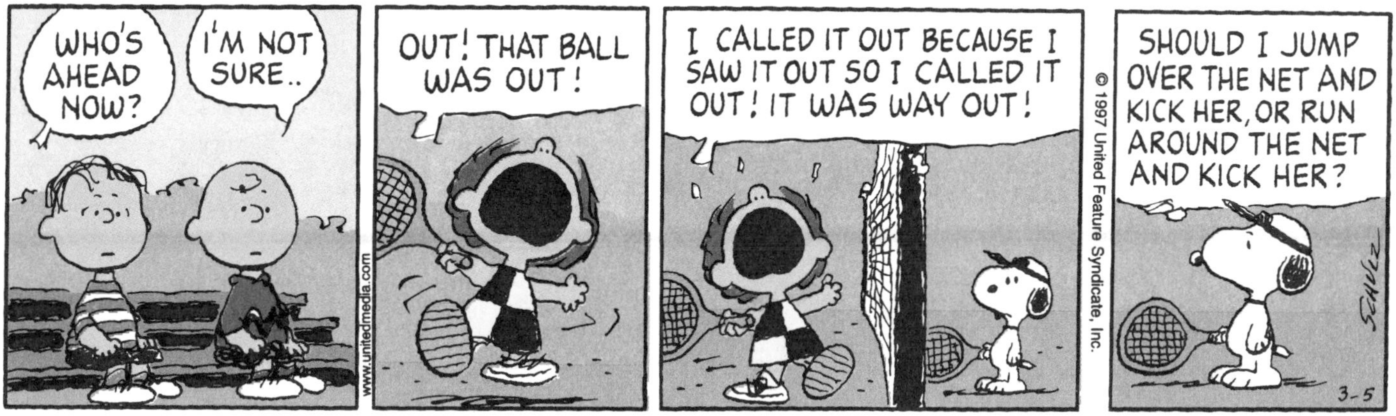
WHO'S AHEAD NOW?
I'M NOT SURE..
OUT! THAT BALL WAS OUT!
I CALLED IT OUT BECAUSE I SAW IT OUT SO I CALLED IT OUT! IT WAS WAY OUT!
SHOULD I JUMP OVER THE NET AND KICK HER, OR RUN AROUND THE NET AND KICK HER?
3-5
© 1997 United Feature Syndicate, Inc.
www.unitedmedia.com
SCHULZ

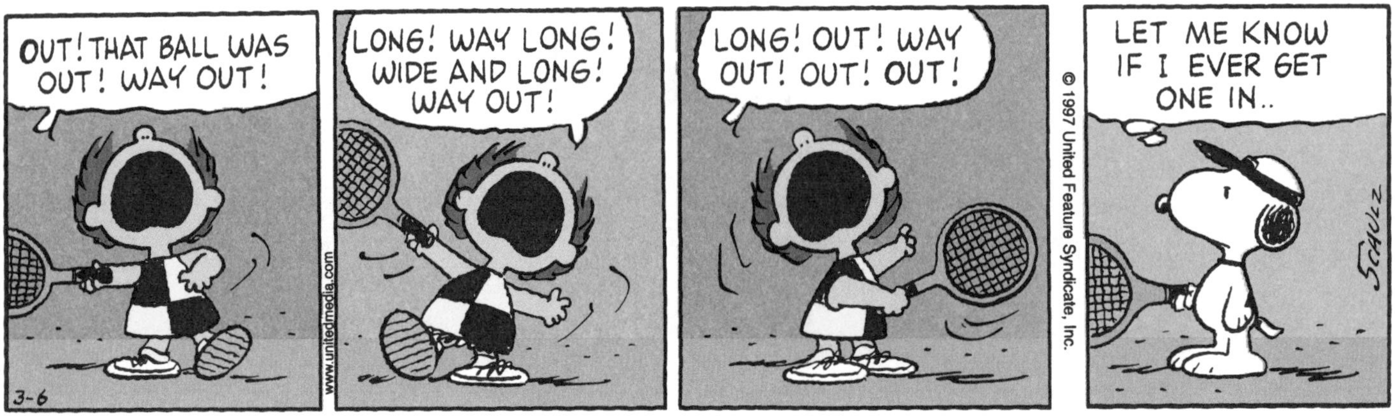
OUT! THAT BALL WAS OUT! WAY OUT!
3-6
www.unitedmedia.com
LONG! WAY LONG! WIDE AND LONG! WAY OUT!
LONG! OUT! WAY OUT! OUT! OUT! OUT!
© 1997 United Feature Syndicate, Inc.
LET ME KNOW IF I EVER GET ONE IN..
SCHULZ

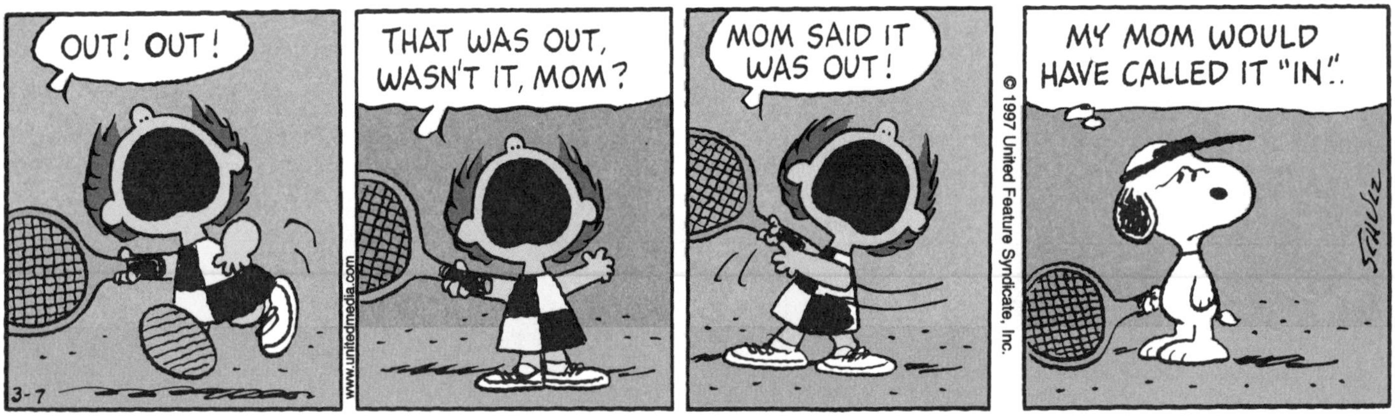
OUT! OUT!
3-7
www.unitedmedia.com
THAT WAS OUT, WASN'T IT, MOM?
MOM SAID IT WAS OUT!
© 1997 United Feature Syndicate, Inc.
MY MOM WOULD HAVE CALLED IT "IN"..
SCHULZ

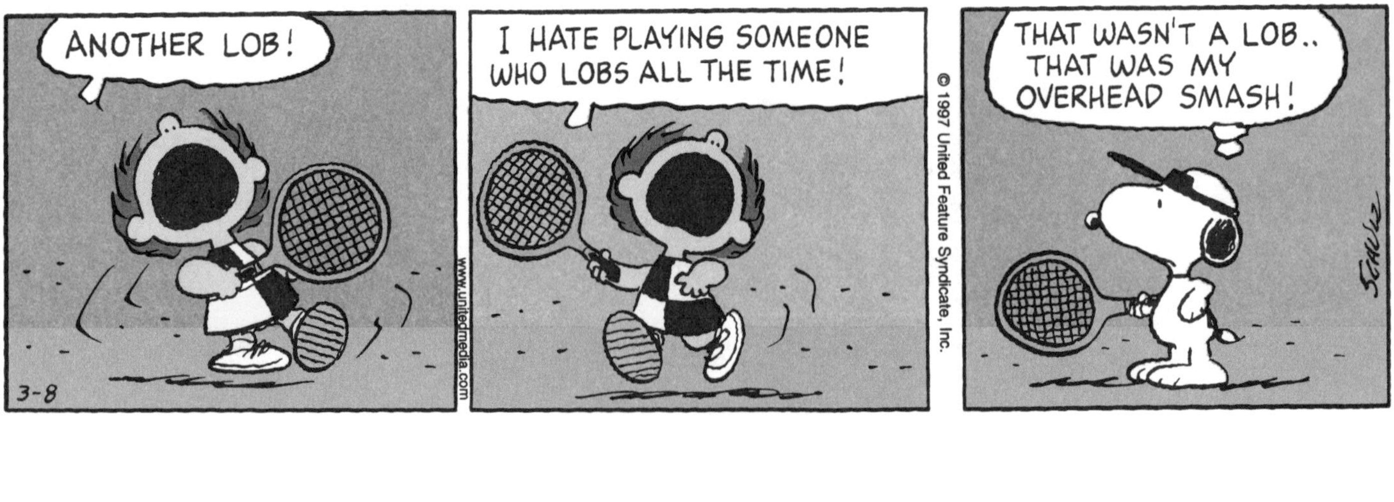
ANOTHER LOB!
3-8
www.unitedmedia.com
I HATE PLAYING SOMEONE WHO LOBS ALL THE TIME!
© 1997 United Feature Syndicate, Inc.
THAT WASN'T A LOB.. THAT WAS MY OVERHEAD SMASH!
SCHULZ

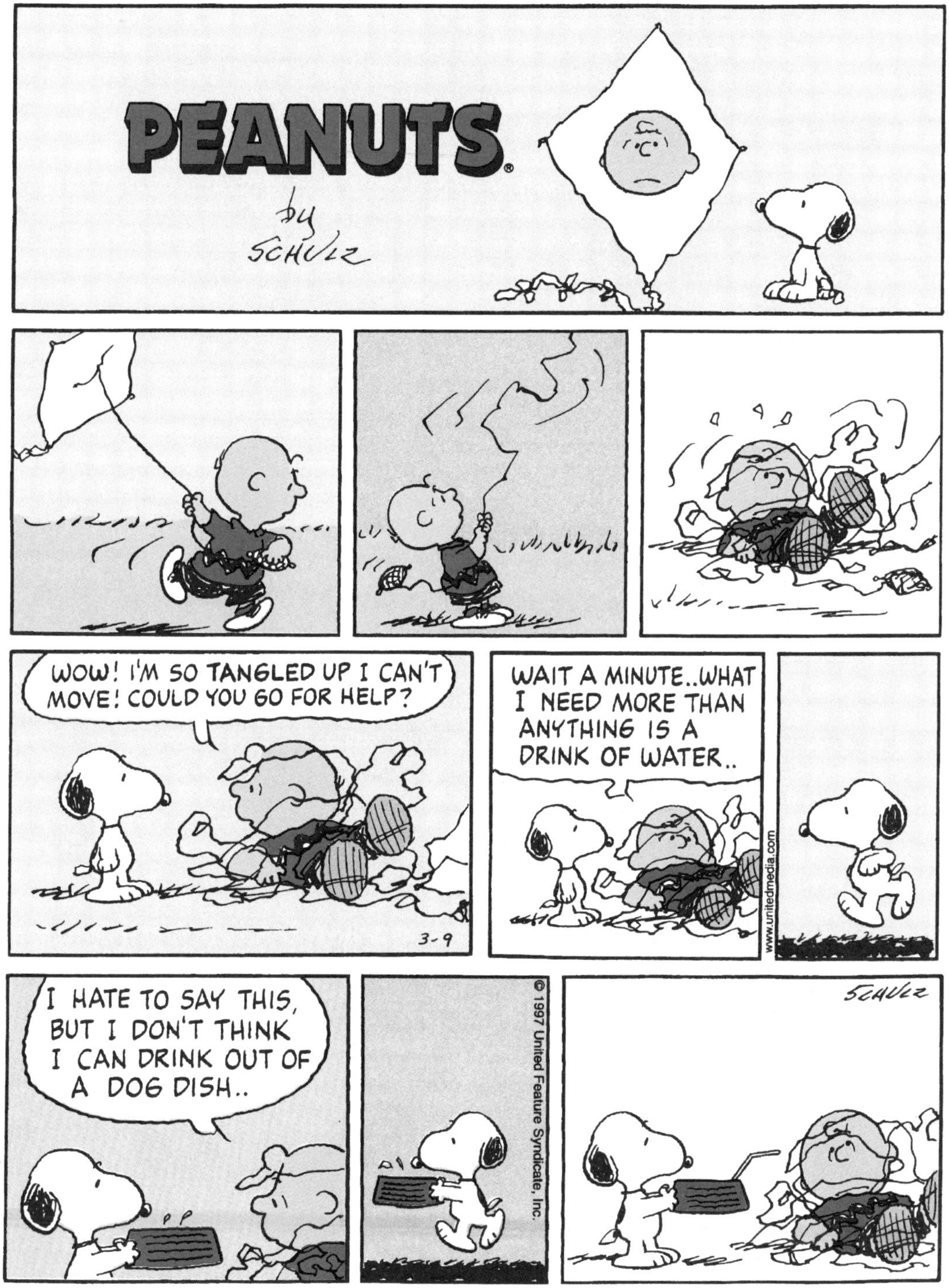
PEANUTS
by SCHULZ
WOW! I'M SO TANGLED UP I CAN'T MOVE! COULD YOU GO FOR HELP?
3-9
WAIT A MINUTE..WHAT I NEED MORE THAN ANYTHING IS A DRINK OF WATER..
www.unitedmedia.com
I HATE TO SAY THIS, BUT I DON'T THINK I CAN DRINK OUT OF A DOG DISH..
© 1997 United Feature Syndicate, Inc.
SCHULZ

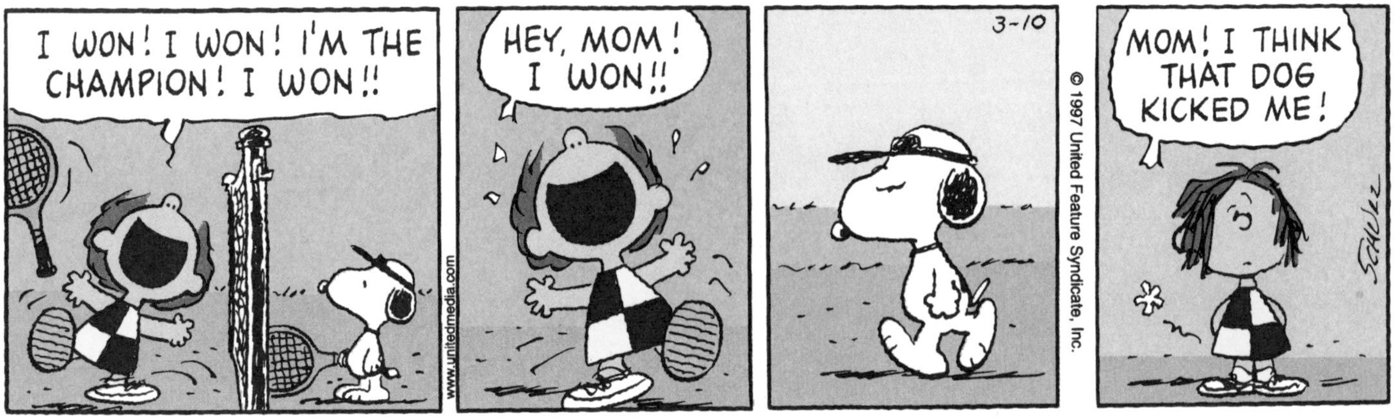
I WON! I WON! I'M THE CHAMPION! I WON!!
HEY, MOM! I WON!!
3-10
MOM! I THINK THAT DOG KICKED ME!
www.unitedmedia.com
© 1997 United Feature Syndicate, Inc.
SCHULZ

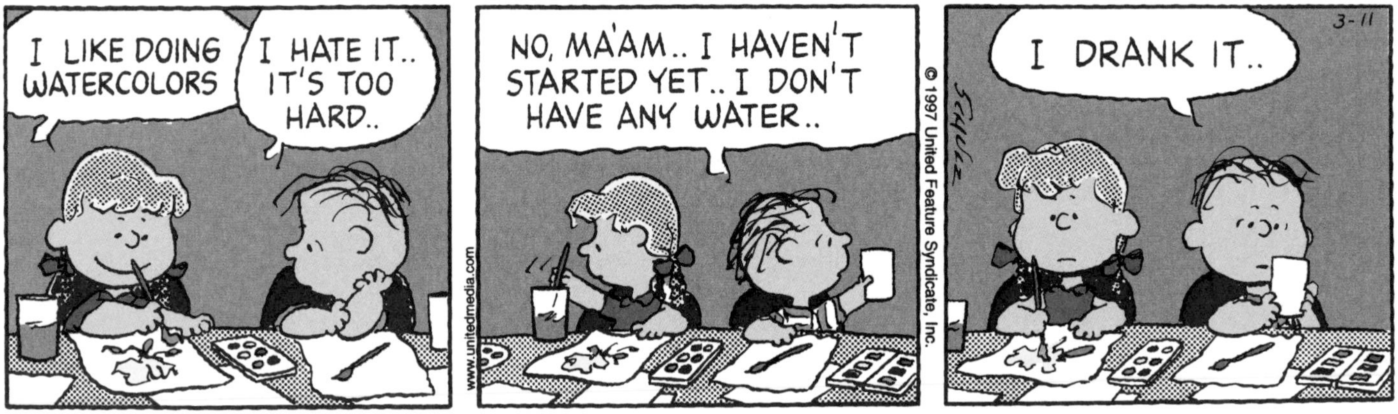
I LIKE DOING WATERCOLORS
I HATE IT.. IT'S TOO HARD..
NO, MA'AM.. I HAVEN'T STARTED YET.. I DON'T HAVE ANY WATER..
I DRANK IT..
3-11
www.unitedmedia.com
© 1997 United Feature Syndicate, Inc.
SCHULZ

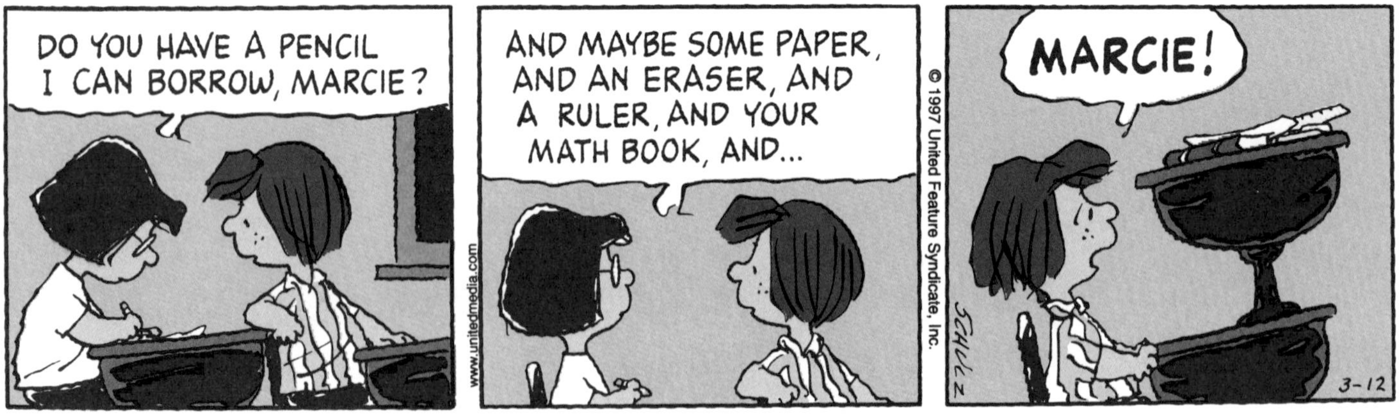
DO YOU HAVE A PENCIL I CAN BORROW, MARCIE?
AND MAYBE SOME PAPER, AND AN ERASER, AND A RULER, AND YOUR MATH BOOK, AND...
MARCIE!
3-12
www.unitedmedia.com
© 1997 United Feature Syndicate, Inc.
SCHULZ

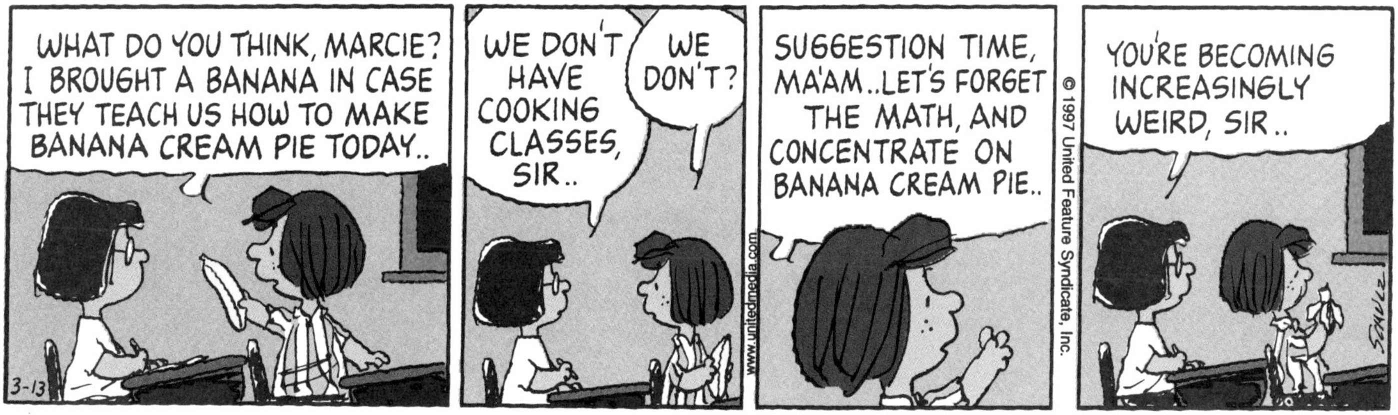
3-13
WHAT DO YOU THINK, MARCIE? I BROUGHT A BANANA IN CASE THEY TEACH US HOW TO MAKE BANANA CREAM PIE TODAY..
WE DON'T HAVE COOKING CLASSES, SIR..
WE DON'T?
www.unitedmedia.com
SUGGESTION TIME, MA'AM..LET'S FORGET THE MATH, AND CONCENTRATE ON BANANA CREAM PIE..
© 1997 United Feature Syndicate, Inc.
YOU'RE BECOMING INCREASINGLY WEIRD, SIR..
SCHULZ

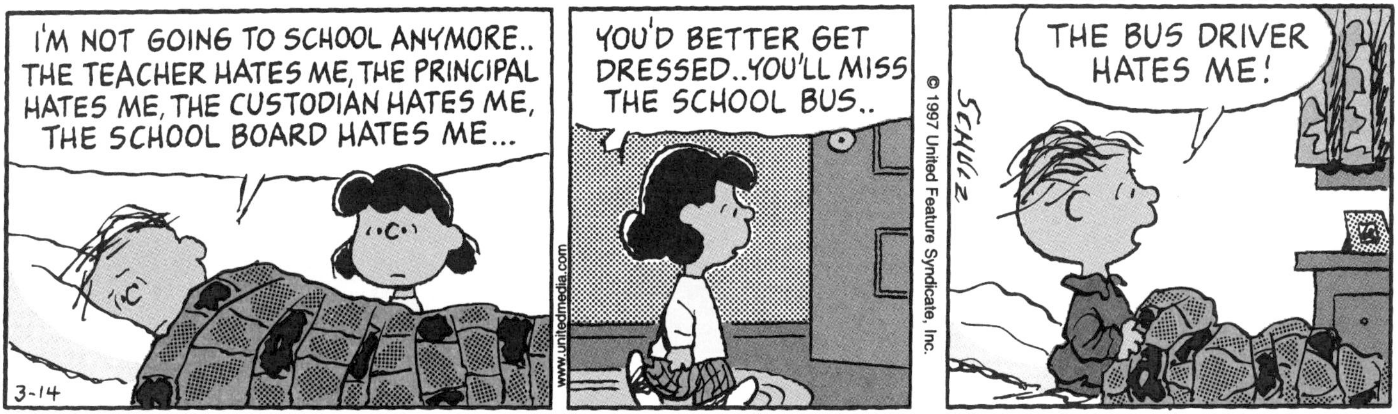
3-14
I'M NOT GOING TO SCHOOL ANYMORE.. THE TEACHER HATES ME, THE PRINCIPAL HATES ME, THE CUSTODIAN HATES ME, THE SCHOOL BOARD HATES ME...
www.unitedmedia.com
YOU'D BETTER GET DRESSED..YOU'LL MISS THE SCHOOL BUS..
© 1997 United Feature Syndicate, Inc.
SCHULZ
THE BUS DRIVER HATES ME!

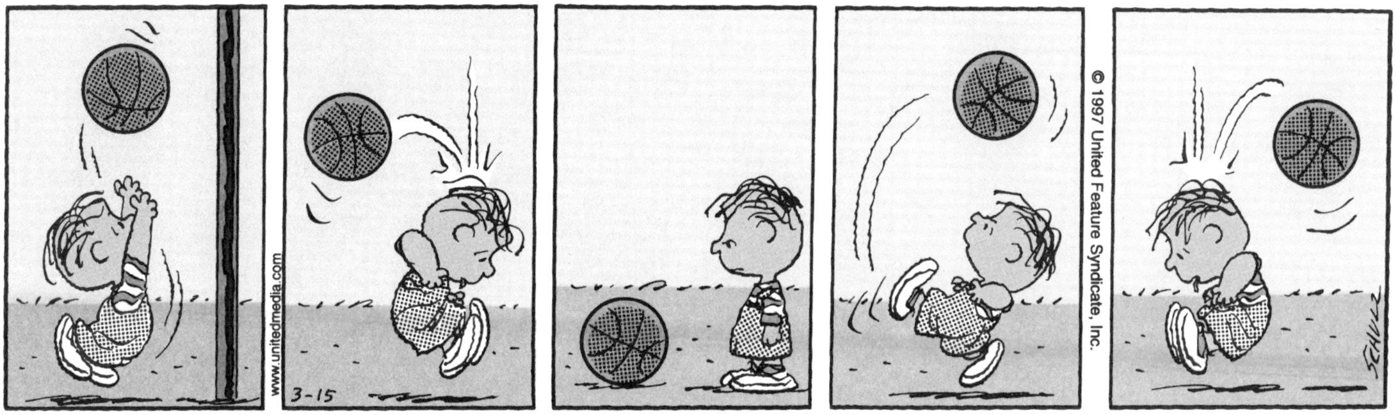
www.unitedmedia.com
3-15
© 1997 United Feature Syndicate, Inc.
SCHULZ

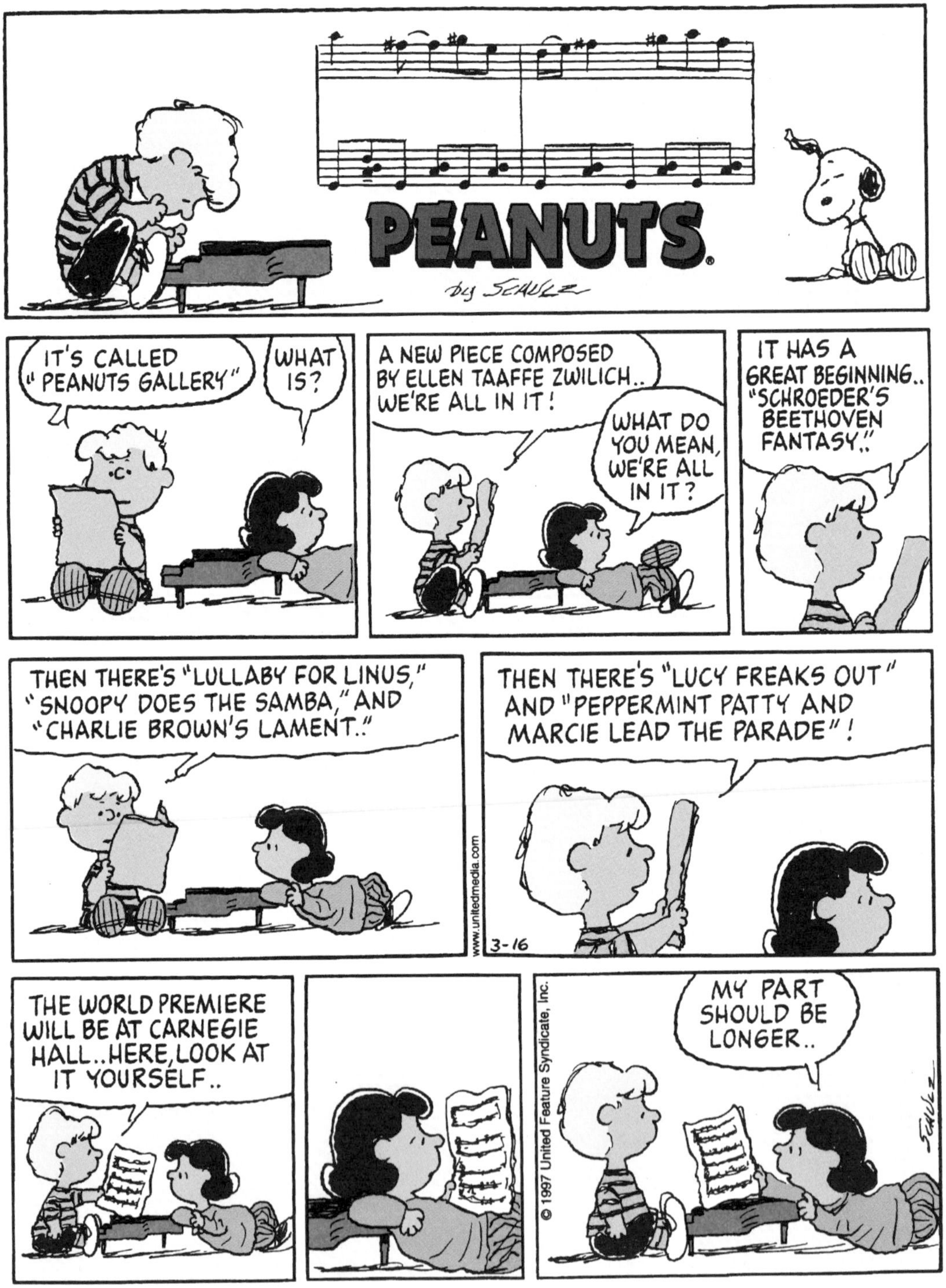
PEANUTS
by SCHULZ
IT'S CALLED "PEANUTS GALLERY"
WHAT IS?
A NEW PIECE COMPOSED BY ELLEN TAAFFE ZWILICH.. WE'RE ALL IN IT!
WHAT DO YOU MEAN, WE'RE ALL IN IT?
IT HAS A GREAT BEGINNING.. "SCHROEDER'S BEETHOVEN FANTASY."
THEN THERE'S "LULLABY FOR LINUS," "SNOOPY DOES THE SAMBA," AND "CHARLIE BROWN'S LAMENT."
www.unitedmedia.com
3-16
THEN THERE'S "LUCY FREAKS OUT" AND "PEPPERMINT PATTY AND MARCIE LEAD THE PARADE"!
THE WORLD PREMIERE WILL BE AT CARNEGIE HALL..HERE, LOOK AT IT YOURSELF..
© 1997 United Feature Syndicate, Inc.
MY PART SHOULD BE LONGER..
SCHULZ

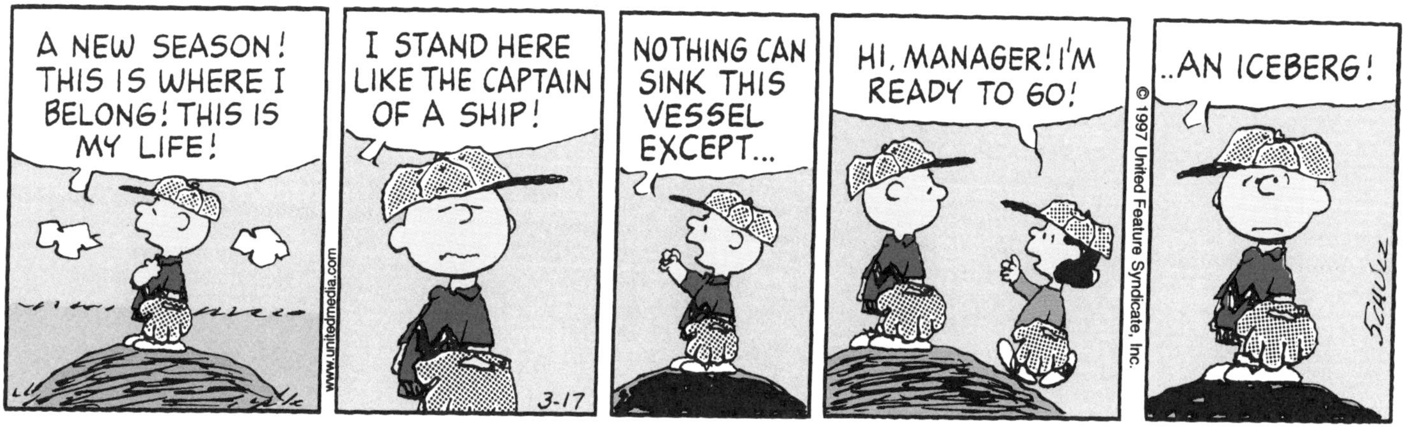
A NEW SEASON! THIS IS WHERE I BELONG! THIS IS MY LIFE!
I STAND HERE LIKE THE CAPTAIN OF A SHIP!
NOTHING CAN SINK THIS VESSEL EXCEPT...
HI, MANAGER! I'M READY TO GO!
..AN ICEBERG!
www.unitedmedia.com
3-17
© 1997 United Feature Syndicate, Inc.
SCHULZ

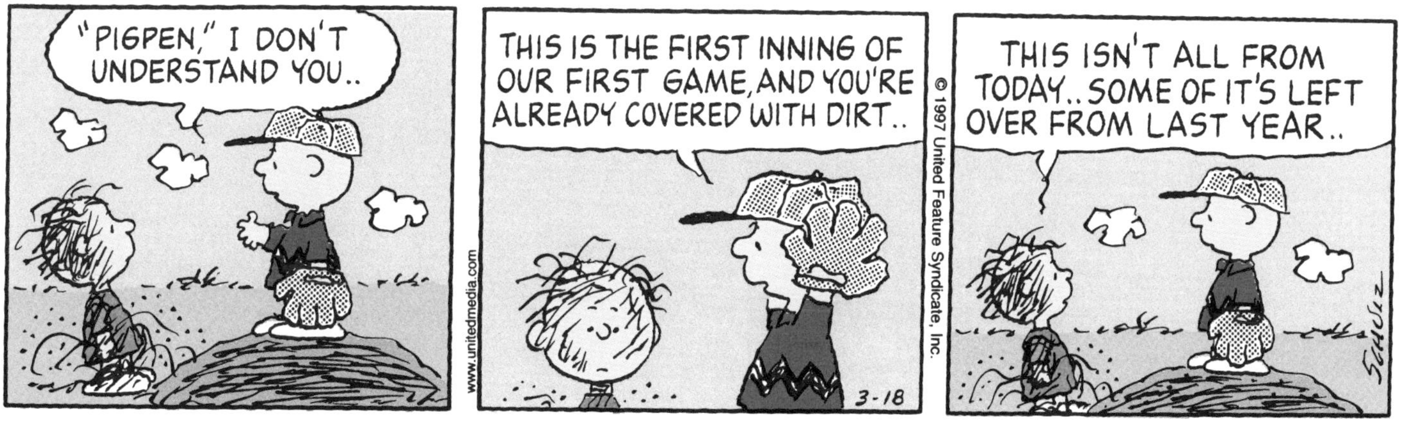
"PIGPEN," I DON'T UNDERSTAND YOU..
THIS IS THE FIRST INNING OF OUR FIRST GAME, AND YOU'RE ALREADY COVERED WITH DIRT..
THIS ISN'T ALL FROM TODAY.. SOME OF IT'S LEFT OVER FROM LAST YEAR..
www.unitedmedia.com
3-18
© 1997 United Feature Syndicate, Inc.
SCHULZ

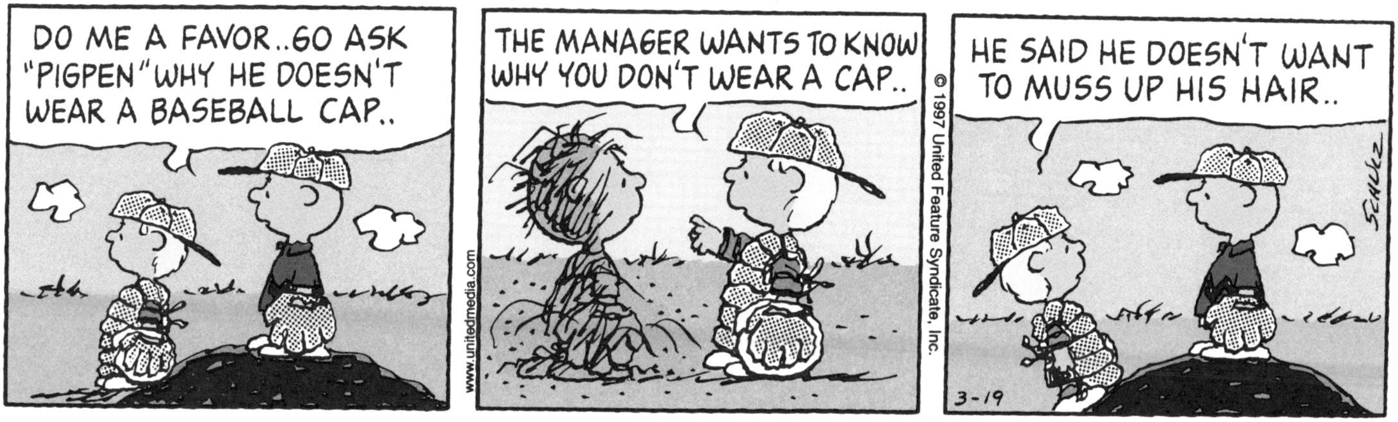
DO ME A FAVOR..GO ASK "PIGPEN" WHY HE DOESN'T WEAR A BASEBALL CAP..
THE MANAGER WANTS TO KNOW WHY YOU DON'T WEAR A CAP..
HE SAID HE DOESN'T WANT TO MUSS UP HIS HAIR..
www.unitedmedia.com
© 1997 United Feature Syndicate, Inc.
3-19
SCHULZ

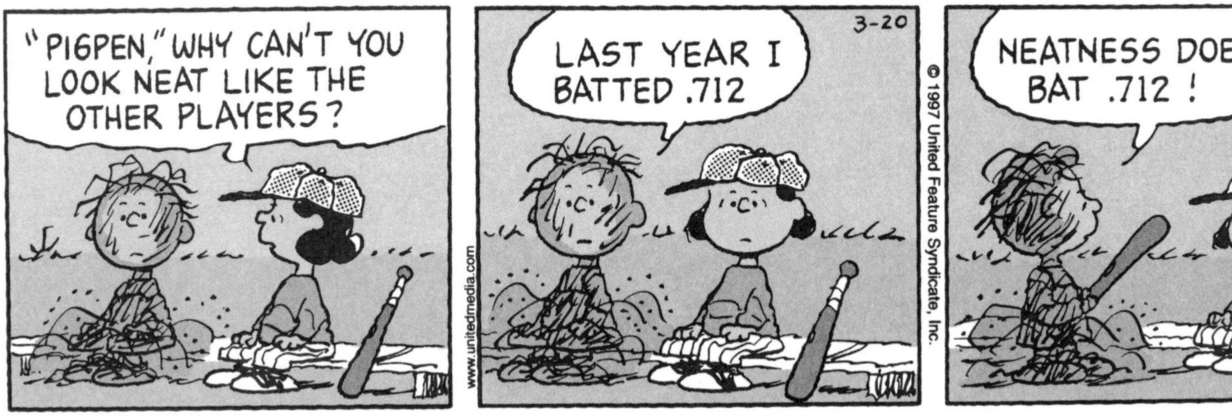
"PIGPEN," WHY CAN'T YOU LOOK NEAT LIKE THE OTHER PLAYERS?
www.unitedmedia.com
3-20
LAST YEAR I BATTED .712
© 1997 United Feature Syndicate, Inc.
NEATNESS DOESN'T BAT .712 !
SCHULZ

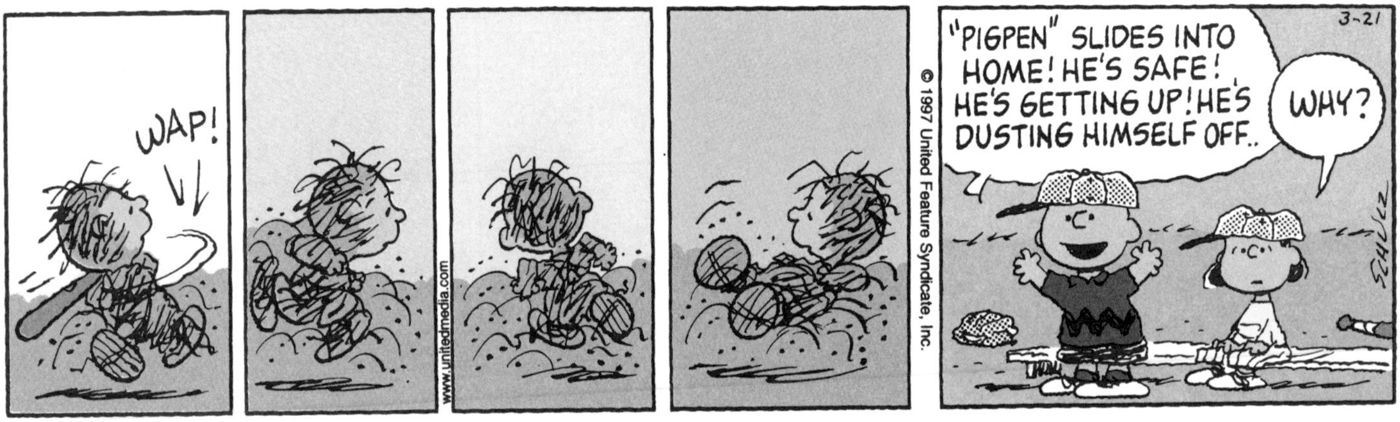
WAP!
www.unitedmedia.com
© 1997 United Feature Syndicate, Inc.
3-21
"PIGPEN" SLIDES INTO HOME! HE'S SAFE! HE'S GETTING UP! HE'S DUSTING HIMSELF OFF..
WHY?
SCHULZ

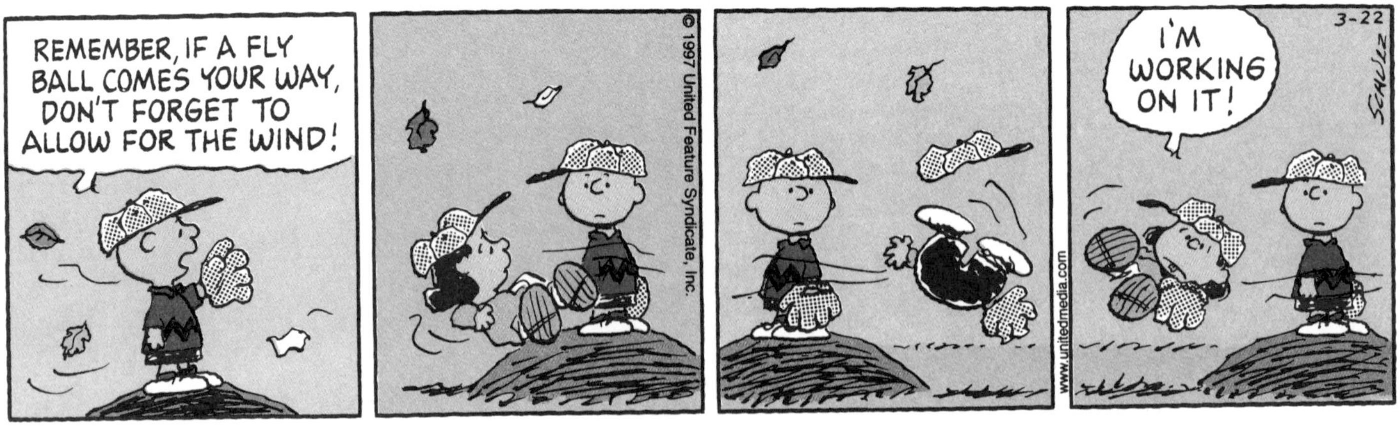
REMEMBER, IF A FLY BALL COMES YOUR WAY, DON'T FORGET TO ALLOW FOR THE WIND!
© 1997 United Feature Syndicate, Inc.
www.unitedmedia.com
3-22
I'M WORKING ON IT!
SCHULZ

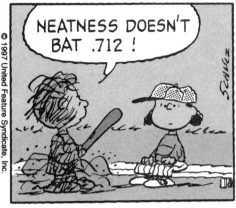

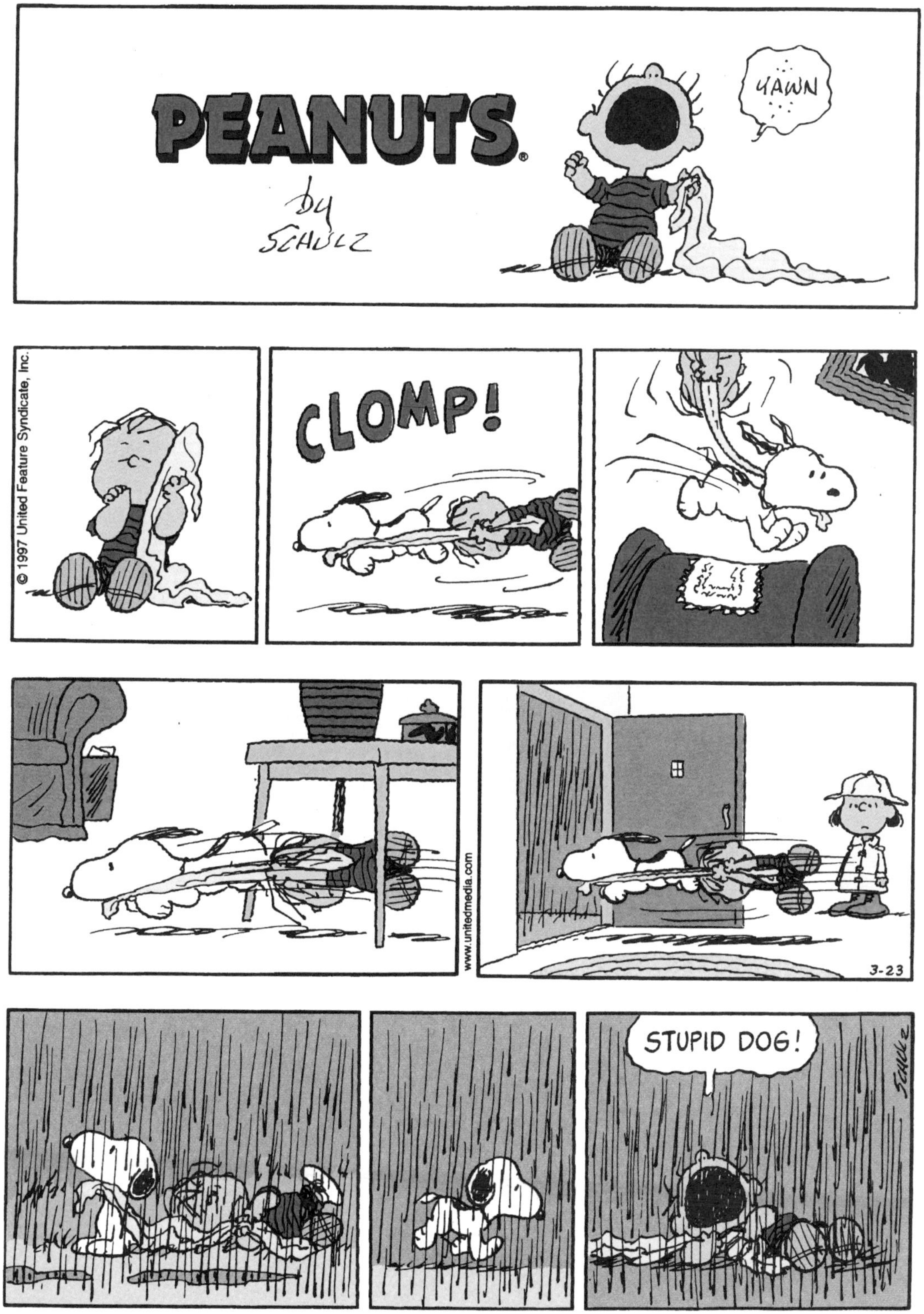
PEANUTS
by SCHULZ
YAWN
© 1997 United Feature Syndicate, Inc.
CLOMP!
www.unitedmedia.com
3-23
STUPID DOG!
SCHULZ

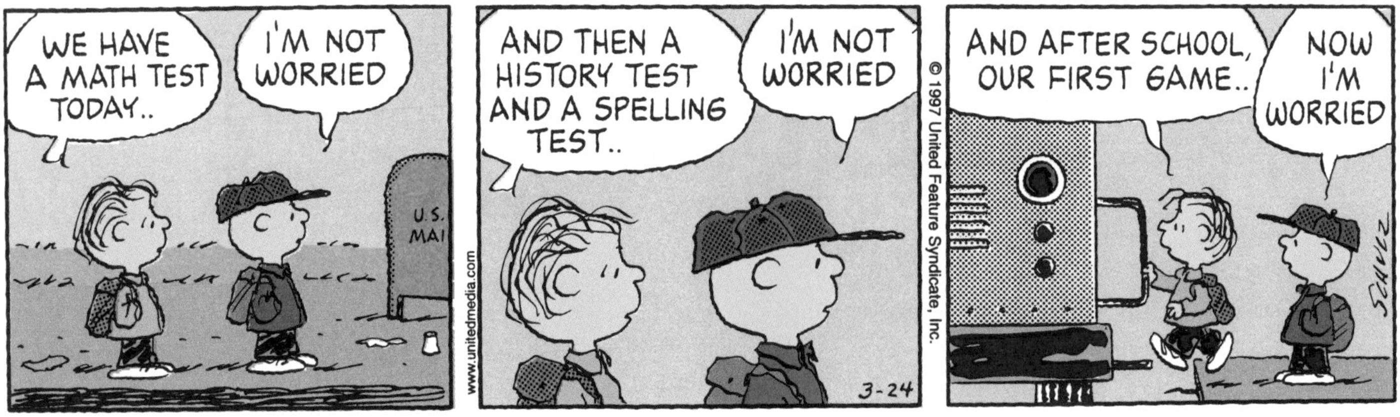
WE HAVE A MATH TEST TODAY..
I'M NOT WORRIED
AND THEN A HISTORY TEST AND A SPELLING TEST..
I'M NOT WORRIED
AND AFTER SCHOOL, OUR FIRST GAME..
NOW I'M WORRIED
U.S. MAI
© 1997 United Feature Syndicate, Inc.
www.unitedmedia.com
3-24
SCHULZ

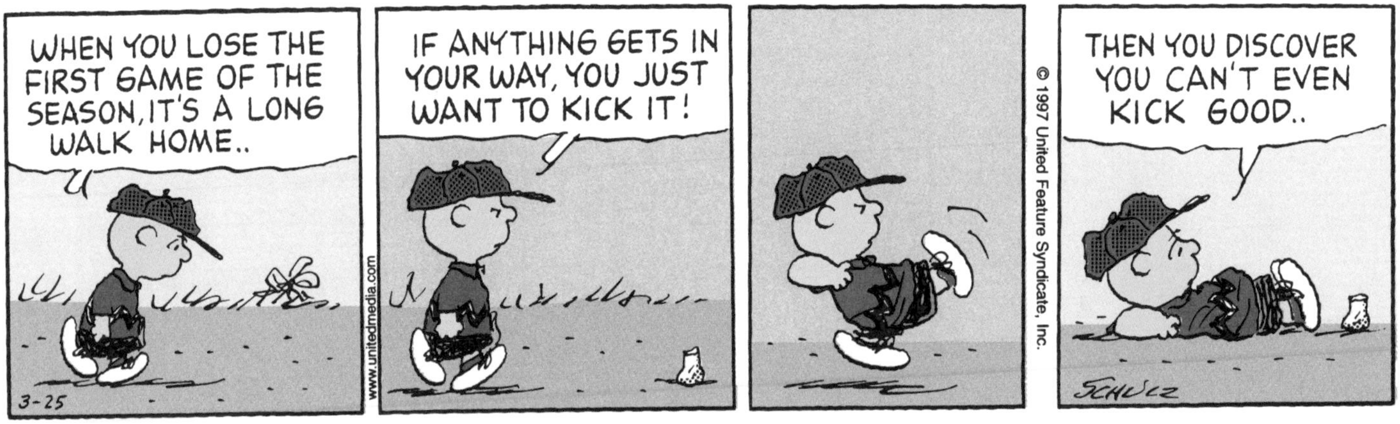
WHEN YOU LOSE THE FIRST GAME OF THE SEASON, IT'S A LONG WALK HOME..
IF ANYTHING GETS IN YOUR WAY, YOU JUST WANT TO KICK IT!
THEN YOU DISCOVER YOU CAN'T EVEN KICK GOOD..
3-25
www.unitedmedia.com
© 1997 United Feature Syndicate, Inc.
SCHULZ

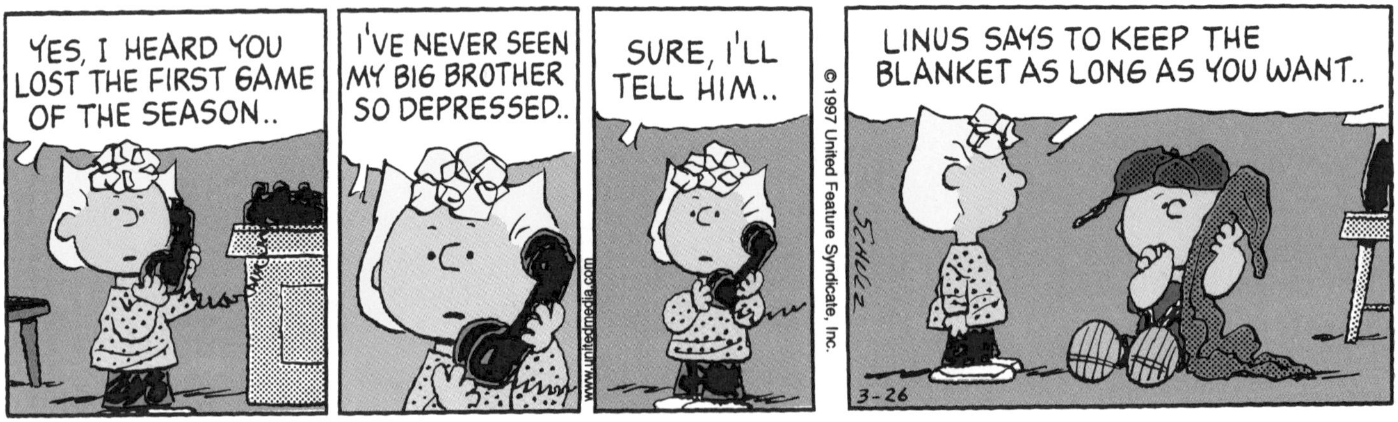
YES, I HEARD YOU LOST THE FIRST GAME OF THE SEASON..
I'VE NEVER SEEN MY BIG BROTHER SO DEPRESSED..
SURE, I'LL TELL HIM..
LINUS SAYS TO KEEP THE BLANKET AS LONG AS YOU WANT..
www.unitedmedia.com
© 1997 United Feature Syndicate, Inc.
SCHULZ
3-26

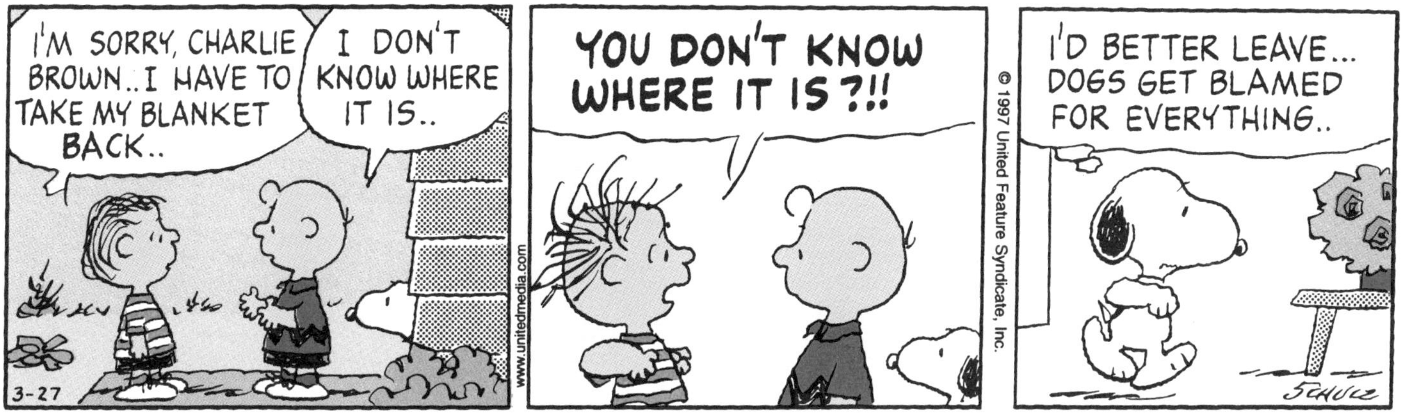
I'M SORRY, CHARLIE BROWN.. I HAVE TO TAKE MY BLANKET BACK..
I DON'T KNOW WHERE IT IS..
YOU DON'T KNOW WHERE IT IS?!!
I'D BETTER LEAVE... DOGS GET BLAMED FOR EVERYTHING..
3-27
www.unitedmedia.com
© 1997 United Feature Syndicate, Inc.
SCHULZ

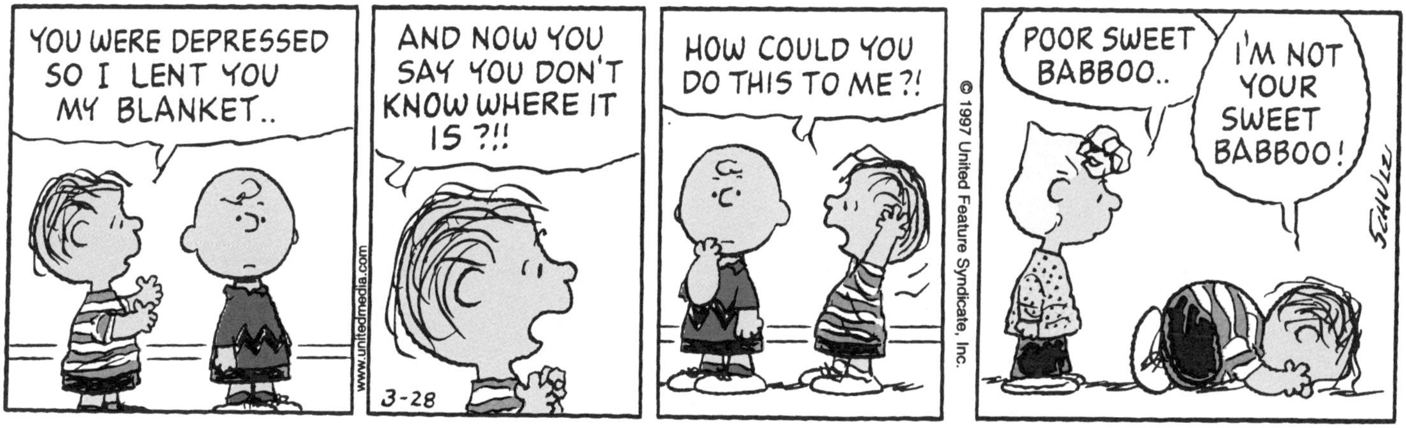
YOU WERE DEPRESSED SO I LENT YOU MY BLANKET..
AND NOW YOU SAY YOU DON'T KNOW WHERE IT IS?!!
HOW COULD YOU DO THIS TO ME?!
POOR SWEET BABBOO..
I'M NOT YOUR SWEET BABBOO!
3-28
www.unitedmedia.com
© 1997 United Feature Syndicate, Inc.
SCHULZ

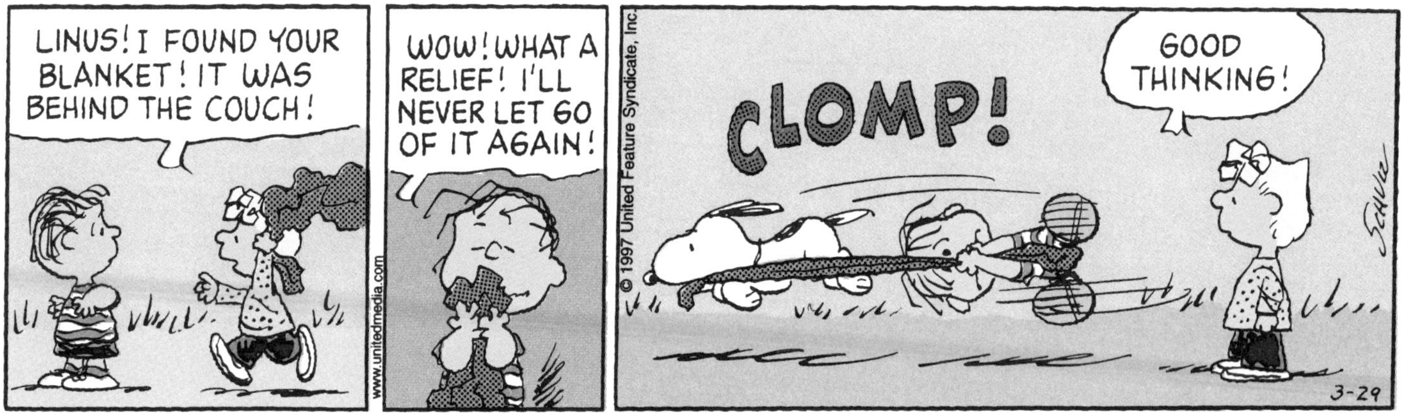
LINUS! I FOUND YOUR BLANKET! IT WAS BEHIND THE COUCH!
WOW! WHAT A RELIEF! I'LL NEVER LET GO OF IT AGAIN!
CLOMP!
GOOD THINKING!
3-29
www.unitedmedia.com
© 1997 United Feature Syndicate, Inc.
SCHULZ

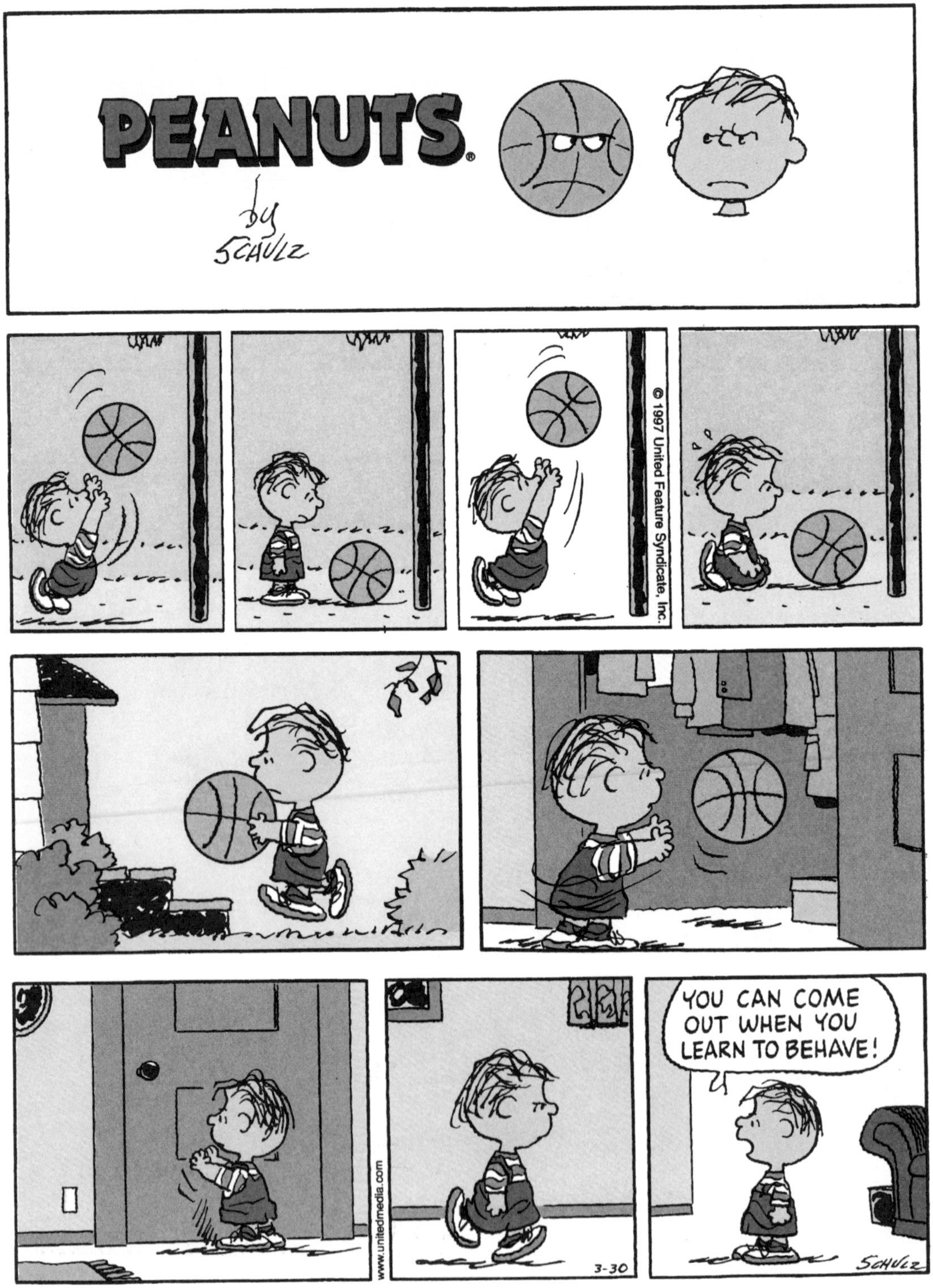
PEANUTS
by SCHULZ
© 1997 United Feature Syndicate, Inc.
www.unitedmedia.com
3-30
YOU CAN COME OUT WHEN YOU LEARN TO BEHAVE!
SCHULZ

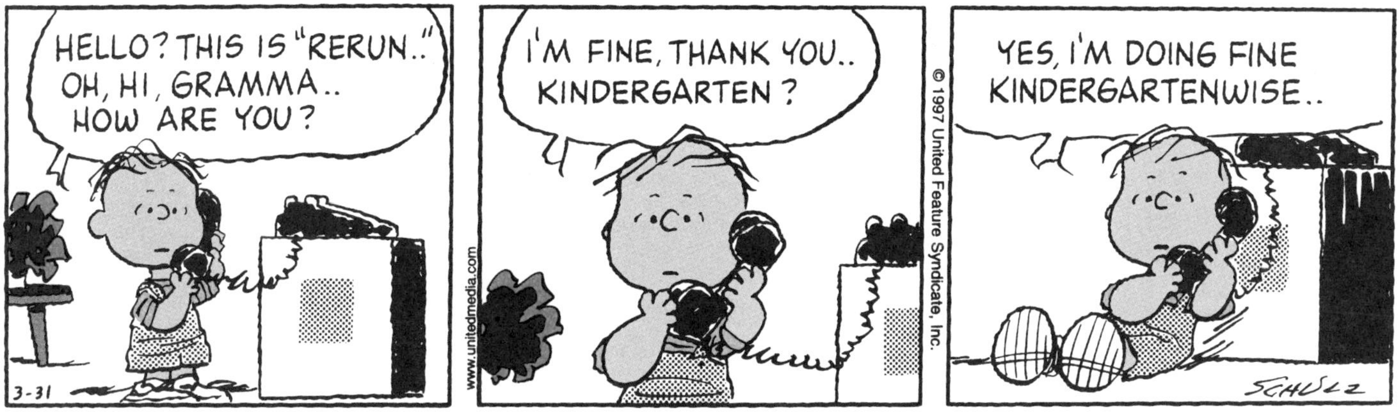
HELLO? THIS IS "RERUN.." OH, HI, GRAMMA.. HOW ARE YOU?
3-31
www.unitedmedia.com
I'M FINE, THANK YOU.. KINDERGARTEN?
© 1997 United Feature Syndicate, Inc.
YES, I'M DOING FINE KINDERGARTENWISE..
SCHULZ

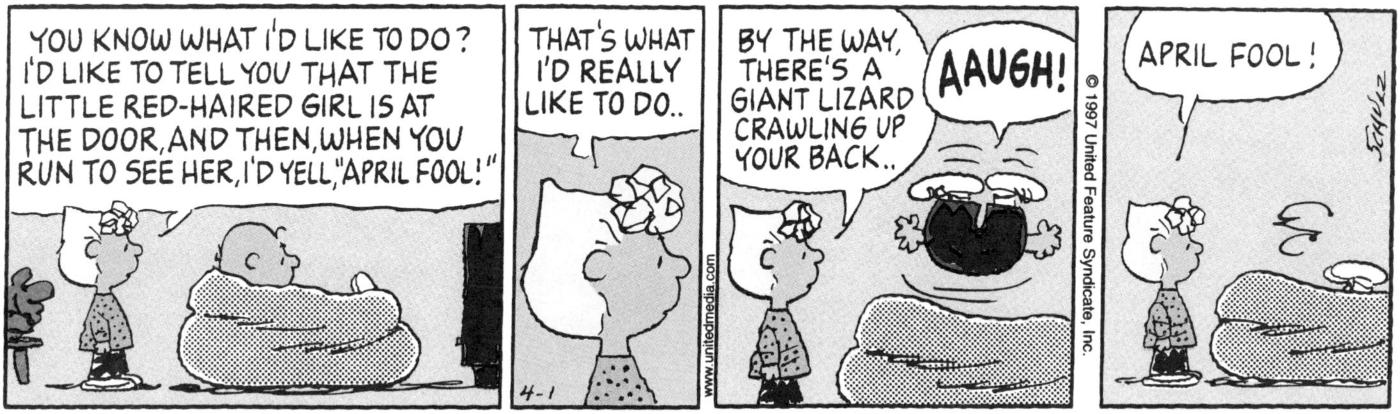
YOU KNOW WHAT I'D LIKE TO DO? I'D LIKE TO TELL YOU THAT THE LITTLE RED-HAIRED GIRL IS AT THE DOOR, AND THEN, WHEN YOU RUN TO SEE HER, I'D YELL, "APRIL FOOL!"
THAT'S WHAT I'D REALLY LIKE TO DO..
4-1
www.unitedmedia.com
BY THE WAY, THERE'S A GIANT LIZARD CRAWLING UP YOUR BACK..
AAUGH!
© 1997 United Feature Syndicate, Inc.
APRIL FOOL!
SCHULZ

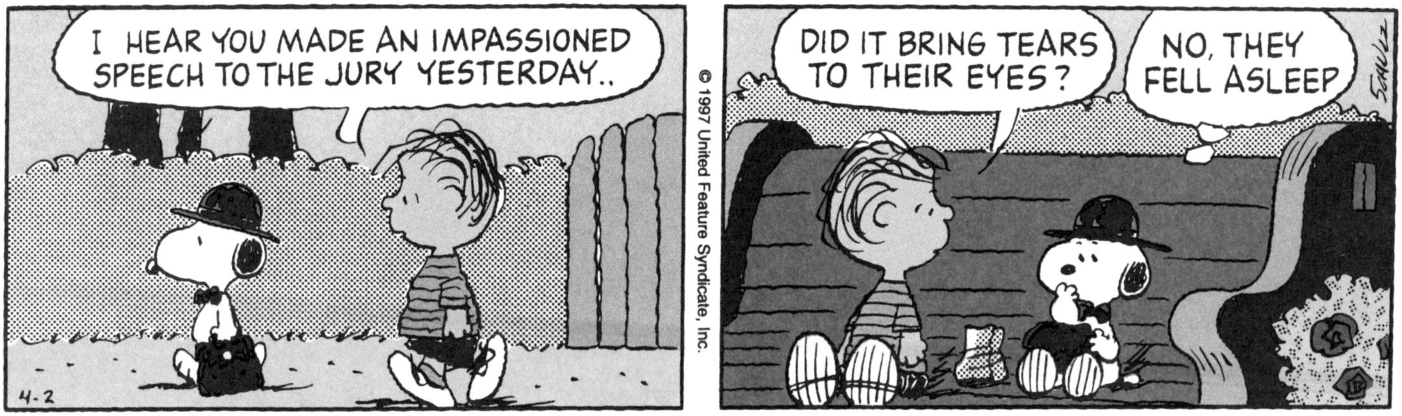
I HEAR YOU MADE AN IMPASSIONED SPEECH TO THE JURY YESTERDAY..
4-2
© 1997 United Feature Syndicate, Inc.
DID IT BRING TEARS TO THEIR EYES?
NO, THEY FELL ASLEEP
SCHULZ

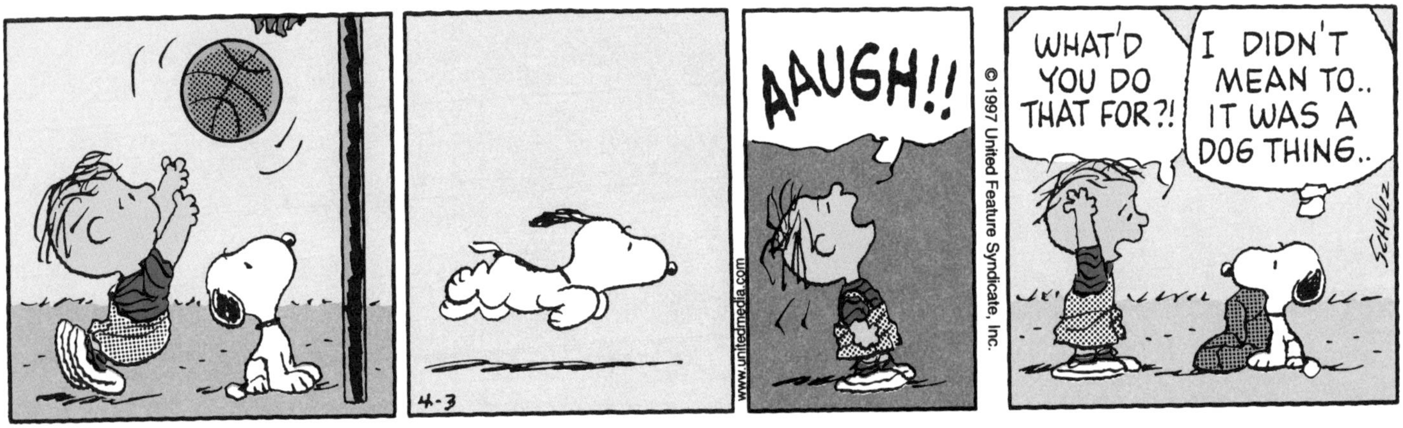
AAUGH!!
WHAT'D YOU DO THAT FOR?!
I DIDN'T MEAN TO.. IT WAS A DOG THING..
© 1997 United Feature Syndicate, Inc.
www.unitedmedia.com
4-3
SCHULZ

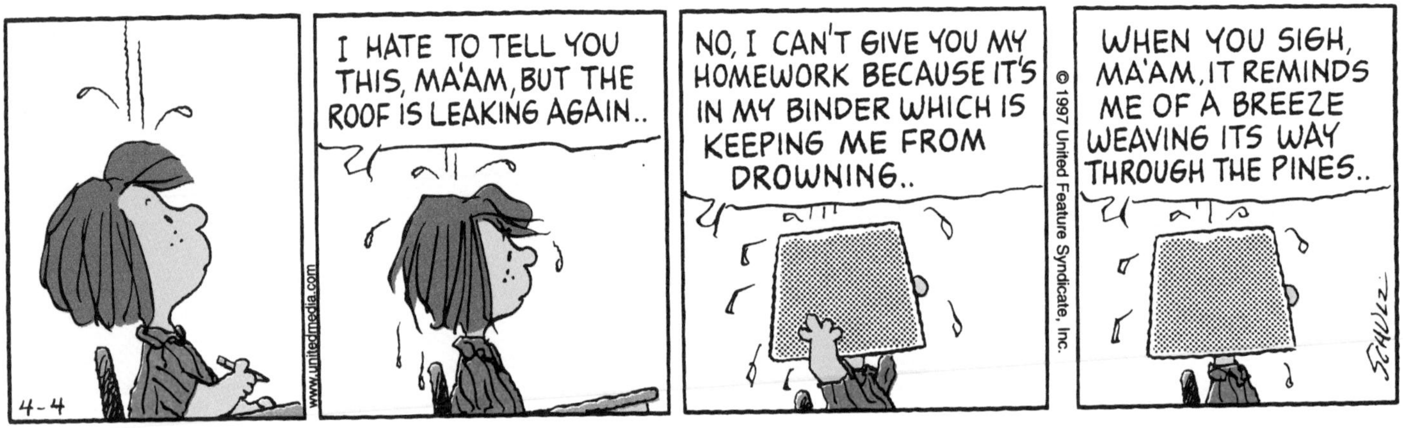
I HATE TO TELL YOU THIS, MA'AM, BUT THE ROOF IS LEAKING AGAIN..
NO, I CAN'T GIVE YOU MY HOMEWORK BECAUSE IT'S IN MY BINDER WHICH IS KEEPING ME FROM DROWNING..
WHEN YOU SIGH, MA'AM, IT REMINDS ME OF A BREEZE WEAVING ITS WAY THROUGH THE PINES..
© 1997 United Feature Syndicate, Inc.
www.unitedmedia.com
4-4
SCHULZ

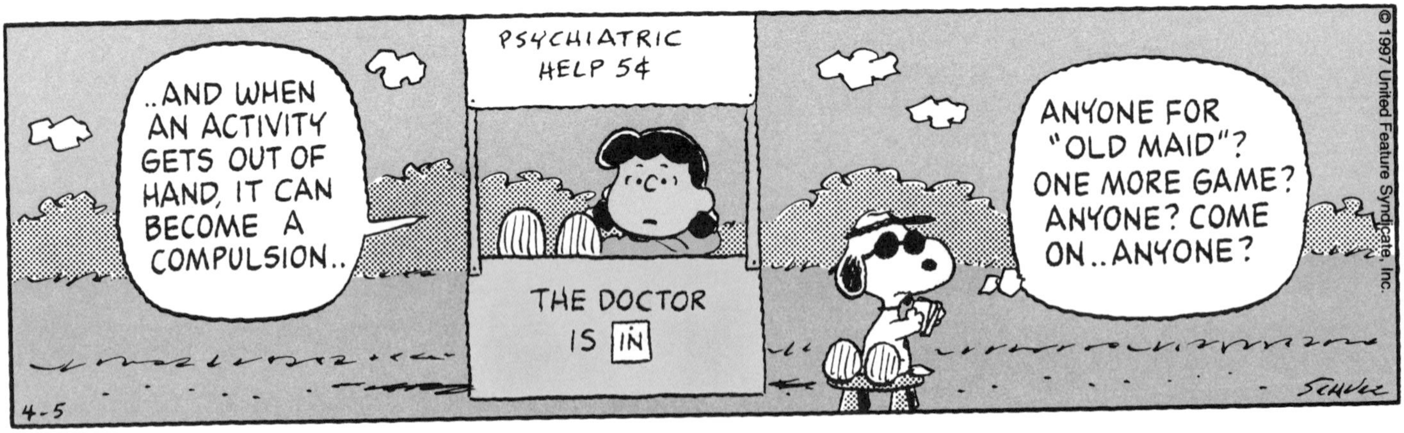
PSYCHIATRIC HELP 5¢
THE DOCTOR IS IN
..AND WHEN AN ACTIVITY GETS OUT OF HAND, IT CAN BECOME A COMPULSION..
ANYONE FOR "OLD MAID"? ONE MORE GAME? ANYONE? COME ON..ANYONE?
© 1997 United Feature Syndicate, Inc.
4-5
SCHULZ

She called him "cute"
PEANUTS
by SCHULZ
© 1997 United Feature Syndicate, Inc.
She called him "adorable,"
and it caused him more trouble than anything that ever happened to him in his whole life.
"adorable" HMM..
THAT'S A PRETTY GOOD BEGINNING..
4-6
www.unitedmedia.com
A GOOD BEGINNING IS VERY IMPORTANT..
I LIKE A GOOD BEGINNING..
THIS ISN'T THE BEGINNING.. THIS IS THE ENDING!
SCHULZ

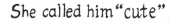

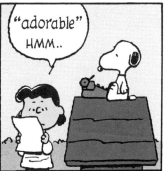

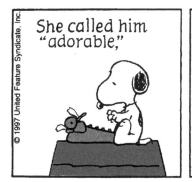

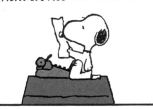

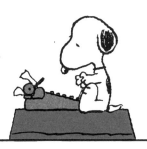

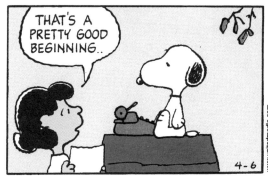

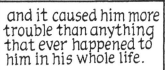

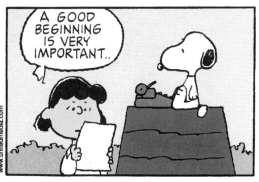

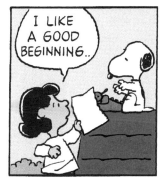

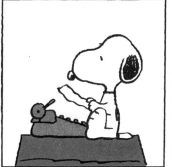

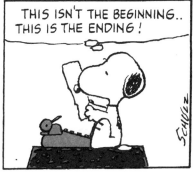

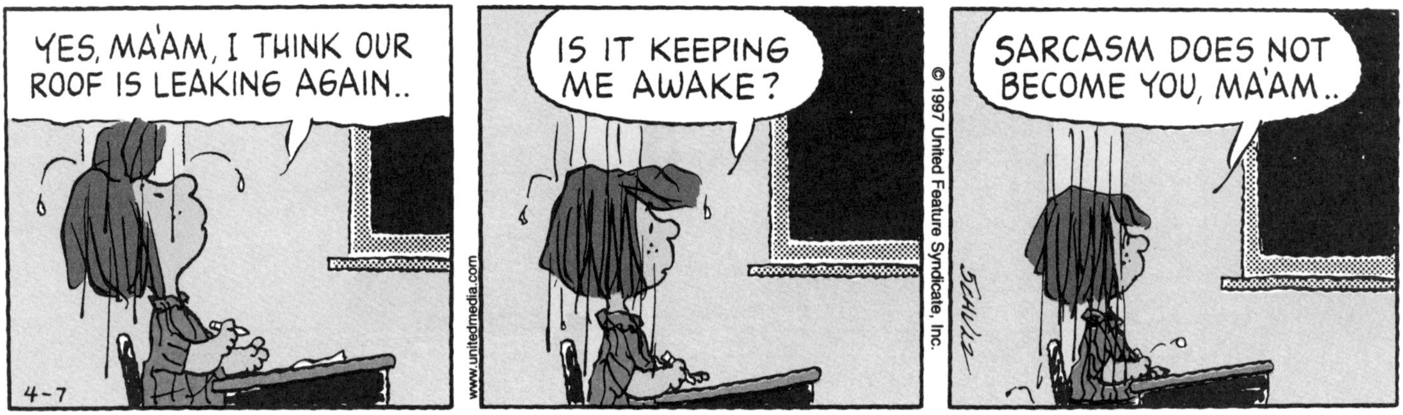
YES, MA'AM, I THINK OUR ROOF IS LEAKING AGAIN..
4-7
IS IT KEEPING ME AWAKE?
www.unitedmedia.com
© 1997 United Feature Syndicate, Inc.
SARCASM DOES NOT BECOME YOU, MA'AM..
SCHULZ

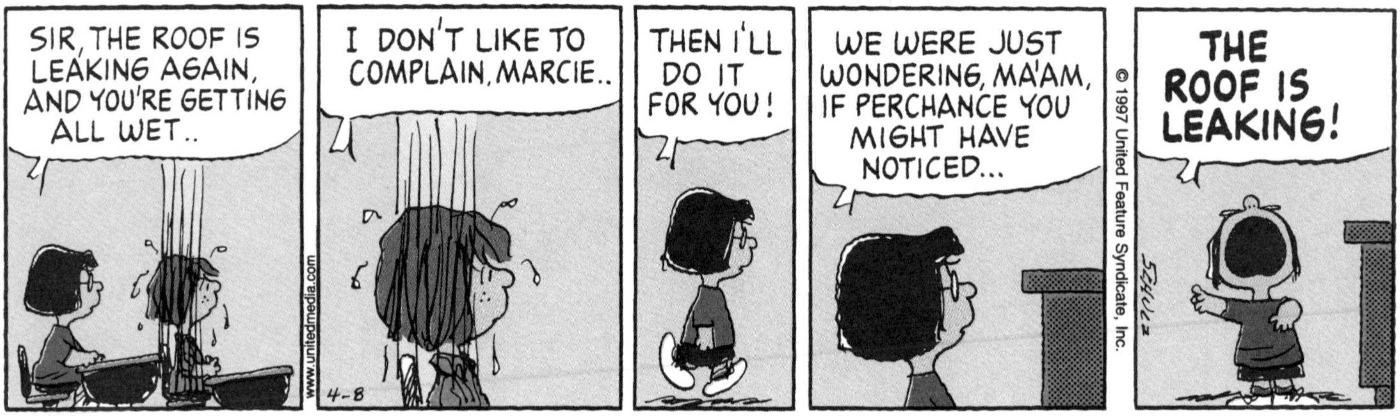
SIR, THE ROOF IS LEAKING AGAIN, AND YOU'RE GETTING ALL WET..
www.unitedmedia.com
I DON'T LIKE TO COMPLAIN, MARCIE..
4-8
THEN I'LL DO IT FOR YOU!
WE WERE JUST WONDERING, MA'AM, IF PERCHANCE YOU MIGHT HAVE NOTICED...
© 1997 United Feature Syndicate, Inc.
SCHULZ
THE ROOF IS LEAKING!

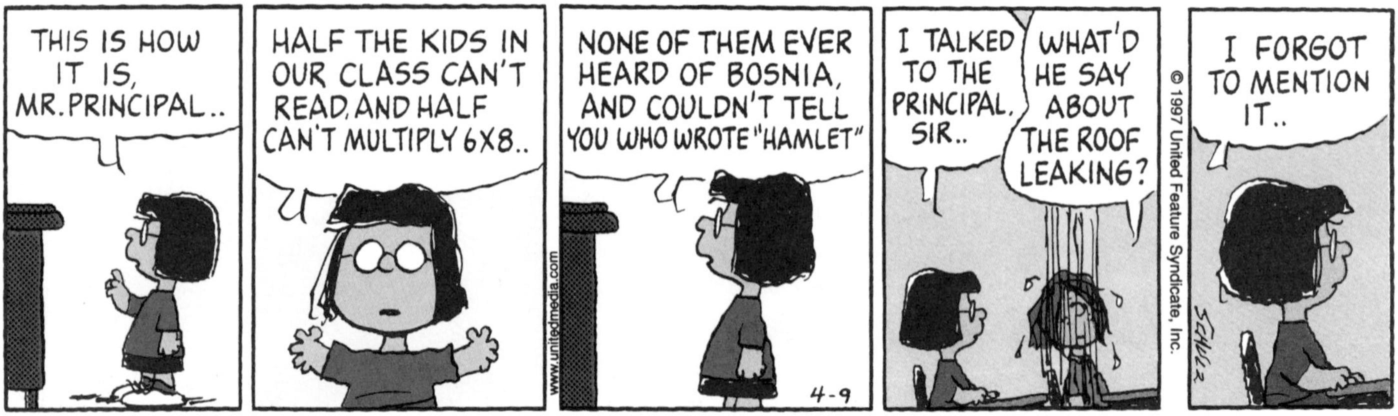
THIS IS HOW IT IS, MR. PRINCIPAL..
HALF THE KIDS IN OUR CLASS CAN'T READ, AND HALF CAN'T MULTIPLY 6X8..
www.unitedmedia.com
NONE OF THEM EVER HEARD OF BOSNIA, AND COULDN'T TELL YOU WHO WROTE "HAMLET"
4-9
I TALKED TO THE PRINCIPAL, SIR..
WHAT'D HE SAY ABOUT THE ROOF LEAKING?
© 1997 United Feature Syndicate, Inc.
SCHULZ
I FORGOT TO MENTION IT..

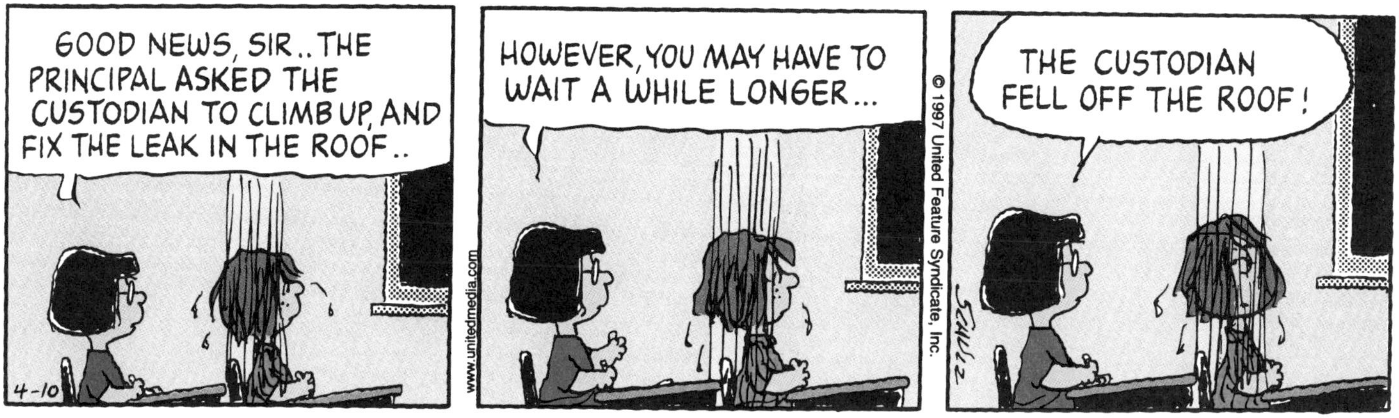
GOOD NEWS, SIR.. THE PRINCIPAL ASKED THE CUSTODIAN TO CLIMB UP, AND FIX THE LEAK IN THE ROOF..
4-10
www.unitedmedia.com
HOWEVER, YOU MAY HAVE TO WAIT A WHILE LONGER...
© 1997 United Feature Syndicate, Inc.
THE CUSTODIAN FELL OFF THE ROOF!

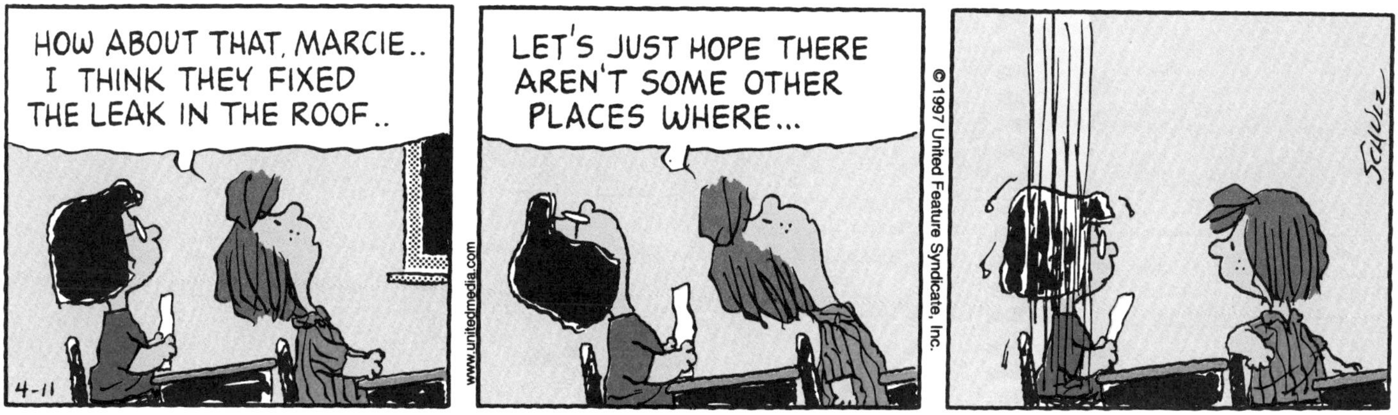
HOW ABOUT THAT, MARCIE.. I THINK THEY FIXED THE LEAK IN THE ROOF..
4-11
www.unitedmedia.com
LET'S JUST HOPE THERE AREN'T SOME OTHER PLACES WHERE...
© 1997 United Feature Syndicate, Inc.

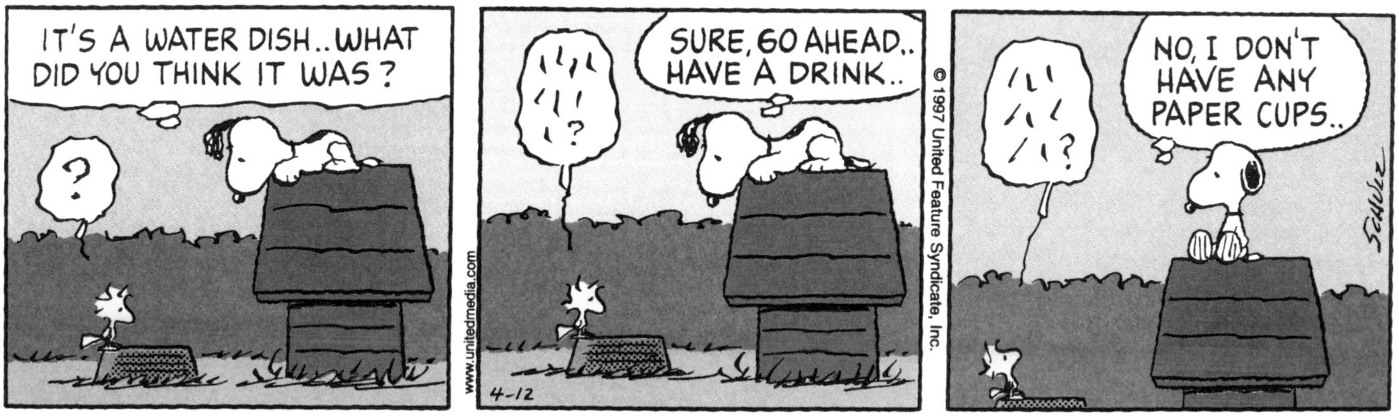
IT'S A WATER DISH.. WHAT DID YOU THINK IT WAS?
?
www.unitedmedia.com
SURE, GO AHEAD.. HAVE A DRINK..
4-12
© 1997 United Feature Syndicate, Inc.
NO, I DON'T HAVE ANY PAPER CUPS..

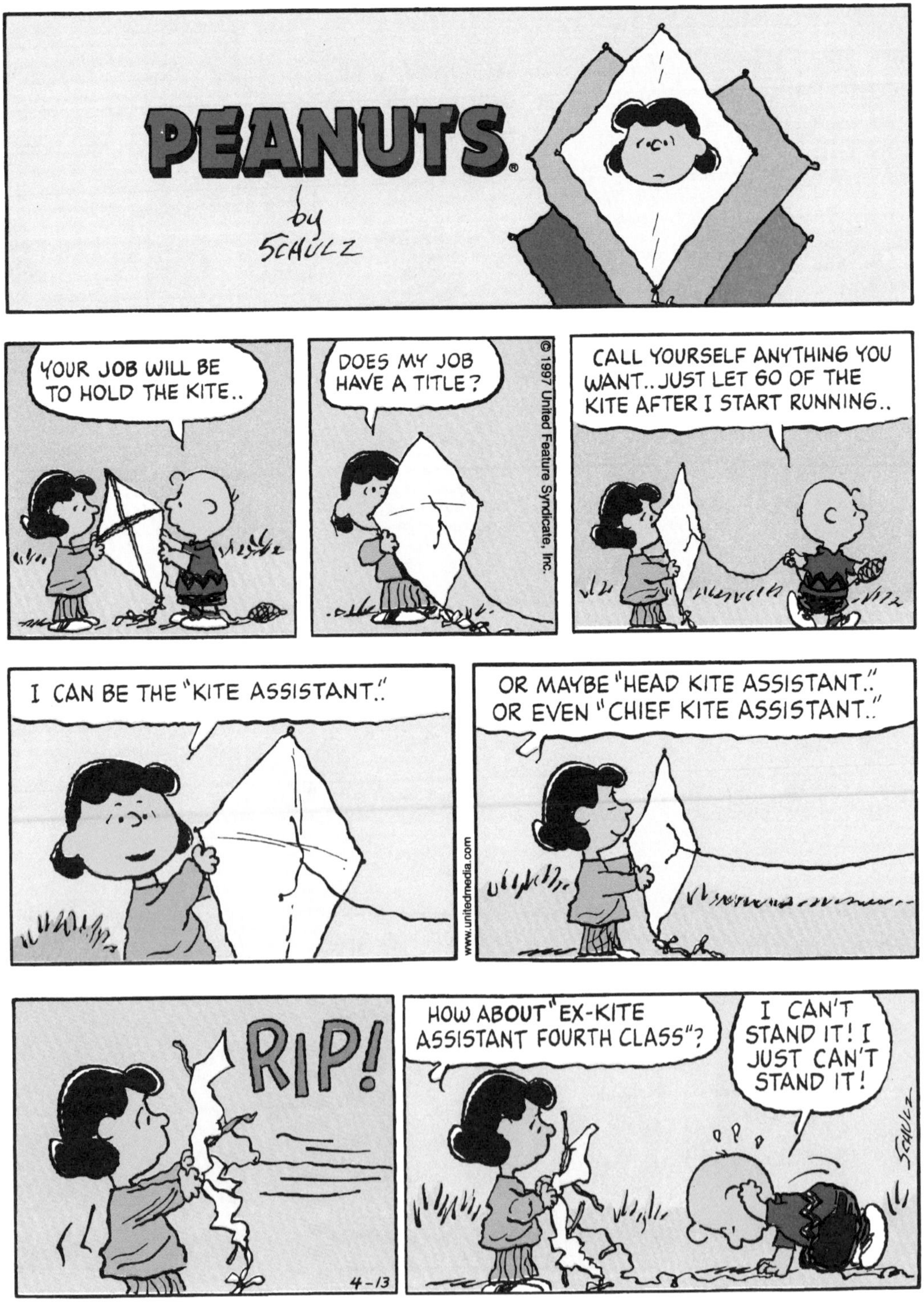
PEANUTS
by SCHULZ
YOUR JOB WILL BE TO HOLD THE KITE..
DOES MY JOB HAVE A TITLE?
© 1997 United Feature Syndicate, Inc.
CALL YOURSELF ANYTHING YOU WANT.. JUST LET GO OF THE KITE AFTER I START RUNNING..
I CAN BE THE "KITE ASSISTANT."
www.unitedmedia.com
OR MAYBE "HEAD KITE ASSISTANT." OR EVEN "CHIEF KITE ASSISTANT."
RIP!
4-13
HOW ABOUT "EX-KITE ASSISTANT FOURTH CLASS"?
I CAN'T STAND IT! I JUST CAN'T STAND IT!
SCHULZ

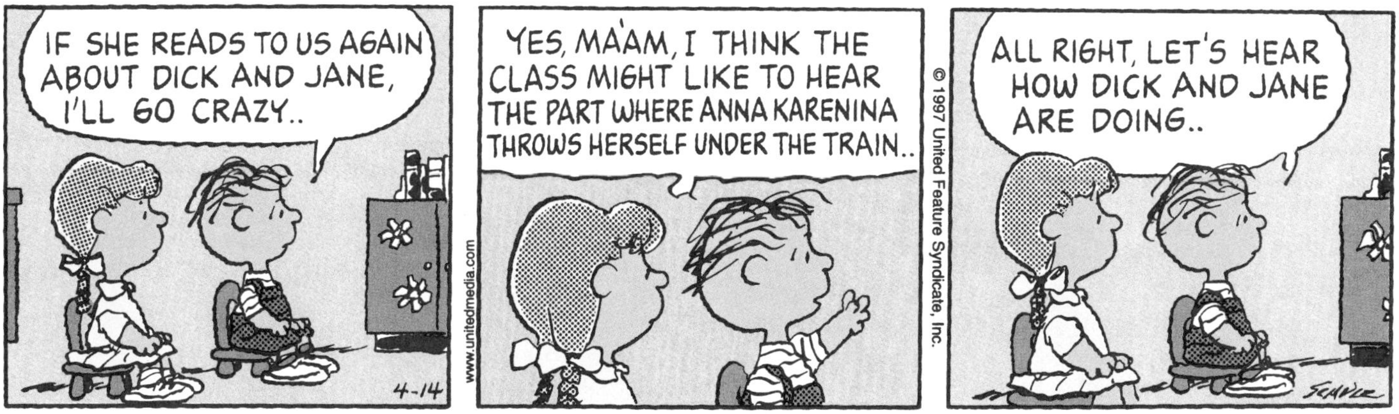
IF SHE READS TO US AGAIN ABOUT DICK AND JANE, I'LL GO CRAZY..
4-14
www.unitedmedia.com
YES, MA'AM, I THINK THE CLASS MIGHT LIKE TO HEAR THE PART WHERE ANNA KARENINA THROWS HERSELF UNDER THE TRAIN..
© 1997 United Feature Syndicate, Inc.
ALL RIGHT, LET'S HEAR HOW DICK AND JANE ARE DOING..
SCHULZ

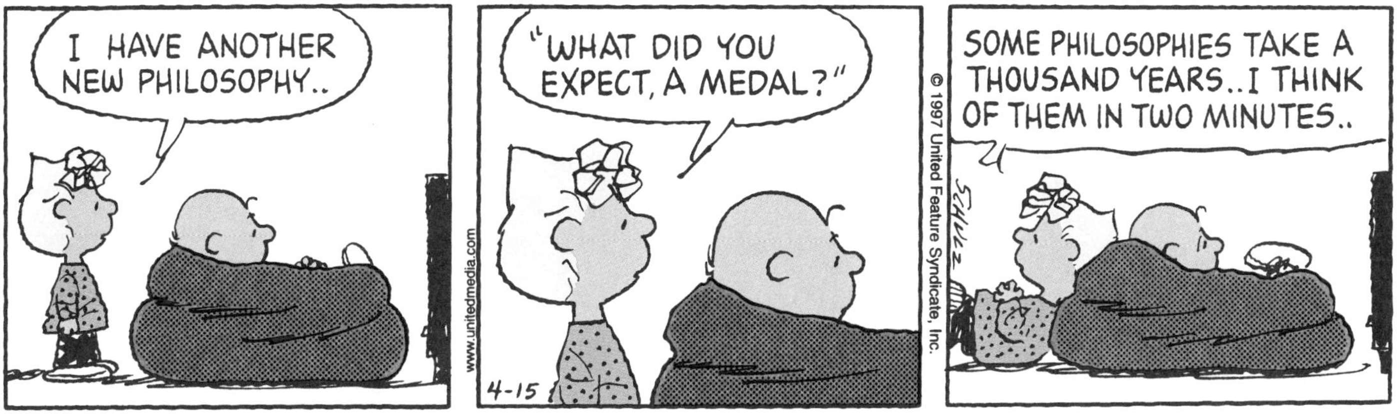
I HAVE ANOTHER NEW PHILOSOPHY..
www.unitedmedia.com
"WHAT DID YOU EXPECT, A MEDAL?"
4-15
© 1997 United Feature Syndicate, Inc.
SOME PHILOSOPHIES TAKE A THOUSAND YEARS..I THINK OF THEM IN TWO MINUTES..
SCHULZ

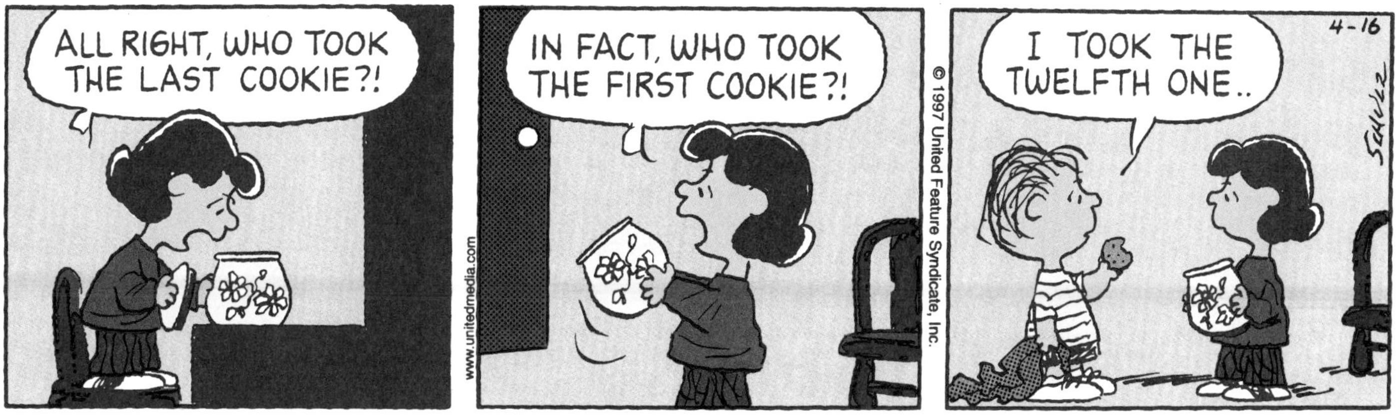
ALL RIGHT, WHO TOOK THE LAST COOKIE?!
www.unitedmedia.com
IN FACT, WHO TOOK THE FIRST COOKIE?!
© 1997 United Feature Syndicate, Inc.
4-16
I TOOK THE TWELFTH ONE..
SCHULZ

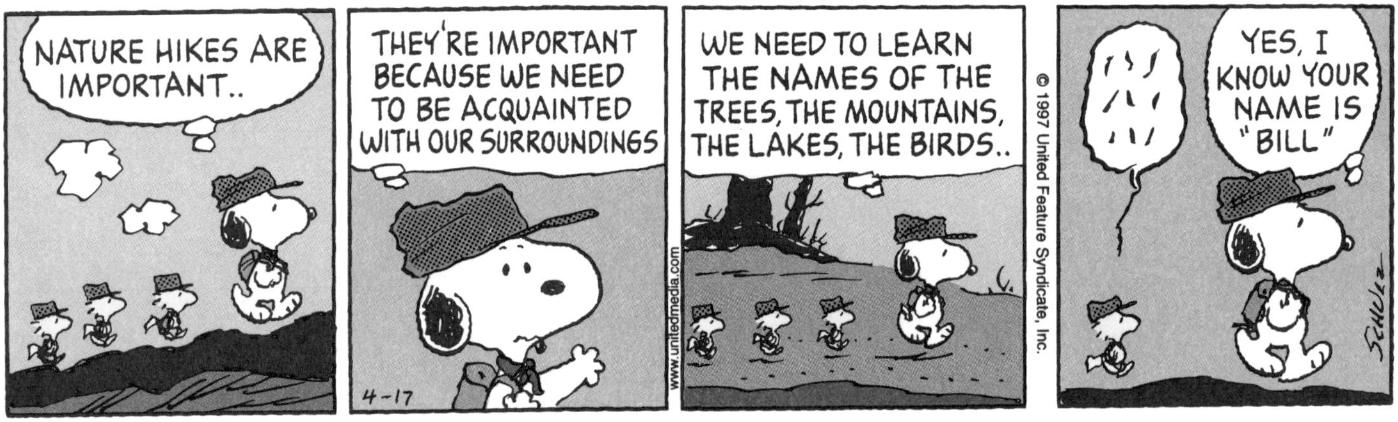
NATURE HIKES ARE IMPORTANT..
THEY'RE IMPORTANT BECAUSE WE NEED TO BE ACQUAINTED WITH OUR SURROUNDINGS
4-17
www.unitedmedia.com
WE NEED TO LEARN THE NAMES OF THE TREES, THE MOUNTAINS, THE LAKES, THE BIRDS..
© 1997 United Feature Syndicate, Inc.
YES, I KNOW YOUR NAME IS "BILL"
SCHULZ

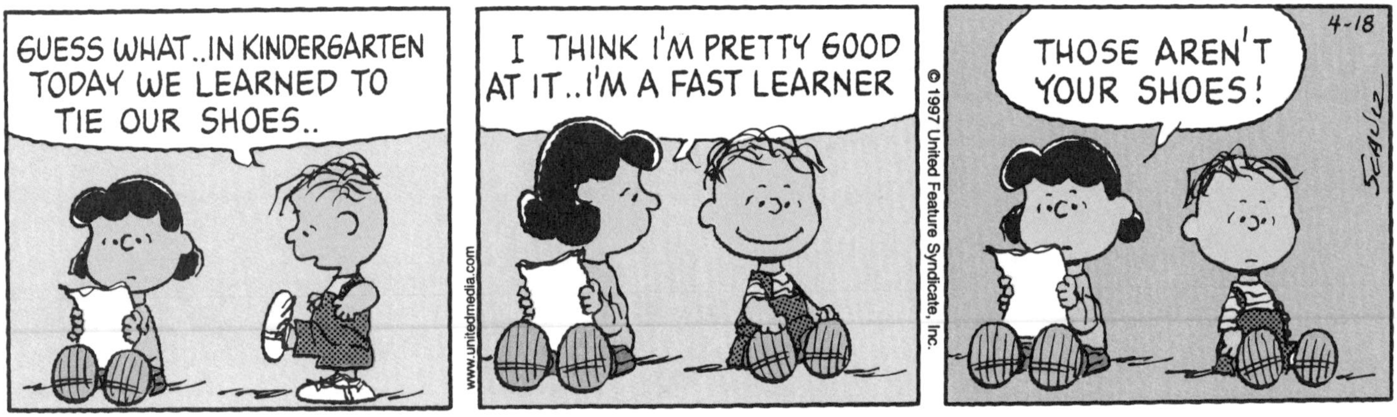
GUESS WHAT..IN KINDERGARTEN TODAY WE LEARNED TO TIE OUR SHOES..
www.unitedmedia.com
I THINK I'M PRETTY GOOD AT IT..I'M A FAST LEARNER
© 1997 United Feature Syndicate, Inc.
4-18
THOSE AREN'T YOUR SHOES!
SCHULZ

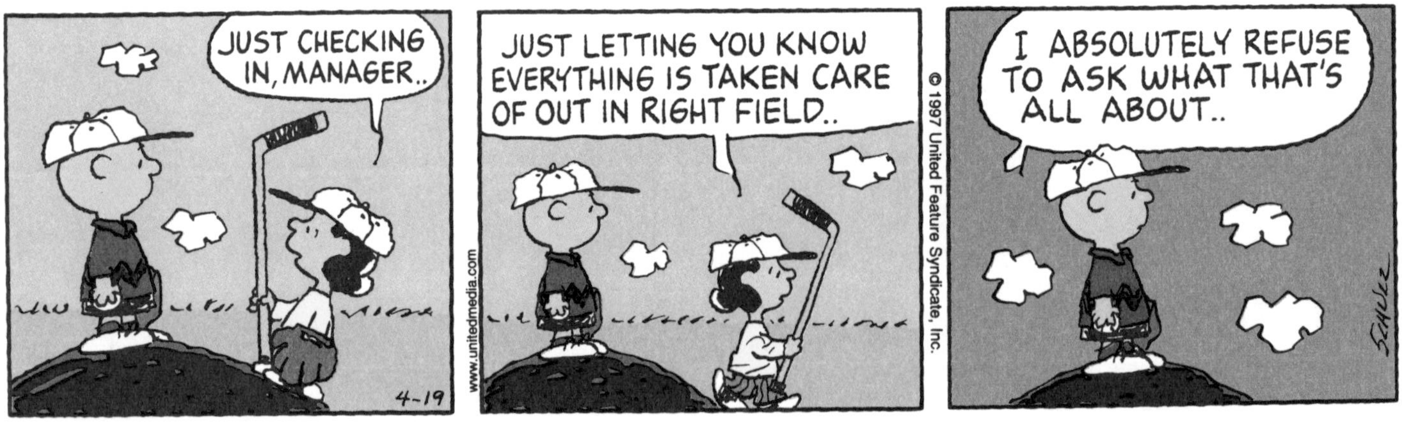
JUST CHECKING IN, MANAGER..
4-19
www.unitedmedia.com
JUST LETTING YOU KNOW EVERYTHING IS TAKEN CARE OF OUT IN RIGHT FIELD..
© 1997 United Feature Syndicate, Inc.
I ABSOLUTELY REFUSE TO ASK WHAT THAT'S ALL ABOUT..
SCHULZ

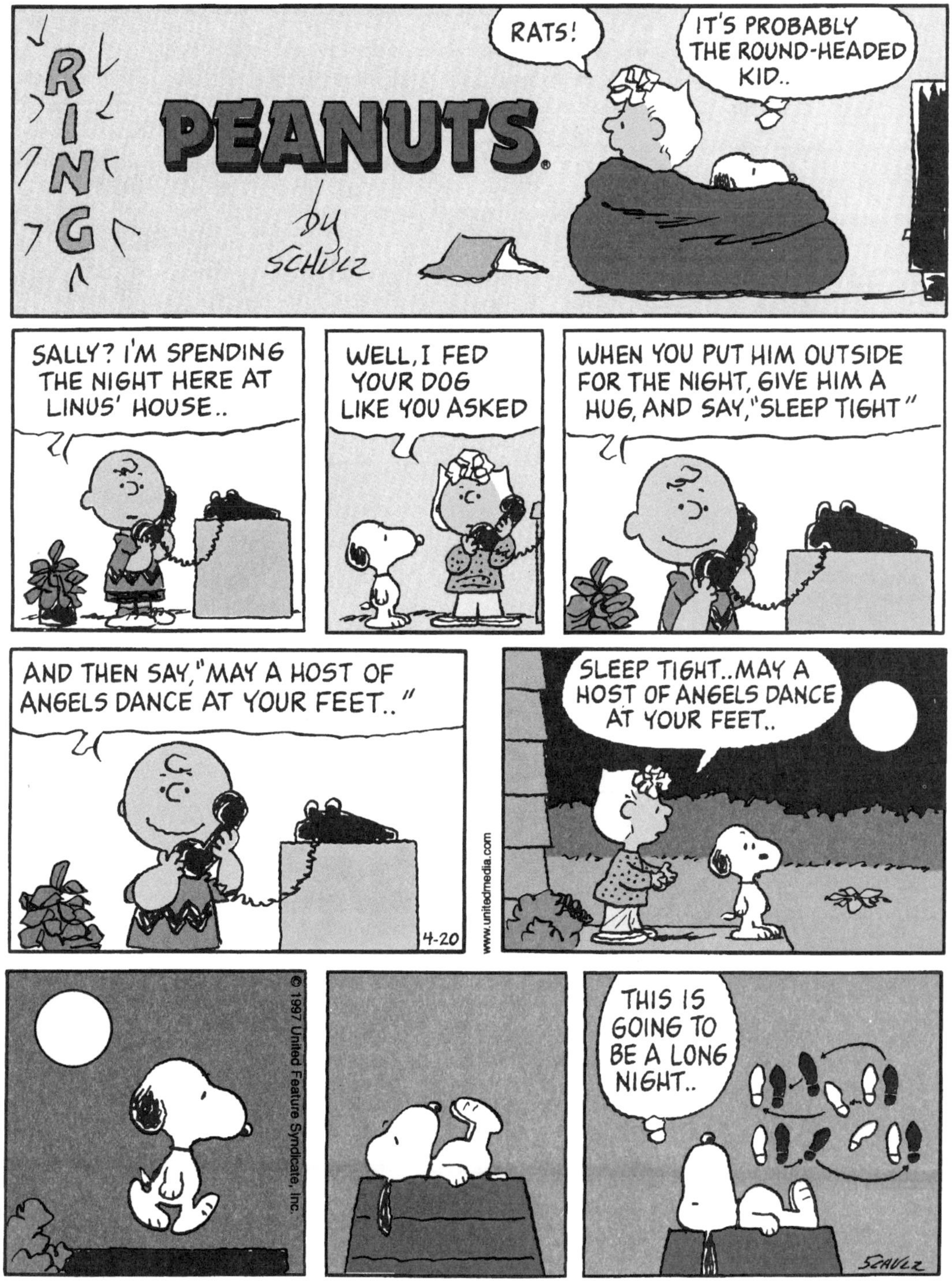
RING
PEANUTS®
by SCHULZ
RATS!
IT'S PROBABLY THE ROUND-HEADED KID..
SALLY? I'M SPENDING THE NIGHT HERE AT LINUS' HOUSE..
WELL, I FED YOUR DOG LIKE YOU ASKED
WHEN YOU PUT HIM OUTSIDE FOR THE NIGHT, GIVE HIM A HUG, AND SAY, "SLEEP TIGHT"
AND THEN SAY, "MAY A HOST OF ANGELS DANCE AT YOUR FEET.."
4-20
www.unitedmedia.com
SLEEP TIGHT..MAY A HOST OF ANGELS DANCE AT YOUR FEET..
© 1997 United Feature Syndicate, Inc.
THIS IS GOING TO BE A LONG NIGHT..
SCHULZ

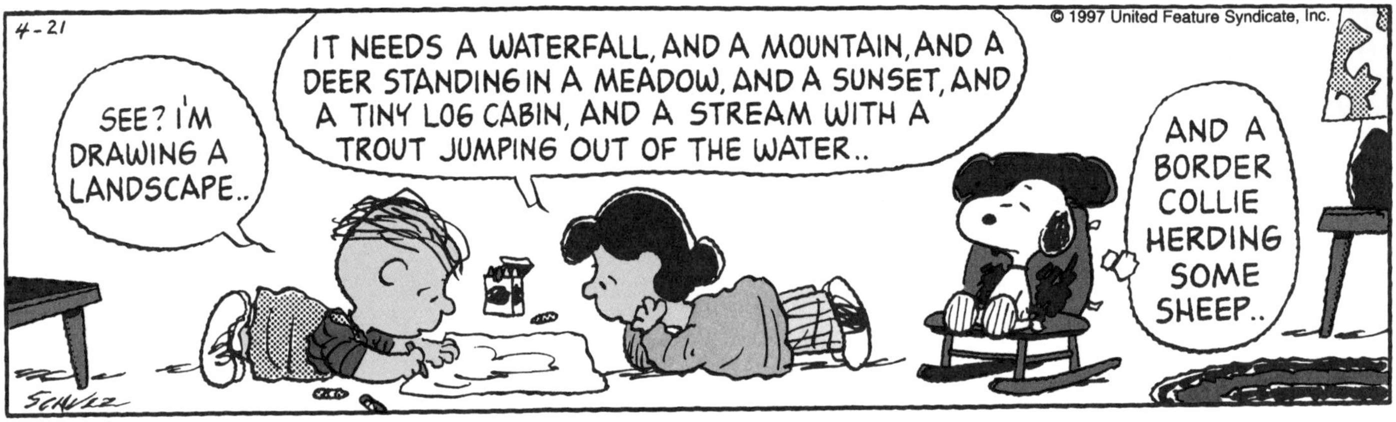
4-21
© 1997 United Feature Syndicate, Inc.
SEE? I'M DRAWING A LANDSCAPE..
IT NEEDS A WATERFALL, AND A MOUNTAIN, AND A DEER STANDING IN A MEADOW, AND A SUNSET, AND A TINY LOG CABIN, AND A STREAM WITH A TROUT JUMPING OUT OF THE WATER..
AND A BORDER COLLIE HERDING SOME SHEEP..
SCHULZ

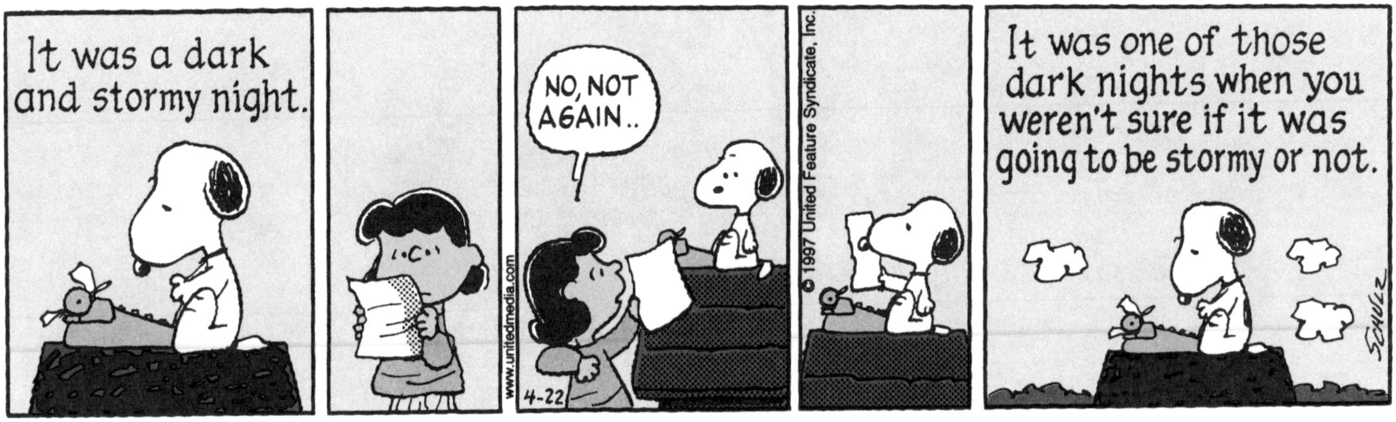
It was a dark and stormy night.
www.unitedmedia.com
4-22
NO, NOT AGAIN..
© 1997 United Feature Syndicate, Inc.
It was one of those dark nights when you weren't sure if it was going to be stormy or not.
SCHULZ

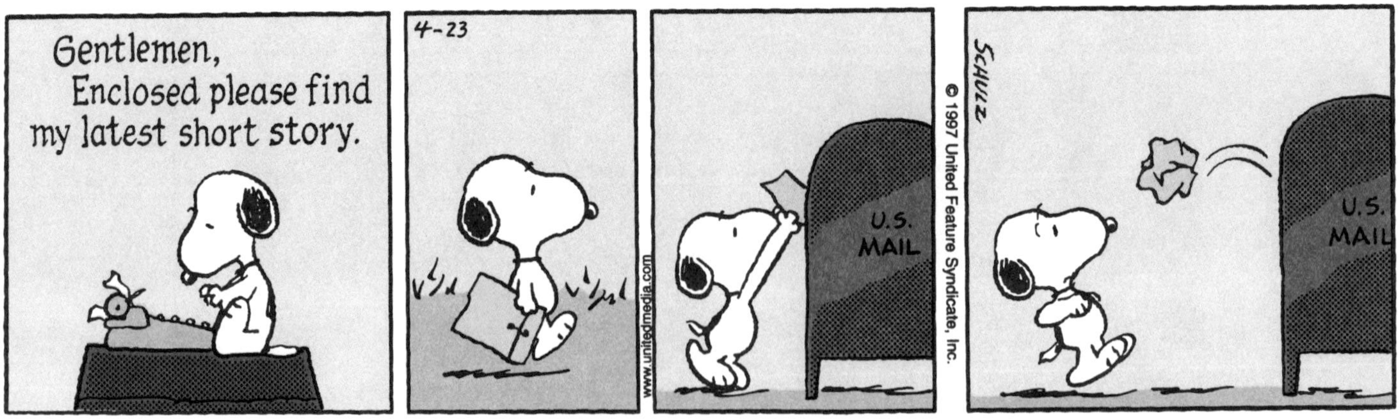
Gentlemen,
Enclosed please find my latest short story.
4-23
www.unitedmedia.com
U.S. MAIL
© 1997 United Feature Syndicate, Inc.
SCHULZ
U.S. MAIL

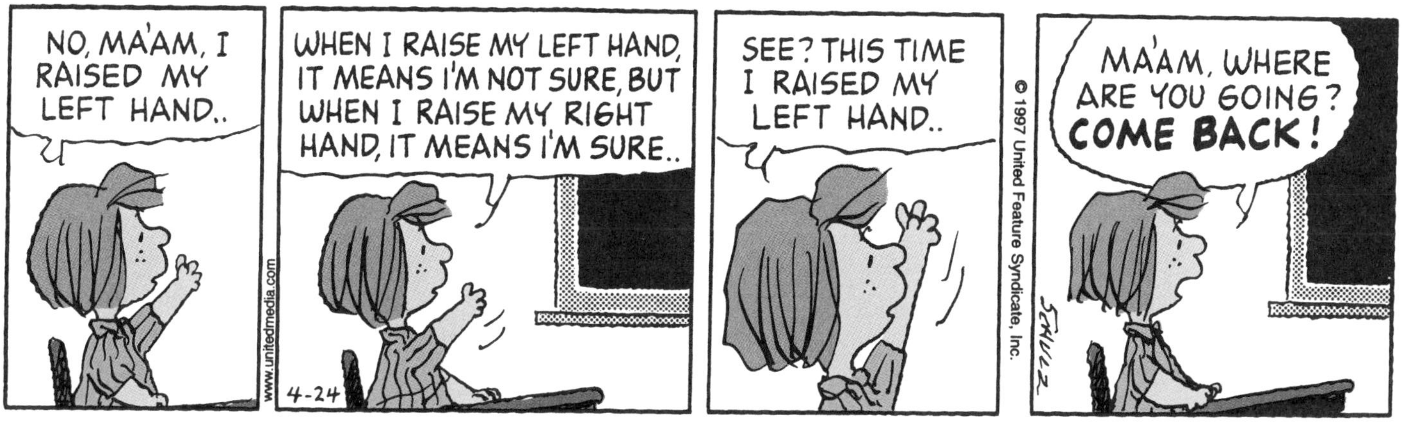
NO, MA'AM, I RAISED MY LEFT HAND..
WHEN I RAISE MY LEFT HAND, IT MEANS I'M NOT SURE, BUT WHEN I RAISE MY RIGHT HAND, IT MEANS I'M SURE..
SEE? THIS TIME I RAISED MY LEFT HAND..
MA'AM, WHERE ARE YOU GOING? **COME BACK!**

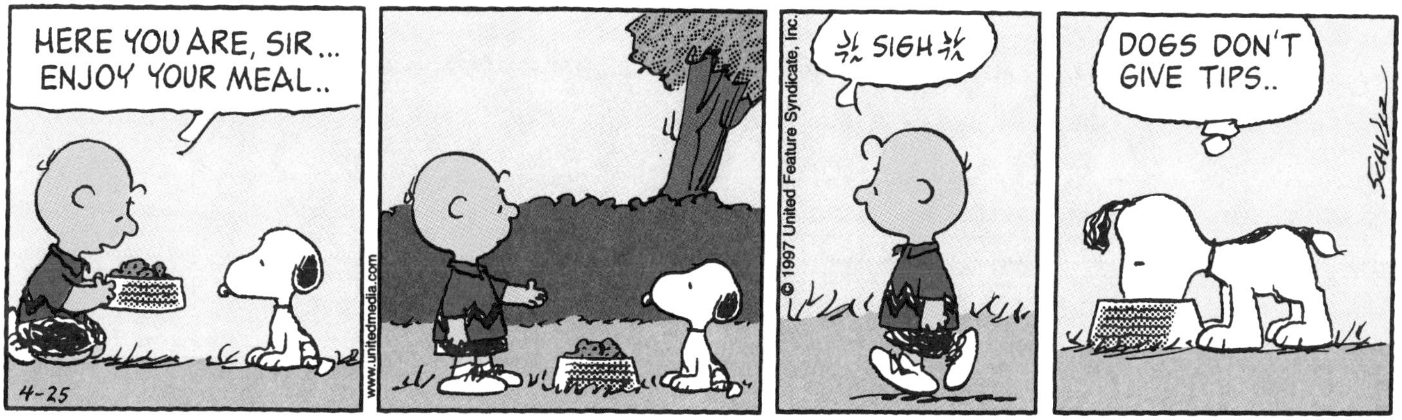
HERE YOU ARE, SIR... ENJOY YOUR MEAL..
SIGH
DOGS DON'T GIVE TIPS..

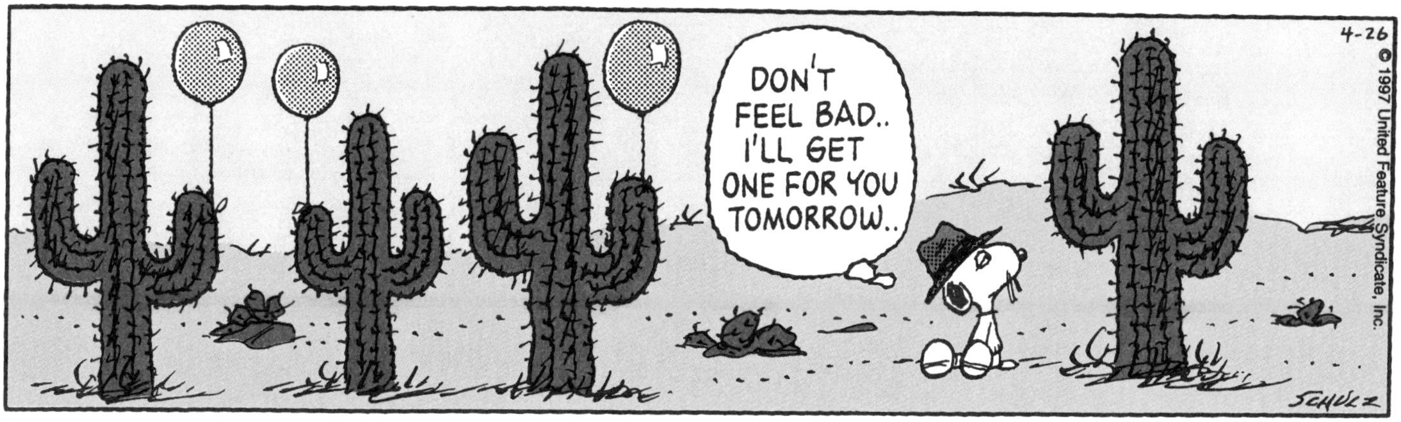
DON'T FEEL BAD.. I'LL GET ONE FOR YOU TOMORROW..

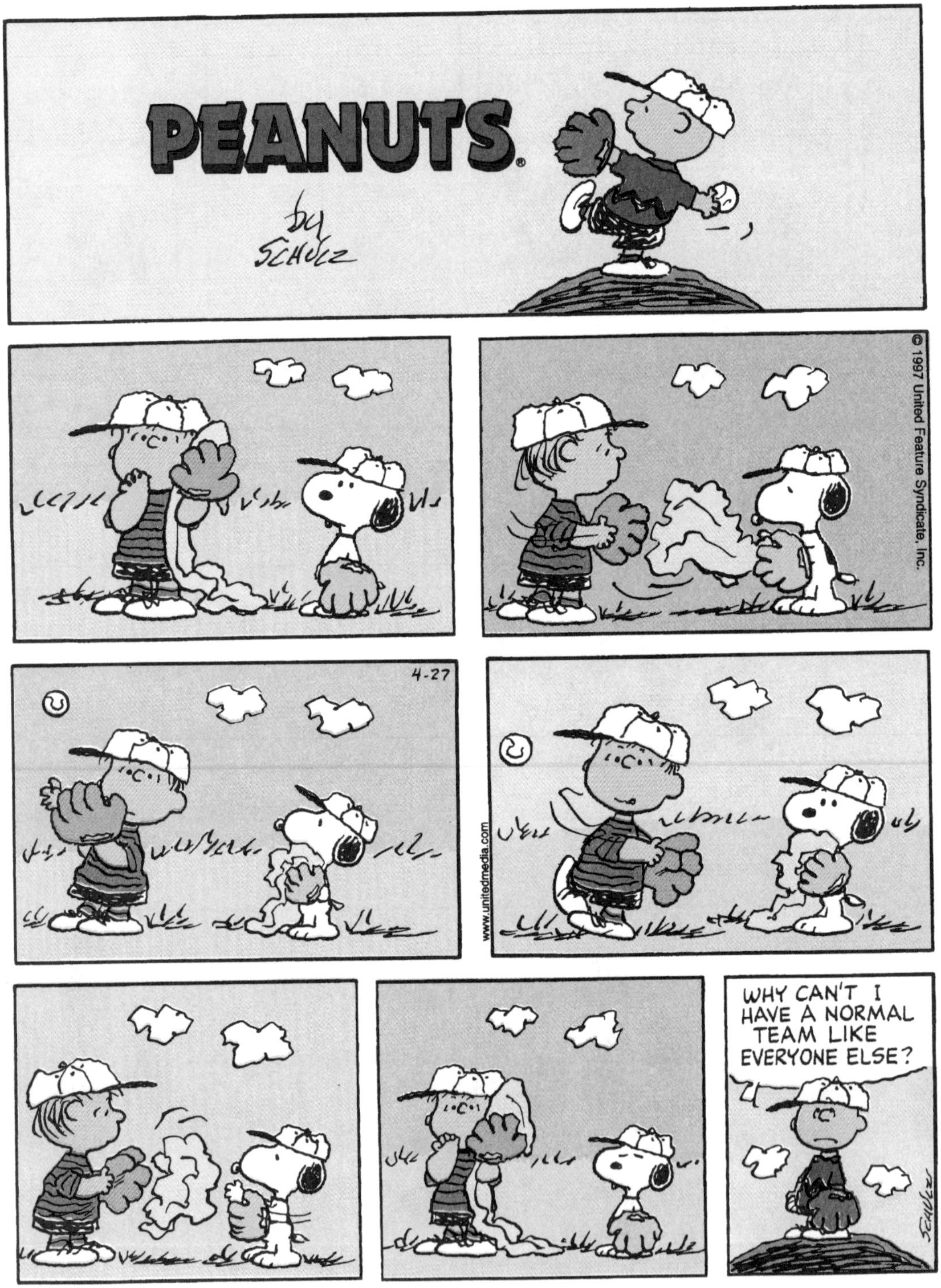
PEANUTS
by SCHULZ
© 1997 United Feature Syndicate, Inc.
4-27
www.unitedmedia.com
WHY CAN'T I HAVE A NORMAL TEAM LIKE EVERYONE ELSE?
SCHULZ

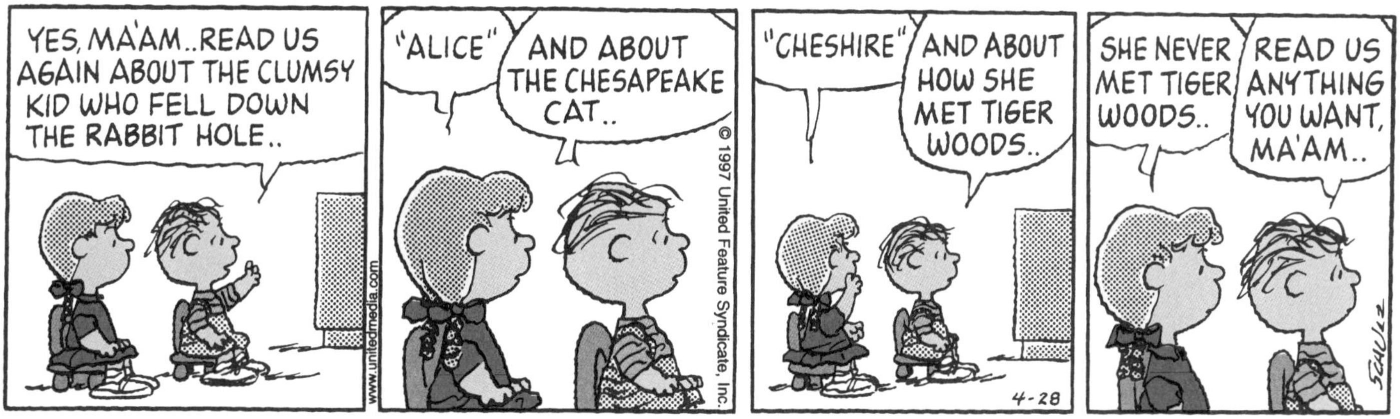
YES, MA'AM..READ US AGAIN ABOUT THE CLUMSY KID WHO FELL DOWN THE RABBIT HOLE..
"ALICE"
AND ABOUT THE CHESAPEAKE CAT..
"CHESHIRE"
AND ABOUT HOW SHE MET TIGER WOODS..
SHE NEVER MET TIGER WOODS..
READ US ANYTHING YOU WANT, MA'AM..
4-28
© 1997 United Feature Syndicate, Inc.
www.unitedmedia.com
SCHULZ

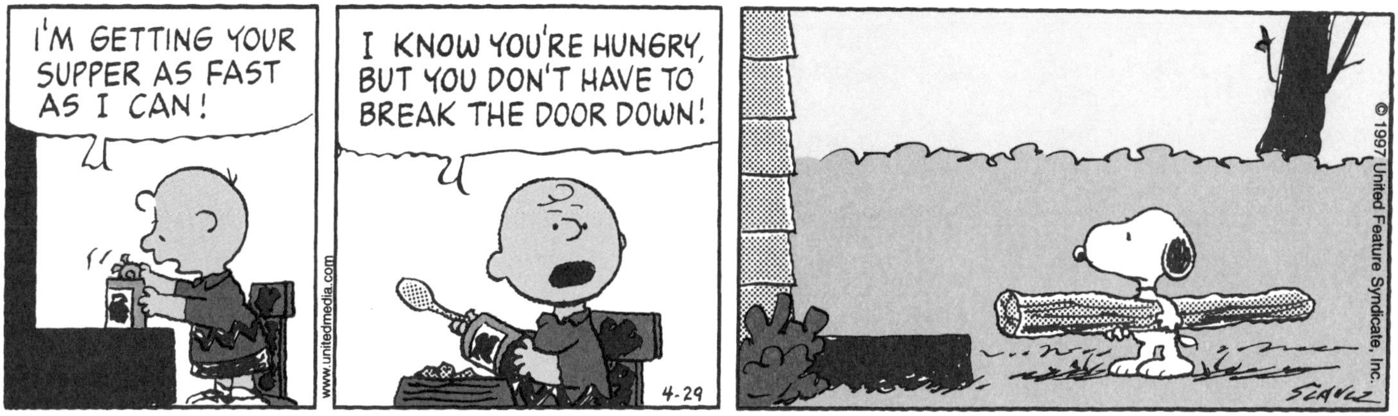
I'M GETTING YOUR SUPPER AS FAST AS I CAN!
I KNOW YOU'RE HUNGRY, BUT YOU DON'T HAVE TO BREAK THE DOOR DOWN!
4-29
© 1997 United Feature Syndicate, Inc.
www.unitedmedia.com
SCHULZ

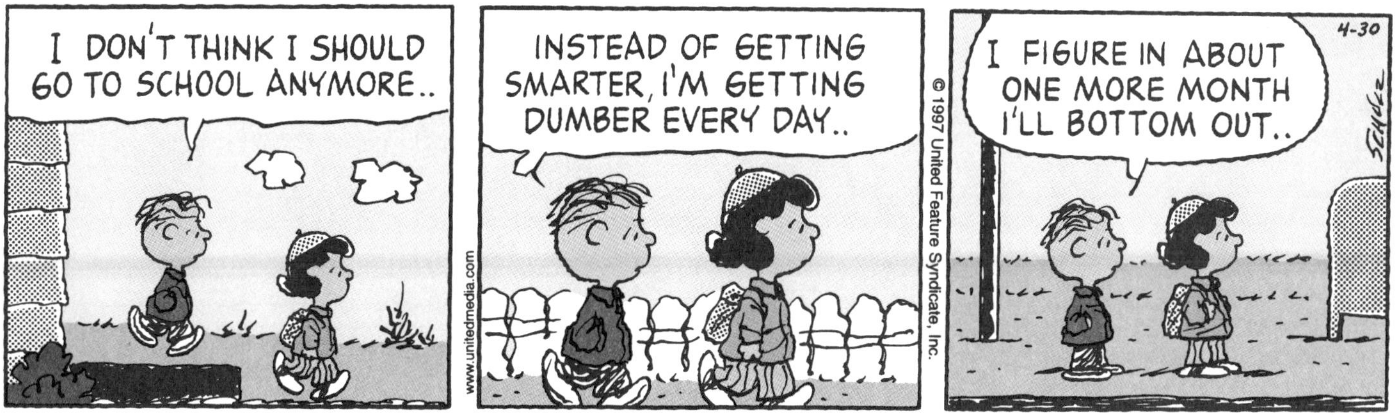
I DON'T THINK I SHOULD GO TO SCHOOL ANYMORE..
INSTEAD OF GETTING SMARTER, I'M GETTING DUMBER EVERY DAY..
I FIGURE IN ABOUT ONE MORE MONTH I'LL BOTTOM OUT..
4-30
© 1997 United Feature Syndicate, Inc.
www.unitedmedia.com
SCHULZ

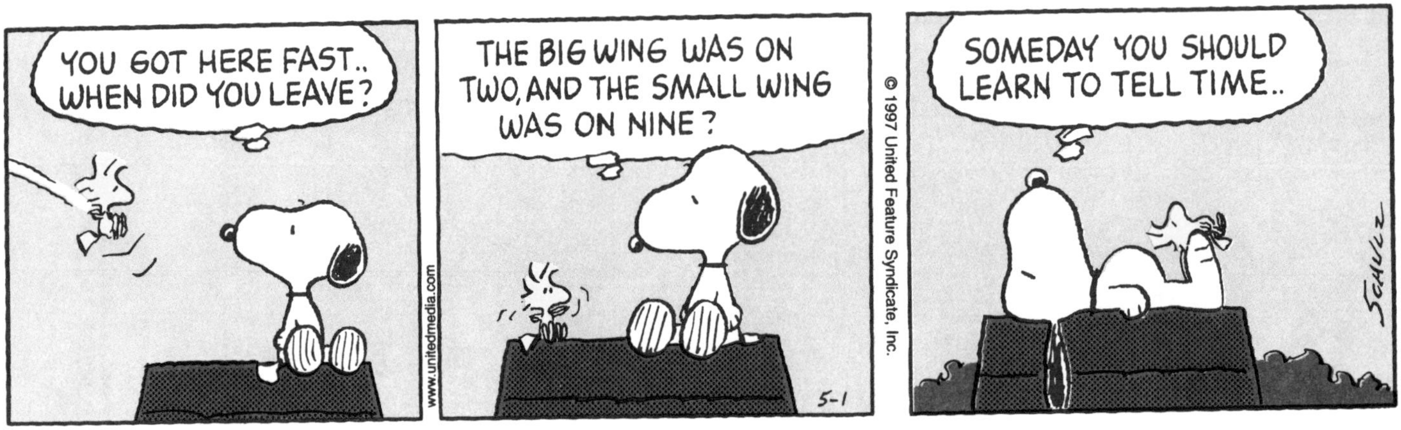
YOU GOT HERE FAST.. WHEN DID YOU LEAVE?
THE BIG WING WAS ON TWO, AND THE SMALL WING WAS ON NINE?
SOMEDAY YOU SHOULD LEARN TO TELL TIME..
www.unitedmedia.com
5-1
© 1997 United Feature Syndicate, Inc.
SCHULZ

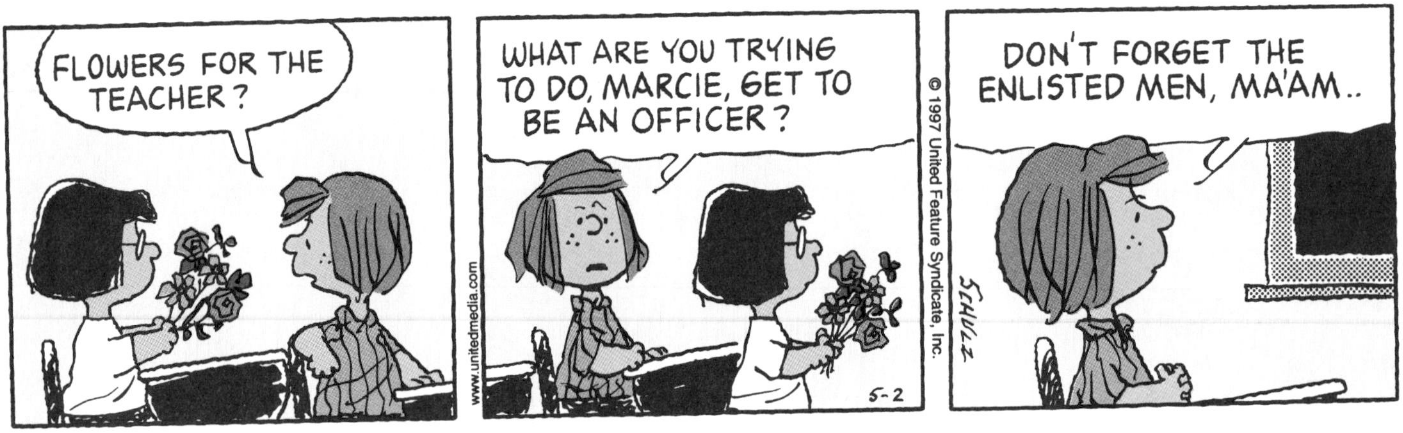
FLOWERS FOR THE TEACHER?
WHAT ARE YOU TRYING TO DO, MARCIE, GET TO BE AN OFFICER?
DON'T FORGET THE ENLISTED MEN, MA'AM..
www.unitedmedia.com
5-2
© 1997 United Feature Syndicate, Inc.
SCHULZ

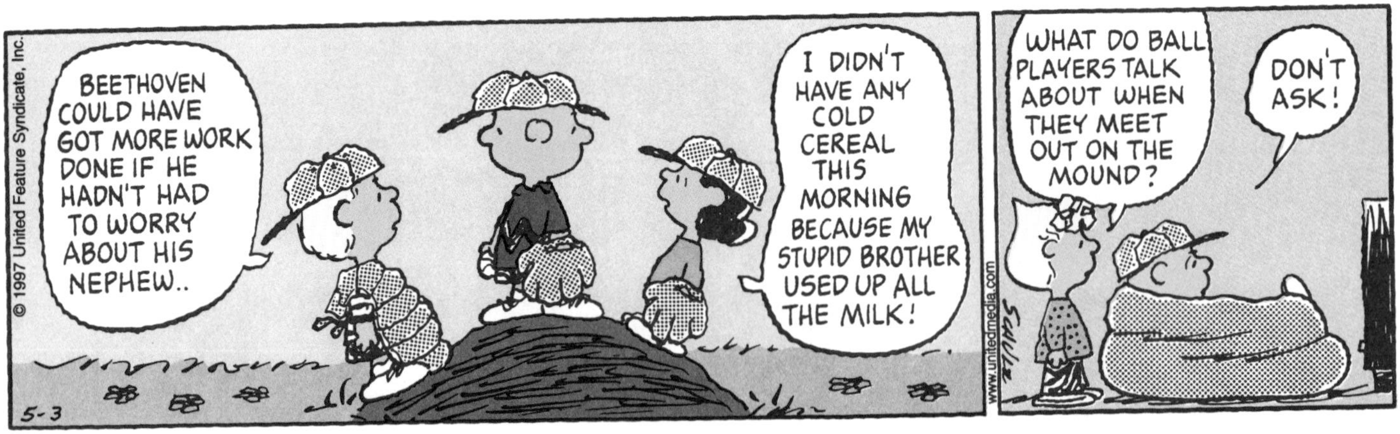
© 1997 United Feature Syndicate, Inc.
BEETHOVEN COULD HAVE GOT MORE WORK DONE IF HE HADN'T HAD TO WORRY ABOUT HIS NEPHEW..
I DIDN'T HAVE ANY COLD CEREAL THIS MORNING BECAUSE MY STUPID BROTHER USED UP ALL THE MILK!
5-3
www.unitedmedia.com
SCHULZ
WHAT DO BALL PLAYERS TALK ABOUT WHEN THEY MEET OUT ON THE MOUND?
DON'T ASK!

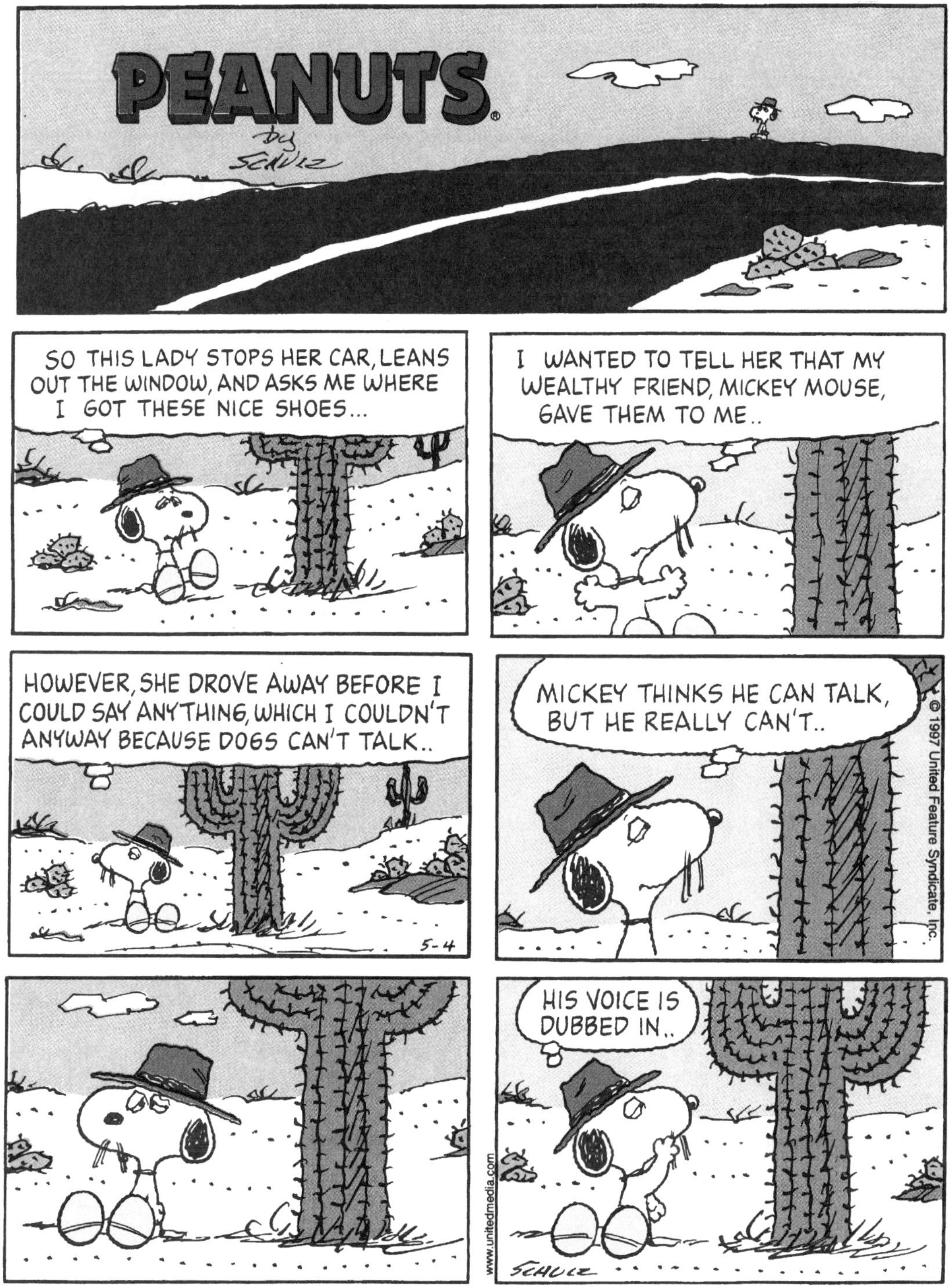
PEANUTS
by SCHULZ
SO THIS LADY STOPS HER CAR, LEANS OUT THE WINDOW, AND ASKS ME WHERE I GOT THESE NICE SHOES...
I WANTED TO TELL HER THAT MY WEALTHY FRIEND, MICKEY MOUSE, GAVE THEM TO ME..
HOWEVER, SHE DROVE AWAY BEFORE I COULD SAY ANYTHING, WHICH I COULDN'T ANYWAY BECAUSE DOGS CAN'T TALK..
5-4
MICKEY THINKS HE CAN TALK, BUT HE REALLY CAN'T..
© 1997 United Feature Syndicate, Inc.
www.unitedmedia.com
HIS VOICE IS DUBBED IN..
SCHULZ

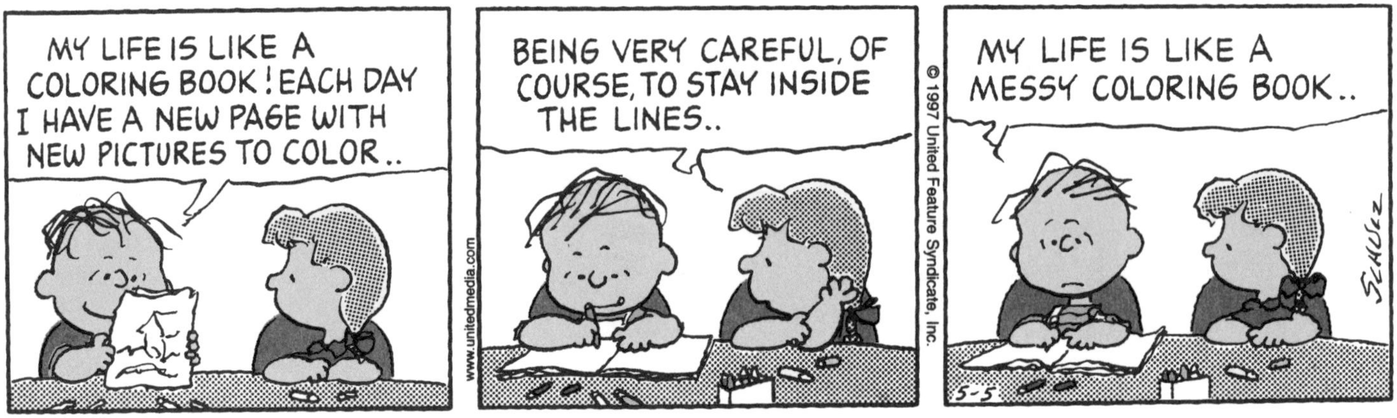
MY LIFE IS LIKE A COLORING BOOK ! EACH DAY I HAVE A NEW PAGE WITH NEW PICTURES TO COLOR..
www.unitedmedia.com
BEING VERY CAREFUL, OF COURSE, TO STAY INSIDE THE LINES..
© 1997 United Feature Syndicate, Inc.
MY LIFE IS LIKE A MESSY COLORING BOOK..
SCHULZ
5-5

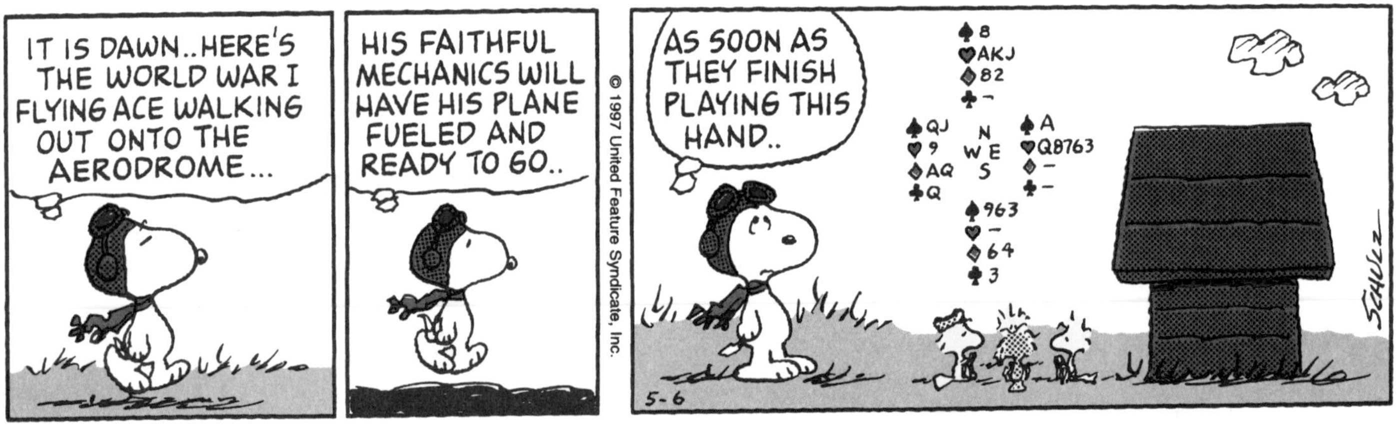
IT IS DAWN..HERE'S THE WORLD WAR I FLYING ACE WALKING OUT ONTO THE AERODROME...
HIS FAITHFUL MECHANICS WILL HAVE HIS PLANE FUELED AND READY TO GO..
© 1997 United Feature Syndicate, Inc.
AS SOON AS THEY FINISH PLAYING THIS HAND..
♠8 ♥AKJ ♦82 ♣–
♠QJ ♥9 ♦AQ ♣Q
N W E S
♠A ♥Q8763 ♦– ♣–
♠963 ♥– ♦64 ♣3
SCHULZ
5-6

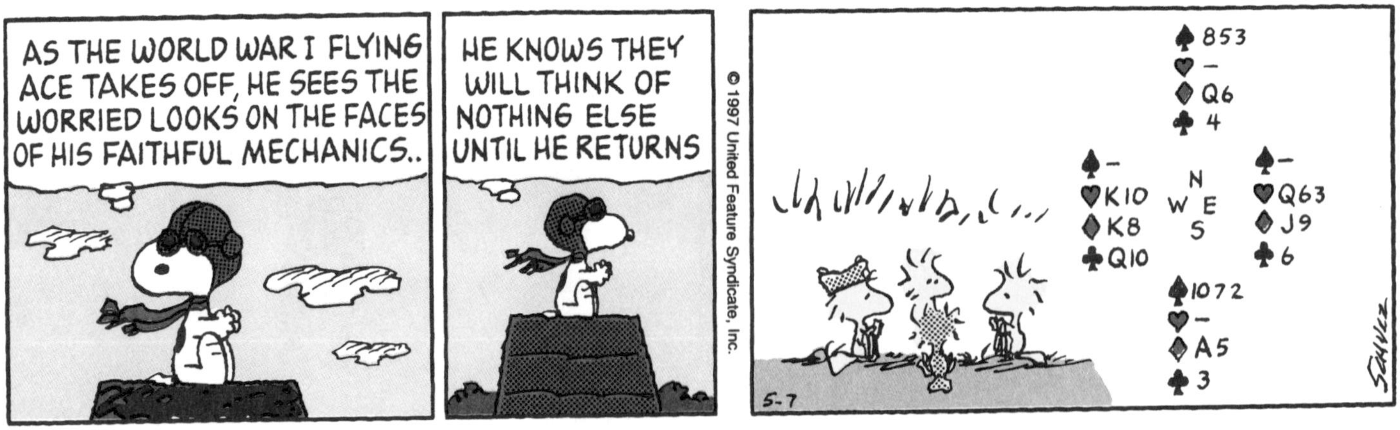
AS THE WORLD WAR I FLYING ACE TAKES OFF, HE SEES THE WORRIED LOOKS ON THE FACES OF HIS FAITHFUL MECHANICS..
HE KNOWS THEY WILL THINK OF NOTHING ELSE UNTIL HE RETURNS
© 1997 United Feature Syndicate, Inc.
♠853 ♥– ♦Q6 ♣4
♠– ♥K10 ♦K8 ♣Q10
N W E S
♠– ♥Q63 ♦J9 ♣6
♠1072 ♥– ♦A5 ♣3
SCHULZ
5-7

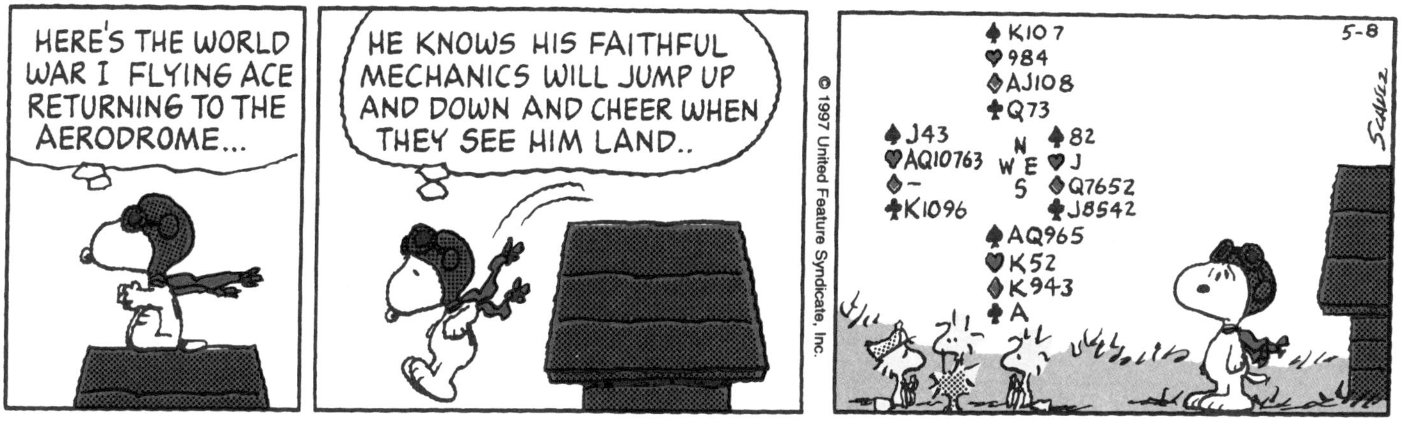
HERE'S THE WORLD WAR I FLYING ACE RETURNING TO THE AERODROME...
HE KNOWS HIS FAITHFUL MECHANICS WILL JUMP UP AND DOWN AND CHEER WHEN THEY SEE HIM LAND..
© 1997 United Feature Syndicate, Inc.
5-8
♠K10 7
♥984
♦AJ108
♣Q73
♠J43
♥AQ10763
♦–
♣K1096
N
W E
S
♠82
♥J
♦Q7652
♣J8542
♠AQ965
♥K52
♦K943
♣A
SCHULZ

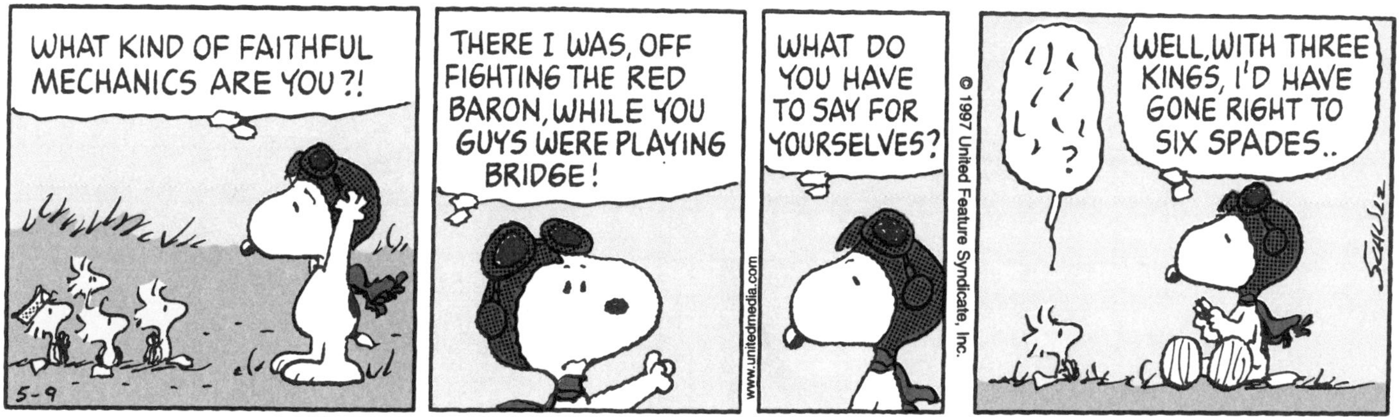
5-9
WHAT KIND OF FAITHFUL MECHANICS ARE YOU?!
THERE I WAS, OFF FIGHTING THE RED BARON, WHILE YOU GUYS WERE PLAYING BRIDGE!
www.unitedmedia.com
WHAT DO YOU HAVE TO SAY FOR YOURSELVES?
© 1997 United Feature Syndicate, Inc.
?
WELL, WITH THREE KINGS, I'D HAVE GONE RIGHT TO SIX SPADES..
SCHULZ

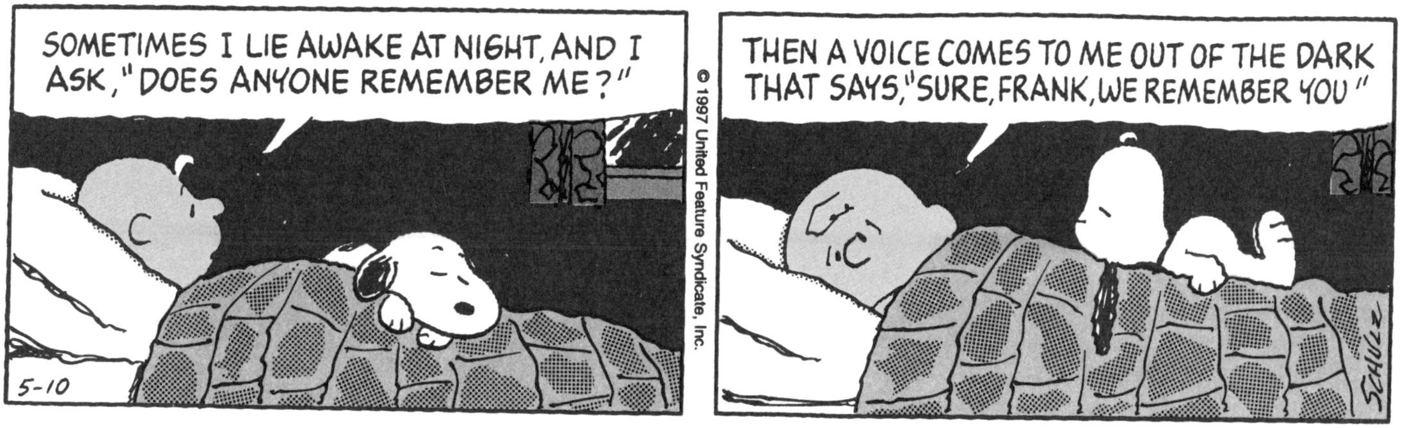
5-10
SOMETIMES I LIE AWAKE AT NIGHT, AND I ASK, "DOES ANYONE REMEMBER ME?"
© 1997 United Feature Syndicate, Inc.
THEN A VOICE COMES TO ME OUT OF THE DARK THAT SAYS, "SURE, FRANK, WE REMEMBER YOU"
SCHULZ

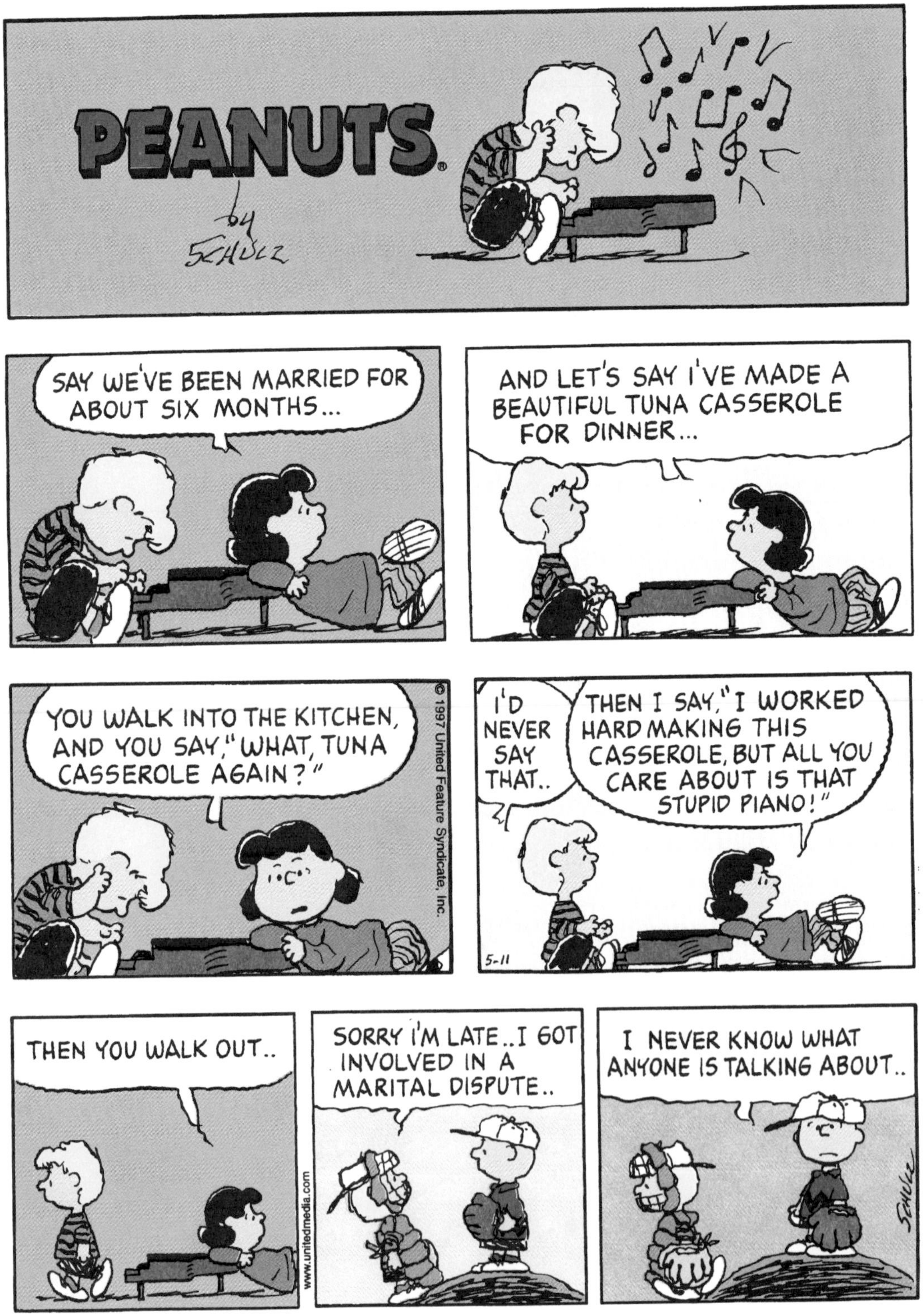
PEANUTS®
by SCHULZ
SAY WE'VE BEEN MARRIED FOR ABOUT SIX MONTHS...
AND LET'S SAY I'VE MADE A BEAUTIFUL TUNA CASSEROLE FOR DINNER...
YOU WALK INTO THE KITCHEN, AND YOU SAY, "WHAT, TUNA CASSEROLE AGAIN?"
© 1997 United Feature Syndicate, Inc.
I'D NEVER SAY THAT..
THEN I SAY, "I WORKED HARD MAKING THIS CASSEROLE, BUT ALL YOU CARE ABOUT IS THAT STUPID PIANO!"
5-11
THEN YOU WALK OUT..
www.unitedmedia.com
SORRY I'M LATE..I GOT INVOLVED IN A MARITAL DISPUTE..
I NEVER KNOW WHAT ANYONE IS TALKING ABOUT..
SCHULZ

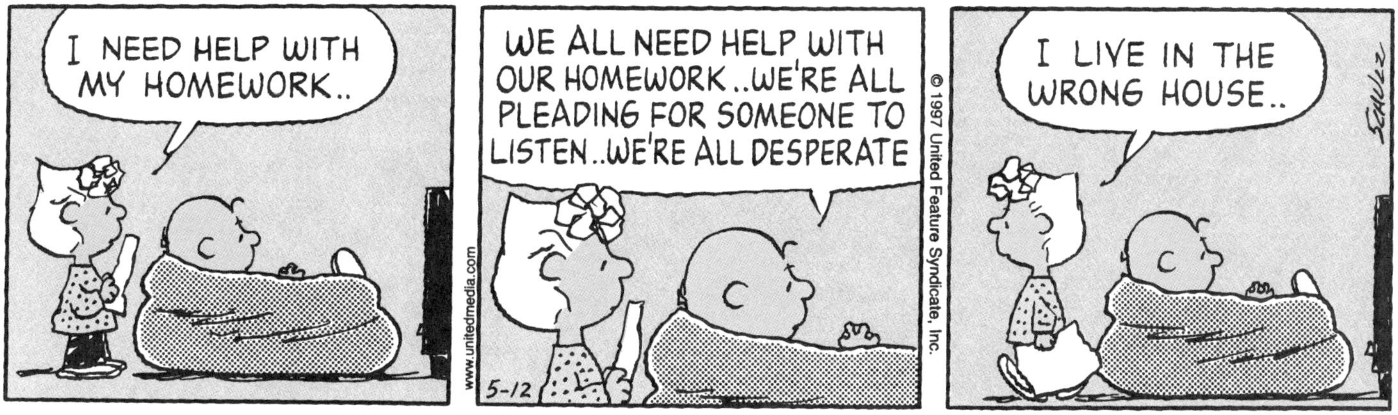
I NEED HELP WITH MY HOMEWORK..
WE ALL NEED HELP WITH OUR HOMEWORK..WE'RE ALL PLEADING FOR SOMEONE TO LISTEN..WE'RE ALL DESPERATE
I LIVE IN THE WRONG HOUSE..
5-12
www.unitedmedia.com
© 1997 United Feature Syndicate, Inc.

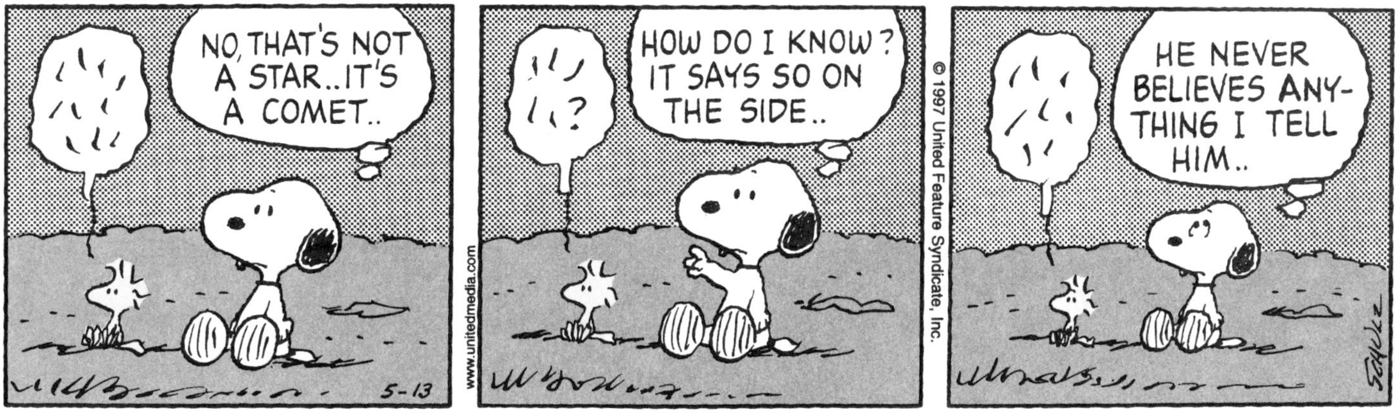
NO, THAT'S NOT A STAR..IT'S A COMET..
?
HOW DO I KNOW? IT SAYS SO ON THE SIDE..
HE NEVER BELIEVES ANYTHING I TELL HIM..
5-13
www.unitedmedia.com
© 1997 United Feature Syndicate, Inc.

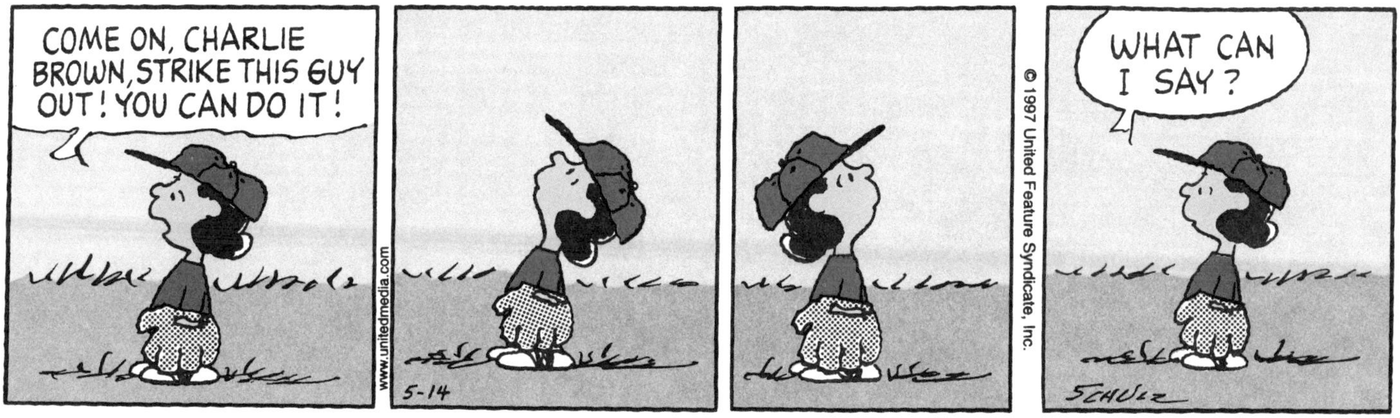
COME ON, CHARLIE BROWN, STRIKE THIS GUY OUT! YOU CAN DO IT!
WHAT CAN I SAY?
5-14
www.unitedmedia.com
© 1997 United Feature Syndicate, Inc.

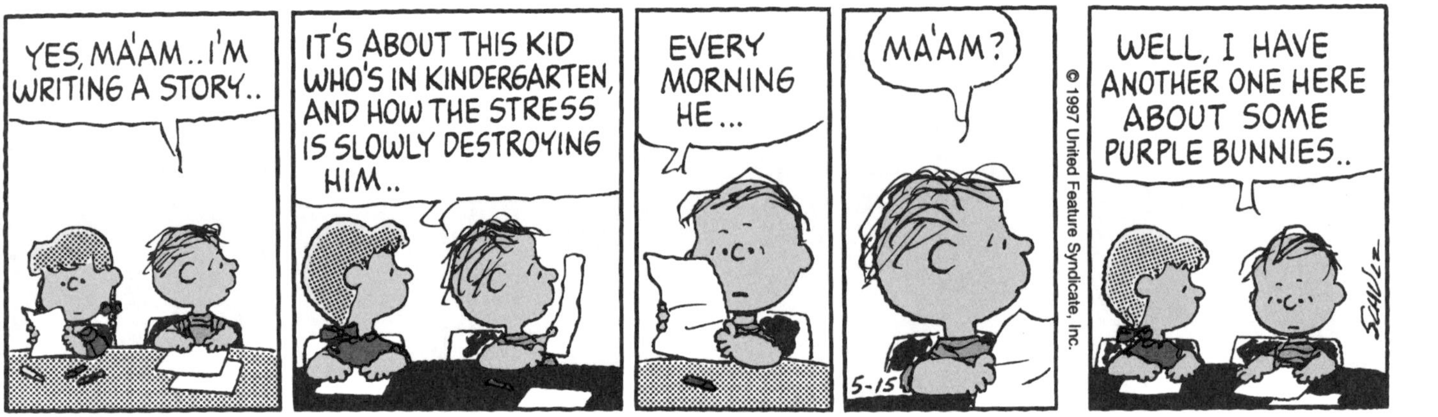
YES, MA'AM..I'M WRITING A STORY..
IT'S ABOUT THIS KID WHO'S IN KINDERGARTEN, AND HOW THE STRESS IS SLOWLY DESTROYING HIM..
EVERY MORNING HE...
MA'AM?
5-15
© 1997 United Feature Syndicate, Inc.
WELL, I HAVE ANOTHER ONE HERE ABOUT SOME PURPLE BUNNIES..
SCHULZ

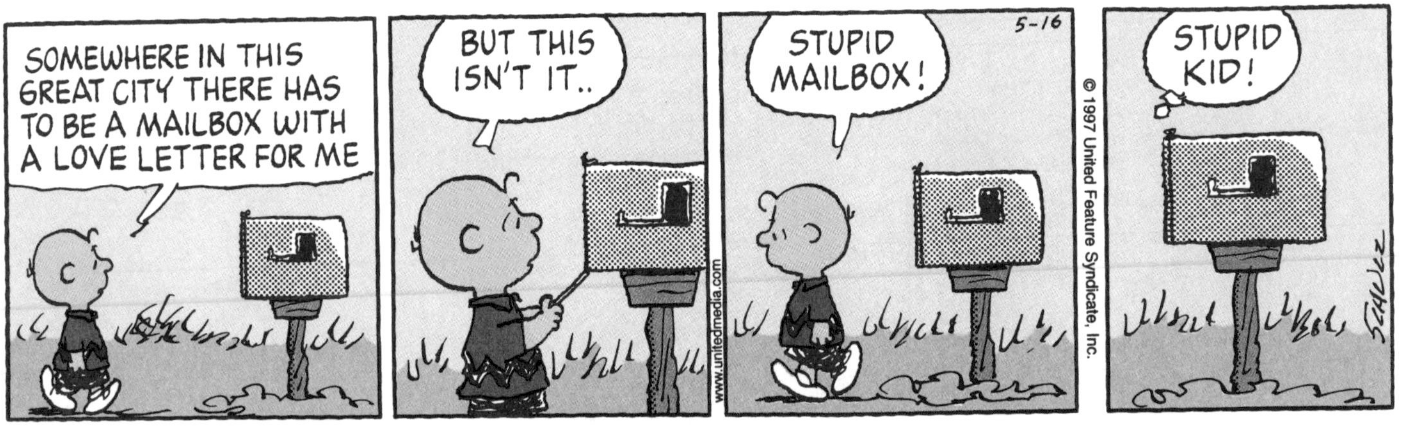
SOMEWHERE IN THIS GREAT CITY THERE HAS TO BE A MAILBOX WITH A LOVE LETTER FOR ME
BUT THIS ISN'T IT..
www.unitedmedia.com
STUPID MAILBOX!
5-16
© 1997 United Feature Syndicate, Inc.
STUPID KID!
SCHULZ

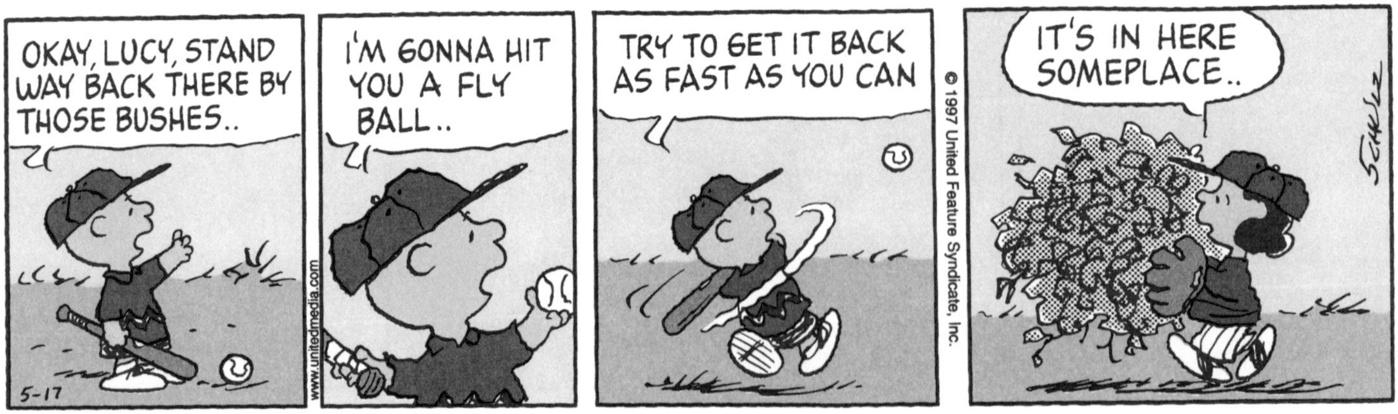
OKAY, LUCY, STAND WAY BACK THERE BY THOSE BUSHES..
5-17
I'M GONNA HIT YOU A FLY BALL..
www.unitedmedia.com
TRY TO GET IT BACK AS FAST AS YOU CAN
© 1997 United Feature Syndicate, Inc.
IT'S IN HERE SOMEPLACE..
SCHULZ

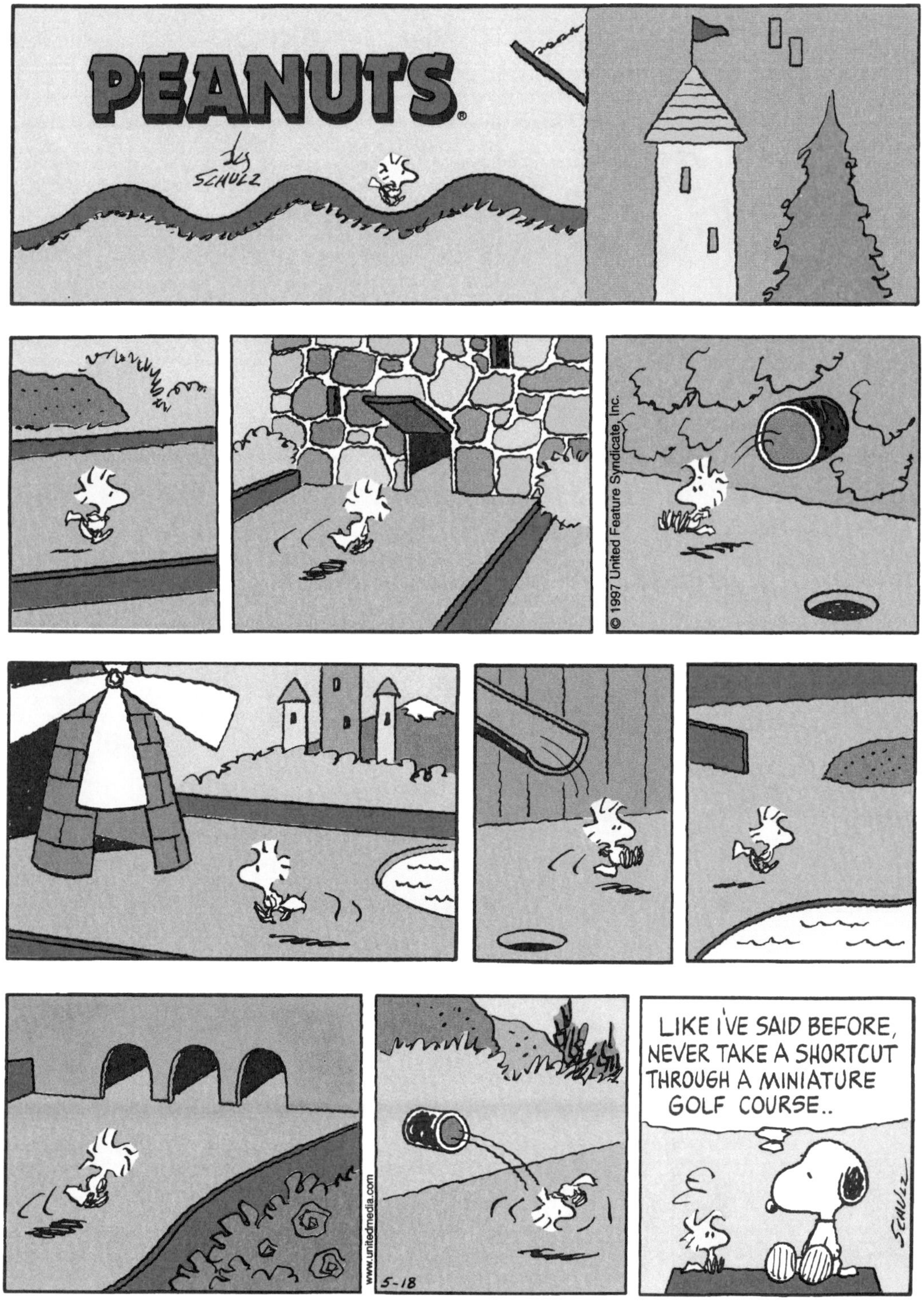
PEANUTS
SCHULZ
© 1997 United Feature Syndicate, Inc.
www.unitedmedia.com
5-18
LIKE I'VE SAID BEFORE, NEVER TAKE A SHORTCUT THROUGH A MINIATURE GOLF COURSE..
SCHULZ

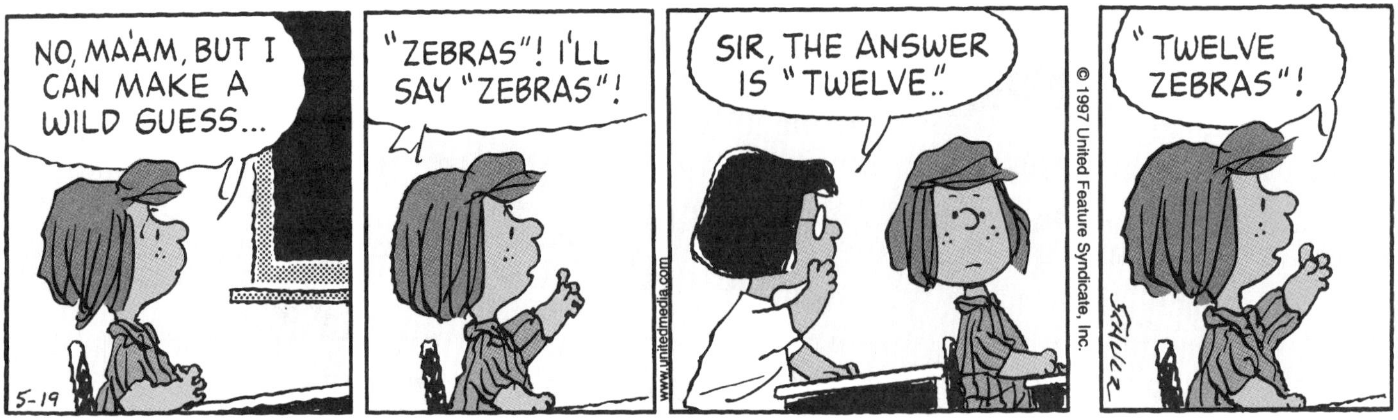
NO, MA'AM, BUT I CAN MAKE A WILD GUESS...
"ZEBRAS"! I'LL SAY "ZEBRAS"!
SIR, THE ANSWER IS "TWELVE."
"TWELVE ZEBRAS"!
5-19
www.unitedmedia.com
© 1997 United Feature Syndicate, Inc.
SCHULZ

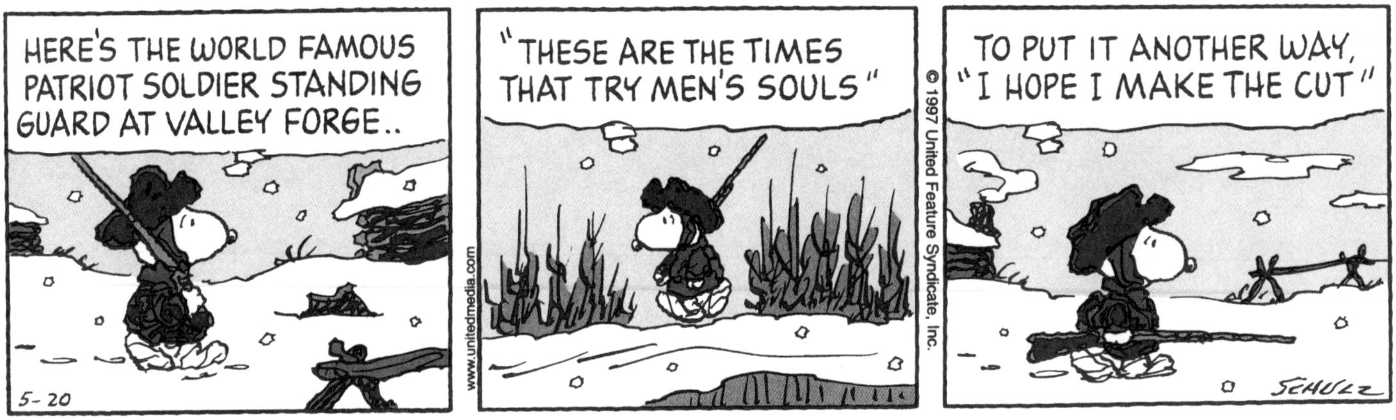
HERE'S THE WORLD FAMOUS PATRIOT SOLDIER STANDING GUARD AT VALLEY FORGE..
"THESE ARE THE TIMES THAT TRY MEN'S SOULS"
TO PUT IT ANOTHER WAY, "I HOPE I MAKE THE CUT"
5-20
www.unitedmedia.com
© 1997 United Feature Syndicate, Inc.
SCHULZ

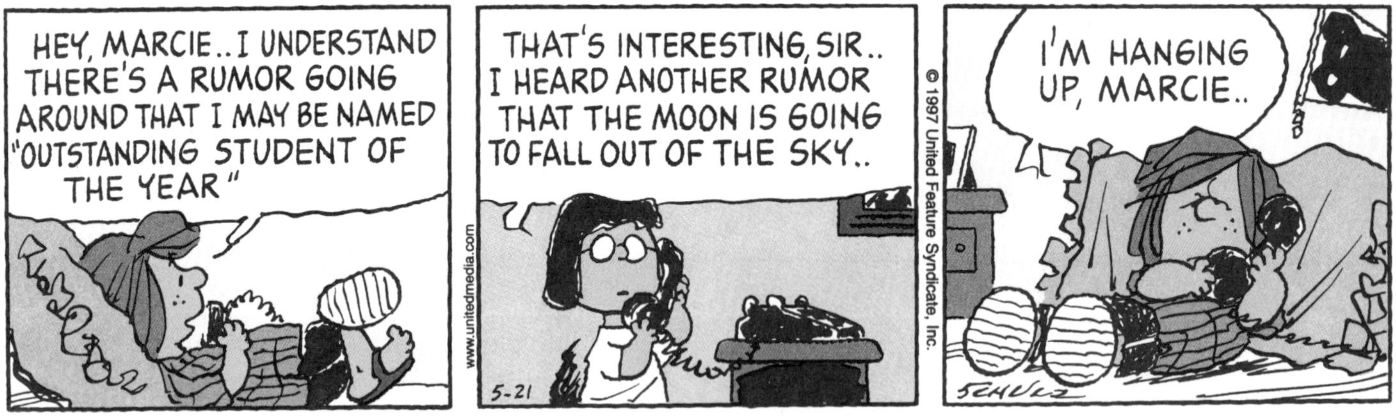
HEY, MARCIE..I UNDERSTAND THERE'S A RUMOR GOING AROUND THAT I MAY BE NAMED "OUTSTANDING STUDENT OF THE YEAR"
THAT'S INTERESTING, SIR.. I HEARD ANOTHER RUMOR THAT THE MOON IS GOING TO FALL OUT OF THE SKY..
I'M HANGING UP, MARCIE..
5-21
www.unitedmedia.com
© 1997 United Feature Syndicate, Inc.
SCHULZ

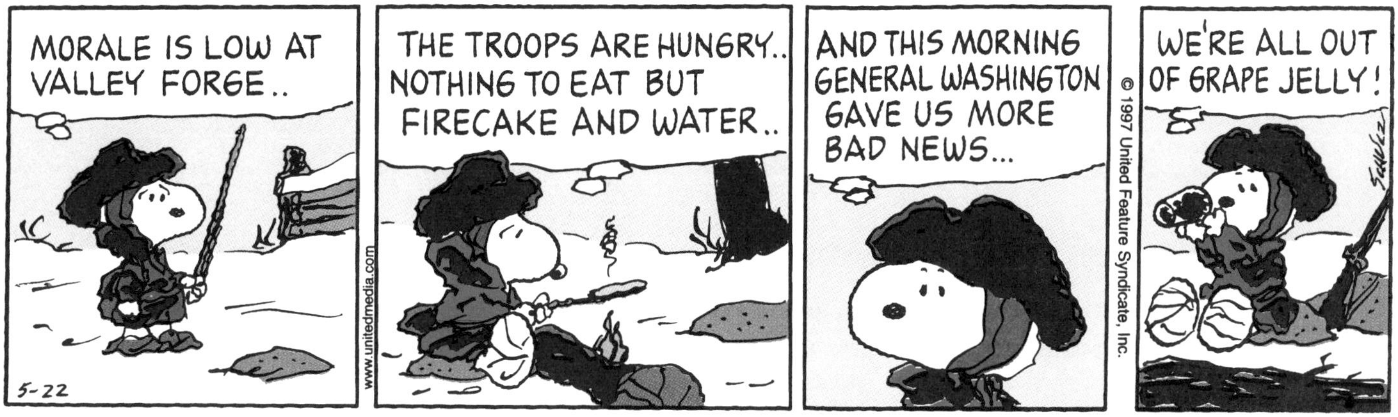
MORALE IS LOW AT VALLEY FORGE..
5-22
THE TROOPS ARE HUNGRY.. NOTHING TO EAT BUT FIRECAKE AND WATER..
AND THIS MORNING GENERAL WASHINGTON GAVE US MORE BAD NEWS...
WE'RE ALL OUT OF GRAPE JELLY!

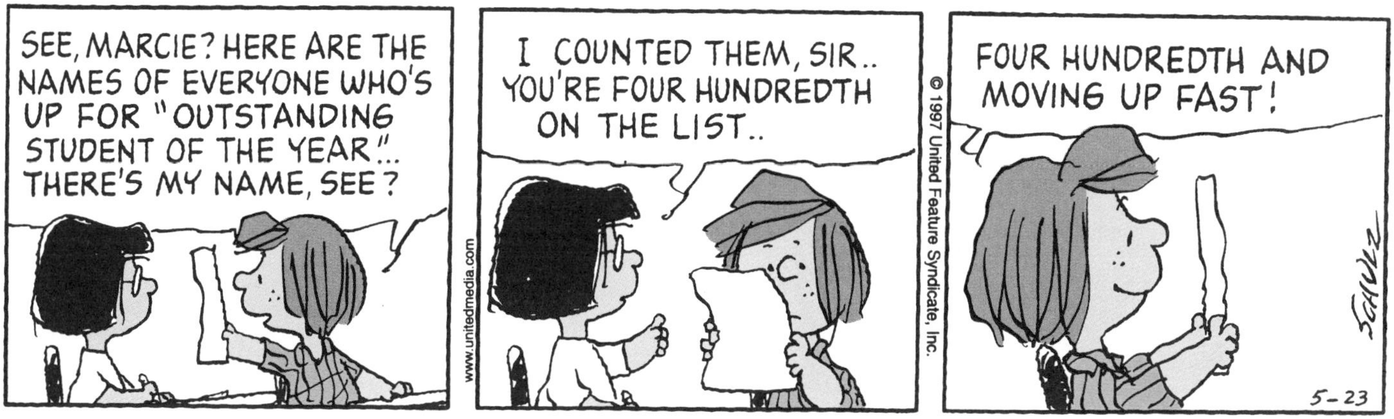
SEE, MARCIE? HERE ARE THE NAMES OF EVERYONE WHO'S UP FOR "OUTSTANDING STUDENT OF THE YEAR"... THERE'S MY NAME, SEE?
I COUNTED THEM, SIR.. YOU'RE FOUR HUNDREDTH ON THE LIST..
FOUR HUNDREDTH AND MOVING UP FAST!
5-23

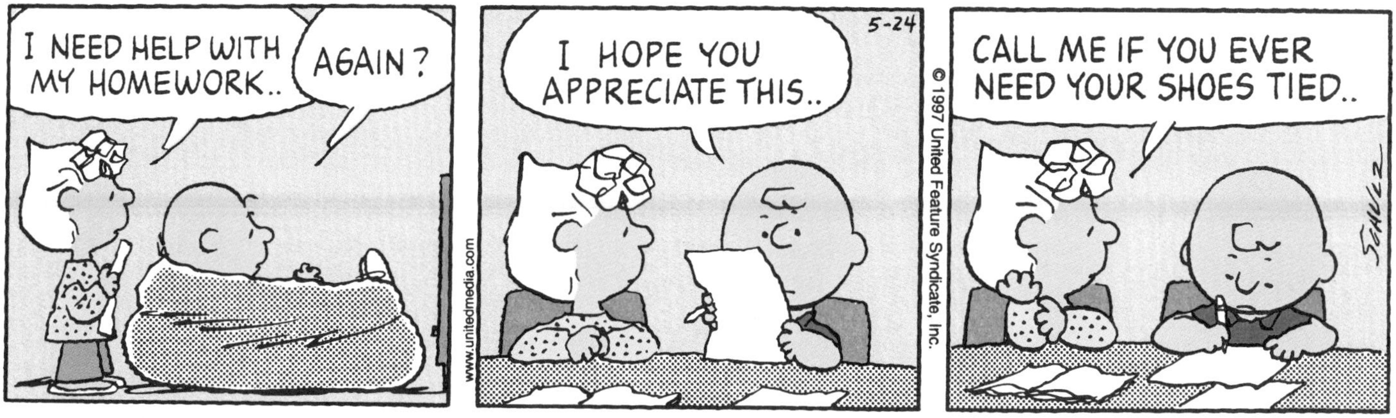
I NEED HELP WITH MY HOMEWORK..
AGAIN?
5-24
I HOPE YOU APPRECIATE THIS..
CALL ME IF YOU EVER NEED YOUR SHOES TIED..

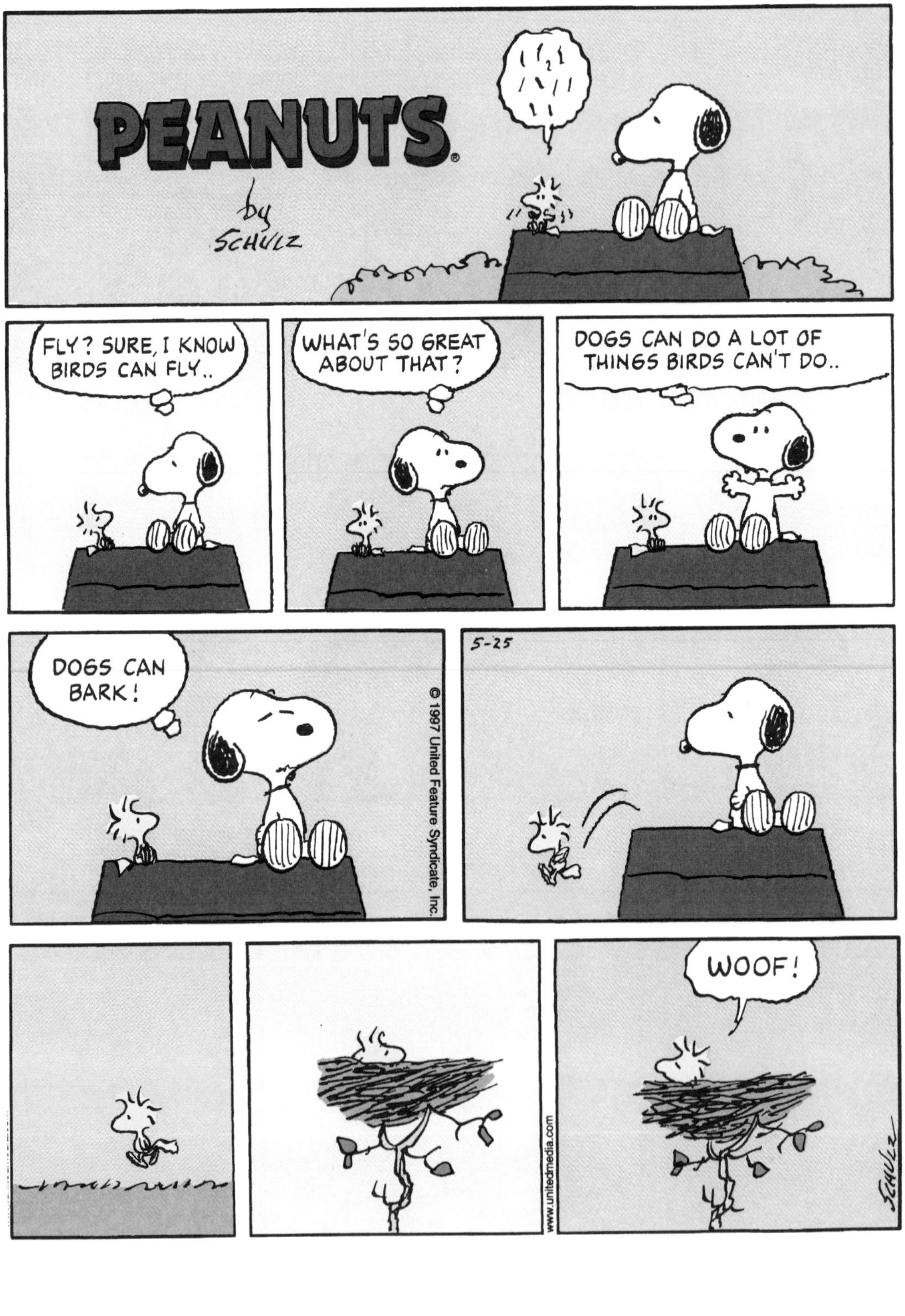
PEANUTS
by SCHULZ
FLY? SURE, I KNOW BIRDS CAN FLY..
WHAT'S SO GREAT ABOUT THAT?
DOGS CAN DO A LOT OF THINGS BIRDS CAN'T DO..
DOGS CAN BARK!
© 1997 United Feature Syndicate, Inc.
5-25
www.unitedmedia.com
WOOF!
SCHULZ

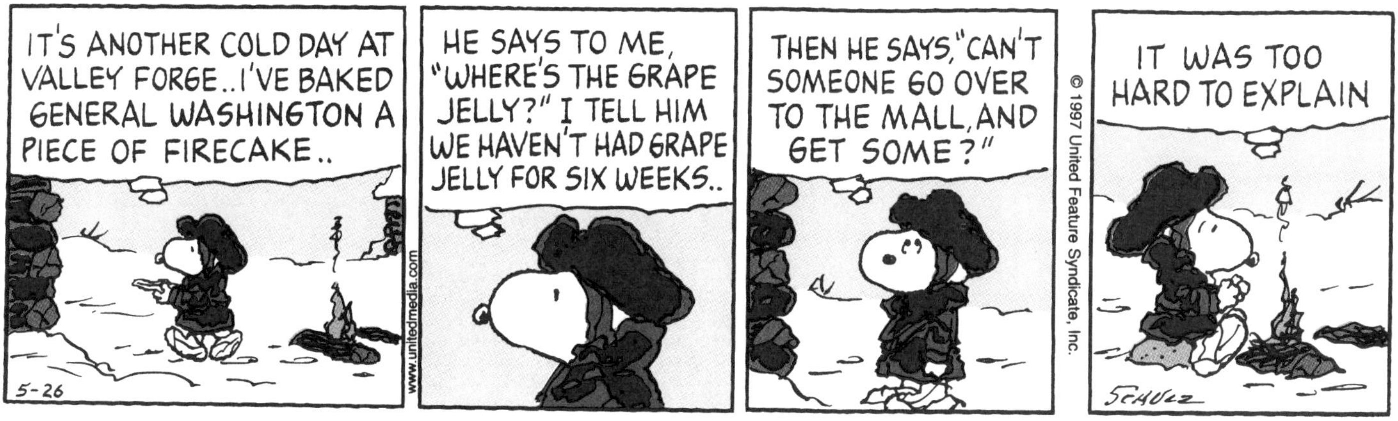
IT'S ANOTHER COLD DAY AT VALLEY FORGE..I'VE BAKED GENERAL WASHINGTON A PIECE OF FIRECAKE..
5-26
www.unitedmedia.com
HE SAYS TO ME, "WHERE'S THE GRAPE JELLY?" I TELL HIM WE HAVEN'T HAD GRAPE JELLY FOR SIX WEEKS..
THEN HE SAYS, "CAN'T SOMEONE GO OVER TO THE MALL, AND GET SOME?"
© 1997 United Feature Syndicate, Inc.
IT WAS TOO HARD TO EXPLAIN
SCHULZ

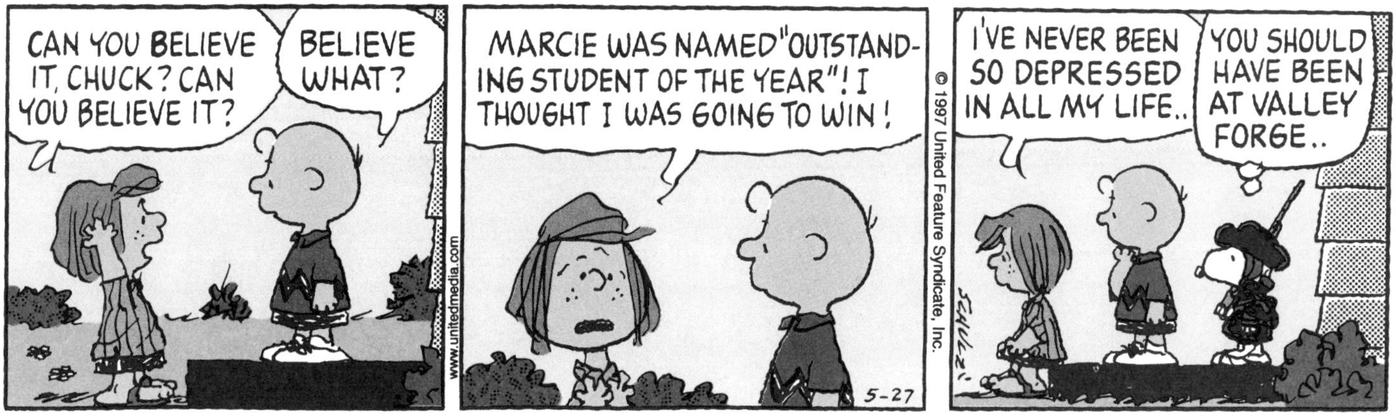
CAN YOU BELIEVE IT, CHUCK? CAN YOU BELIEVE IT?
BELIEVE WHAT?
www.unitedmedia.com
MARCIE WAS NAMED "OUTSTANDING STUDENT OF THE YEAR"! I THOUGHT I WAS GOING TO WIN!
5-27
© 1997 United Feature Syndicate, Inc.
I'VE NEVER BEEN SO DEPRESSED IN ALL MY LIFE..
YOU SHOULD HAVE BEEN AT VALLEY FORGE..
SCHULZ

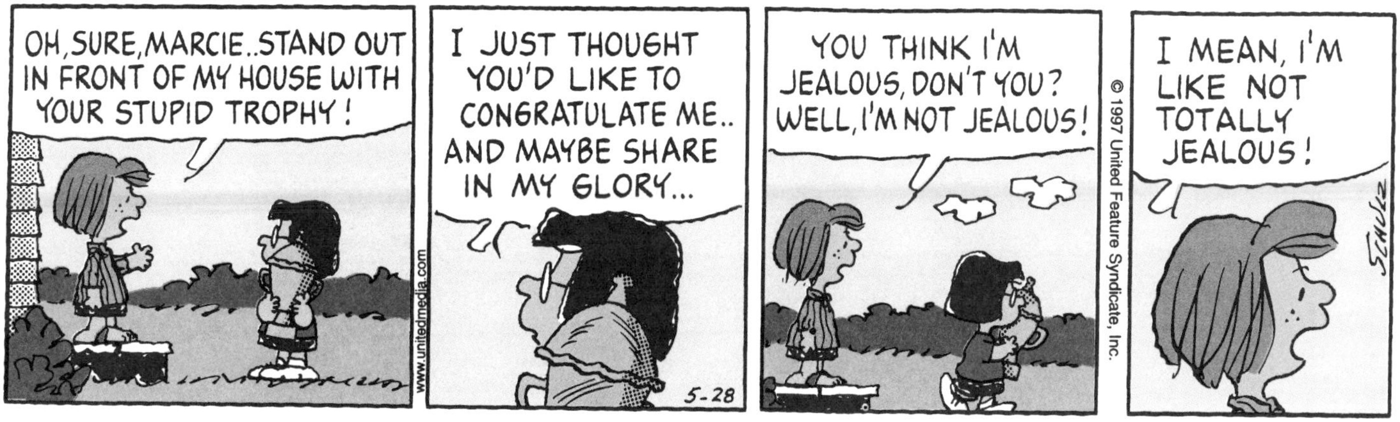
OH, SURE, MARCIE..STAND OUT IN FRONT OF MY HOUSE WITH YOUR STUPID TROPHY!
www.unitedmedia.com
I JUST THOUGHT YOU'D LIKE TO CONGRATULATE ME.. AND MAYBE SHARE IN MY GLORY...
5-28
YOU THINK I'M JEALOUS, DON'T YOU? WELL, I'M NOT JEALOUS!
© 1997 United Feature Syndicate, Inc.
I MEAN, I'M LIKE NOT TOTALLY JEALOUS!
SCHULZ

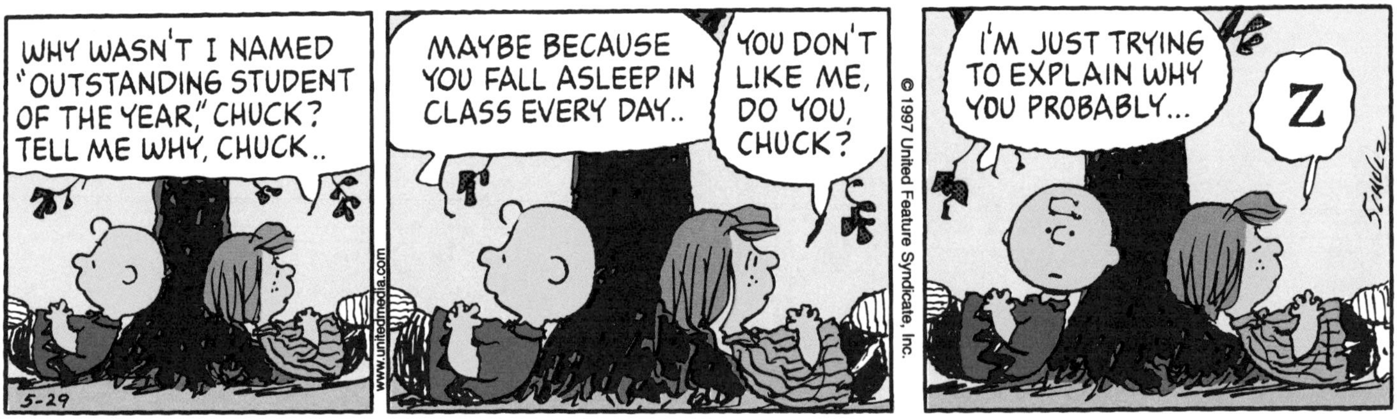
WHY WASN'T I NAMED "OUTSTANDING STUDENT OF THE YEAR," CHUCK? TELL ME WHY, CHUCK..
5-29
www.unitedmedia.com
MAYBE BECAUSE YOU FALL ASLEEP IN CLASS EVERY DAY..
YOU DON'T LIKE ME, DO YOU, CHUCK?
© 1997 United Feature Syndicate, Inc.
I'M JUST TRYING TO EXPLAIN WHY YOU PROBABLY...
Z
SCHULZ

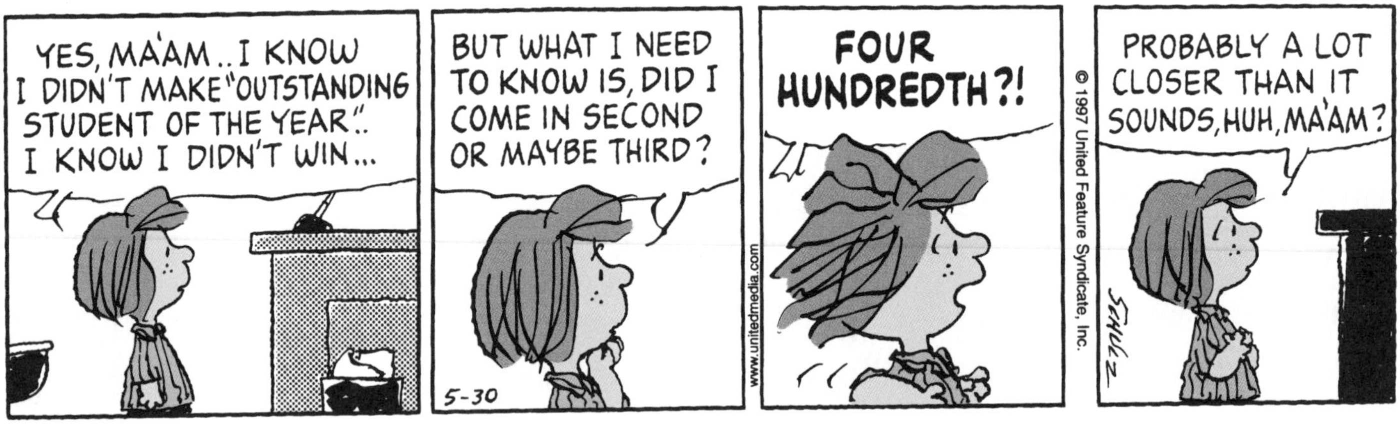
YES, MA'AM..I KNOW I DIDN'T MAKE "OUTSTANDING STUDENT OF THE YEAR".. I KNOW I DIDN'T WIN...
BUT WHAT I NEED TO KNOW IS, DID I COME IN SECOND OR MAYBE THIRD?
5-30
www.unitedmedia.com
FOUR HUNDREDTH?!
© 1997 United Feature Syndicate, Inc.
SCHULZ
PROBABLY A LOT CLOSER THAN IT SOUNDS, HUH, MA'AM?

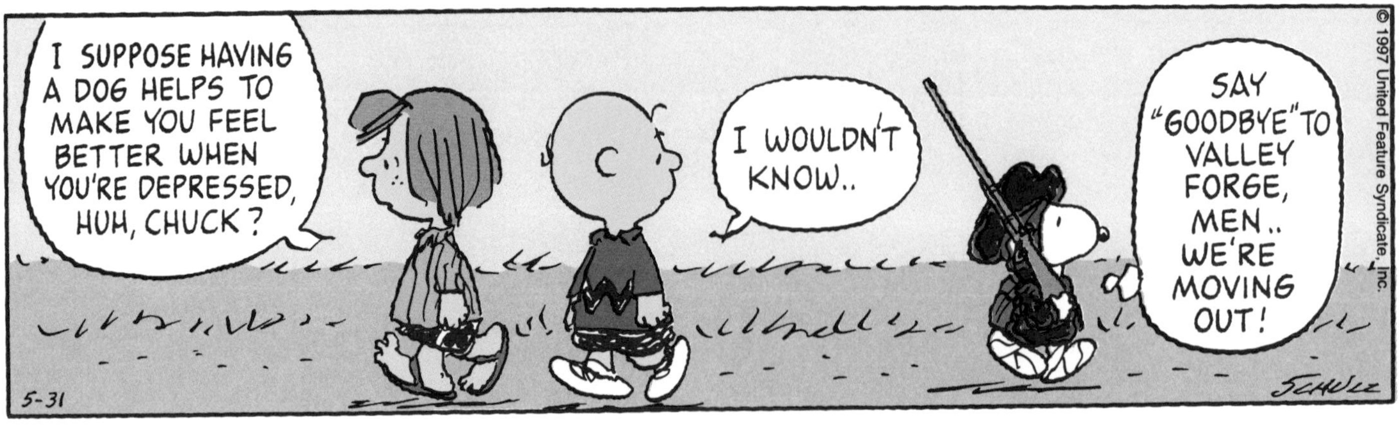
I SUPPOSE HAVING A DOG HELPS TO MAKE YOU FEEL BETTER WHEN YOU'RE DEPRESSED, HUH, CHUCK?
I WOULDN'T KNOW..
SAY "GOODBYE" TO VALLEY FORGE, MEN.. WE'RE MOVING OUT!
© 1997 United Feature Syndicate, Inc.
5-31
SCHULZ

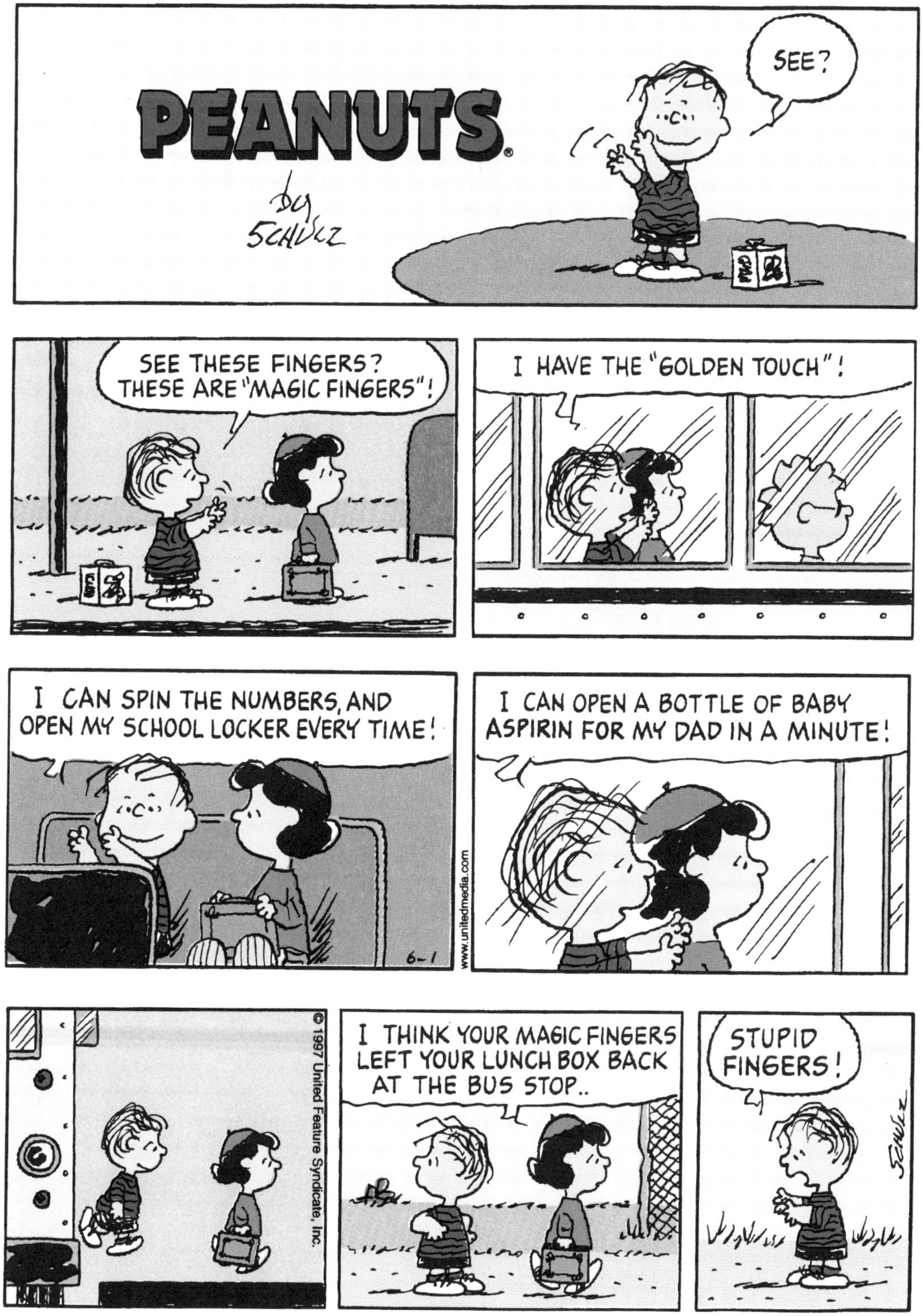
PEANUTS
by SCHULZ
SEE?
SEE THESE FINGERS? THESE ARE "MAGIC FINGERS"!
I HAVE THE "GOLDEN TOUCH"!
I CAN SPIN THE NUMBERS, AND OPEN MY SCHOOL LOCKER EVERY TIME!
6-1
www.unitedmedia.com
I CAN OPEN A BOTTLE OF BABY ASPIRIN FOR MY DAD IN A MINUTE!
© 1997 United Feature Syndicate, Inc.
I THINK YOUR MAGIC FINGERS LEFT YOUR LUNCH BOX BACK AT THE BUS STOP..
STUPID FINGERS!
SCHULZ

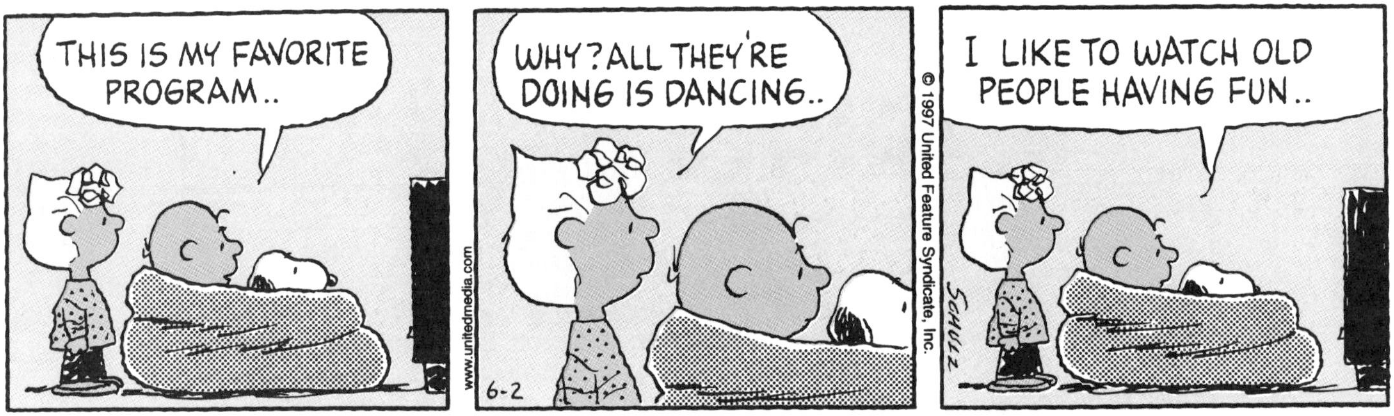
THIS IS MY FAVORITE PROGRAM..
WHY? ALL THEY'RE DOING IS DANCING..
I LIKE TO WATCH OLD PEOPLE HAVING FUN..
www.unitedmedia.com
6-2
© 1997 United Feature Syndicate, Inc.
SCHULZ

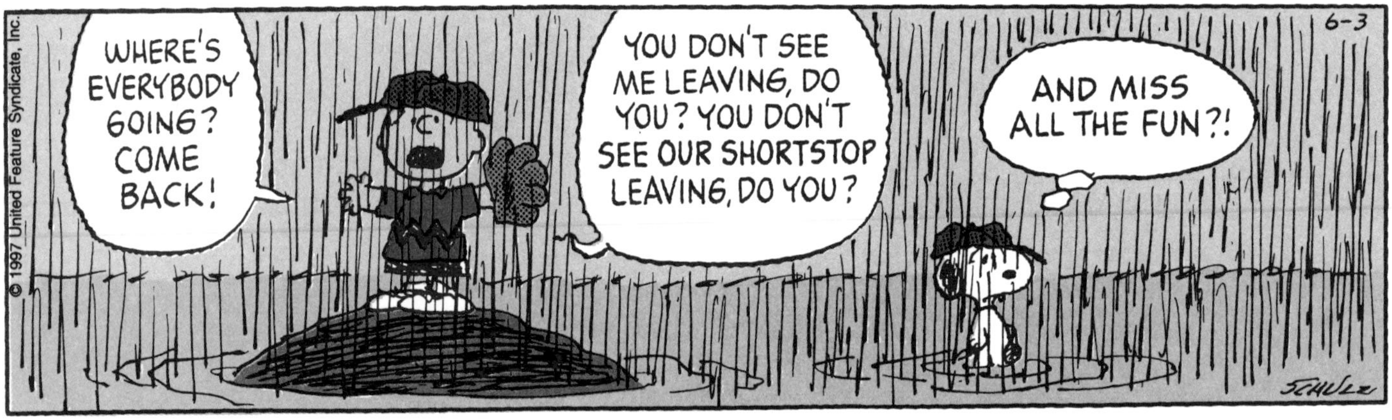
© 1997 United Feature Syndicate, Inc.
WHERE'S EVERYBODY GOING? COME BACK!
YOU DON'T SEE ME LEAVING, DO YOU? YOU DON'T SEE OUR SHORTSTOP LEAVING, DO YOU?
AND MISS ALL THE FUN?!
6-3
SCHULZ

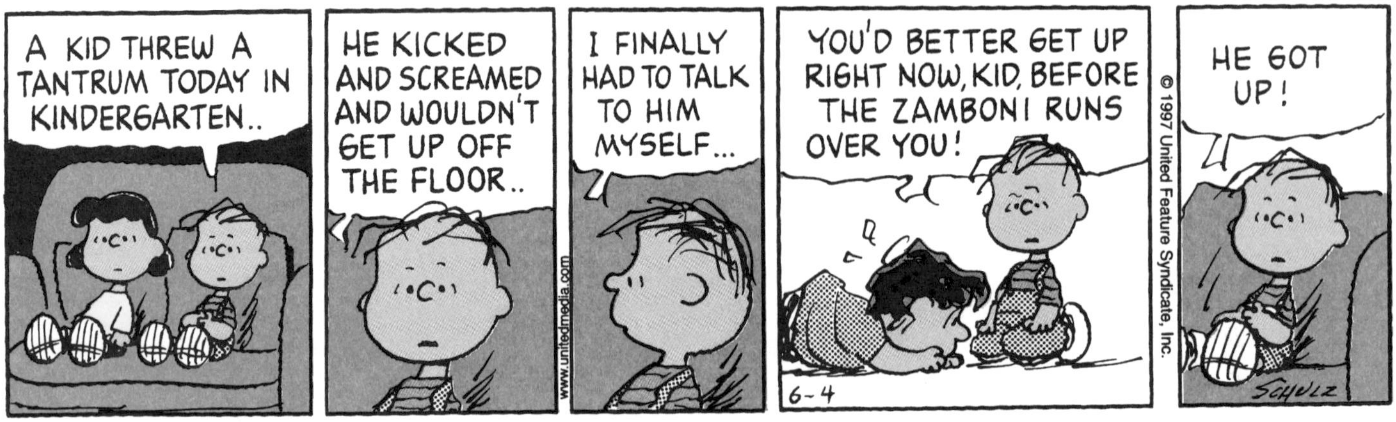
A KID THREW A TANTRUM TODAY IN KINDERGARTEN..
HE KICKED AND SCREAMED AND WOULDN'T GET UP OFF THE FLOOR..
www.unitedmedia.com
I FINALLY HAD TO TALK TO HIM MYSELF...
YOU'D BETTER GET UP RIGHT NOW, KID, BEFORE THE ZAMBONI RUNS OVER YOU!
6-4
© 1997 United Feature Syndicate, Inc.
HE GOT UP!
SCHULZ

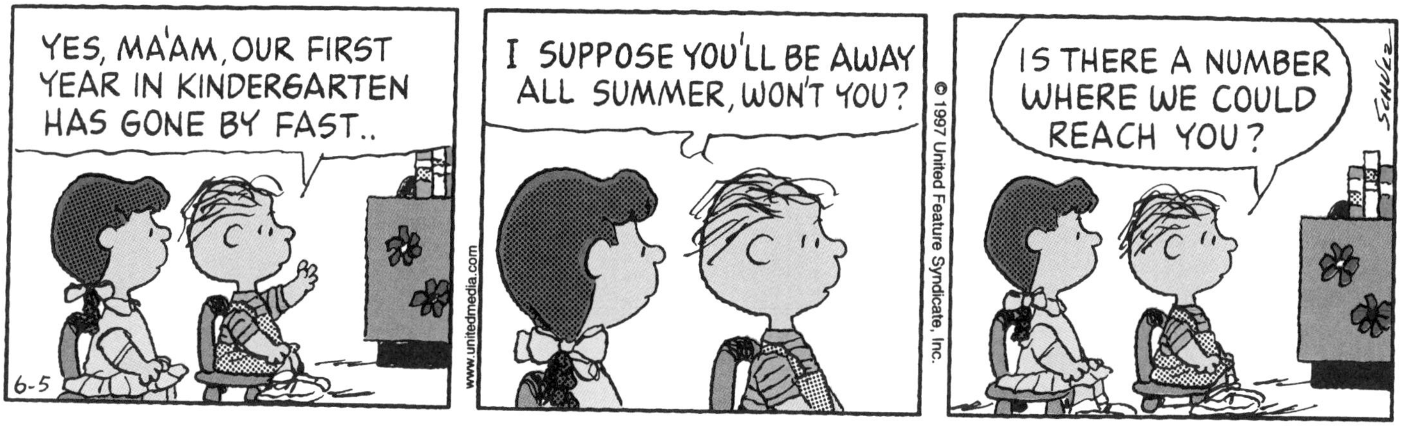
YES, MA'AM, OUR FIRST YEAR IN KINDERGARTEN HAS GONE BY FAST..
6-5
www.unitedmedia.com
I SUPPOSE YOU'LL BE AWAY ALL SUMMER, WON'T YOU?
© 1997 United Feature Syndicate, Inc.
IS THERE A NUMBER WHERE WE COULD REACH YOU?
SCHULZ

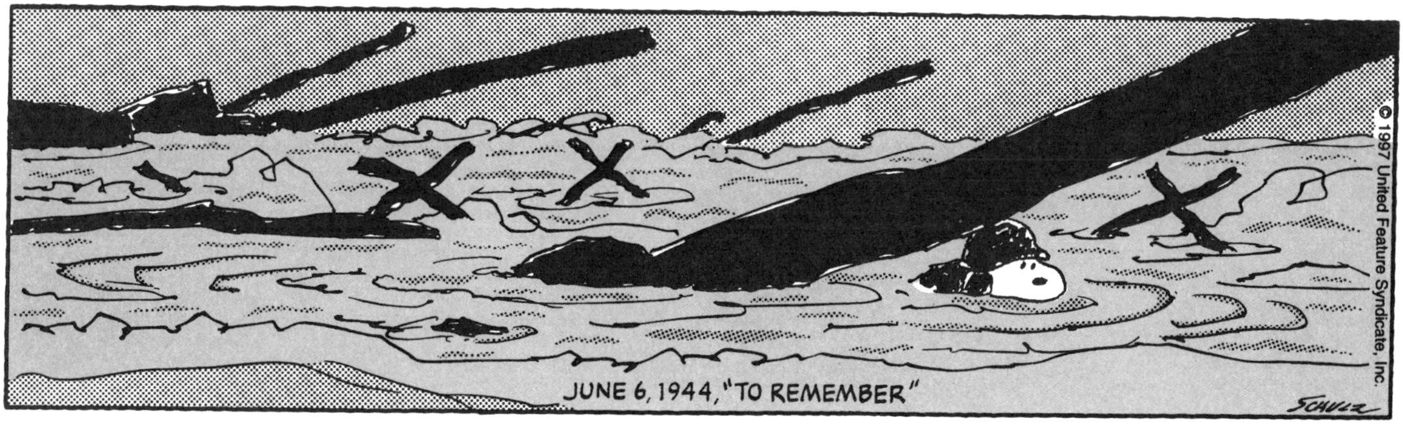
JUNE 6, 1944, "TO REMEMBER"
© 1997 United Feature Syndicate, Inc.
SCHULZ

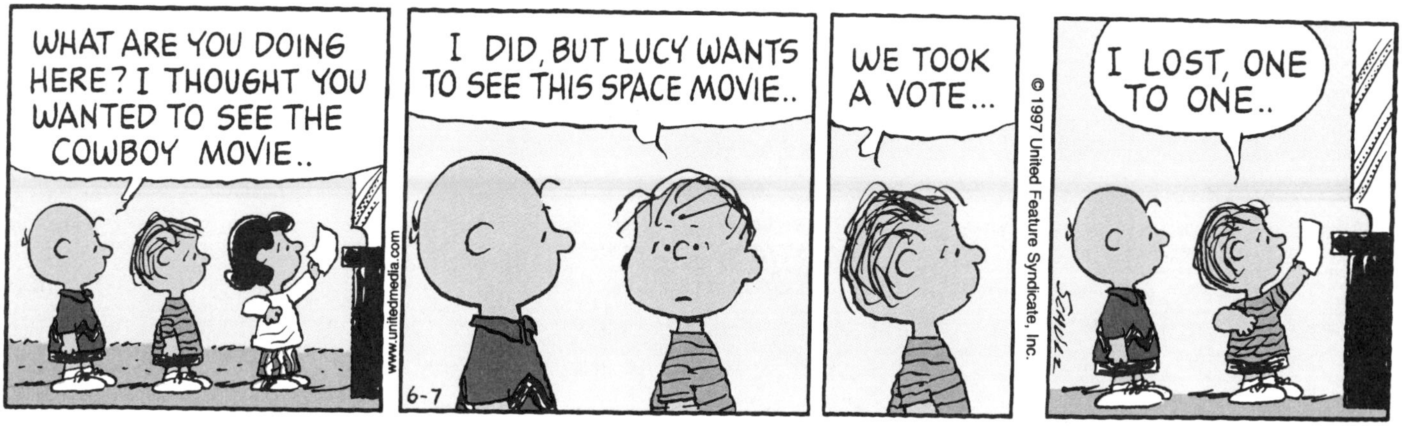
WHAT ARE YOU DOING HERE? I THOUGHT YOU WANTED TO SEE THE COWBOY MOVIE..
www.unitedmedia.com
I DID, BUT LUCY WANTS TO SEE THIS SPACE MOVIE..
6-7
WE TOOK A VOTE...
© 1997 United Feature Syndicate, Inc.
I LOST, ONE TO ONE..
SCHULZ

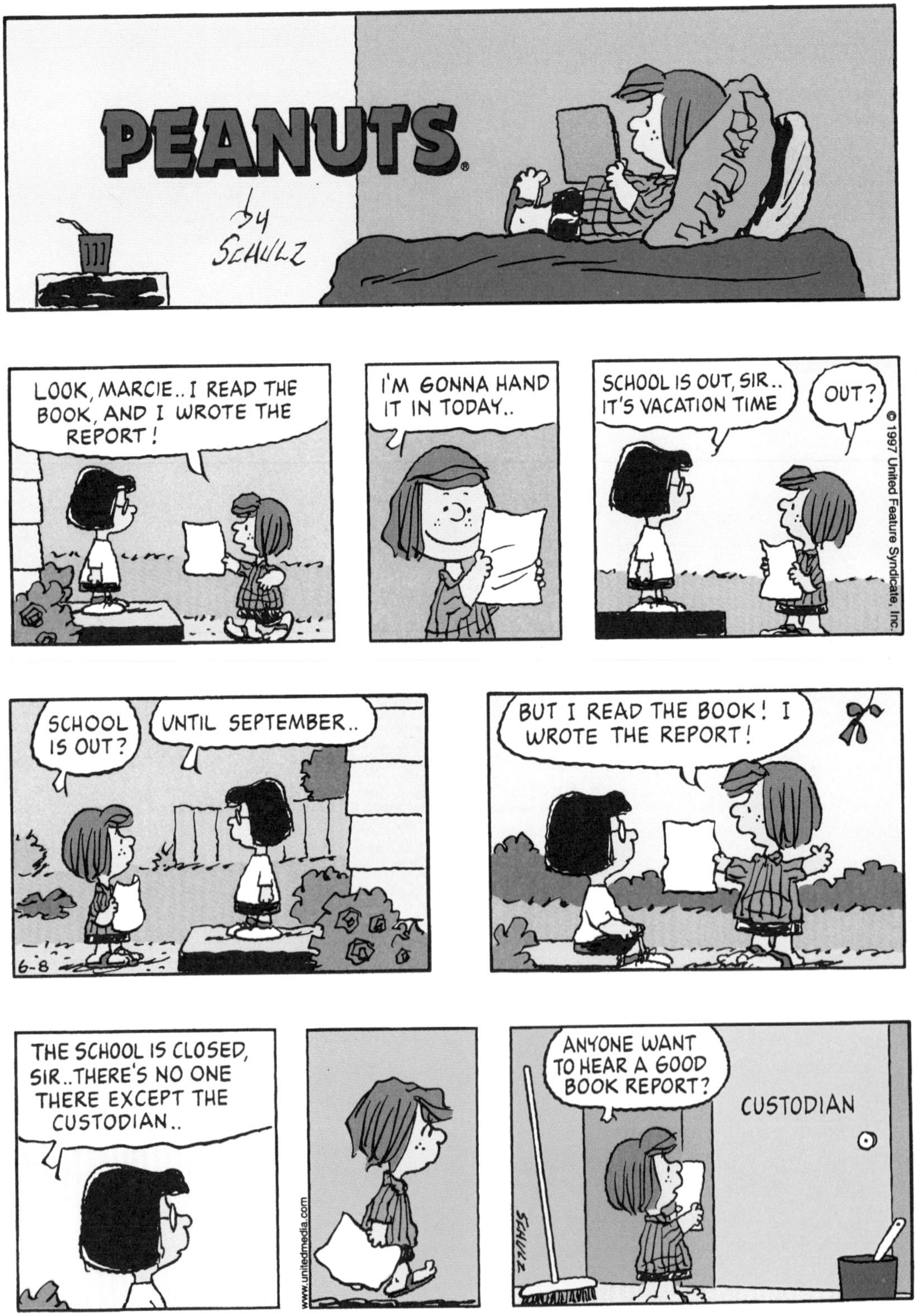
PEANUTS
by SCHULZ
LOOK, MARCIE.. I READ THE BOOK, AND I WROTE THE REPORT!
I'M GONNA HAND IT IN TODAY..
SCHOOL IS OUT, SIR.. IT'S VACATION TIME
OUT?
© 1997 United Feature Syndicate, Inc.
SCHOOL IS OUT?
UNTIL SEPTEMBER..
6-8
BUT I READ THE BOOK! I WROTE THE REPORT!
THE SCHOOL IS CLOSED, SIR.. THERE'S NO ONE THERE EXCEPT THE CUSTODIAN..
www.unitedmedia.com
ANYONE WANT TO HEAR A GOOD BOOK REPORT?
CUSTODIAN
SCHULZ

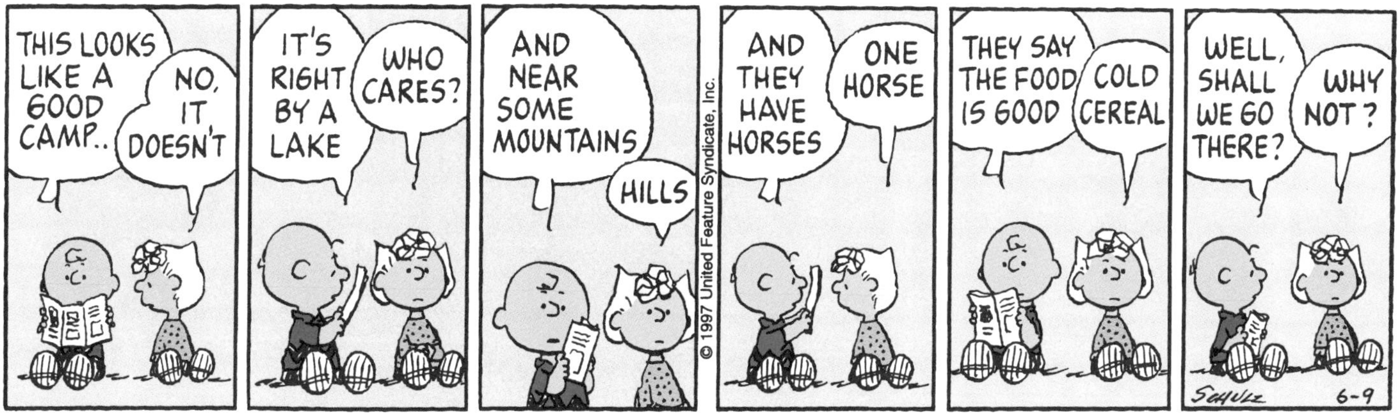
THIS LOOKS LIKE A GOOD CAMP..
NO, IT DOESN'T
IT'S RIGHT BY A LAKE
WHO CARES?
AND NEAR SOME MOUNTAINS
HILLS
AND THEY HAVE HORSES
ONE HORSE
THEY SAY THE FOOD IS GOOD
COLD CEREAL
WELL, SHALL WE GO THERE?
WHY NOT?
© 1997 United Feature Syndicate, Inc.
SCHULZ 6-9

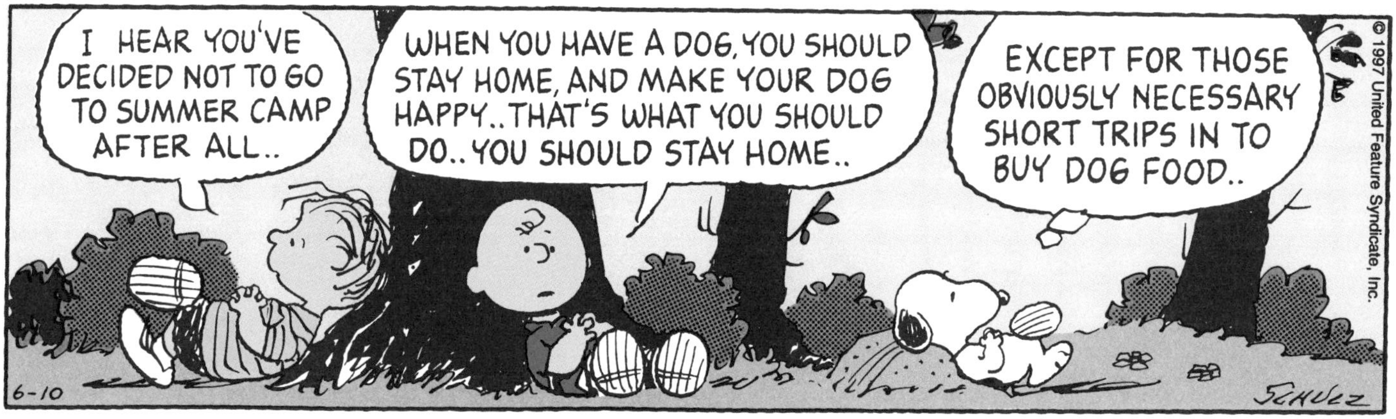
I HEAR YOU'VE DECIDED NOT TO GO TO SUMMER CAMP AFTER ALL..
WHEN YOU HAVE A DOG, YOU SHOULD STAY HOME, AND MAKE YOUR DOG HAPPY..THAT'S WHAT YOU SHOULD DO.. YOU SHOULD STAY HOME..
EXCEPT FOR THOSE OBVIOUSLY NECESSARY SHORT TRIPS IN TO BUY DOG FOOD..
© 1997 United Feature Syndicate, Inc.
6-10
SCHULZ

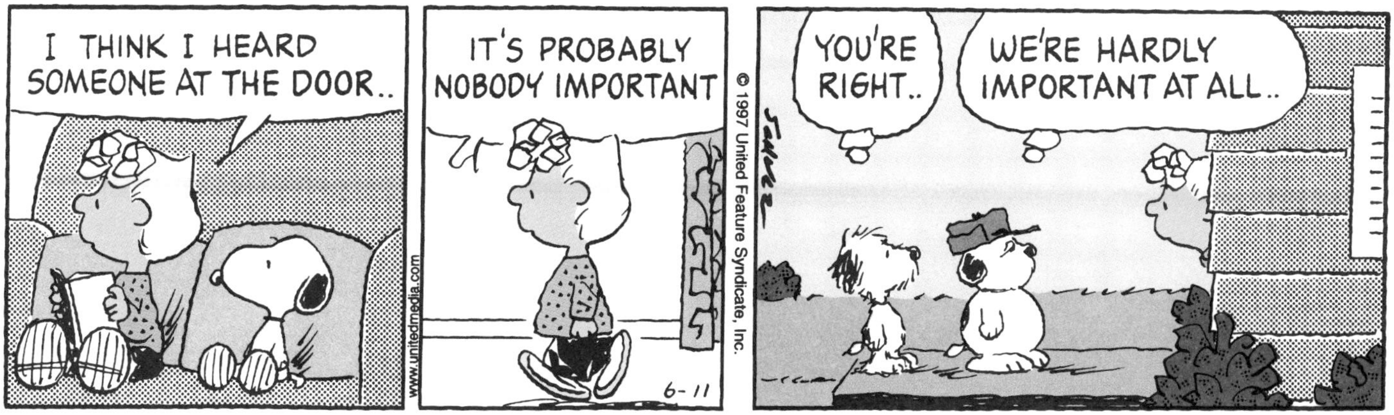
I THINK I HEARD SOMEONE AT THE DOOR..
www.unitedmedia.com
IT'S PROBABLY NOBODY IMPORTANT
6-11
© 1997 United Feature Syndicate, Inc.
SCHULZ
YOU'RE RIGHT..
WE'RE HARDLY IMPORTANT AT ALL..

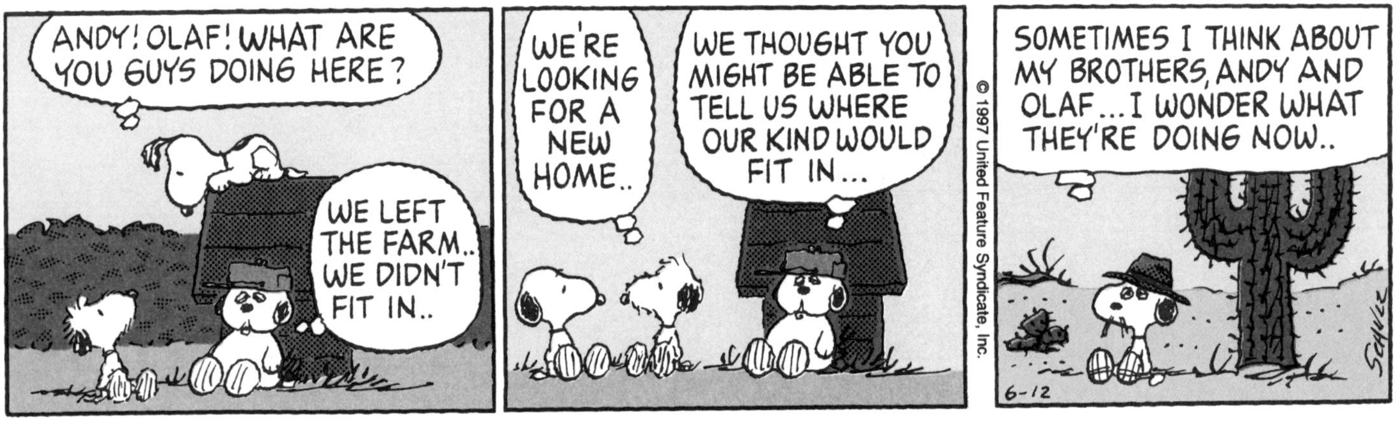
ANDY! OLAF! WHAT ARE YOU GUYS DOING HERE?
WE LEFT THE FARM.. WE DIDN'T FIT IN..
WE'RE LOOKING FOR A NEW HOME..
WE THOUGHT YOU MIGHT BE ABLE TO TELL US WHERE OUR KIND WOULD FIT IN...
© 1997 United Feature Syndicate, Inc.
SOMETIMES I THINK ABOUT MY BROTHERS, ANDY AND OLAF... I WONDER WHAT THEY'RE DOING NOW..
6-12
SCHULZ

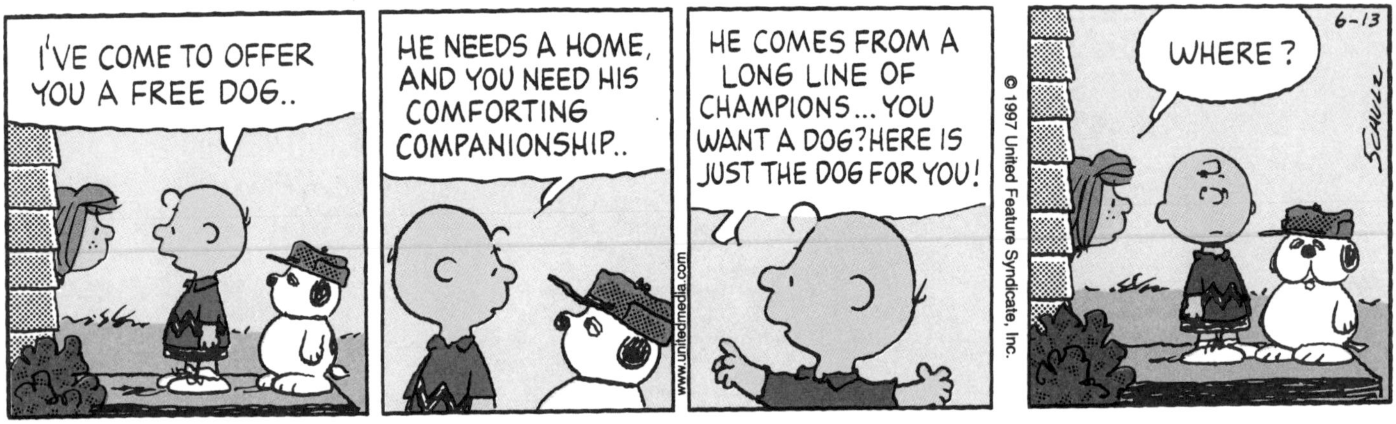
I'VE COME TO OFFER YOU A FREE DOG..
HE NEEDS A HOME, AND YOU NEED HIS COMFORTING COMPANIONSHIP..
www.unitedmedia.com
HE COMES FROM A LONG LINE OF CHAMPIONS... YOU WANT A DOG? HERE IS JUST THE DOG FOR YOU!
© 1997 United Feature Syndicate, Inc.
6-13
WHERE?
SCHULZ

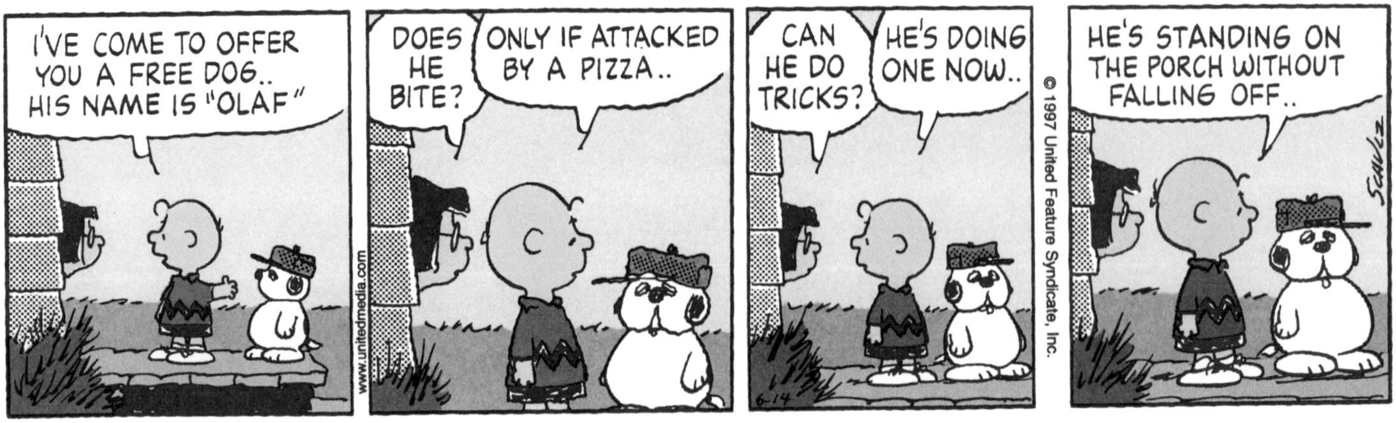
I'VE COME TO OFFER YOU A FREE DOG.. HIS NAME IS "OLAF"
www.unitedmedia.com
DOES HE BITE?
ONLY IF ATTACKED BY A PIZZA..
CAN HE DO TRICKS?
HE'S DOING ONE NOW..
6-14
© 1997 United Feature Syndicate, Inc.
HE'S STANDING ON THE PORCH WITHOUT FALLING OFF..
SCHULZ

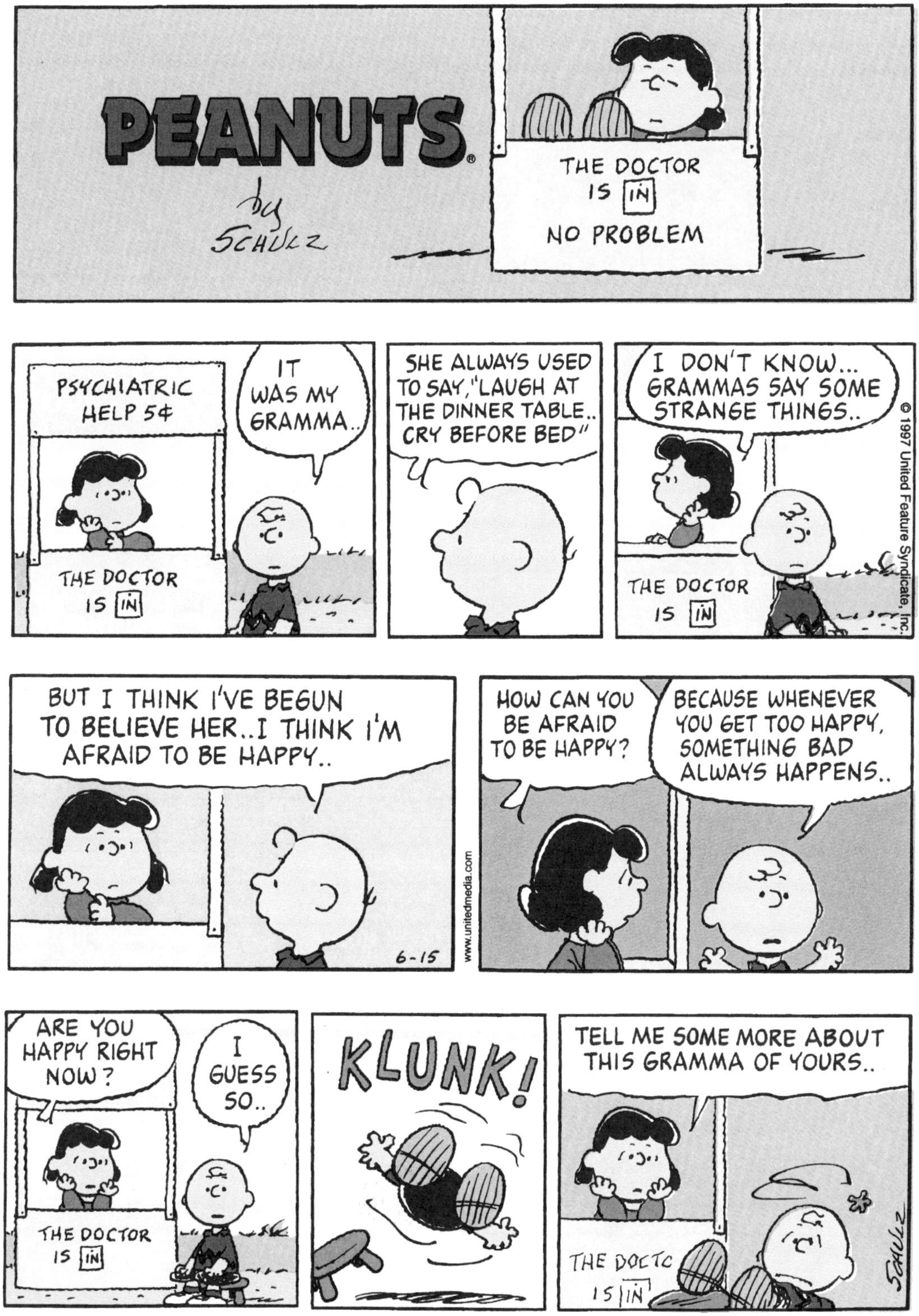
PEANUTS
by SCHULZ
THE DOCTOR IS IN
NO PROBLEM
PSYCHIATRIC HELP 5¢
THE DOCTOR IS IN
IT WAS MY GRAMMA..
SHE ALWAYS USED TO SAY, "LAUGH AT THE DINNER TABLE.. CRY BEFORE BED"
I DON'T KNOW... GRAMMAS SAY SOME STRANGE THINGS..
THE DOCTOR IS IN
© 1997 United Feature Syndicate, Inc.
BUT I THINK I'VE BEGUN TO BELIEVE HER..I THINK I'M AFRAID TO BE HAPPY..
6-15
www.unitedmedia.com
HOW CAN YOU BE AFRAID TO BE HAPPY?
BECAUSE WHENEVER YOU GET TOO HAPPY, SOMETHING BAD ALWAYS HAPPENS..
ARE YOU HAPPY RIGHT NOW?
I GUESS SO..
THE DOCTOR IS IN
KLUNK!
TELL ME SOME MORE ABOUT THIS GRAMMA OF YOURS..
THE DOCTC IS IN
SCHULZ

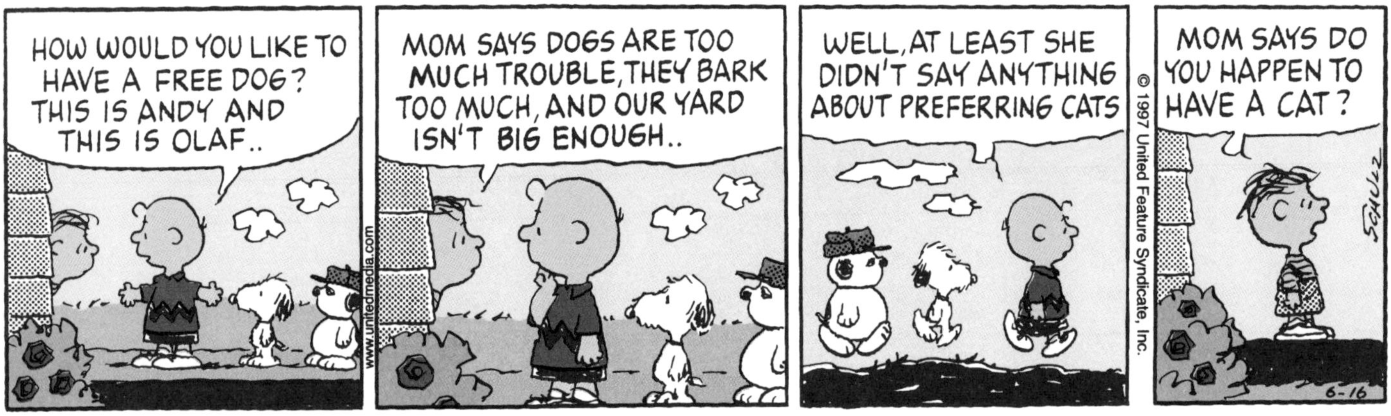
HOW WOULD YOU LIKE TO HAVE A FREE DOG? THIS IS ANDY AND THIS IS OLAF..
MOM SAYS DOGS ARE TOO MUCH TROUBLE, THEY BARK TOO MUCH, AND OUR YARD ISN'T BIG ENOUGH..
WELL, AT LEAST SHE DIDN'T SAY ANYTHING ABOUT PREFERRING CATS
MOM SAYS DO YOU HAPPEN TO HAVE A CAT?
www.unitedmedia.com
© 1997 United Feature Syndicate, Inc.
SCHULZ
6-16

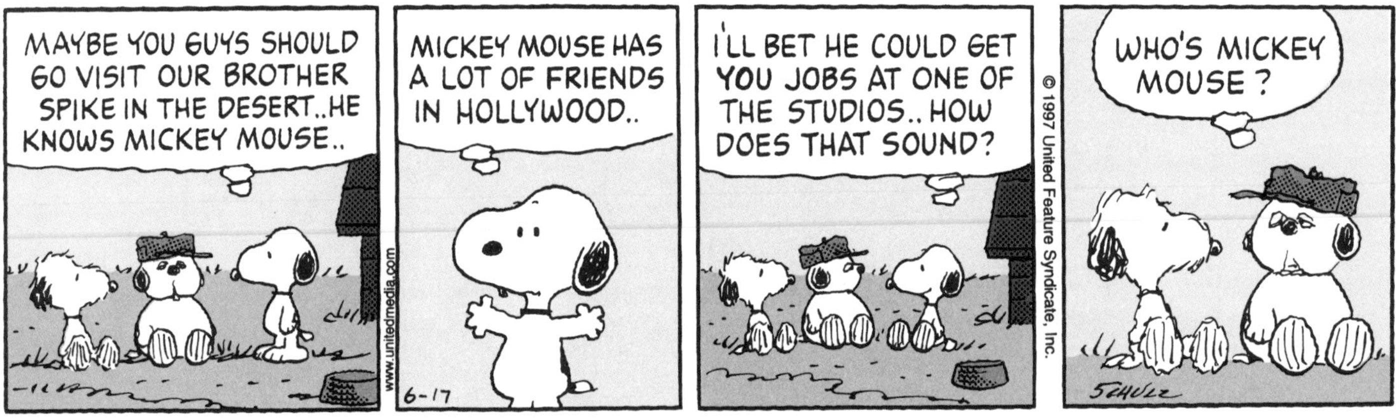
MAYBE YOU GUYS SHOULD GO VISIT OUR BROTHER SPIKE IN THE DESERT..HE KNOWS MICKEY MOUSE..
MICKEY MOUSE HAS A LOT OF FRIENDS IN HOLLYWOOD..
I'LL BET HE COULD GET YOU JOBS AT ONE OF THE STUDIOS.. HOW DOES THAT SOUND?
WHO'S MICKEY MOUSE?
www.unitedmedia.com
6-17
© 1997 United Feature Syndicate, Inc.
SCHULZ

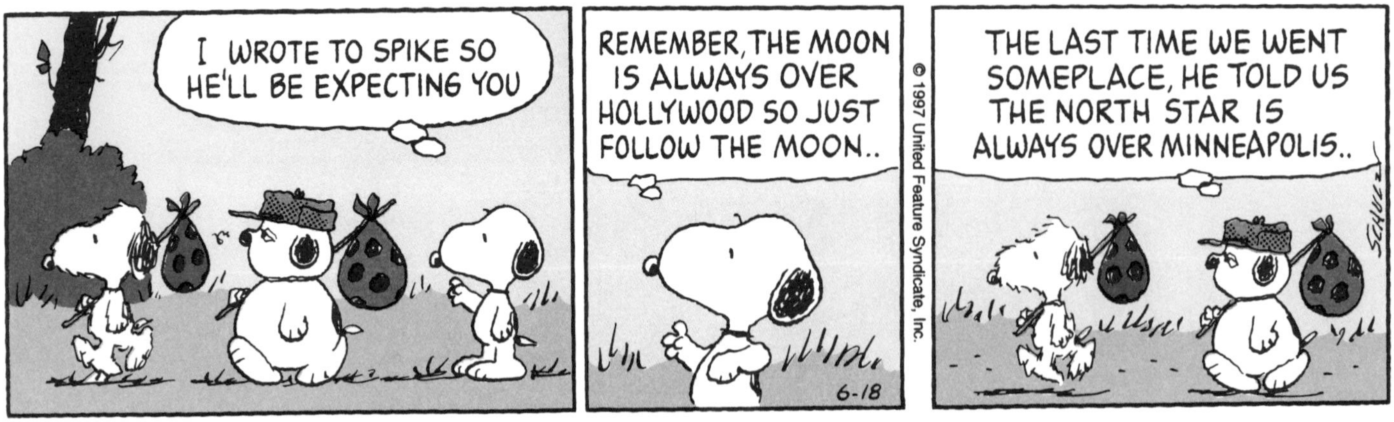
I WROTE TO SPIKE SO HE'LL BE EXPECTING YOU
REMEMBER, THE MOON IS ALWAYS OVER HOLLYWOOD SO JUST FOLLOW THE MOON..
THE LAST TIME WE WENT SOMEPLACE, HE TOLD US THE NORTH STAR IS ALWAYS OVER MINNEAPOLIS..
6-18
© 1997 United Feature Syndicate, Inc.
SCHULZ

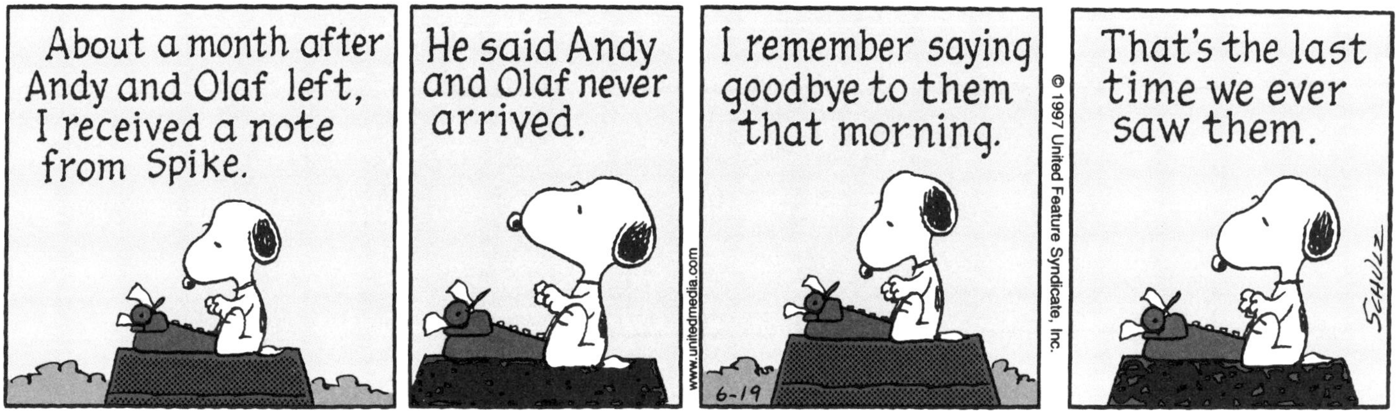
About a month after Andy and Olaf left, I received a note from Spike.
He said Andy and Olaf never arrived.
I remember saying goodbye to them that morning.
© 1997 United Feature Syndicate, Inc.
That's the last time we ever saw them.

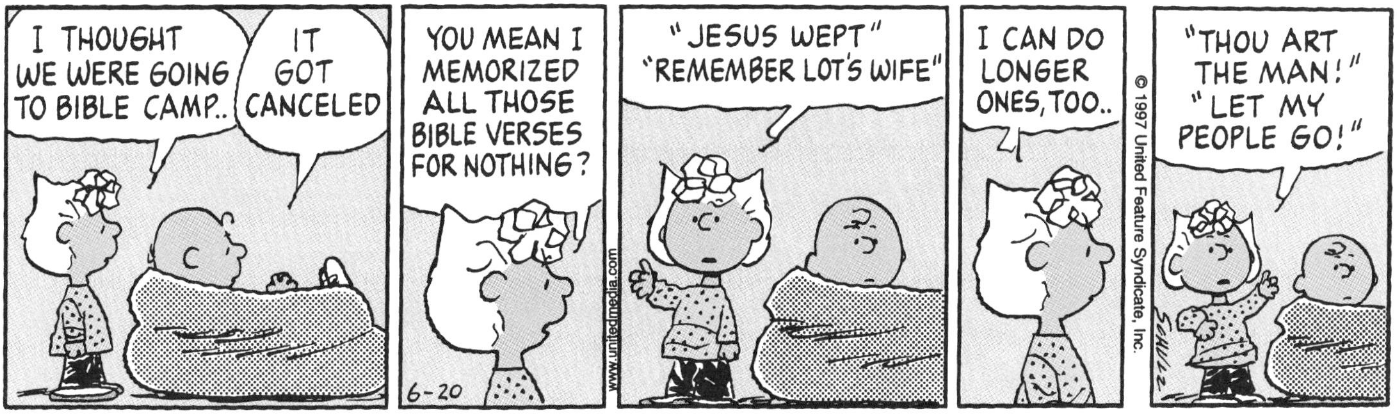
I THOUGHT WE WERE GOING TO BIBLE CAMP..
IT GOT CANCELED
YOU MEAN I MEMORIZED ALL THOSE BIBLE VERSES FOR NOTHING?
"JESUS WEPT" "REMEMBER LOT'S WIFE"
I CAN DO LONGER ONES, TOO..
© 1997 United Feature Syndicate, Inc.
"THOU ART THE MAN!" "LET MY PEOPLE GO!"

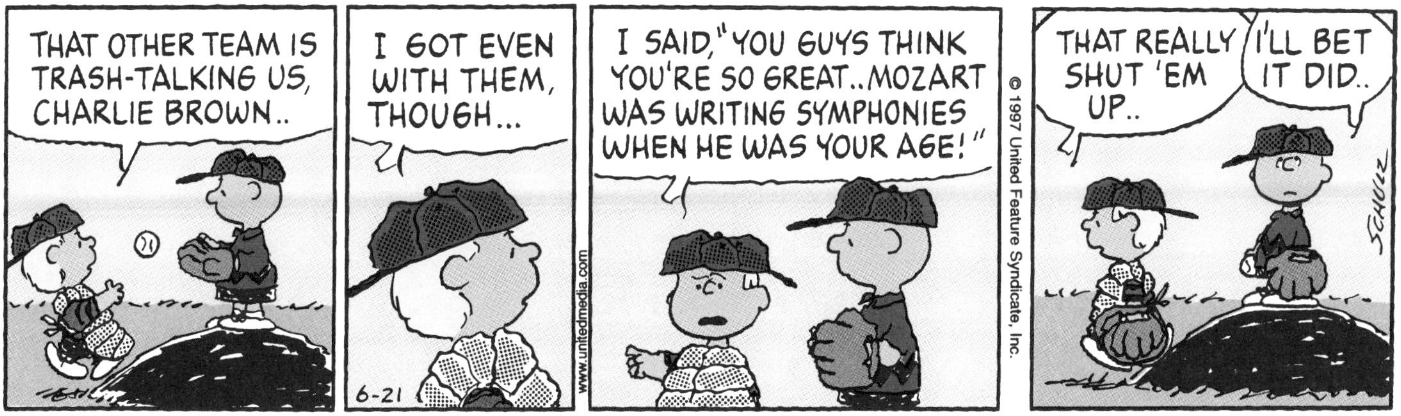
THAT OTHER TEAM IS TRASH-TALKING US, CHARLIE BROWN..
I GOT EVEN WITH THEM, THOUGH...
I SAID, "YOU GUYS THINK YOU'RE SO GREAT..MOZART WAS WRITING SYMPHONIES WHEN HE WAS YOUR AGE!"
© 1997 United Feature Syndicate, Inc.
THAT REALLY SHUT 'EM UP..
I'LL BET IT DID..

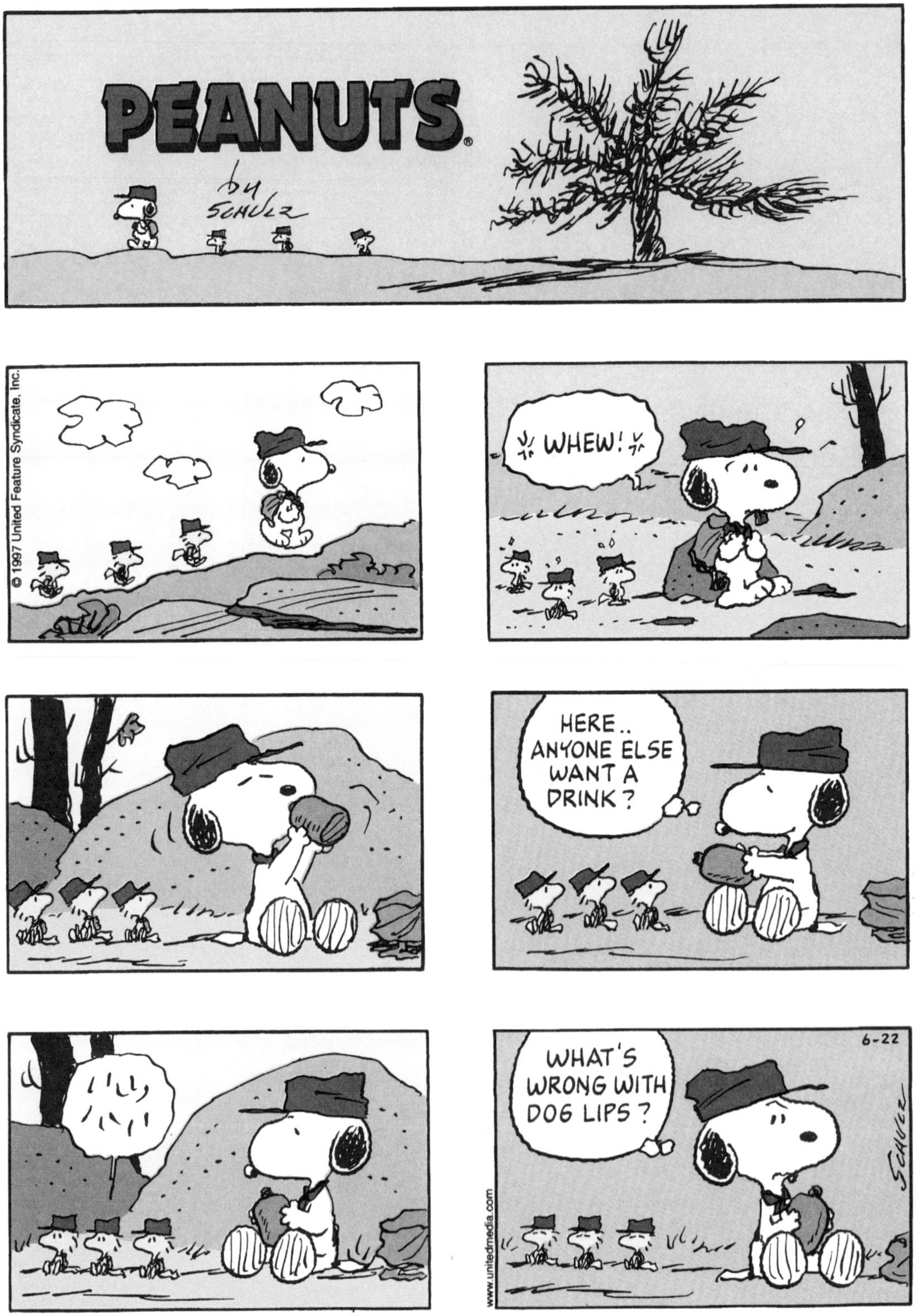
PEANUTS
by Schulz
© 1997 United Feature Syndicate, Inc.
WHEW!
HERE.. ANYONE ELSE WANT A DRINK?
6-22
WHAT'S WRONG WITH DOG LIPS?
SCHULZ
www.unitedmedia.com

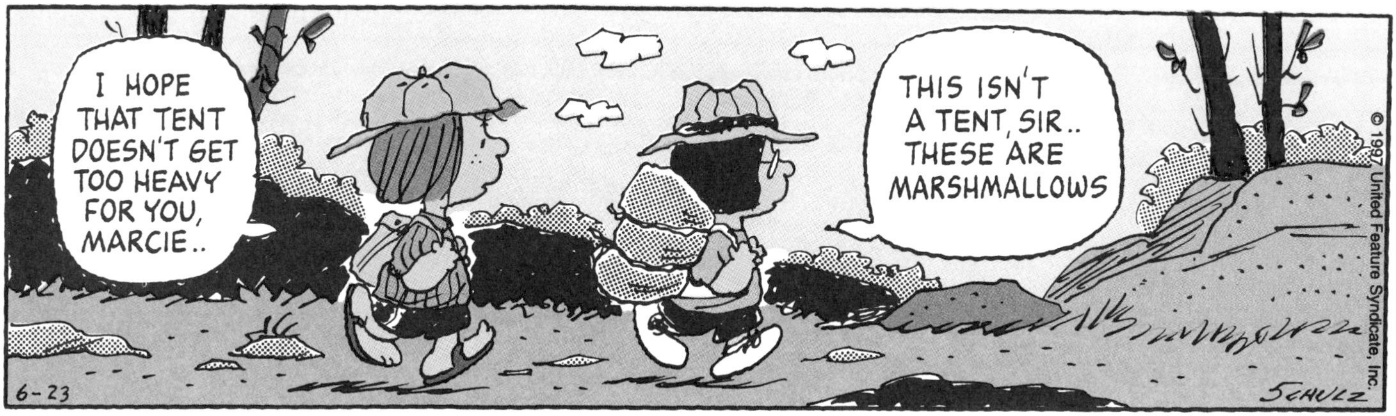
I HOPE THAT TENT DOESN'T GET TOO HEAVY FOR YOU, MARCIE..
THIS ISN'T A TENT, SIR.. THESE ARE MARSHMALLOWS
© 1997 United Feature Syndicate, Inc.
6-23
SCHULZ

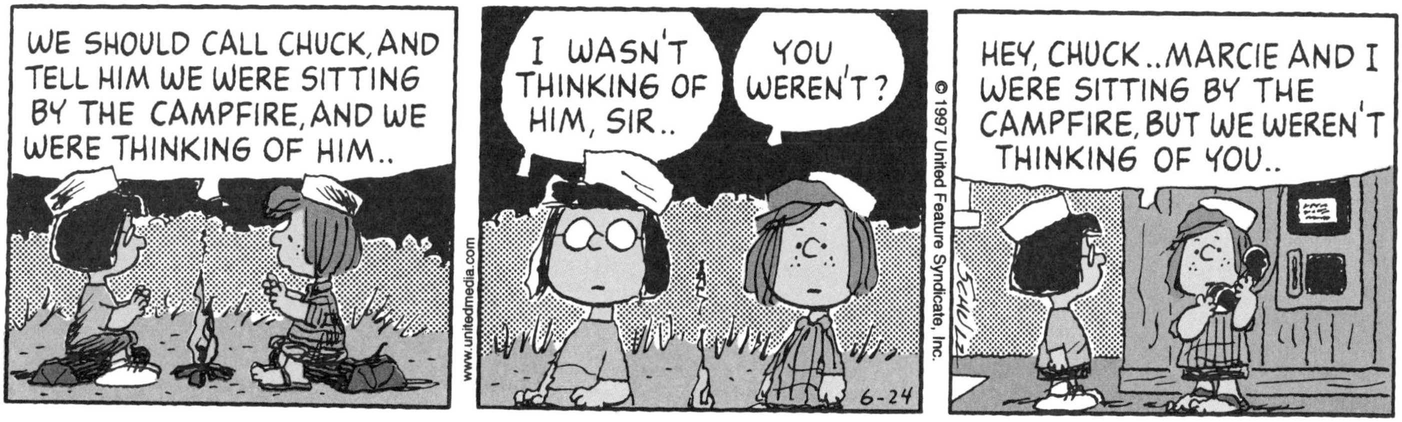
WE SHOULD CALL CHUCK, AND TELL HIM WE WERE SITTING BY THE CAMPFIRE, AND WE WERE THINKING OF HIM..
www.unitedmedia.com
I WASN'T THINKING OF HIM, SIR..
YOU WEREN'T?
6-24
© 1997 United Feature Syndicate, Inc.
SCHULZ
HEY, CHUCK..MARCIE AND I WERE SITTING BY THE CAMPFIRE, BUT WE WEREN'T THINKING OF YOU..

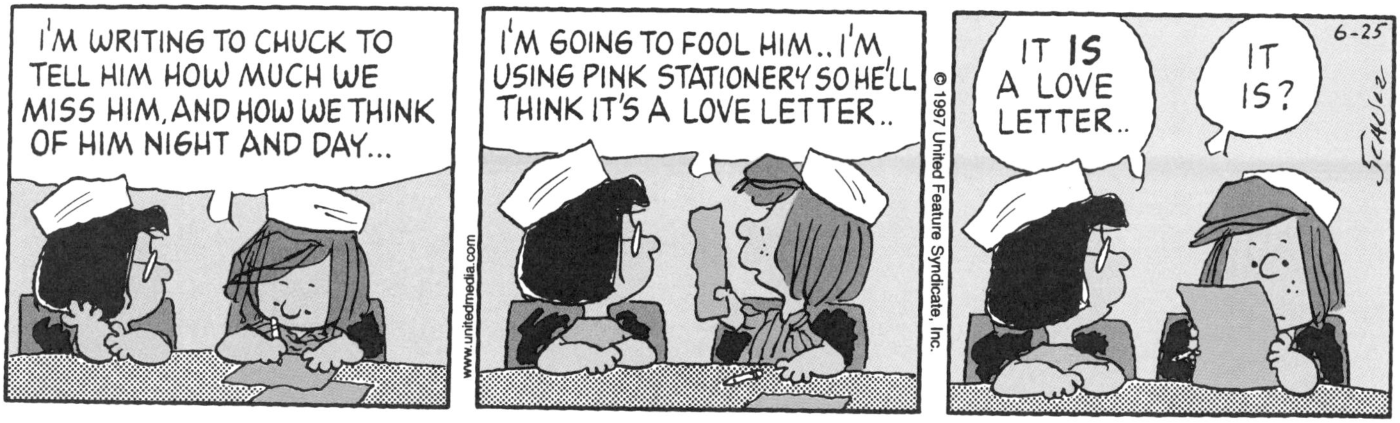
I'M WRITING TO CHUCK TO TELL HIM HOW MUCH WE MISS HIM, AND HOW WE THINK OF HIM NIGHT AND DAY...
www.unitedmedia.com
I'M GOING TO FOOL HIM..I'M USING PINK STATIONERY SO HE'LL THINK IT'S A LOVE LETTER..
© 1997 United Feature Syndicate, Inc.
IT IS A LOVE LETTER..
IT IS?
6-25
SCHULZ

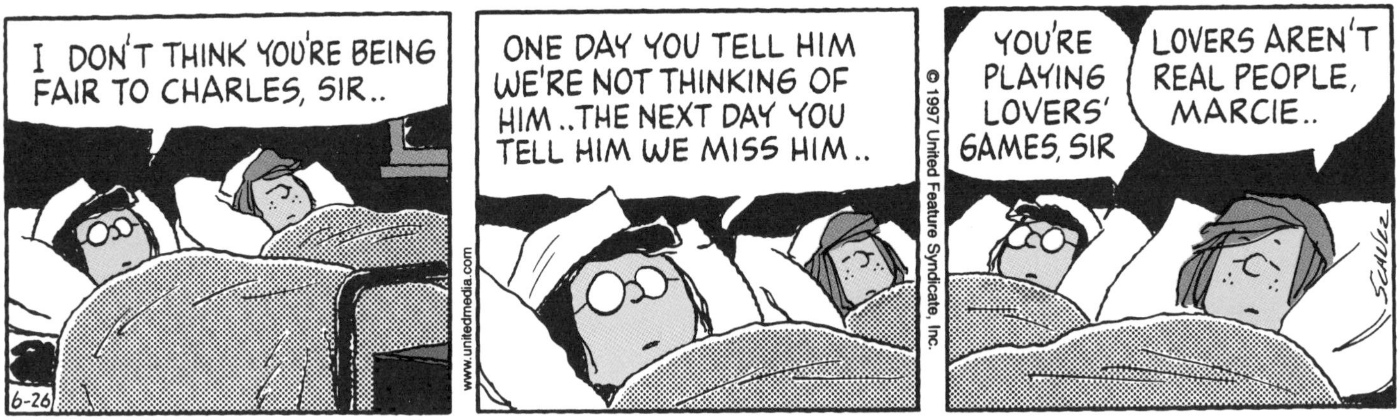
I DON'T THINK YOU'RE BEING FAIR TO CHARLES, SIR..
ONE DAY YOU TELL HIM WE'RE NOT THINKING OF HIM..THE NEXT DAY YOU TELL HIM WE MISS HIM..
YOU'RE PLAYING LOVERS' GAMES, SIR
LOVERS AREN'T REAL PEOPLE, MARCIE..
6-26
www.unitedmedia.com
© 1997 United Feature Syndicate, Inc.
SCHULZ

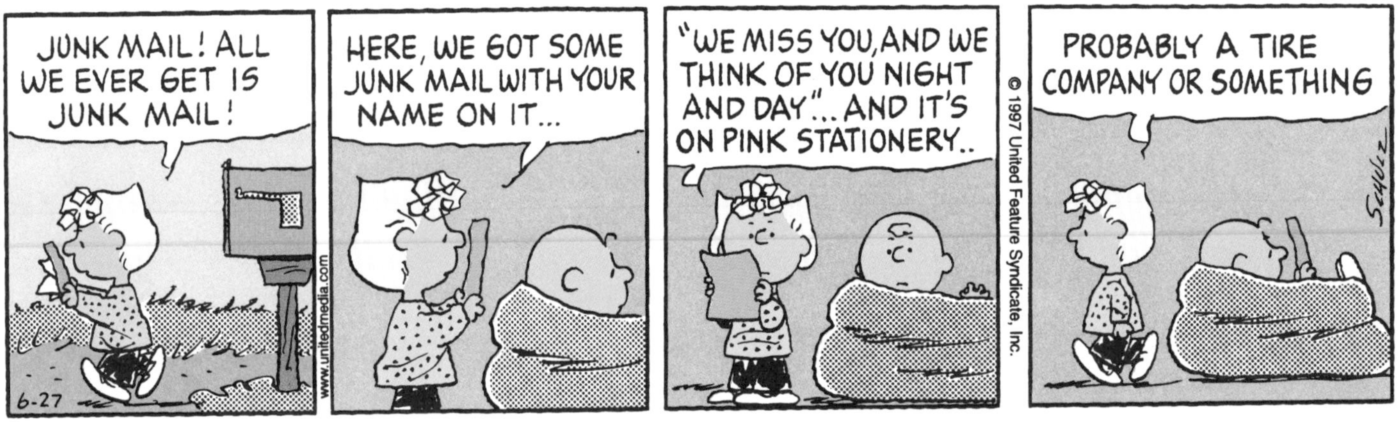
JUNK MAIL! ALL WE EVER GET IS JUNK MAIL!
HERE, WE GOT SOME JUNK MAIL WITH YOUR NAME ON IT...
"WE MISS YOU, AND WE THINK OF YOU NIGHT AND DAY"... AND IT'S ON PINK STATIONERY..
PROBABLY A TIRE COMPANY OR SOMETHING
6-27
www.unitedmedia.com
© 1997 United Feature Syndicate, Inc.
SCHULZ

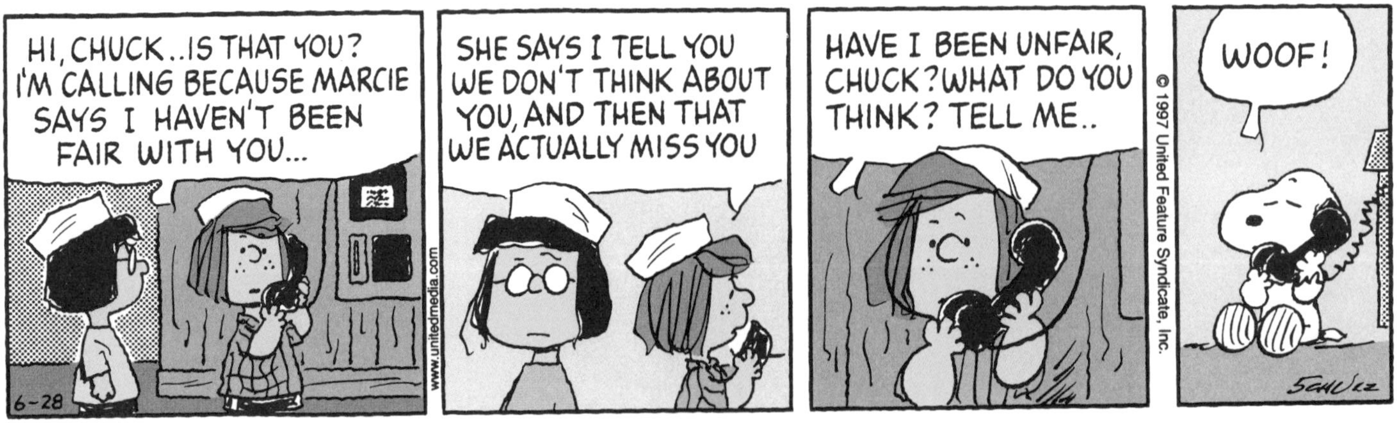
HI, CHUCK..IS THAT YOU? I'M CALLING BECAUSE MARCIE SAYS I HAVEN'T BEEN FAIR WITH YOU...
SHE SAYS I TELL YOU WE DON'T THINK ABOUT YOU, AND THEN THAT WE ACTUALLY MISS YOU
HAVE I BEEN UNFAIR, CHUCK? WHAT DO YOU THINK? TELL ME..
WOOF!
6-28
www.unitedmedia.com
© 1997 United Feature Syndicate, Inc.
SCHULZ

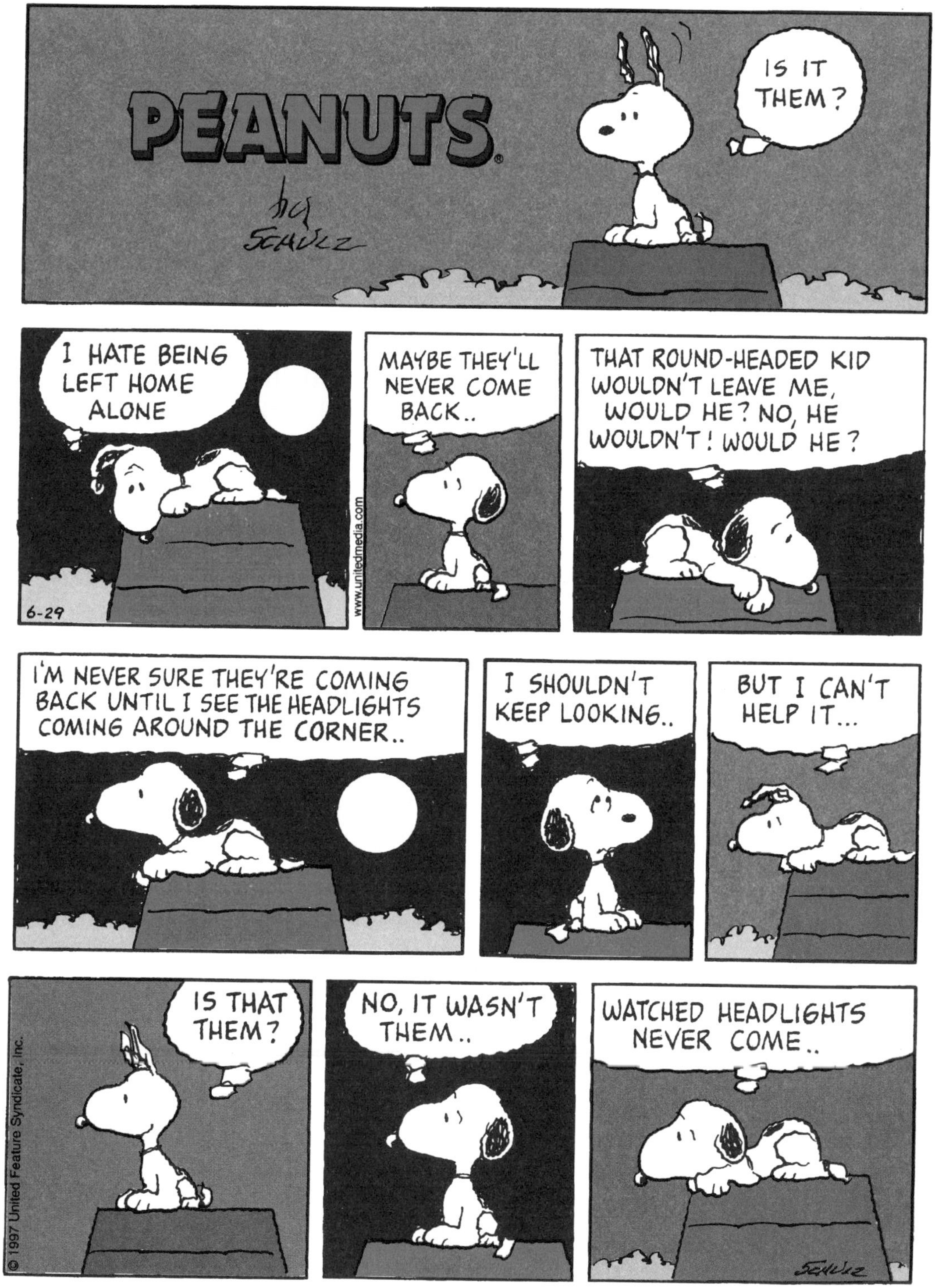
PEANUTS
by SCHULZ
IS IT THEM?
I HATE BEING LEFT HOME ALONE
6-29
www.unitedmedia.com
MAYBE THEY'LL NEVER COME BACK..
THAT ROUND-HEADED KID WOULDN'T LEAVE ME, WOULD HE? NO, HE WOULDN'T! WOULD HE?
I'M NEVER SURE THEY'RE COMING BACK UNTIL I SEE THE HEADLIGHTS COMING AROUND THE CORNER..
I SHOULDN'T KEEP LOOKING..
BUT I CAN'T HELP IT...
© 1997 United Feature Syndicate, Inc.
IS THAT THEM?
NO, IT WASN'T THEM..
WATCHED HEADLIGHTS NEVER COME..
SCHULZ

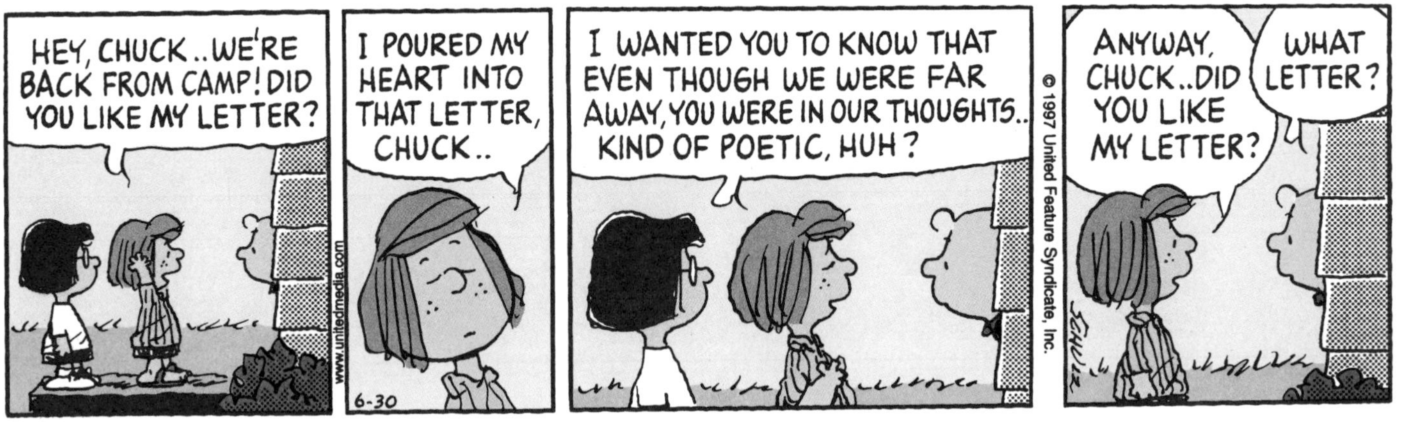
HEY, CHUCK..WE'RE BACK FROM CAMP! DID YOU LIKE MY LETTER?
www.unitedmedia.com
I POURED MY HEART INTO THAT LETTER, CHUCK..
6-30
I WANTED YOU TO KNOW THAT EVEN THOUGH WE WERE FAR AWAY, YOU WERE IN OUR THOUGHTS.. KIND OF POETIC, HUH?
© 1997 United Feature Syndicate, Inc.
ANYWAY, CHUCK..DID YOU LIKE MY LETTER?
WHAT LETTER?
SCHULZ

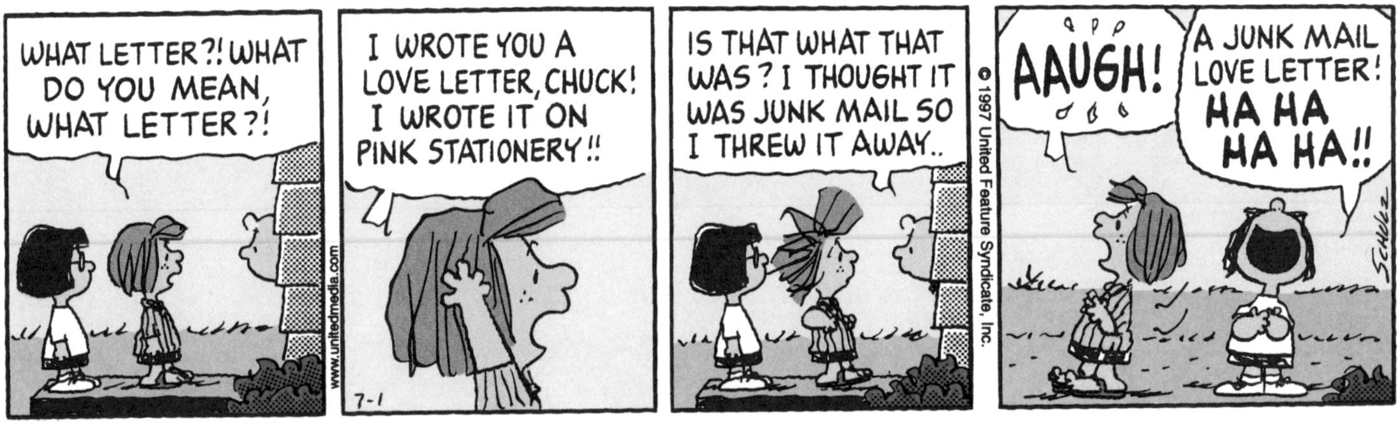
WHAT LETTER?! WHAT DO YOU MEAN, WHAT LETTER?!
www.unitedmedia.com
I WROTE YOU A LOVE LETTER, CHUCK! I WROTE IT ON PINK STATIONERY!!
7-1
IS THAT WHAT THAT WAS? I THOUGHT IT WAS JUNK MAIL SO I THREW IT AWAY..
© 1997 United Feature Syndicate, Inc.
AAUGH!
A JUNK MAIL LOVE LETTER! HA HA HA HA!!
SCHULZ

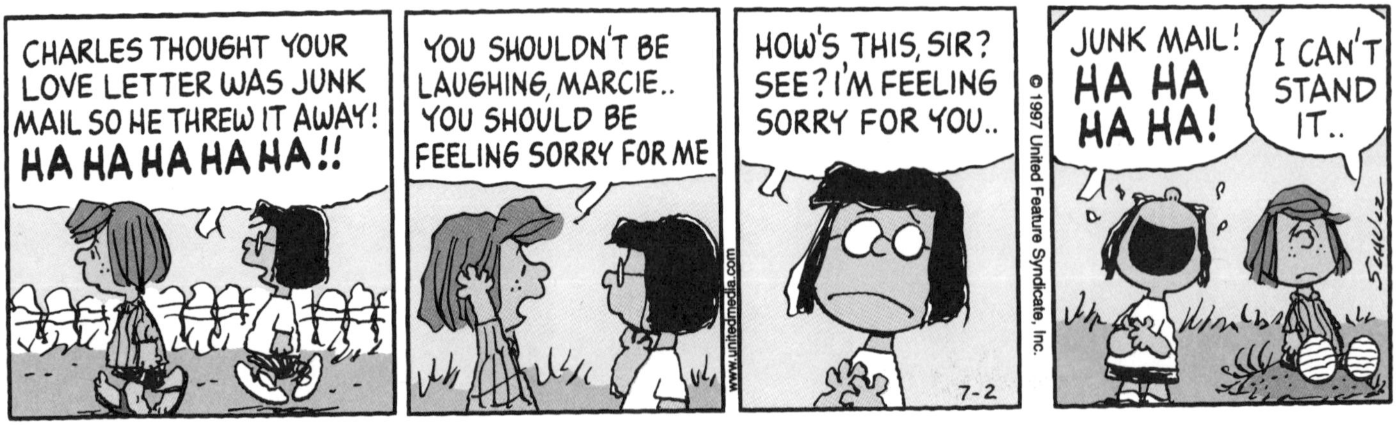
CHARLES THOUGHT YOUR LOVE LETTER WAS JUNK MAIL SO HE THREW IT AWAY! HA HA HA HA HA HA!!
YOU SHOULDN'T BE LAUGHING, MARCIE.. YOU SHOULD BE FEELING SORRY FOR ME
www.unitedmedia.com
HOW'S THIS, SIR? SEE? I'M FEELING SORRY FOR YOU..
7-2
© 1997 United Feature Syndicate, Inc.
JUNK MAIL! HA HA HA HA!
I CAN'T STAND IT..
SCHULZ

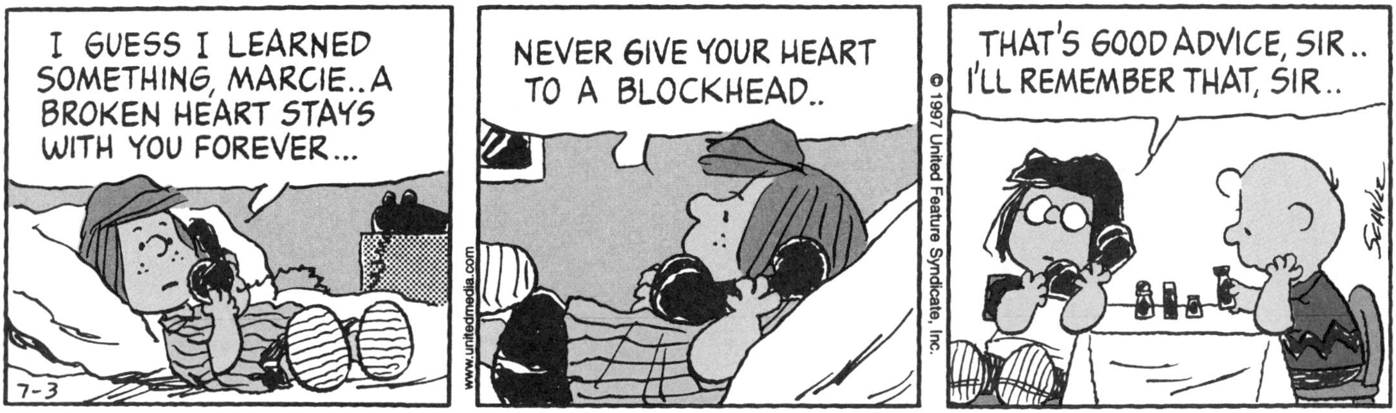
7-3
I GUESS I LEARNED SOMETHING, MARCIE.. A BROKEN HEART STAYS WITH YOU FOREVER...
NEVER GIVE YOUR HEART TO A BLOCKHEAD..
THAT'S GOOD ADVICE, SIR.. I'LL REMEMBER THAT, SIR..
www.unitedmedia.com
© 1997 United Feature Syndicate, Inc.
SCHULZ

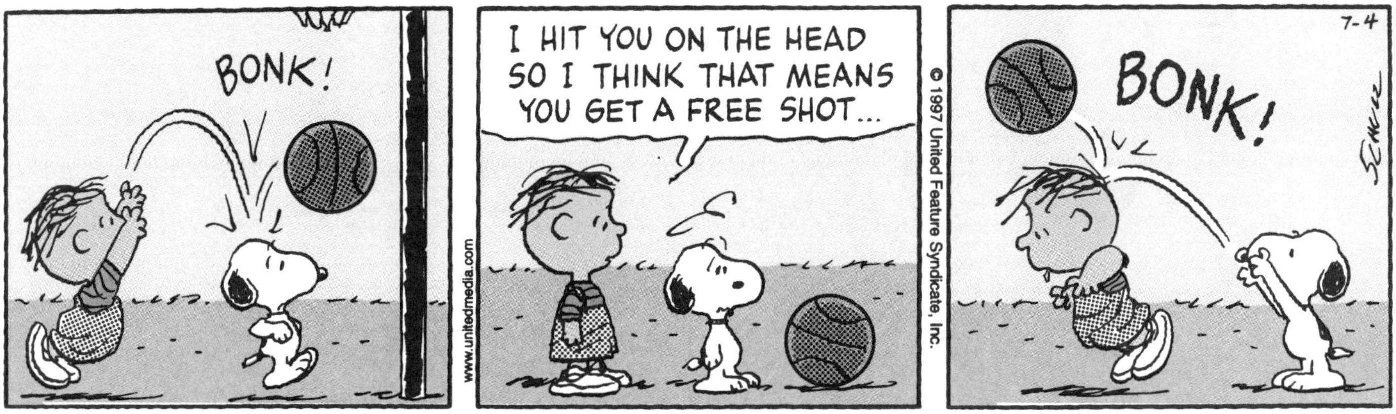
BONK!
I HIT YOU ON THE HEAD SO I THINK THAT MEANS YOU GET A FREE SHOT...
7-4
BONK!
www.unitedmedia.com
© 1997 United Feature Syndicate, Inc.
SCHULZ

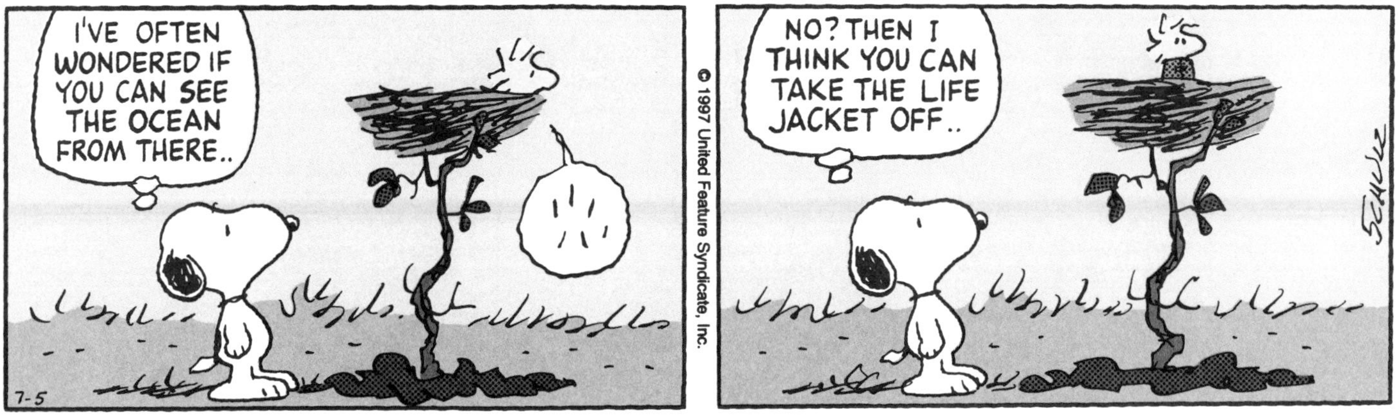
I'VE OFTEN WONDERED IF YOU CAN SEE THE OCEAN FROM THERE..
NO? THEN I THINK YOU CAN TAKE THE LIFE JACKET OFF..
7-5
© 1997 United Feature Syndicate, Inc.
SCHULZ

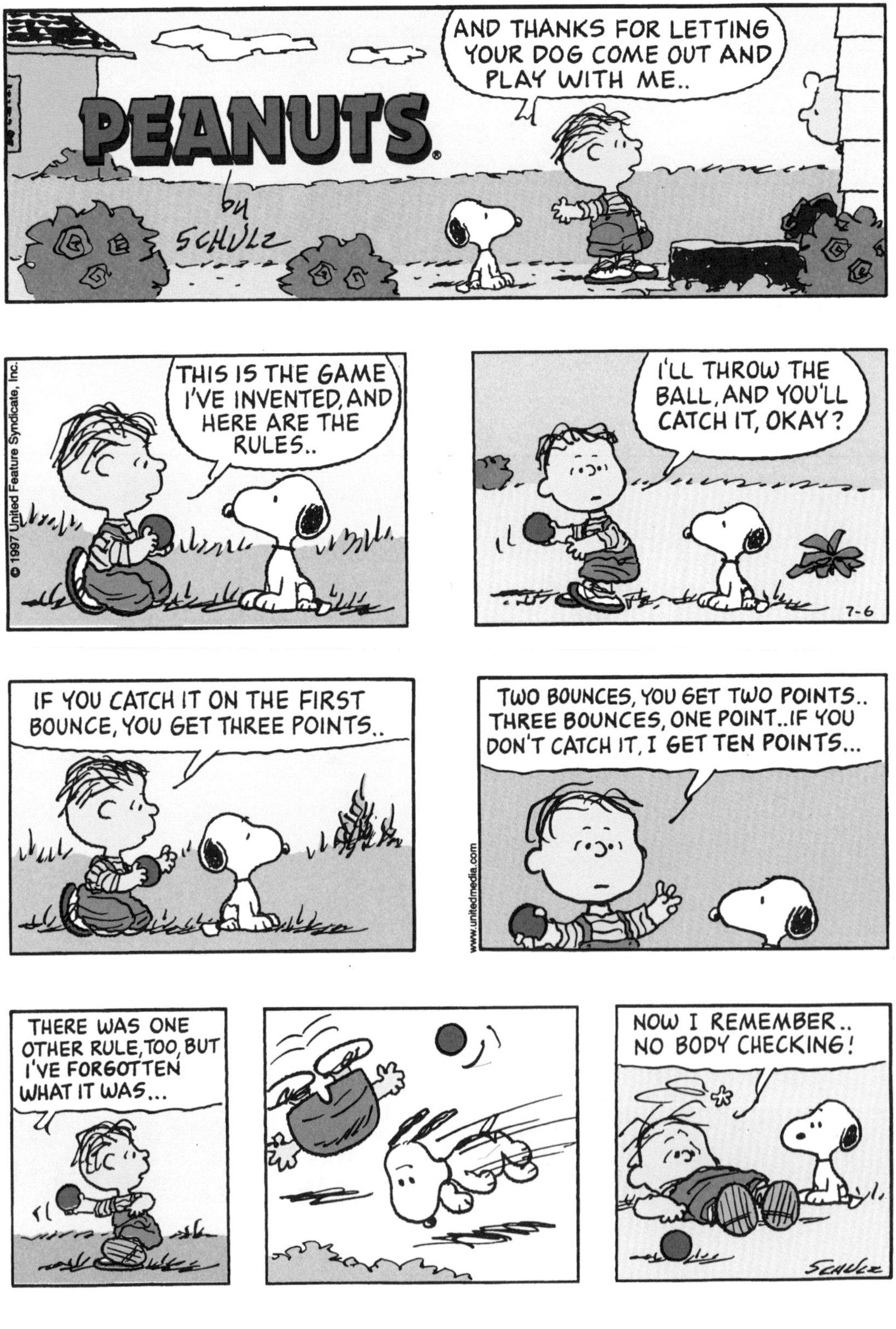
PEANUTS
by SCHULZ
AND THANKS FOR LETTING YOUR DOG COME OUT AND PLAY WITH ME..
© 1997 United Feature Syndicate, Inc.
THIS IS THE GAME I'VE INVENTED, AND HERE ARE THE RULES..
I'LL THROW THE BALL, AND YOU'LL CATCH IT, OKAY?
7-6
IF YOU CATCH IT ON THE FIRST BOUNCE, YOU GET THREE POINTS..
www.unitedmedia.com
TWO BOUNCES, YOU GET TWO POINTS.. THREE BOUNCES, ONE POINT..IF YOU DON'T CATCH IT, I GET TEN POINTS...
THERE WAS ONE OTHER RULE, TOO, BUT I'VE FORGOTTEN WHAT IT WAS...
NOW I REMEMBER.. NO BODY CHECKING!
SCHULZ

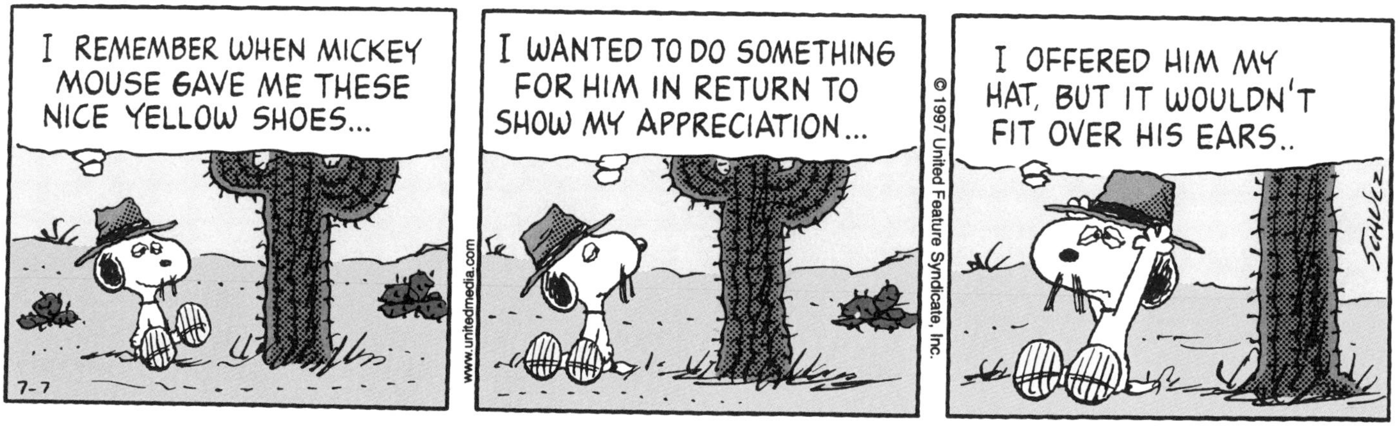
I REMEMBER WHEN MICKEY MOUSE GAVE ME THESE NICE YELLOW SHOES...
7-7
www.unitedmedia.com
I WANTED TO DO SOMETHING FOR HIM IN RETURN TO SHOW MY APPRECIATION...
© 1997 United Feature Syndicate, Inc.
I OFFERED HIM MY HAT, BUT IT WOULDN'T FIT OVER HIS EARS..
SCHULZ

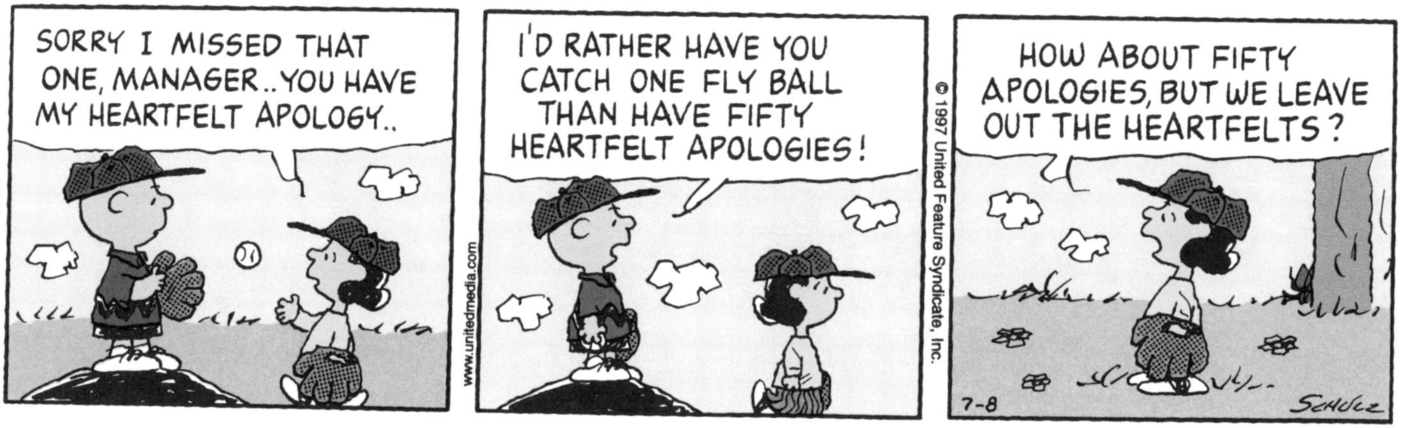
SORRY I MISSED THAT ONE, MANAGER.. YOU HAVE MY HEARTFELT APOLOGY..
www.unitedmedia.com
I'D RATHER HAVE YOU CATCH ONE FLY BALL THAN HAVE FIFTY HEARTFELT APOLOGIES!
© 1997 United Feature Syndicate, Inc.
HOW ABOUT FIFTY APOLOGIES, BUT WE LEAVE OUT THE HEARTFELTS?
7-8
SCHULZ

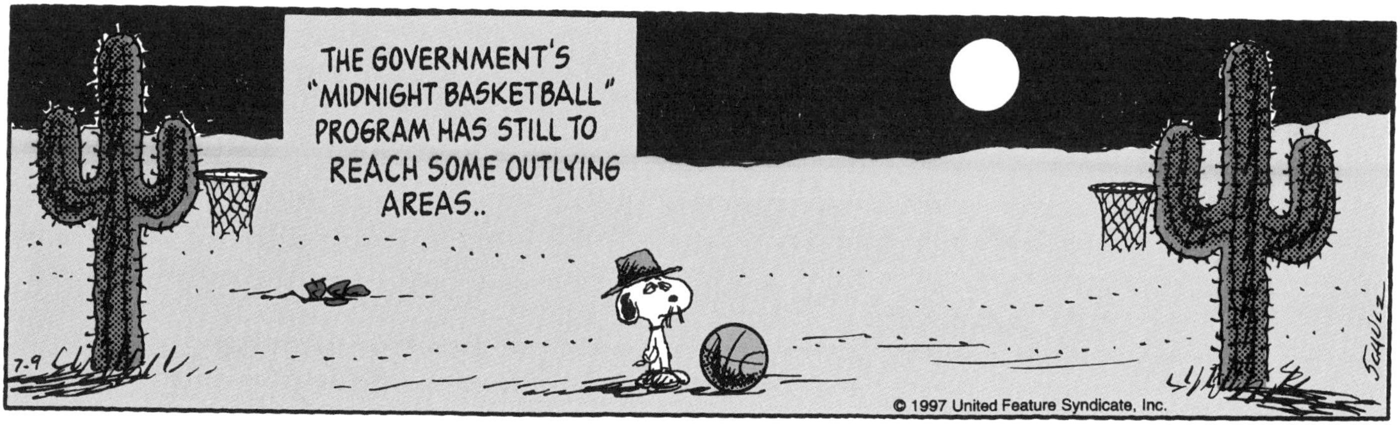
THE GOVERNMENT'S "MIDNIGHT BASKETBALL" PROGRAM HAS STILL TO REACH SOME OUTLYING AREAS..
7-9
SCHULZ
© 1997 United Feature Syndicate, Inc.

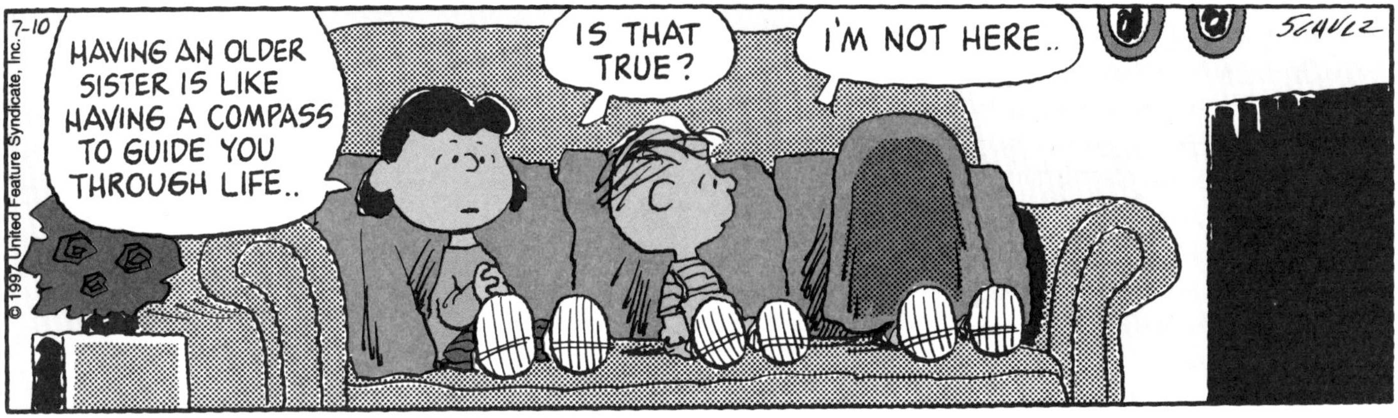
7-10
© 1997 United Feature Syndicate, Inc.
HAVING AN OLDER SISTER IS LIKE HAVING A COMPASS TO GUIDE YOU THROUGH LIFE..
IS THAT TRUE?
I'M NOT HERE..
SCHULZ

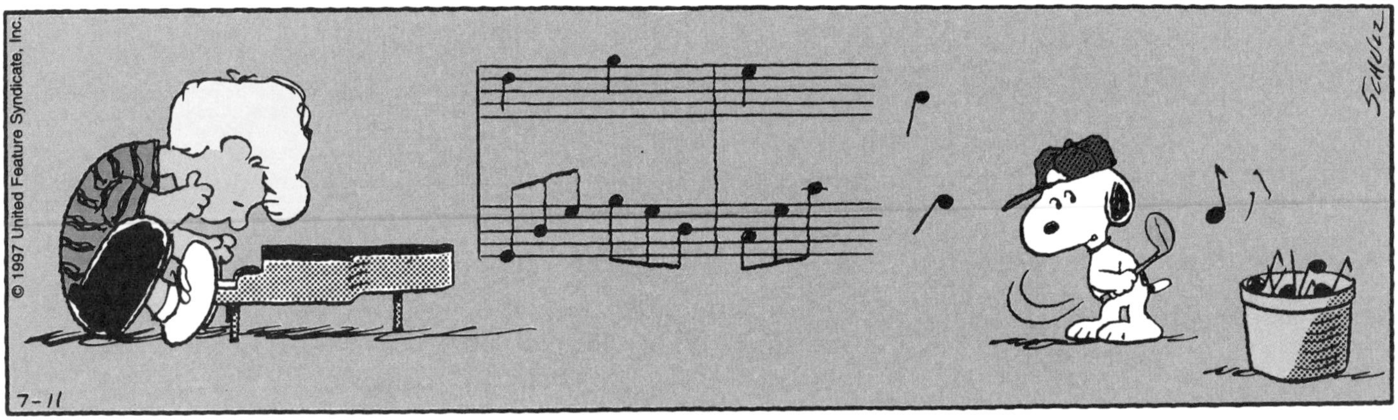
© 1997 United Feature Syndicate, Inc.
SCHULZ
7-11

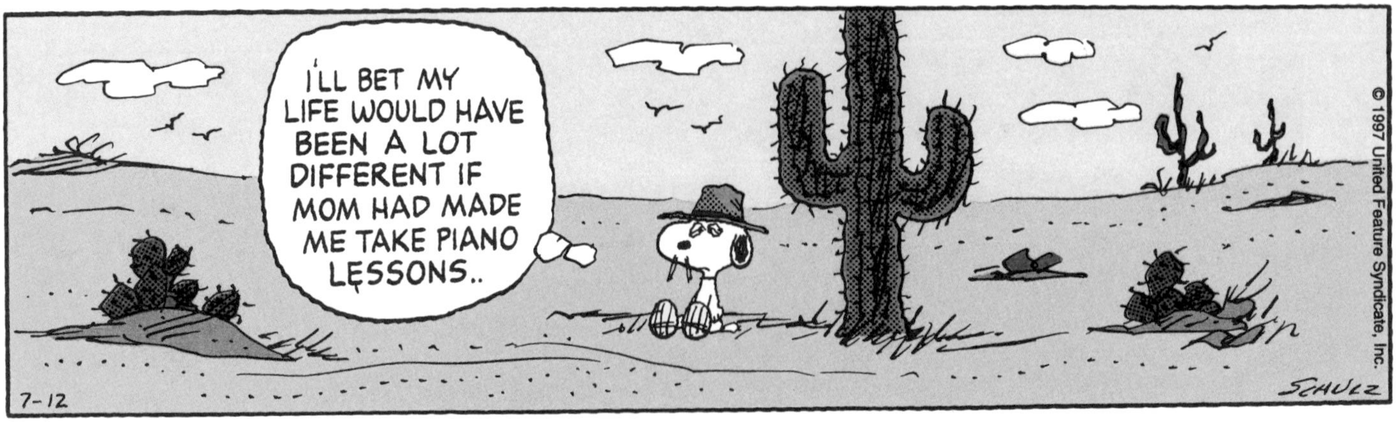
I'LL BET MY LIFE WOULD HAVE BEEN A LOT DIFFERENT IF MOM HAD MADE ME TAKE PIANO LESSONS..
© 1997 United Feature Syndicate, Inc.
7-12
SCHULZ

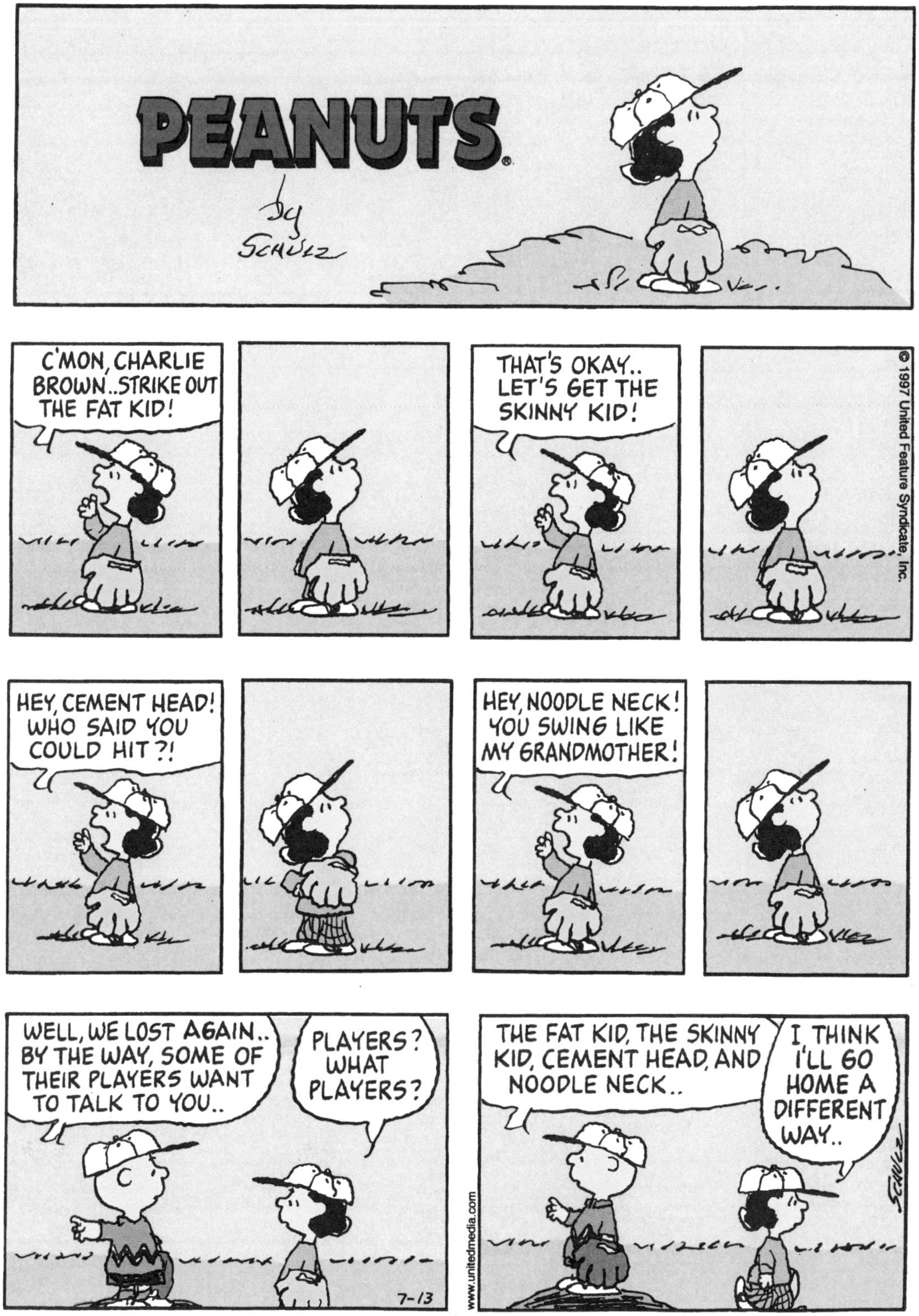
PEANUTS
by SCHULZ
C'MON, CHARLIE BROWN..STRIKE OUT THE FAT KID!
THAT'S OKAY.. LET'S GET THE SKINNY KID!
© 1997 United Feature Syndicate, Inc.
HEY, CEMENT HEAD! WHO SAID YOU COULD HIT?!
HEY, NOODLE NECK! YOU SWING LIKE MY GRANDMOTHER!
WELL, WE LOST AGAIN.. BY THE WAY, SOME OF THEIR PLAYERS WANT TO TALK TO YOU..
PLAYERS? WHAT PLAYERS?
7-13
www.unitedmedia.com
THE FAT KID, THE SKINNY KID, CEMENT HEAD, AND NOODLE NECK..
I THINK I'LL GO HOME A DIFFERENT WAY..
SCHULZ

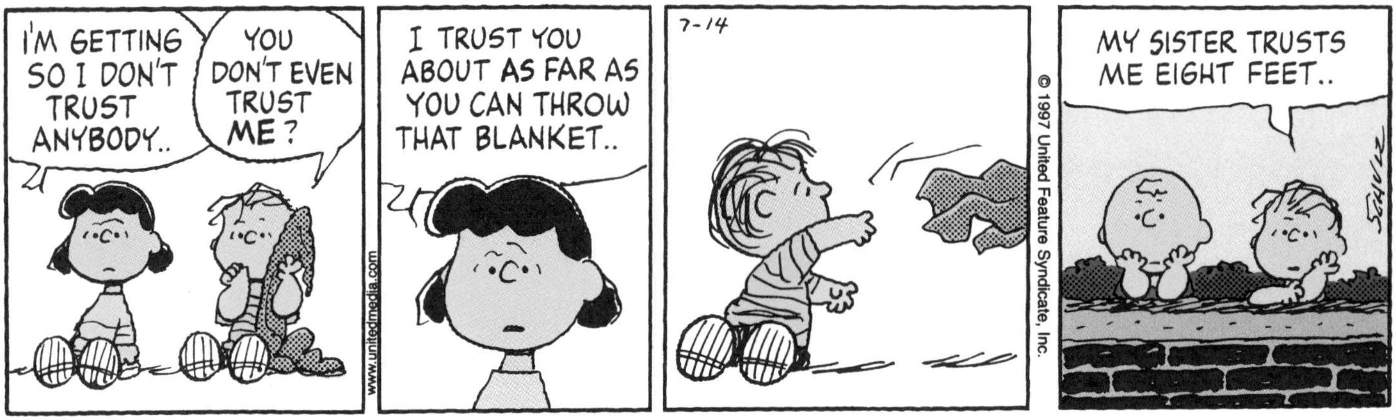
I'M GETTING SO I DON'T TRUST ANYBODY..
YOU DON'T EVEN TRUST ME?
I TRUST YOU ABOUT AS FAR AS YOU CAN THROW THAT BLANKET..
7-14
MY SISTER TRUSTS ME EIGHT FEET..
SCHULZ
www.unitedmedia.com
© 1997 United Feature Syndicate, Inc.

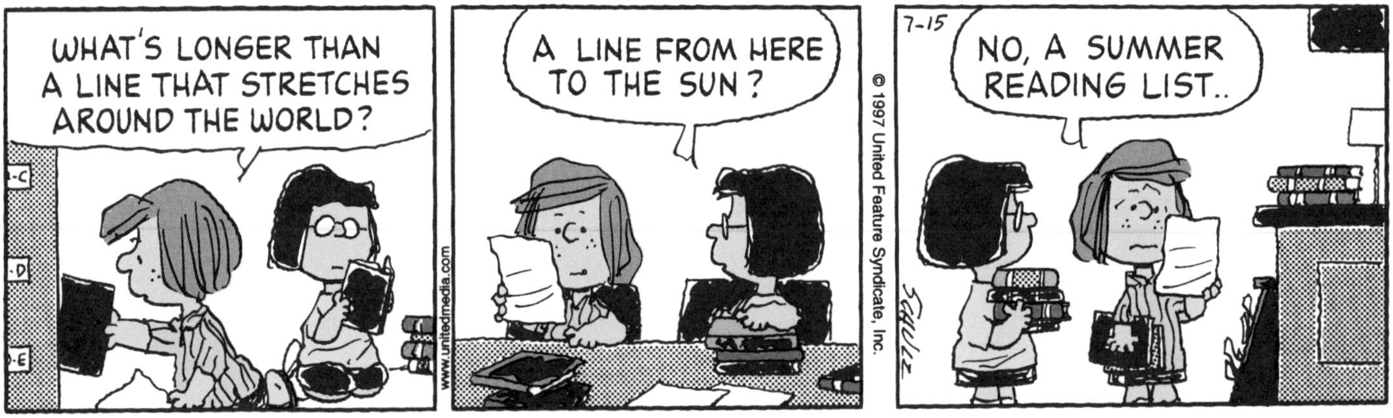
WHAT'S LONGER THAN A LINE THAT STRETCHES AROUND THE WORLD?
A LINE FROM HERE TO THE SUN?
7-15
NO, A SUMMER READING LIST..
SCHULZ
www.unitedmedia.com
© 1997 United Feature Syndicate, Inc.

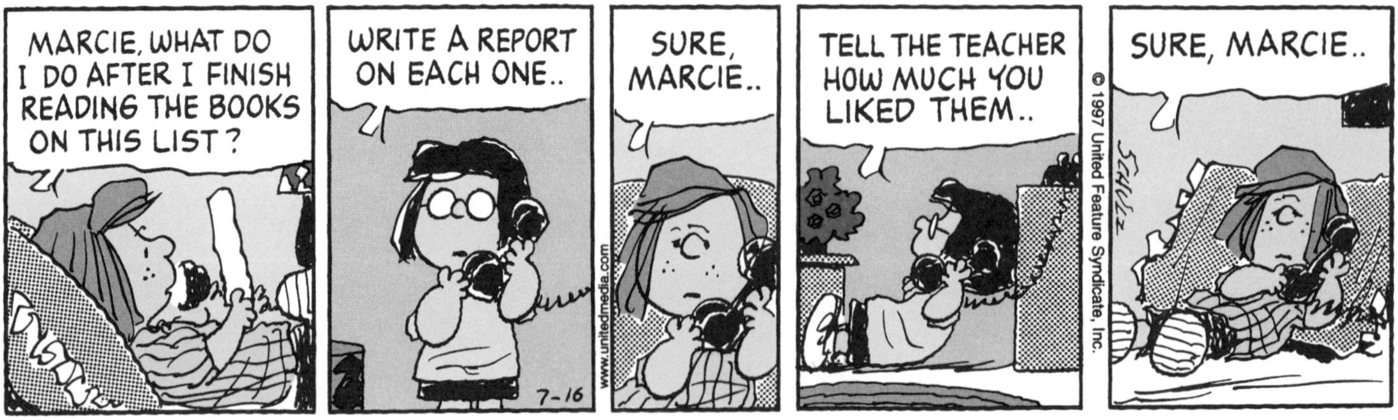
MARCIE, WHAT DO I DO AFTER I FINISH READING THE BOOKS ON THIS LIST?
WRITE A REPORT ON EACH ONE..
7-16
SURE, MARCIE..
TELL THE TEACHER HOW MUCH YOU LIKED THEM..
SURE, MARCIE..
SCHULZ
www.unitedmedia.com
© 1997 United Feature Syndicate, Inc.

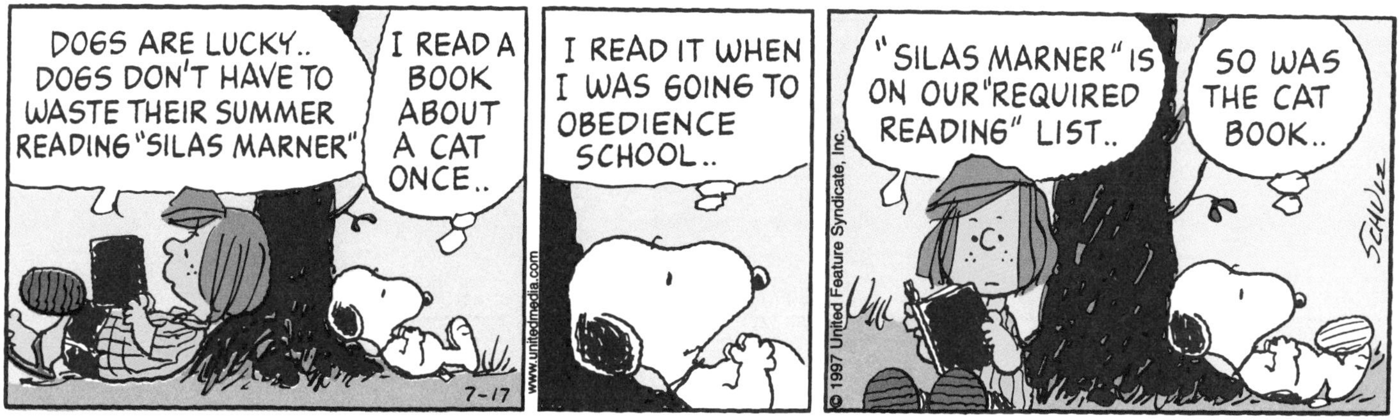
DOGS ARE LUCKY.. DOGS DON'T HAVE TO WASTE THEIR SUMMER READING "SILAS MARNER"
I READ A BOOK ABOUT A CAT ONCE..
7-17
www.unitedmedia.com
I READ IT WHEN I WAS GOING TO OBEDIENCE SCHOOL..
© 1997 United Feature Syndicate, Inc.
"SILAS MARNER" IS ON OUR "REQUIRED READING" LIST..
SO WAS THE CAT BOOK..
SCHULZ

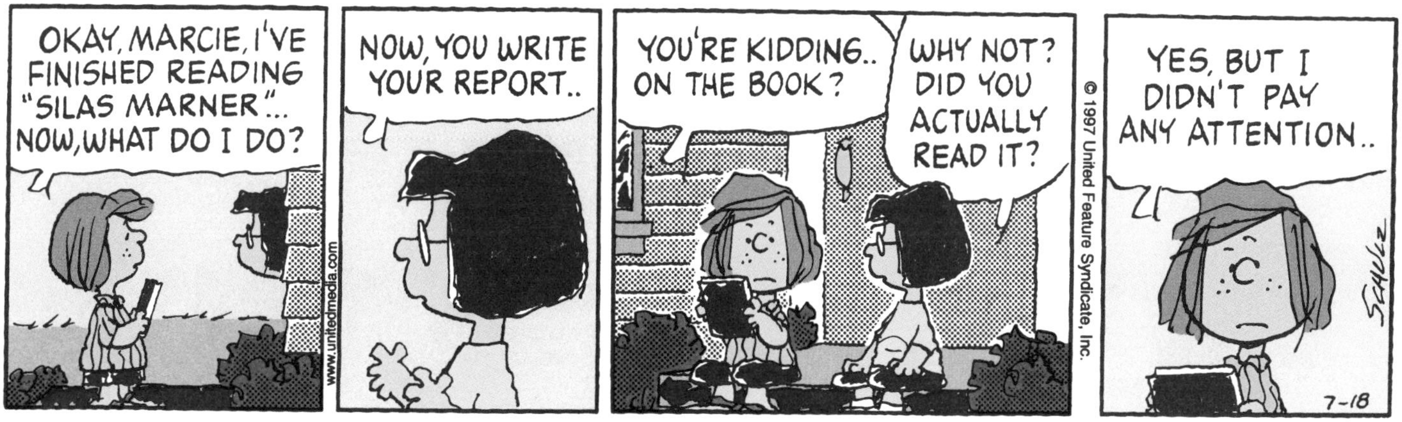
OKAY, MARCIE, I'VE FINISHED READING "SILAS MARNER"... NOW, WHAT DO I DO?
www.unitedmedia.com
NOW, YOU WRITE YOUR REPORT..
YOU'RE KIDDING.. ON THE BOOK?
WHY NOT? DID YOU ACTUALLY READ IT?
© 1997 United Feature Syndicate, Inc.
YES, BUT I DIDN'T PAY ANY ATTENTION..
SCHULZ
7-18

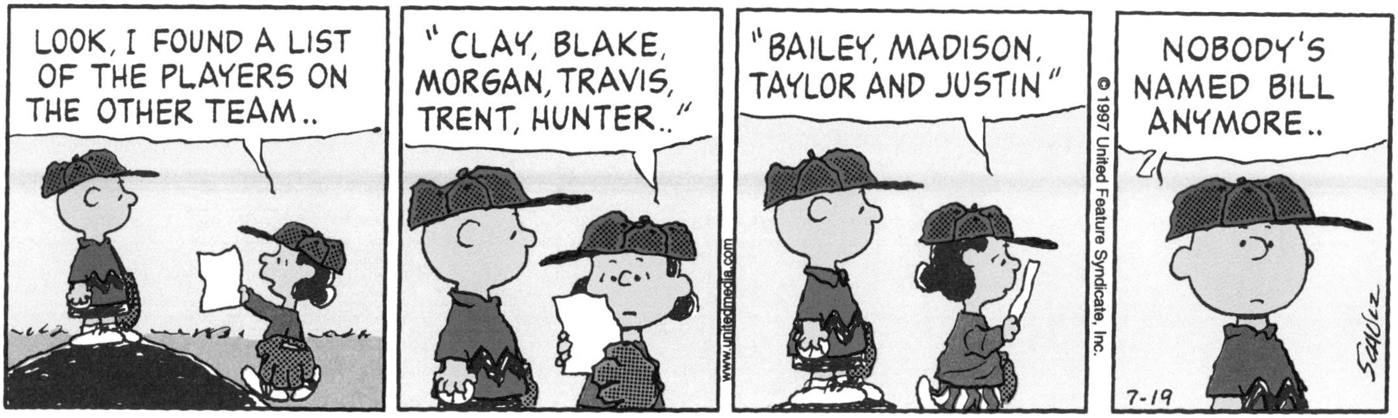
LOOK, I FOUND A LIST OF THE PLAYERS ON THE OTHER TEAM..
"CLAY, BLAKE, MORGAN, TRAVIS, TRENT, HUNTER.."
www.unitedmedia.com
"BAILEY, MADISON, TAYLOR AND JUSTIN"
© 1997 United Feature Syndicate, Inc.
NOBODY'S NAMED BILL ANYMORE..
SCHULZ
7-19

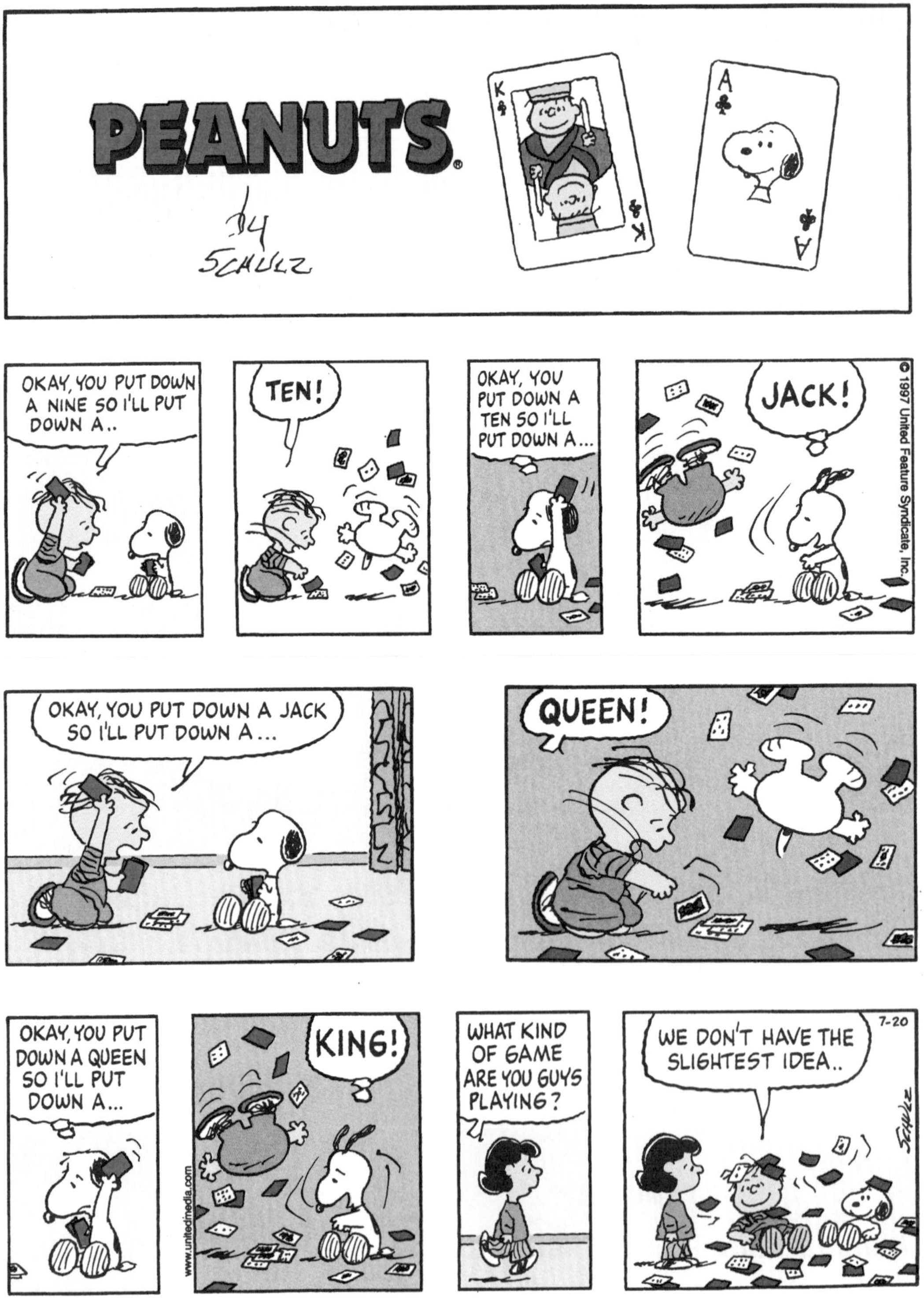
PEANUTS
by SCHULZ
K
A
OKAY, YOU PUT DOWN A NINE SO I'LL PUT DOWN A..
TEN!
OKAY, YOU PUT DOWN A TEN SO I'LL PUT DOWN A...
JACK!
© 1997 United Feature Syndicate, Inc.
OKAY, YOU PUT DOWN A JACK SO I'LL PUT DOWN A...
QUEEN!
OKAY, YOU PUT DOWN A QUEEN SO I'LL PUT DOWN A...
KING!
www.unitedmedia.com
WHAT KIND OF GAME ARE YOU GUYS PLAYING?
7-20
WE DON'T HAVE THE SLIGHTEST IDEA..
SCHULZ

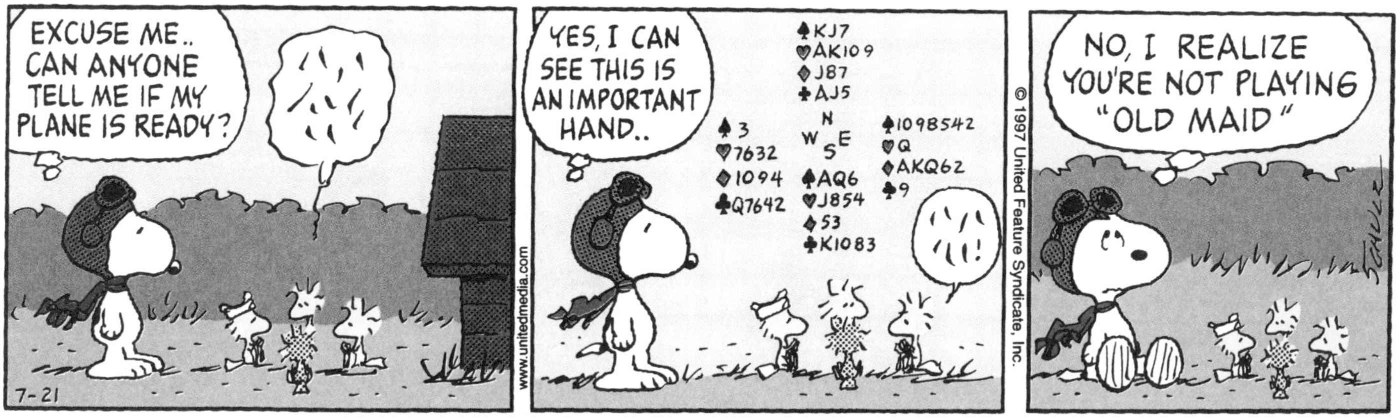
EXCUSE ME.. CAN ANYONE TELL ME IF MY PLANE IS READY?
7-21
www.unitedmedia.com
YES, I CAN SEE THIS IS AN IMPORTANT HAND..
♠KJ7
♥AK109
♦J87
♣AJ5
N
W E
S
♠3
♥7632
♦1094
♣Q7642
♠1098542
♥Q
♦AKQ62
♣9
♠AQ6
♥J854
♦53
♣K1083
© 1997 United Feature Syndicate, Inc.
NO, I REALIZE YOU'RE NOT PLAYING "OLD MAID"
SCHULZ

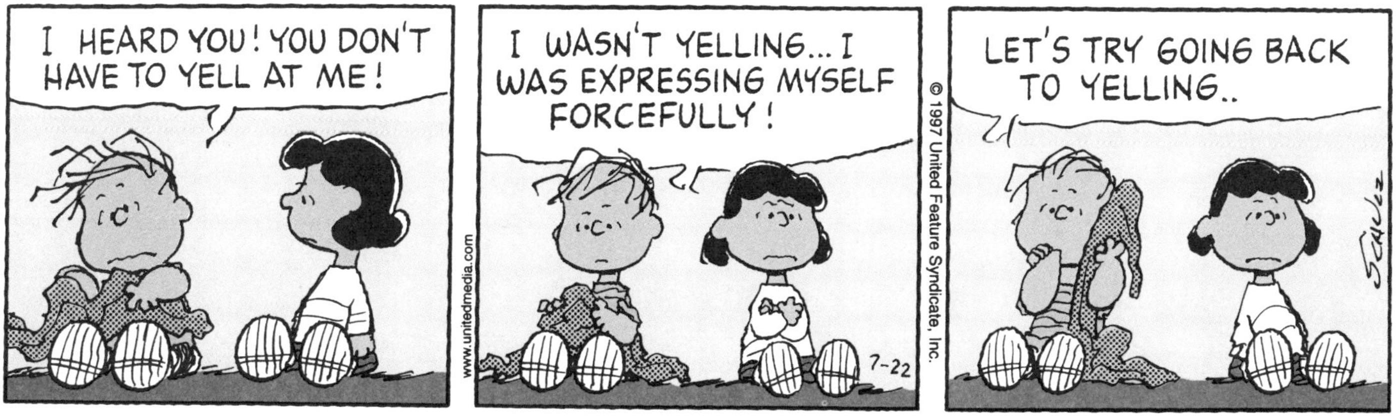
I HEARD YOU! YOU DON'T HAVE TO YELL AT ME!
www.unitedmedia.com
I WASN'T YELLING... I WAS EXPRESSING MYSELF FORCEFULLY!
7-22
© 1997 United Feature Syndicate, Inc.
LET'S TRY GOING BACK TO YELLING..
SCHULZ

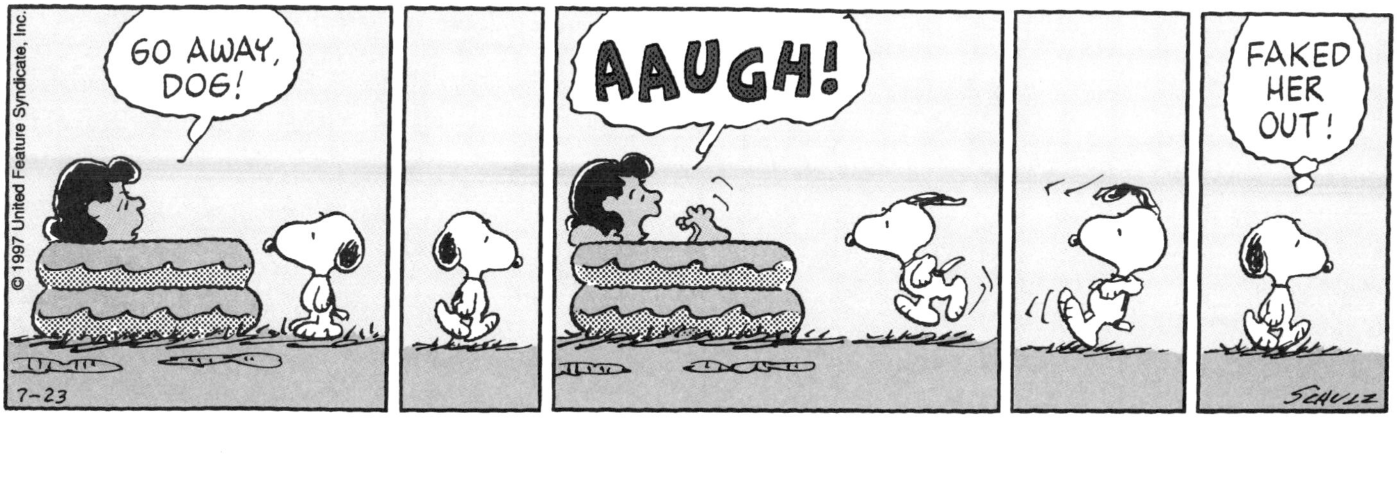
© 1997 United Feature Syndicate, Inc.
GO AWAY, DOG!
7-23
AAUGH!
FAKED HER OUT!
SCHULZ

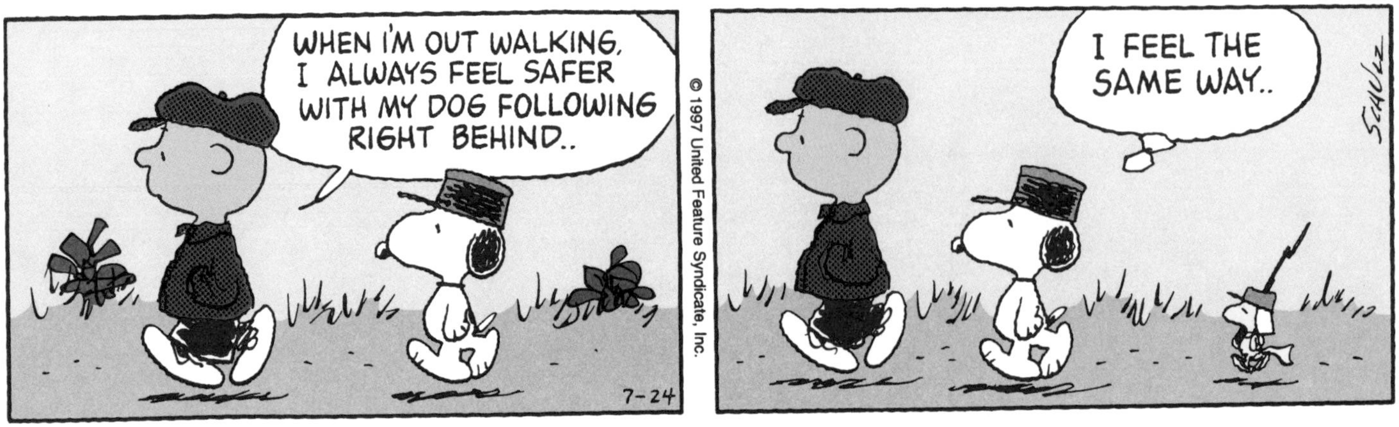
WHEN I'M OUT WALKING, I ALWAYS FEEL SAFER WITH MY DOG FOLLOWING RIGHT BEHIND..
© 1997 United Feature Syndicate, Inc.
7-24
I FEEL THE SAME WAY..
SCHULZ

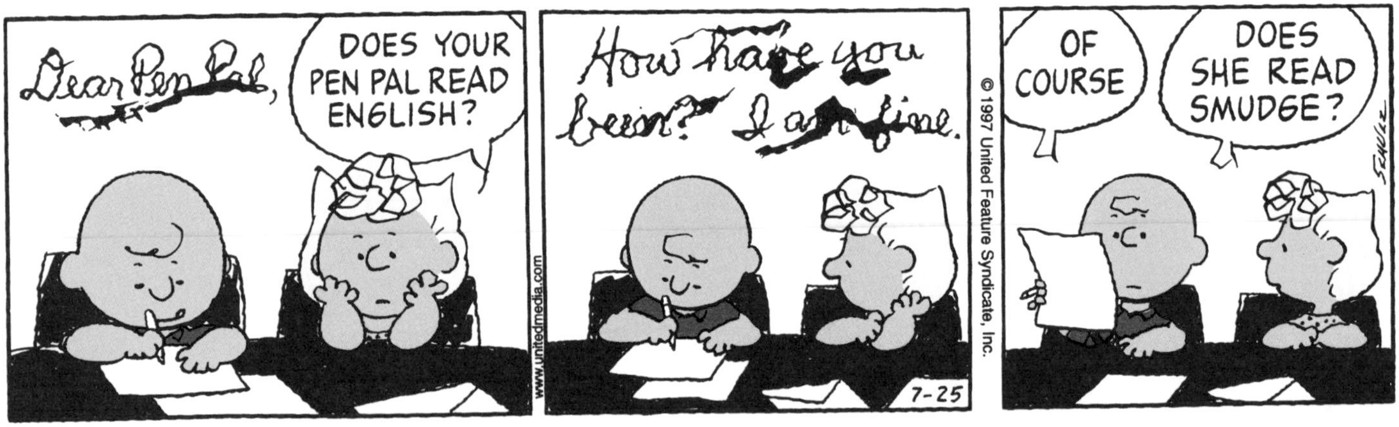
Dear Pen Pal,
DOES YOUR PEN PAL READ ENGLISH?
www.unitedmedia.com
How have you been? I am fine.
7-25
© 1997 United Feature Syndicate, Inc.
OF COURSE
DOES SHE READ SMUDGE?
SCHULZ

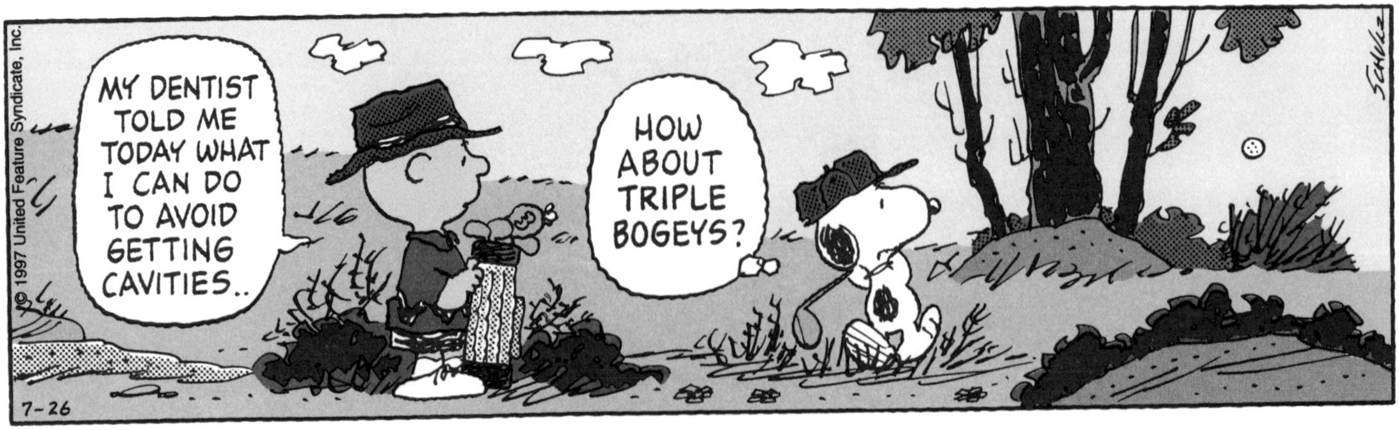
© 1997 United Feature Syndicate, Inc.
MY DENTIST TOLD ME TODAY WHAT I CAN DO TO AVOID GETTING CAVITIES..
HOW ABOUT TRIPLE BOGEYS?
SCHULZ
7-26

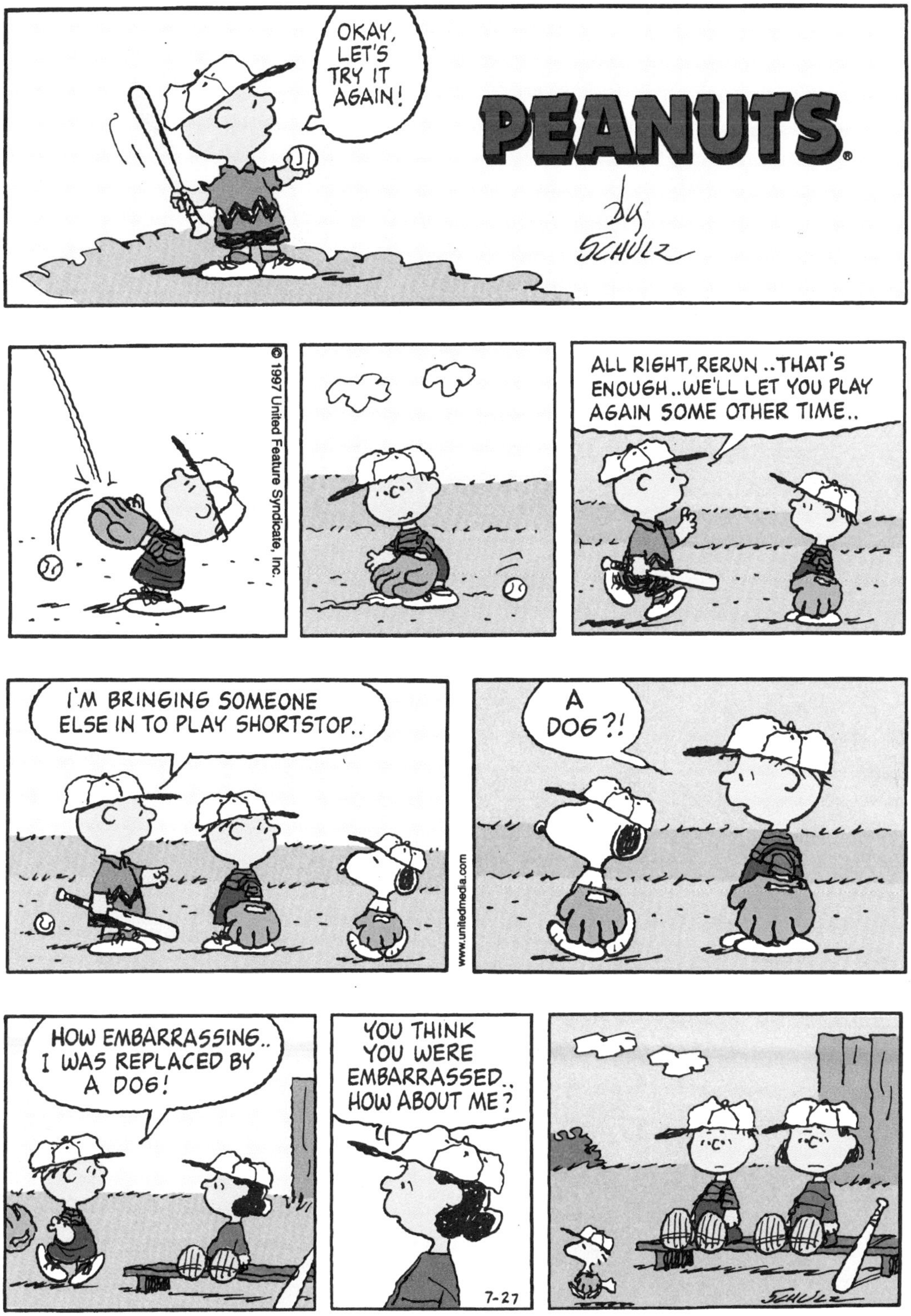
OKAY, LET'S TRY IT AGAIN!
PEANUTS
by SCHULZ
© 1997 United Feature Syndicate, Inc.
ALL RIGHT, RERUN ..THAT'S ENOUGH..WE'LL LET YOU PLAY AGAIN SOME OTHER TIME..
I'M BRINGING SOMEONE ELSE IN TO PLAY SHORTSTOP..
www.unitedmedia.com
A DOG?!
HOW EMBARRASSING.. I WAS REPLACED BY A DOG!
YOU THINK YOU WERE EMBARRASSED.. HOW ABOUT ME?
7-27
SCHULZ

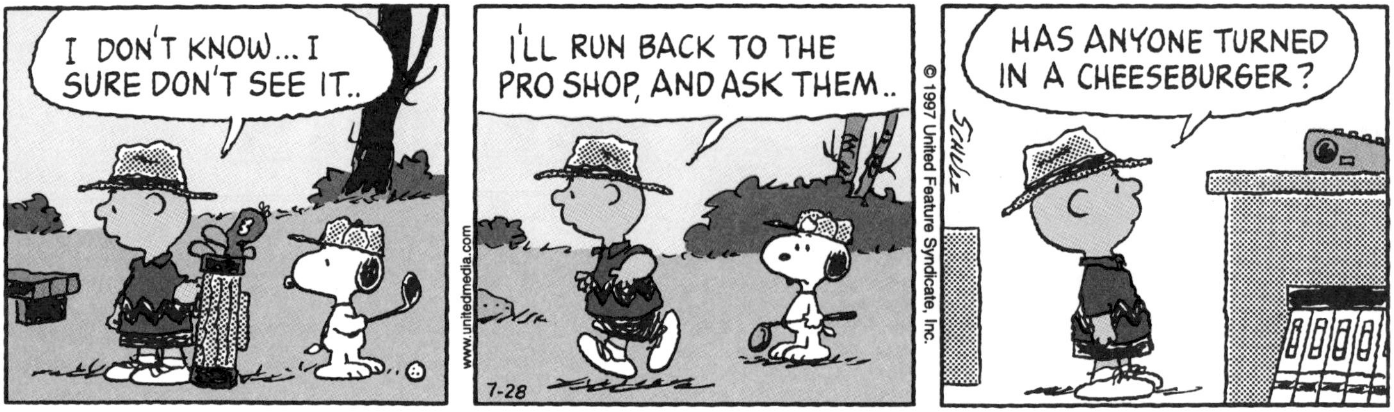
I DON'T KNOW... I SURE DON'T SEE IT..
www.unitedmedia.com
I'LL RUN BACK TO THE PRO SHOP, AND ASK THEM..
7-28
© 1997 United Feature Syndicate, Inc.
SCHULZ
HAS ANYONE TURNED IN A CHEESEBURGER?

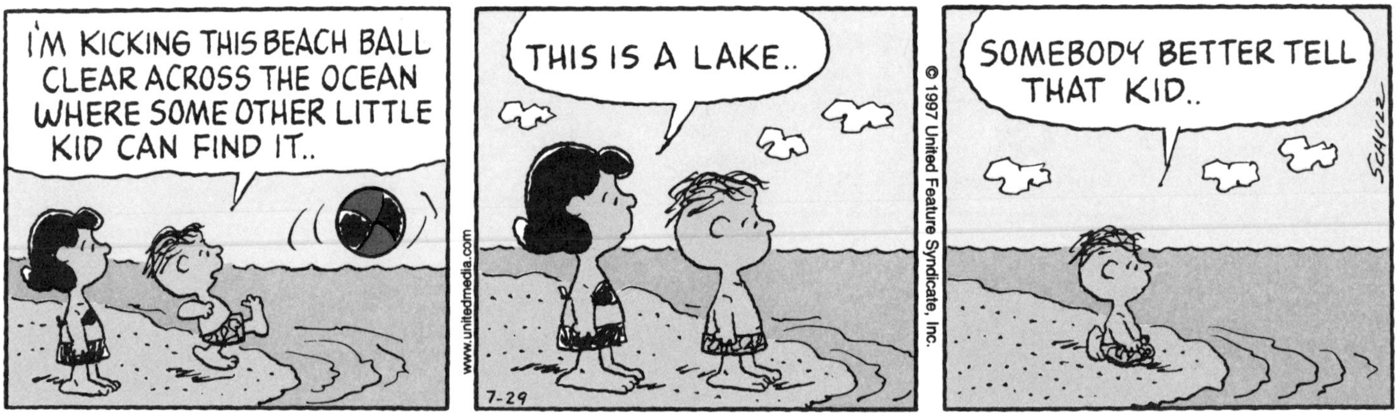
I'M KICKING THIS BEACH BALL CLEAR ACROSS THE OCEAN WHERE SOME OTHER LITTLE KID CAN FIND IT..
www.unitedmedia.com
THIS IS A LAKE..
7-29
© 1997 United Feature Syndicate, Inc.
SOMEBODY BETTER TELL THAT KID..
SCHULZ

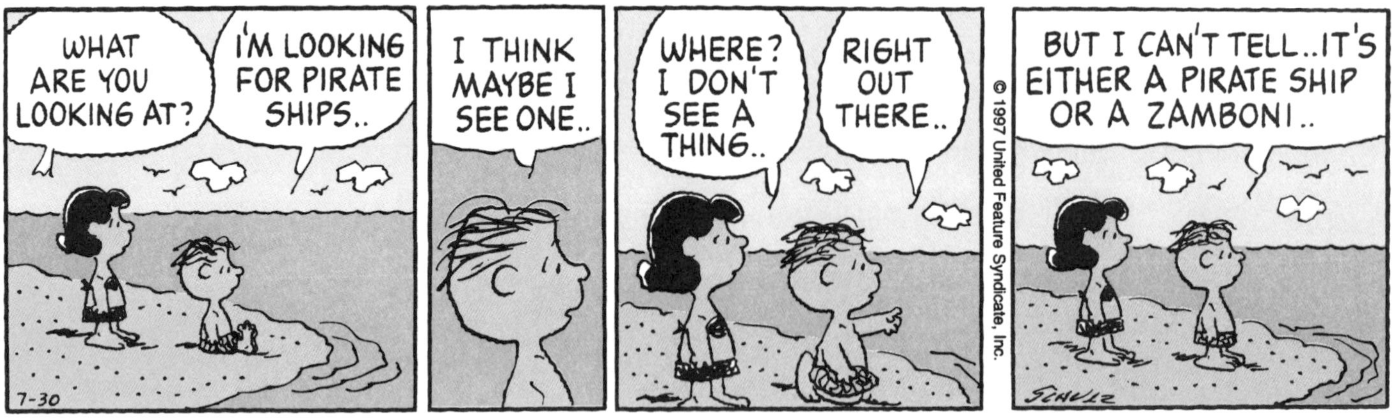
WHAT ARE YOU LOOKING AT?
I'M LOOKING FOR PIRATE SHIPS..
7-30
I THINK MAYBE I SEE ONE..
WHERE? I DON'T SEE A THING..
RIGHT OUT THERE..
© 1997 United Feature Syndicate, Inc.
BUT I CAN'T TELL..IT'S EITHER A PIRATE SHIP OR A ZAMBONI..
SCHULZ

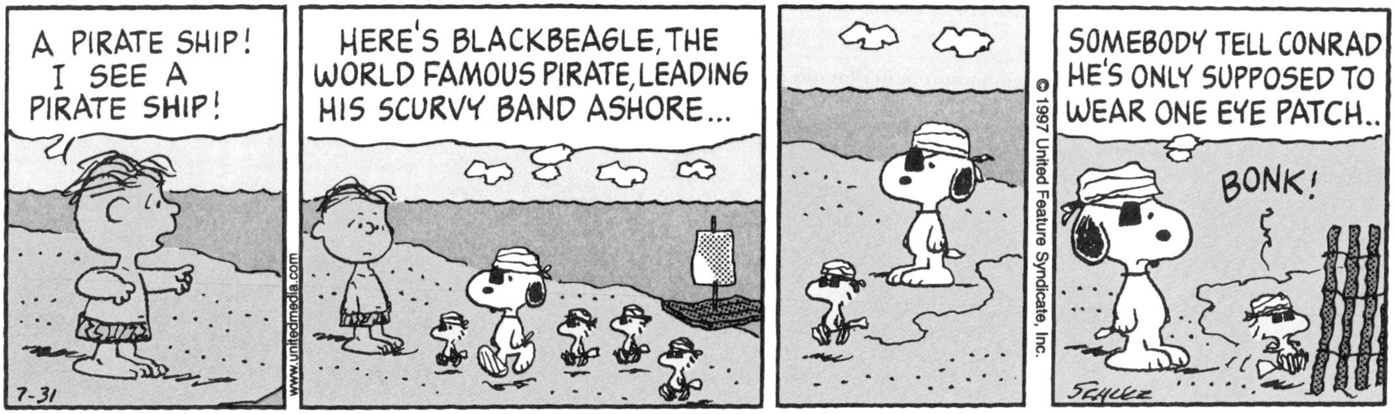
7-31
A PIRATE SHIP! I SEE A PIRATE SHIP!
www.unitedmedia.com
HERE'S BLACKBEAGLE, THE WORLD FAMOUS PIRATE, LEADING HIS SCURVY BAND ASHORE...
© 1997 United Feature Syndicate, Inc.
SOMEBODY TELL CONRAD HE'S ONLY SUPPOSED TO WEAR ONE EYE PATCH..
BONK!
SCHULZ

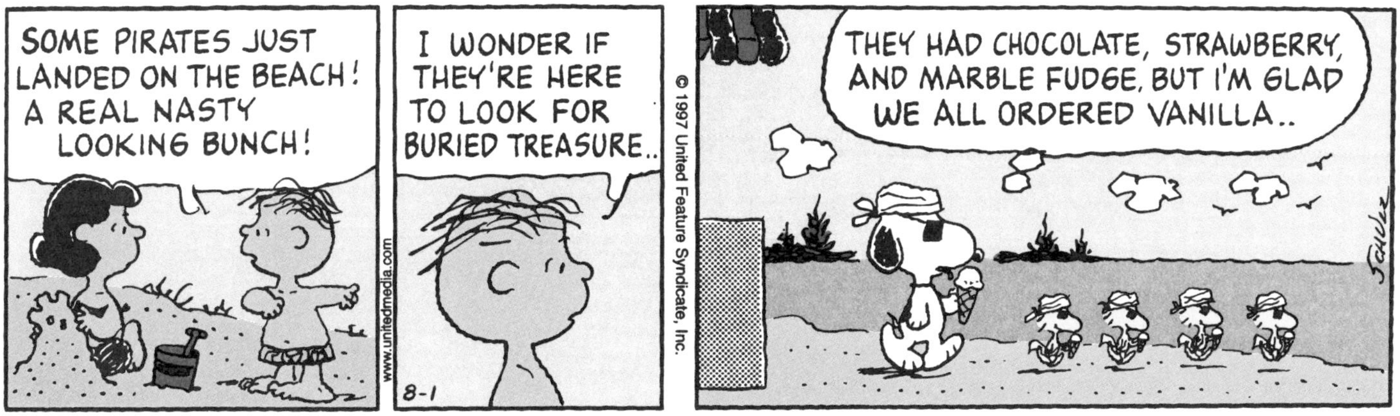
SOME PIRATES JUST LANDED ON THE BEACH! A REAL NASTY LOOKING BUNCH!
www.unitedmedia.com
8-1
I WONDER IF THEY'RE HERE TO LOOK FOR BURIED TREASURE..
© 1997 United Feature Syndicate, Inc.
THEY HAD CHOCOLATE, STRAWBERRY, AND MARBLE FUDGE, BUT I'M GLAD WE ALL ORDERED VANILLA..
SCHULZ

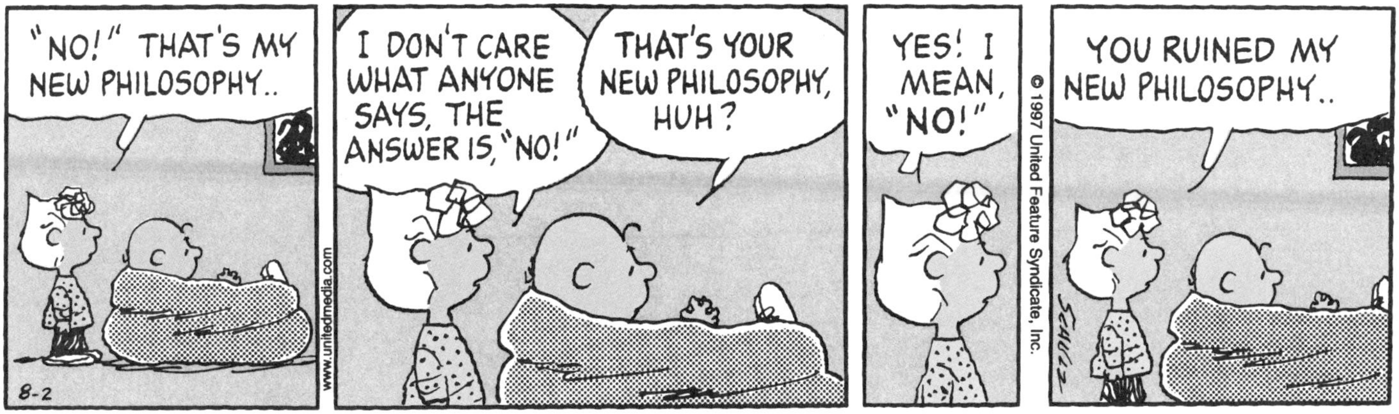
"NO!" THAT'S MY NEW PHILOSOPHY..
8-2
www.unitedmedia.com
I DON'T CARE WHAT ANYONE SAYS, THE ANSWER IS, "NO!"
THAT'S YOUR NEW PHILOSOPHY, HUH?
YES! I MEAN, "NO!"
© 1997 United Feature Syndicate, Inc.
YOU RUINED MY NEW PHILOSOPHY..
SCHULZ

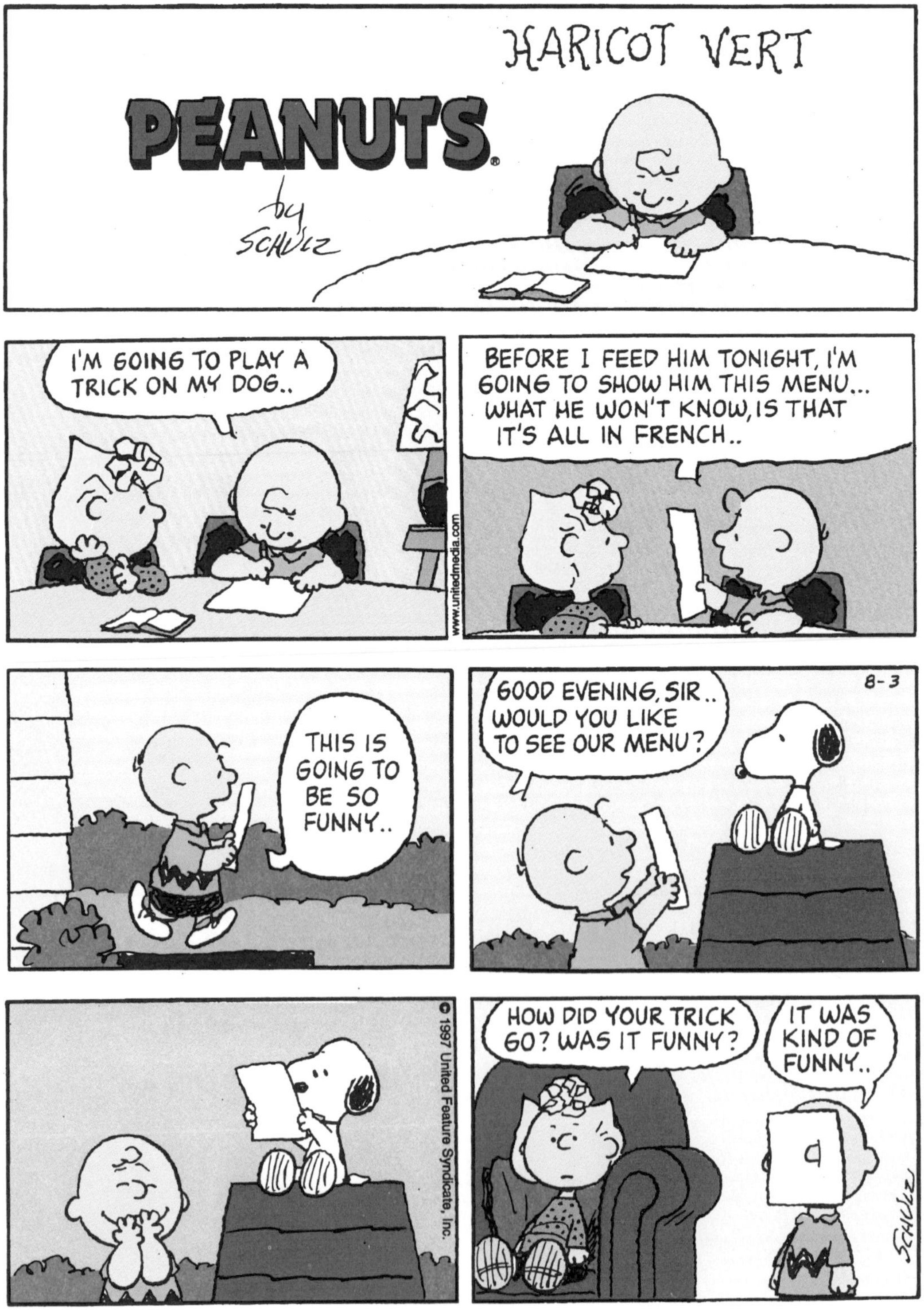
HARICOT VERT
PEANUTS
by SCHULZ
I'M GOING TO PLAY A TRICK ON MY DOG..
www.unitedmedia.com
BEFORE I FEED HIM TONIGHT, I'M GOING TO SHOW HIM THIS MENU... WHAT HE WON'T KNOW, IS THAT IT'S ALL IN FRENCH..
THIS IS GOING TO BE SO FUNNY..
8-3
GOOD EVENING, SIR.. WOULD YOU LIKE TO SEE OUR MENU?
© 1997 United Feature Syndicate, Inc.
HOW DID YOUR TRICK GO? WAS IT FUNNY?
IT WAS KIND OF FUNNY..
SCHULZ

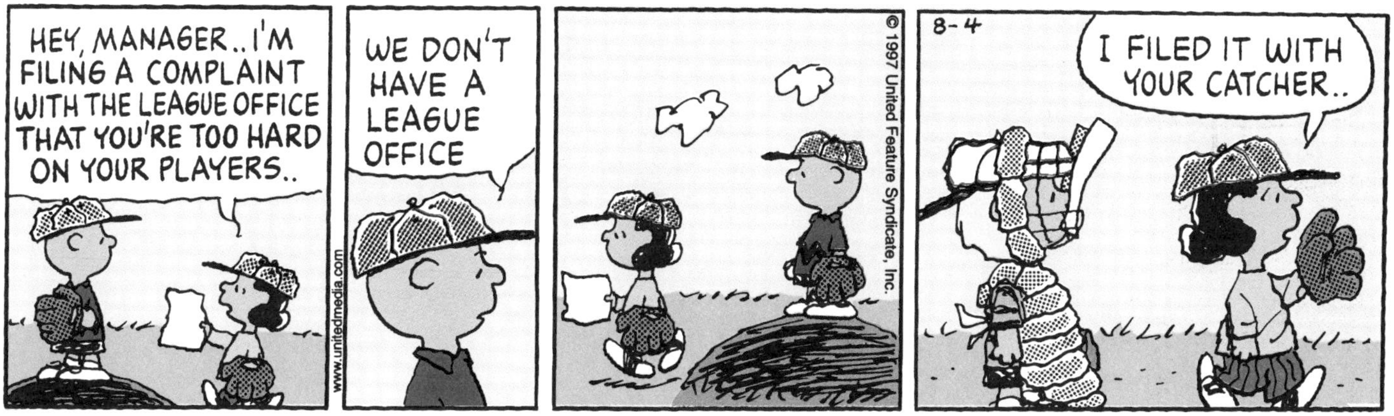
HEY, MANAGER.. I'M FILING A COMPLAINT WITH THE LEAGUE OFFICE THAT YOU'RE TOO HARD ON YOUR PLAYERS..
www.unitedmedia.com
WE DON'T HAVE A LEAGUE OFFICE
© 1997 United Feature Syndicate, Inc.
8-4
I FILED IT WITH YOUR CATCHER..

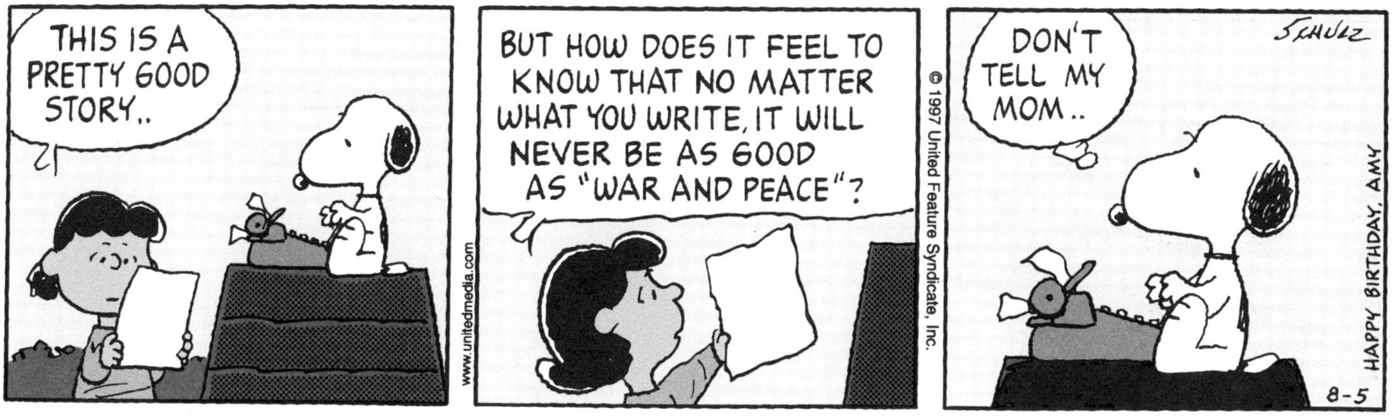
THIS IS A PRETTY GOOD STORY..
www.unitedmedia.com
BUT HOW DOES IT FEEL TO KNOW THAT NO MATTER WHAT YOU WRITE, IT WILL NEVER BE AS GOOD AS "WAR AND PEACE"?
© 1997 United Feature Syndicate, Inc.
DON'T TELL MY MOM..
SCHULZ
HAPPY BIRTHDAY, AMY
8-5

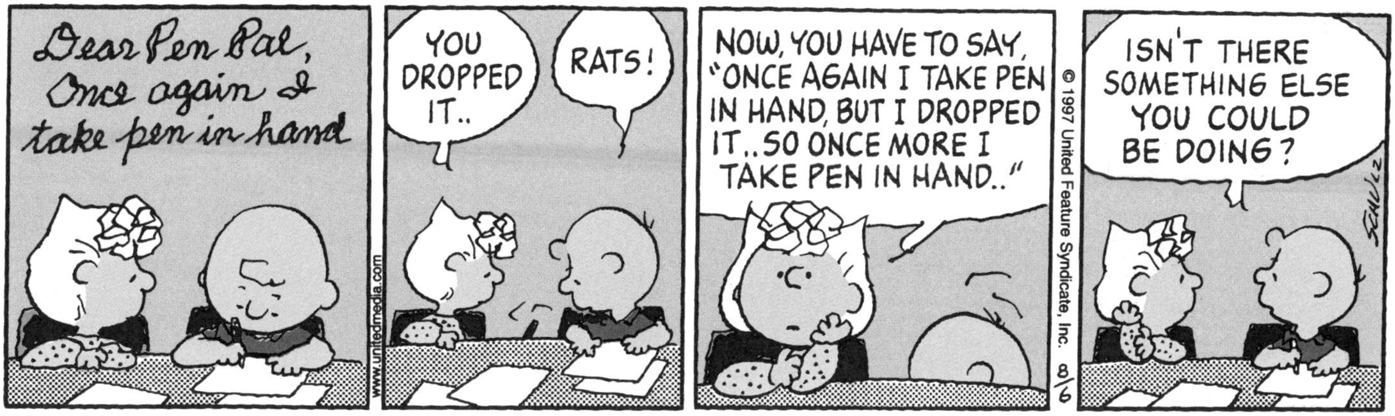
Dear Pen Pal, Once again I take pen in hand
www.unitedmedia.com
YOU DROPPED IT..
RATS!
NOW, YOU HAVE TO SAY, "ONCE AGAIN I TAKE PEN IN HAND, BUT I DROPPED IT.. SO ONCE MORE I TAKE PEN IN HAND.."
© 1997 United Feature Syndicate, Inc.
8/6
ISN'T THERE SOMETHING ELSE YOU COULD BE DOING?
SCHULZ

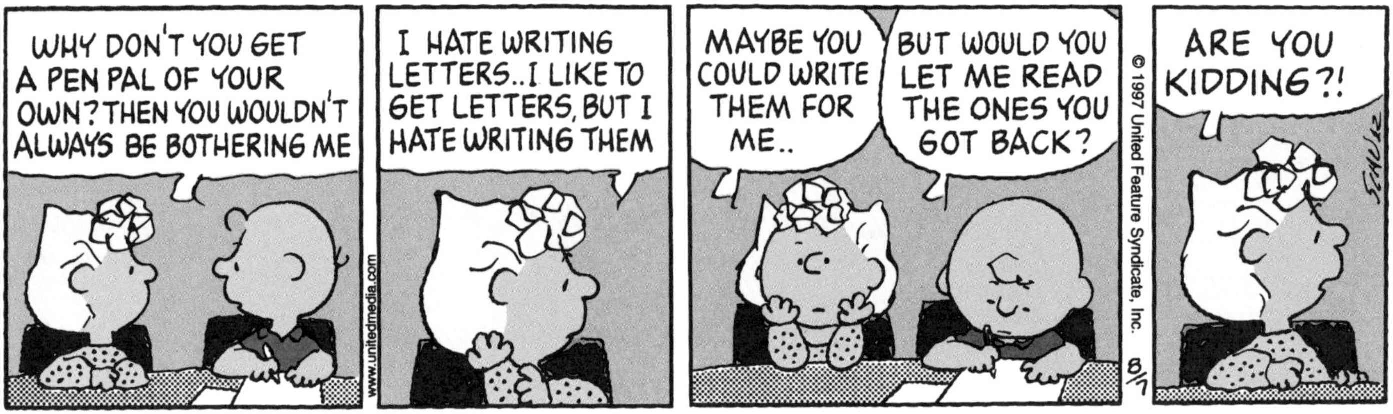
WHY DON'T YOU GET A PEN PAL OF YOUR OWN? THEN YOU WOULDN'T ALWAYS BE BOTHERING ME
www.unitedmedia.com
I HATE WRITING LETTERS..I LIKE TO GET LETTERS, BUT I HATE WRITING THEM
MAYBE YOU COULD WRITE THEM FOR ME..
BUT WOULD YOU LET ME READ THE ONES YOU GOT BACK?
© 1997 United Feature Syndicate, Inc.
8/7
ARE YOU KIDDING?!
SCHULZ

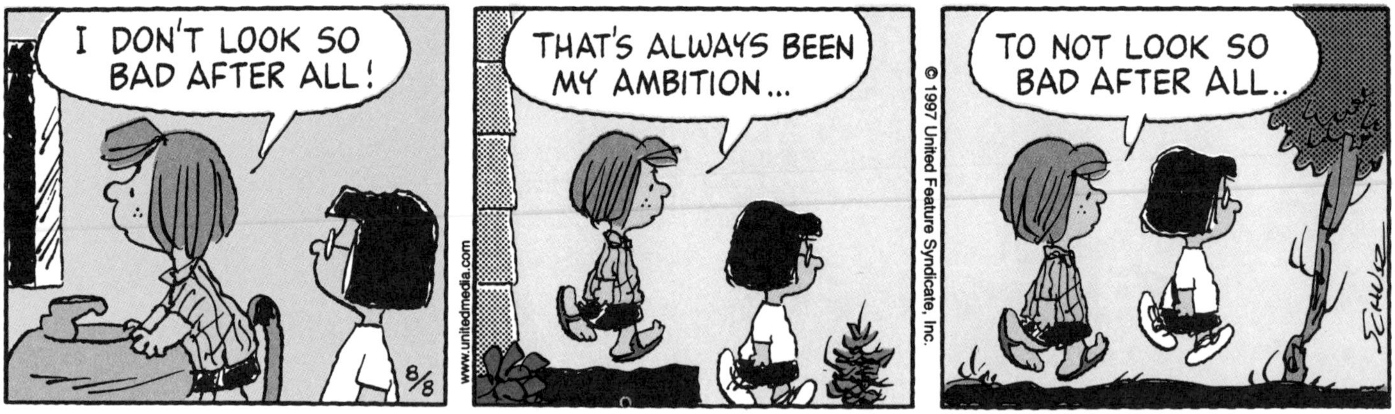
I DON'T LOOK SO BAD AFTER ALL!
8/8
www.unitedmedia.com
THAT'S ALWAYS BEEN MY AMBITION...
© 1997 United Feature Syndicate, Inc.
TO NOT LOOK SO BAD AFTER ALL..
SCHULZ

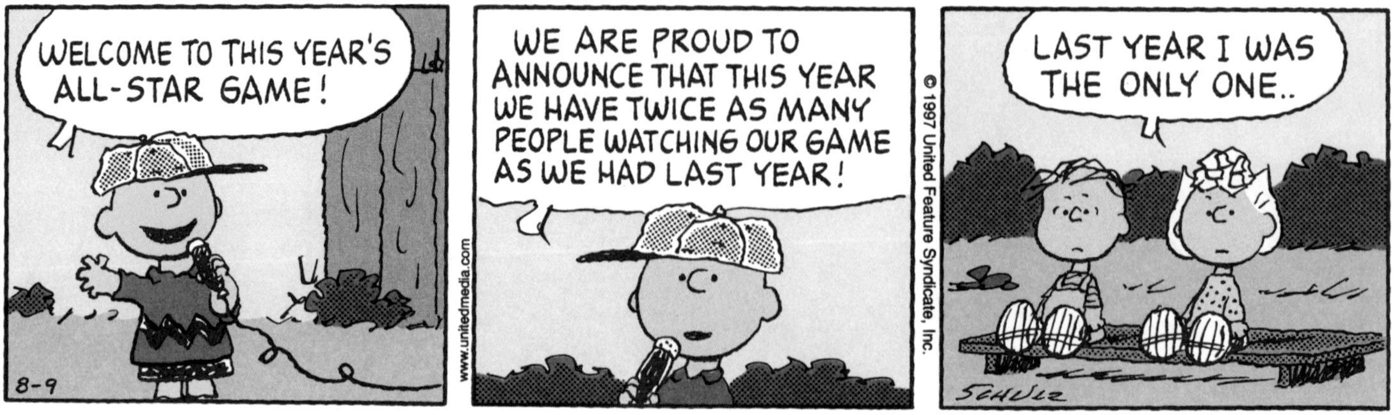
WELCOME TO THIS YEAR'S ALL-STAR GAME!
8-9
www.unitedmedia.com
WE ARE PROUD TO ANNOUNCE THAT THIS YEAR WE HAVE TWICE AS MANY PEOPLE WATCHING OUR GAME AS WE HAD LAST YEAR!
© 1997 United Feature Syndicate, Inc.
LAST YEAR I WAS THE ONLY ONE..
SCHULZ

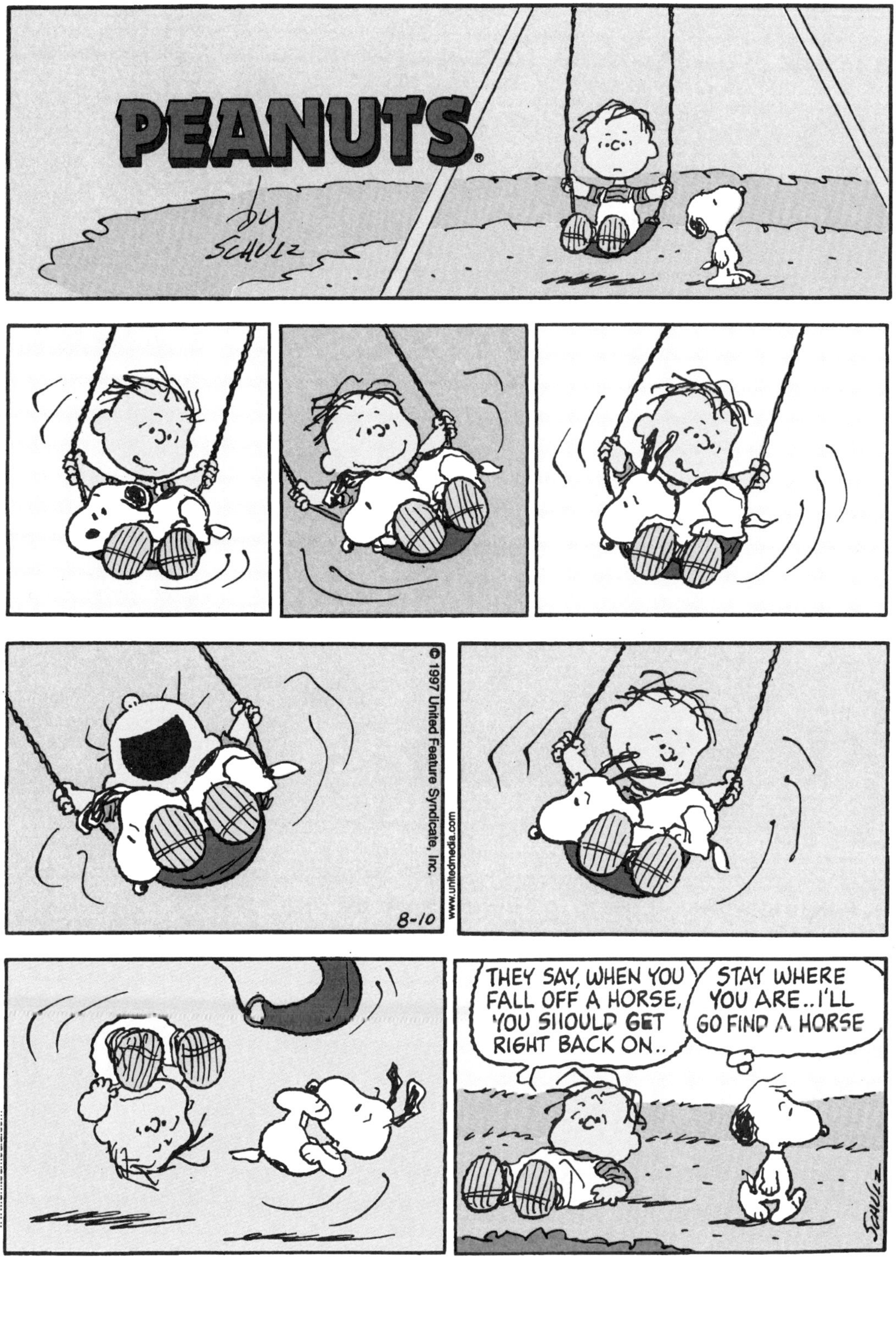
PEANUTS
by SCHULZ
© 1997 United Feature Syndicate, Inc.
www.unitedmedia.com
8-10
THEY SAY, WHEN YOU FALL OFF A HORSE, YOU SHOULD GET RIGHT BACK ON..
STAY WHERE YOU ARE.. I'LL GO FIND A HORSE
SCHULZ

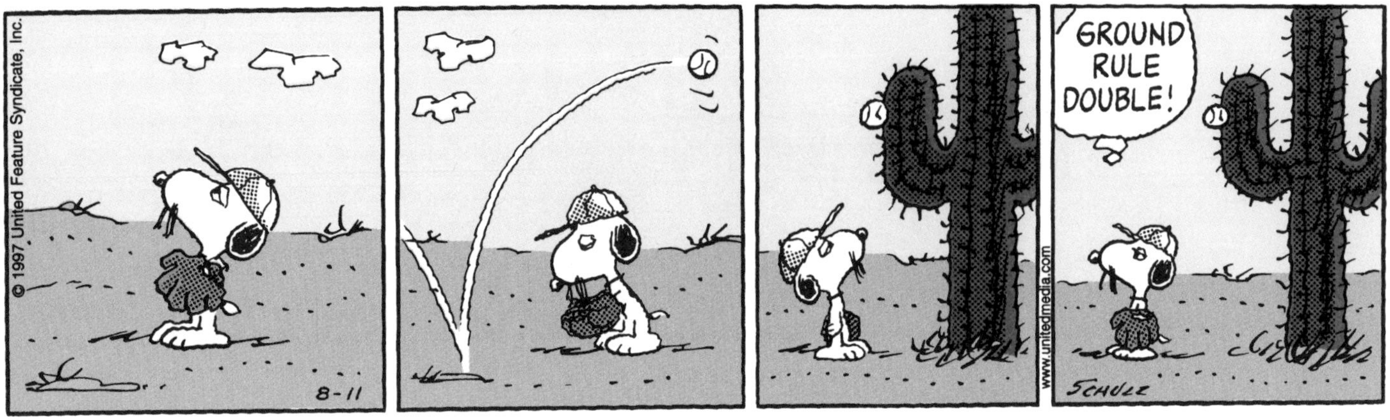
GROUND RULE DOUBLE!

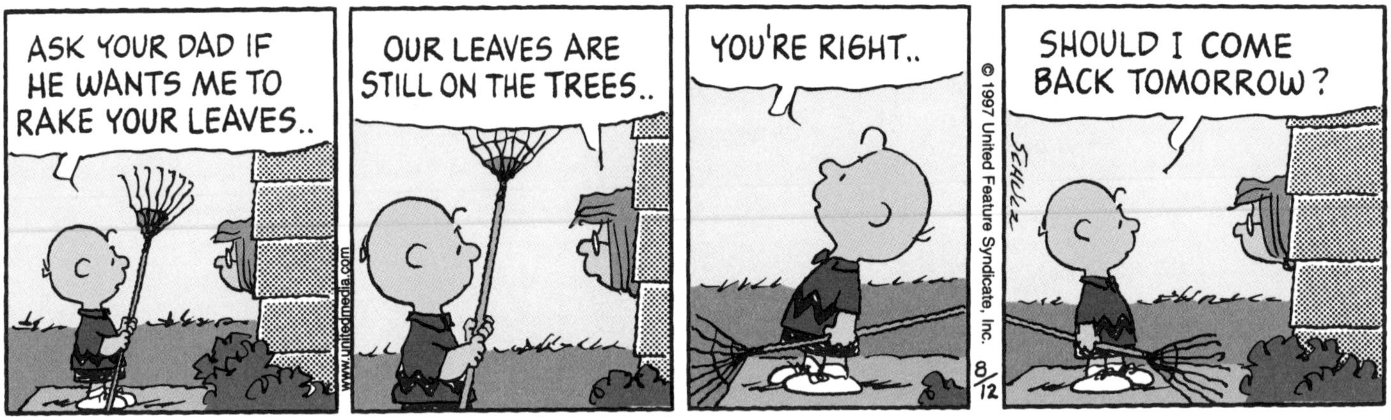
ASK YOUR DAD IF HE WANTS ME TO RAKE YOUR LEAVES..
OUR LEAVES ARE STILL ON THE TREES..
YOU'RE RIGHT..
SHOULD I COME BACK TOMORROW?

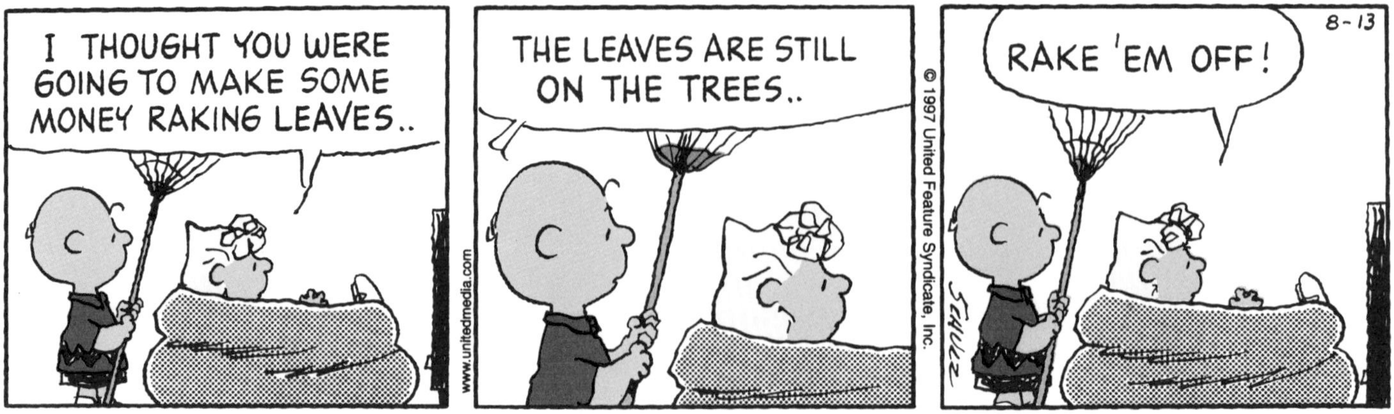
I THOUGHT YOU WERE GOING TO MAKE SOME MONEY RAKING LEAVES..
THE LEAVES ARE STILL ON THE TREES..
RAKE 'EM OFF!

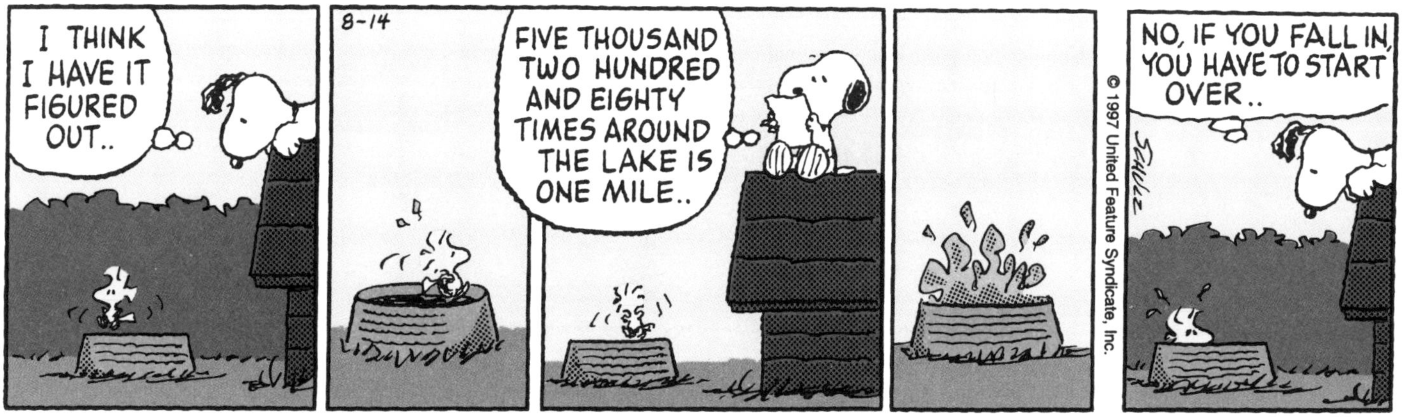
I THINK I HAVE IT FIGURED OUT..
8-14
FIVE THOUSAND TWO HUNDRED AND EIGHTY TIMES AROUND THE LAKE IS ONE MILE..
© 1997 United Feature Syndicate, Inc.
SCHULZ
NO, IF YOU FALL IN, YOU HAVE TO START OVER..

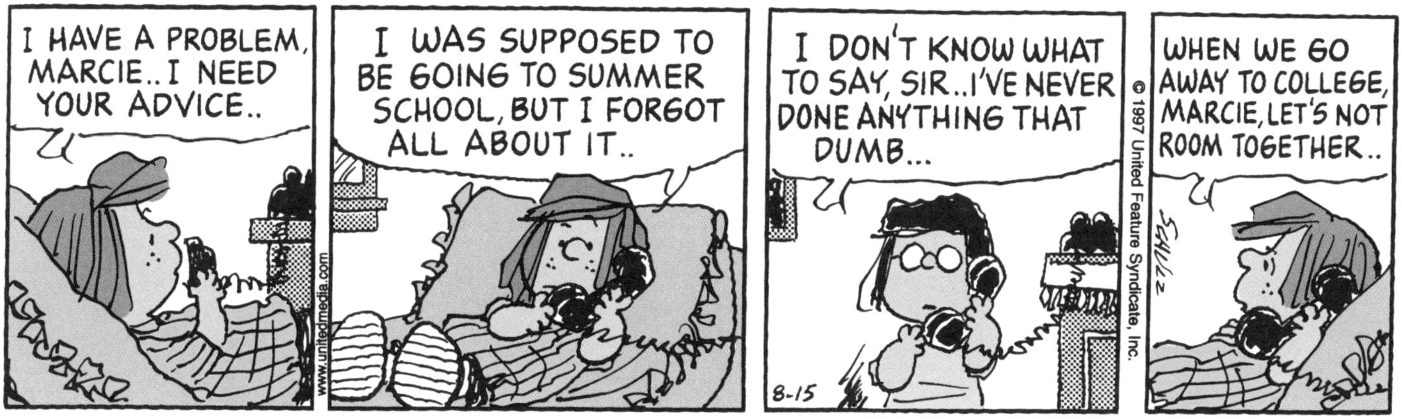
I HAVE A PROBLEM, MARCIE.. I NEED YOUR ADVICE..
www.unitedmedia.com
I WAS SUPPOSED TO BE GOING TO SUMMER SCHOOL, BUT I FORGOT ALL ABOUT IT..
I DON'T KNOW WHAT TO SAY, SIR.. I'VE NEVER DONE ANYTHING THAT DUMB...
8-15
© 1997 United Feature Syndicate, Inc.
SCHULZ
WHEN WE GO AWAY TO COLLEGE, MARCIE, LET'S NOT ROOM TOGETHER..

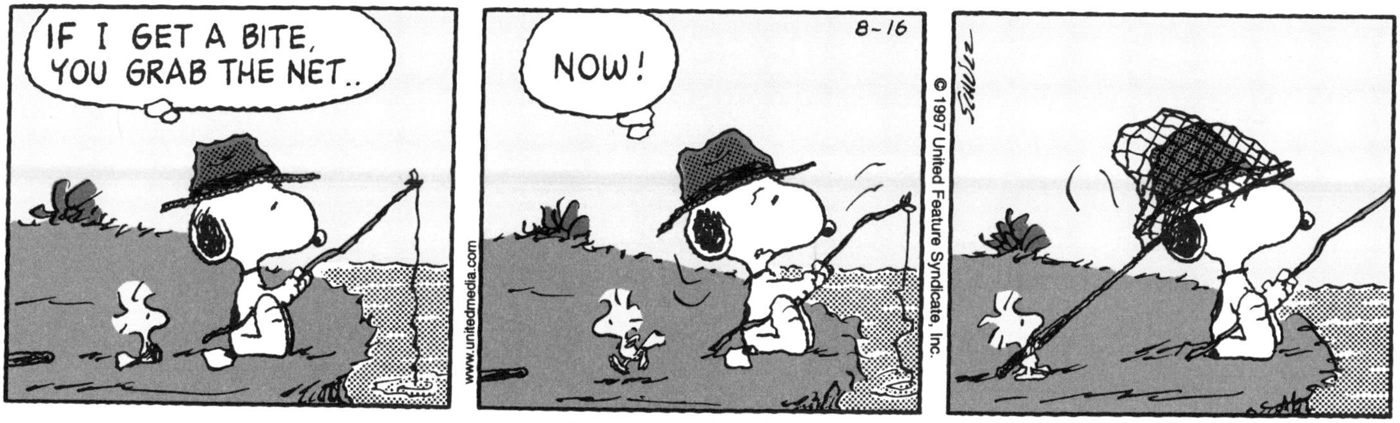
IF I GET A BITE, YOU GRAB THE NET..
www.unitedmedia.com
NOW!
8-16
© 1997 United Feature Syndicate, Inc.
SCHULZ

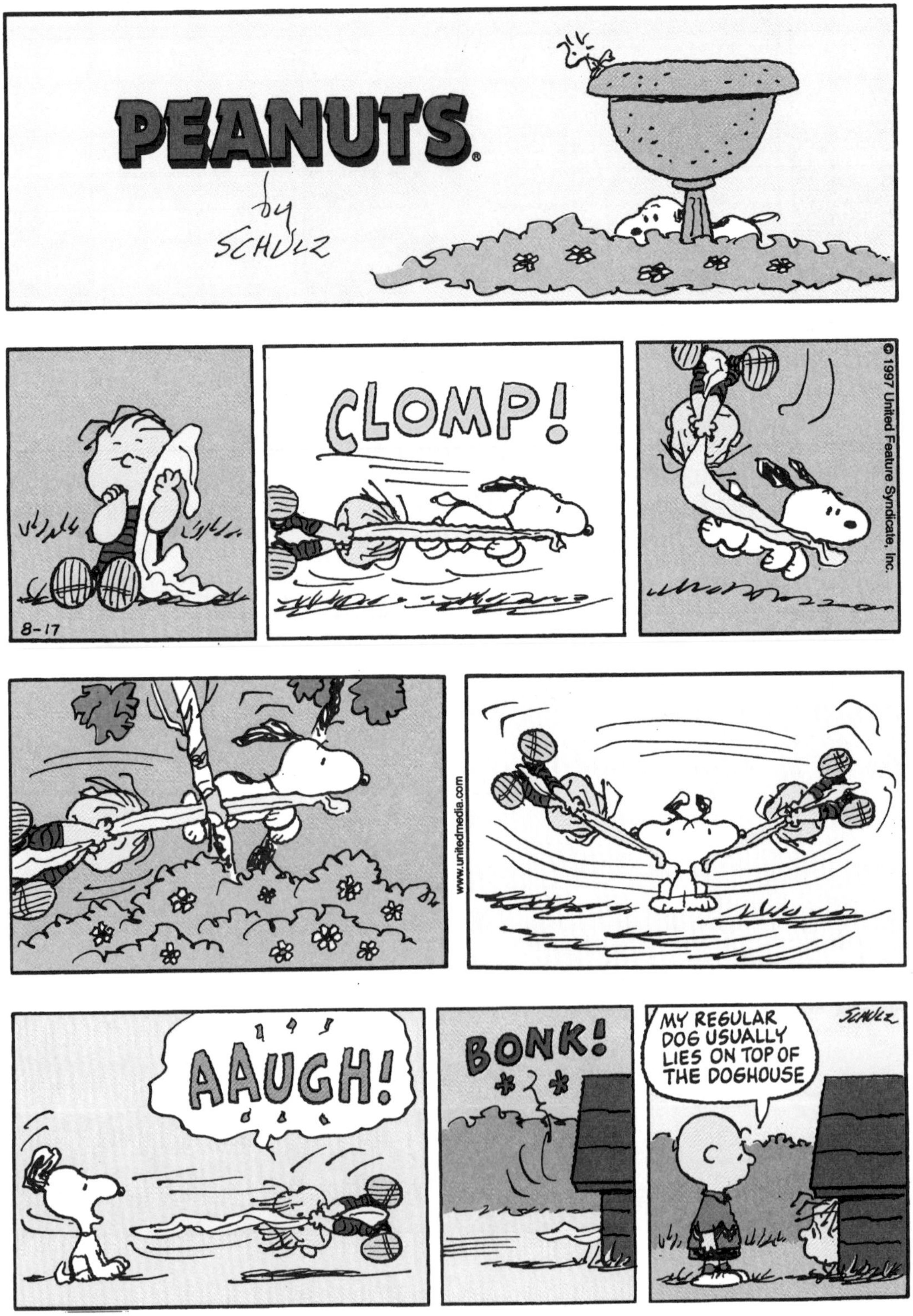
PEANUTS®
by SCHULZ
8-17
CLOMP!
© 1997 United Feature Syndicate, Inc.
www.unitedmedia.com
AAUGH!
BONK!
SCHULZ
MY REGULAR DOG USUALLY LIES ON TOP OF THE DOGHOUSE

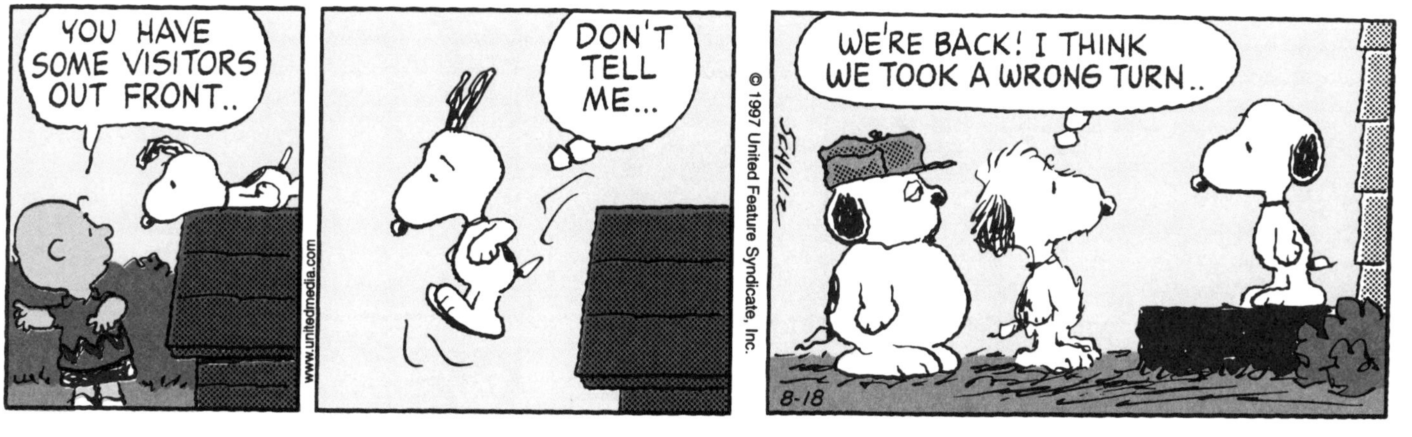
YOU HAVE SOME VISITORS OUT FRONT..
DON'T TELL ME...
© 1997 United Feature Syndicate, Inc.
www.unitedmedia.com
WE'RE BACK! I THINK WE TOOK A WRONG TURN..
SCHULZ
8-18

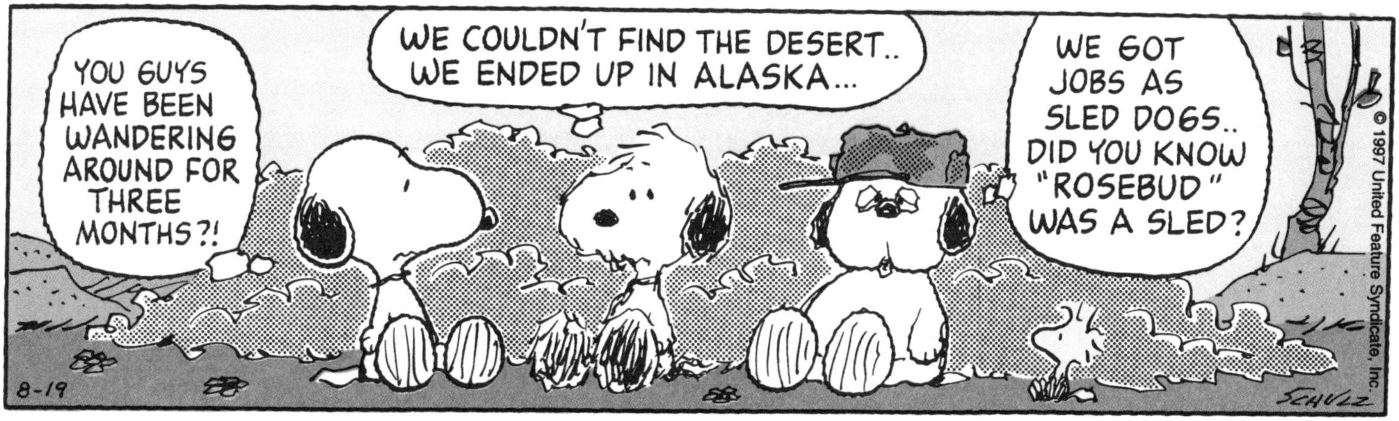
YOU GUYS HAVE BEEN WANDERING AROUND FOR THREE MONTHS?!
WE COULDN'T FIND THE DESERT.. WE ENDED UP IN ALASKA...
WE GOT JOBS AS SLED DOGS.. DID YOU KNOW "ROSEBUD" WAS A SLED?
© 1997 United Feature Syndicate, Inc.
8-19
SCHULZ

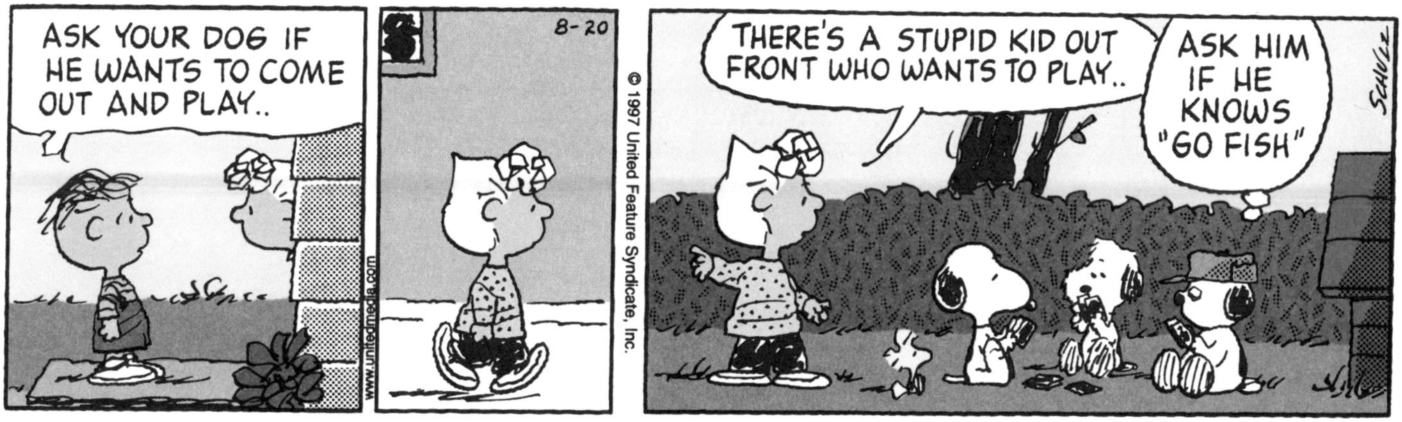
ASK YOUR DOG IF HE WANTS TO COME OUT AND PLAY..
www.unitedmedia.com
8-20
© 1997 United Feature Syndicate, Inc.
THERE'S A STUPID KID OUT FRONT WHO WANTS TO PLAY..
ASK HIM IF HE KNOWS "GO FISH"
SCHULZ

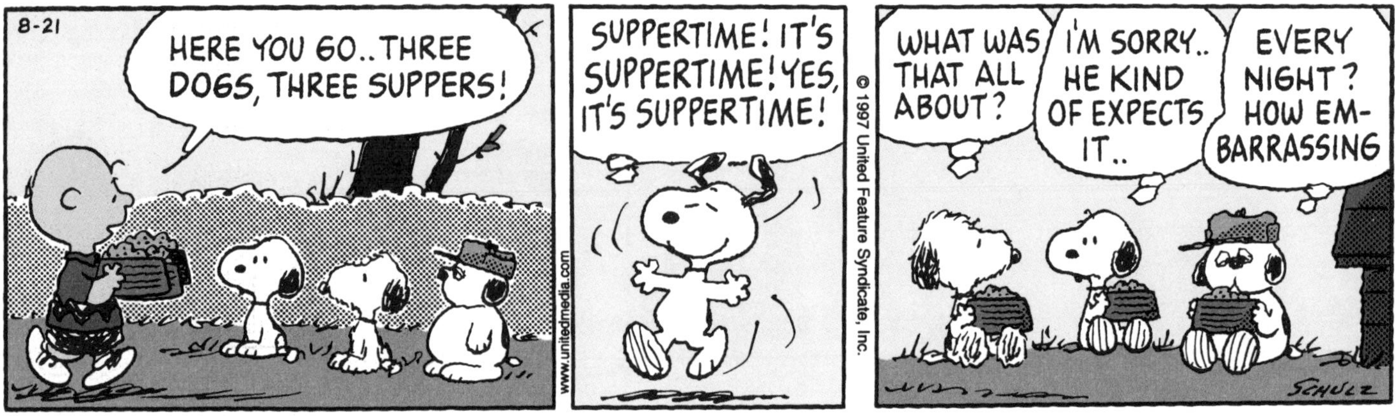
8-21
HERE YOU GO.. THREE DOGS, THREE SUPPERS!
www.unitedmedia.com
SUPPERTIME! IT'S SUPPERTIME! YES, IT'S SUPPERTIME!
© 1997 United Feature Syndicate, Inc.
WHAT WAS THAT ALL ABOUT?
I'M SORRY.. HE KIND OF EXPECTS IT..
EVERY NIGHT? HOW EM-BARRASSING
SCHULZ

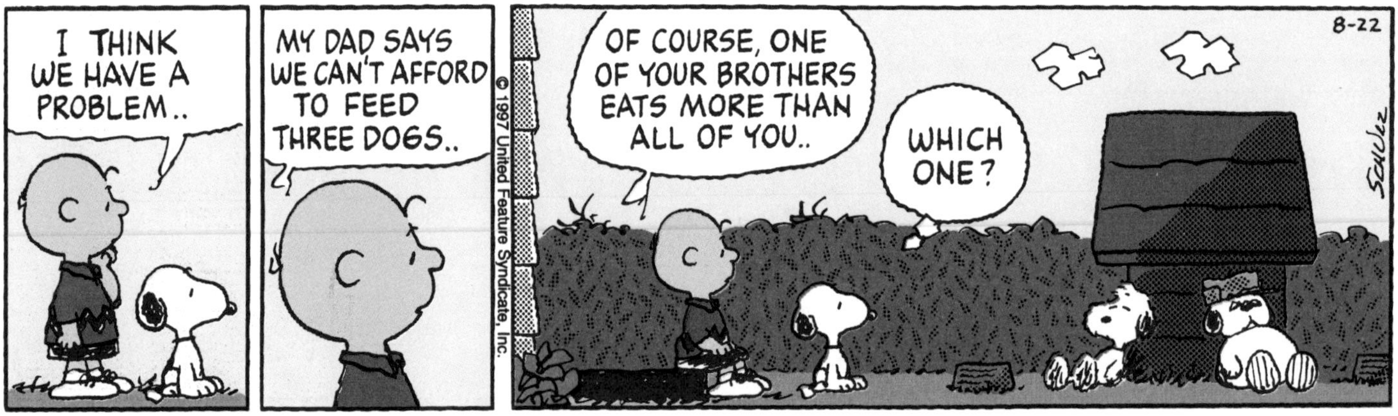
I THINK WE HAVE A PROBLEM..
MY DAD SAYS WE CAN'T AFFORD TO FEED THREE DOGS..
© 1997 United Feature Syndicate, Inc.
8-22
OF COURSE, ONE OF YOUR BROTHERS EATS MORE THAN ALL OF YOU..
WHICH ONE?
SCHULZ

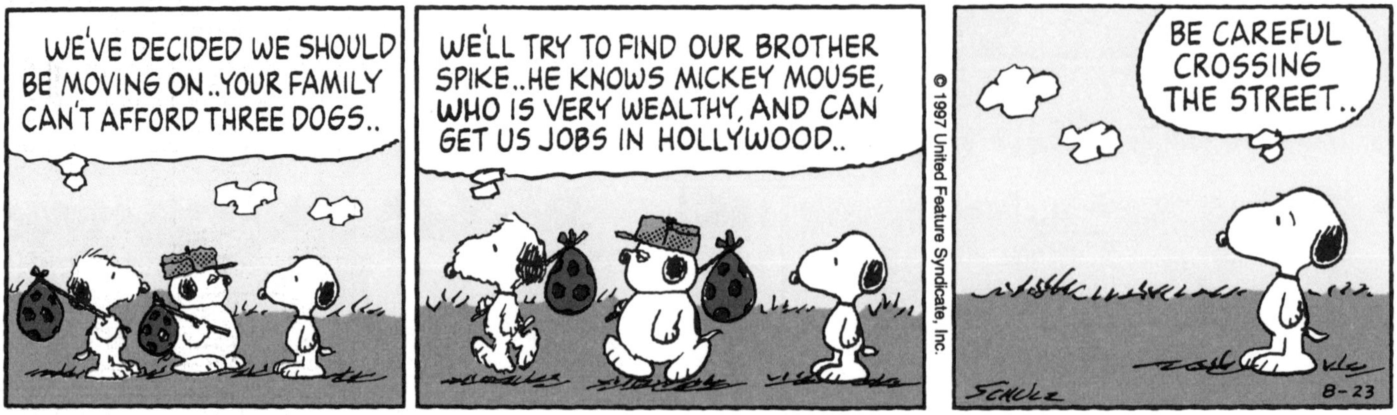
WE'VE DECIDED WE SHOULD BE MOVING ON.. YOUR FAMILY CAN'T AFFORD THREE DOGS..
WE'LL TRY TO FIND OUR BROTHER SPIKE.. HE KNOWS MICKEY MOUSE, WHO IS VERY WEALTHY, AND CAN GET US JOBS IN HOLLYWOOD..
© 1997 United Feature Syndicate, Inc.
BE CAREFUL CROSSING THE STREET..
SCHULZ
8-23

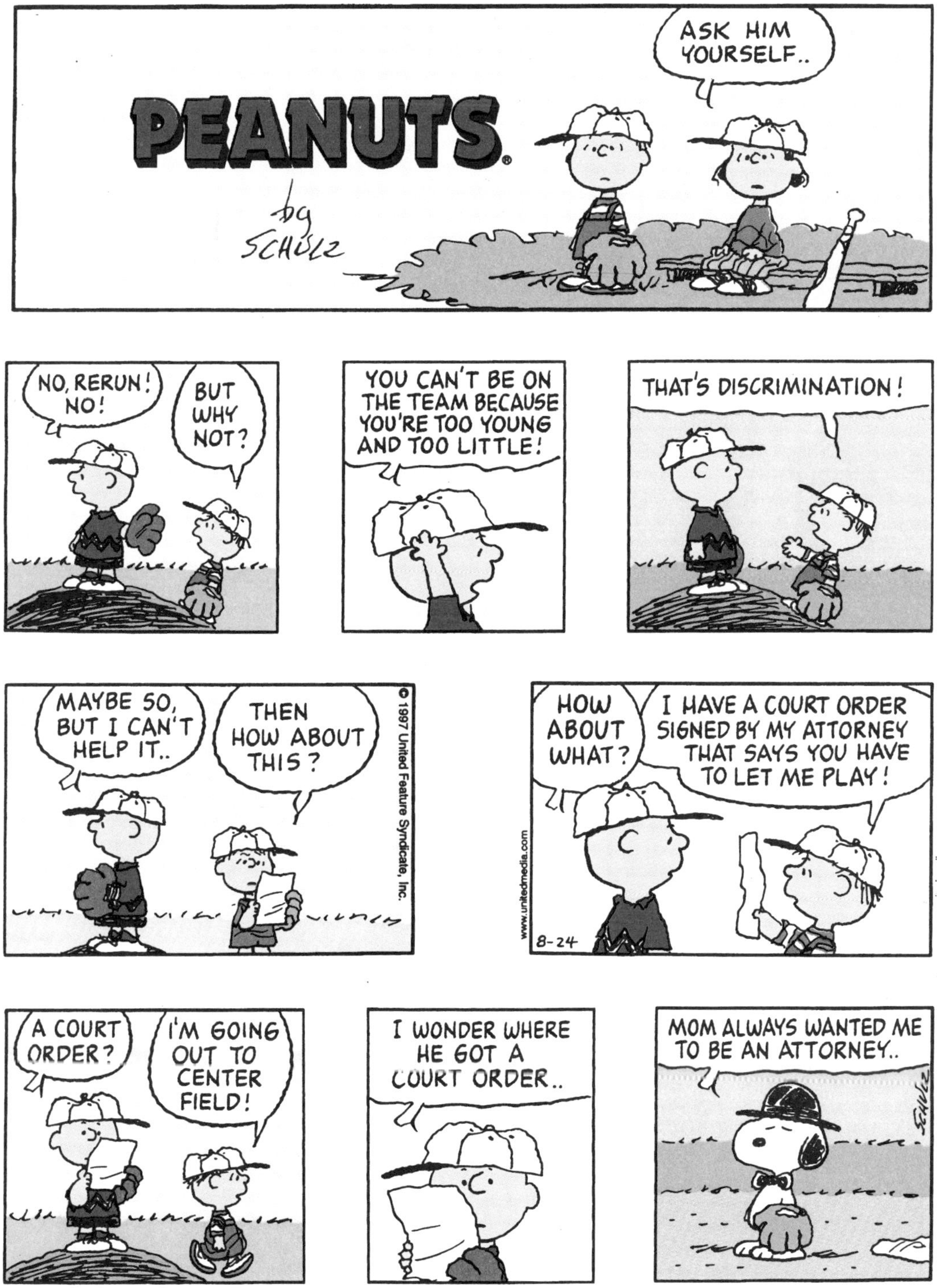
PEANUTS
by SCHULZ
ASK HIM YOURSELF..
NO, RERUN! NO!
BUT WHY NOT?
YOU CAN'T BE ON THE TEAM BECAUSE YOU'RE TOO YOUNG AND TOO LITTLE!
THAT'S DISCRIMINATION!
MAYBE SO, BUT I CAN'T HELP IT..
THEN HOW ABOUT THIS?
© 1997 United Feature Syndicate, Inc.
www.unitedmedia.com
HOW ABOUT WHAT?
I HAVE A COURT ORDER SIGNED BY MY ATTORNEY THAT SAYS YOU HAVE TO LET ME PLAY!
8-24
A COURT ORDER?
I'M GOING OUT TO CENTER FIELD!
I WONDER WHERE HE GOT A COURT ORDER..
MOM ALWAYS WANTED ME TO BE AN ATTORNEY..
SCHULZ

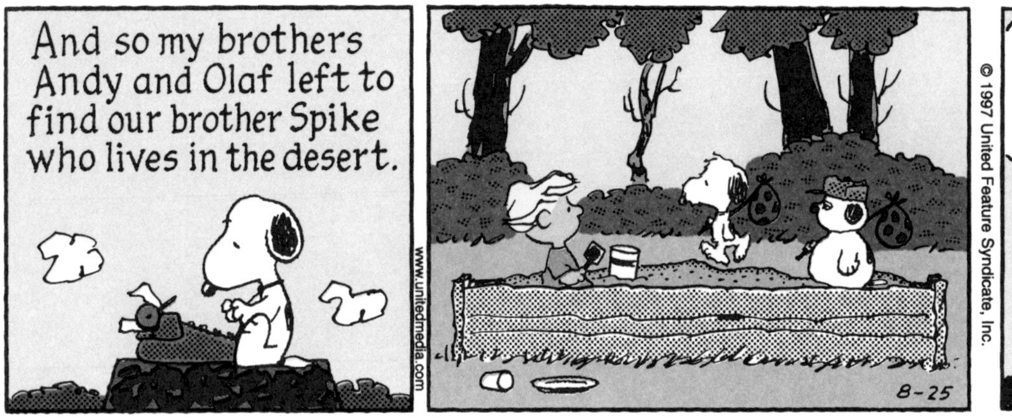
And so my brothers Andy and Olaf left to find our brother Spike who lives in the desert.
www.unitedmedia.com
8-25
© 1997 United Feature Syndicate, Inc.
I DON'T THINK THAT WAS A DESERT..
THAT KID LOOKED AT ME REAL FUNNY..
SCHULZ

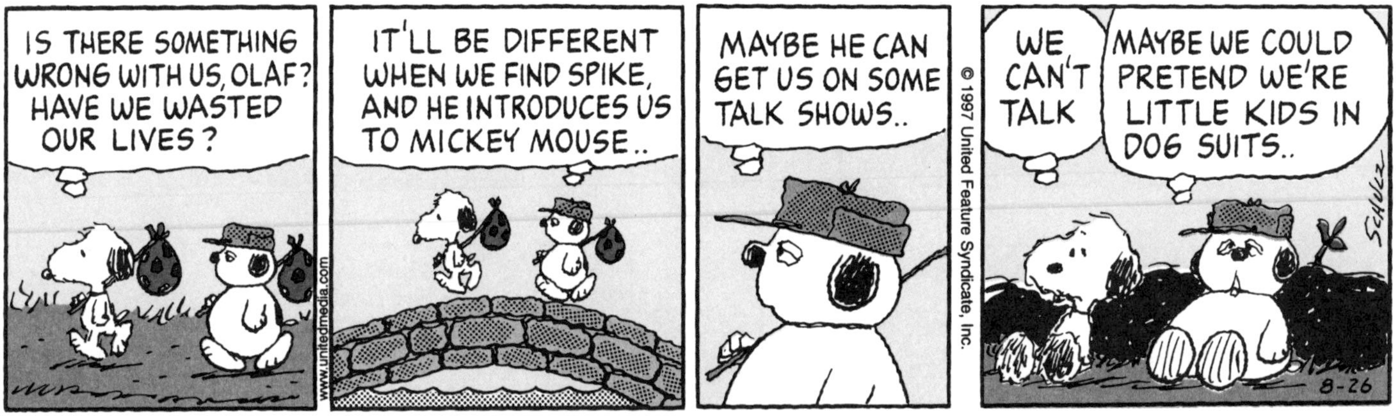
IS THERE SOMETHING WRONG WITH US, OLAF? HAVE WE WASTED OUR LIVES?
www.unitedmedia.com
IT'LL BE DIFFERENT WHEN WE FIND SPIKE, AND HE INTRODUCES US TO MICKEY MOUSE..
MAYBE HE CAN GET US ON SOME TALK SHOWS..
© 1997 United Feature Syndicate, Inc.
WE CAN'T TALK
MAYBE WE COULD PRETEND WE'RE LITTLE KIDS IN DOG SUITS..
SCHULZ
8-26

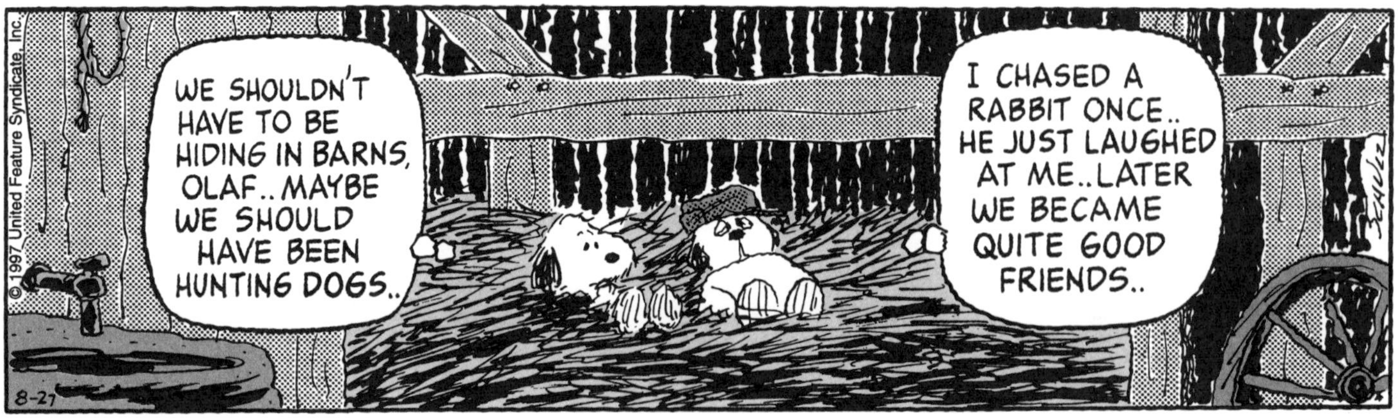
© 1997 United Feature Syndicate, Inc.
WE SHOULDN'T HAVE TO BE HIDING IN BARNS, OLAF.. MAYBE WE SHOULD HAVE BEEN HUNTING DOGS..
I CHASED A RABBIT ONCE.. HE JUST LAUGHED AT ME.. LATER WE BECAME QUITE GOOD FRIENDS..
SCHULZ
8-27

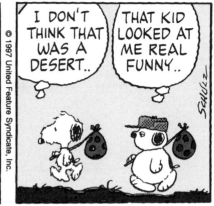

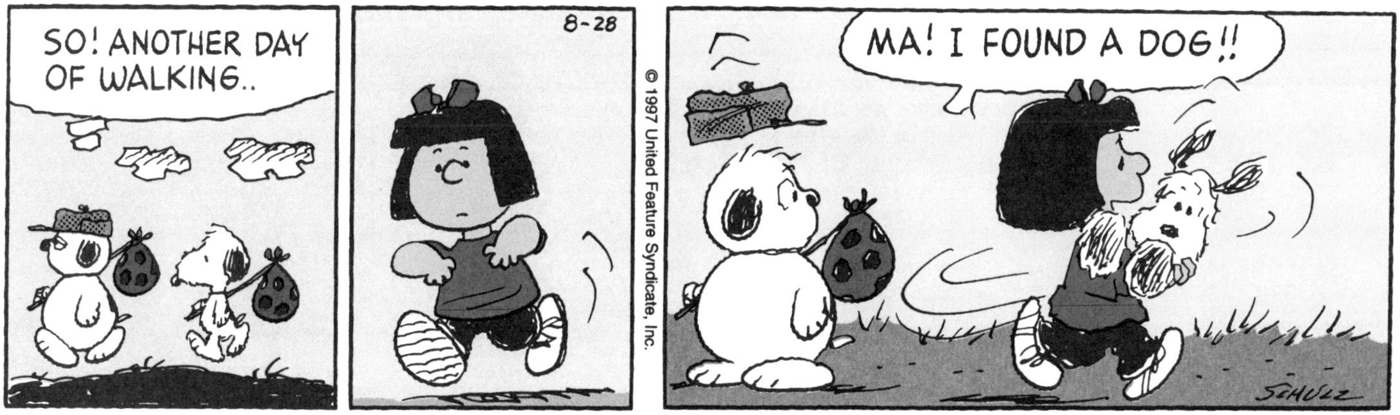
SO! ANOTHER DAY OF WALKING..
8-28
© 1997 United Feature Syndicate, Inc.
MA! I FOUND A DOG!!
SCHULZ

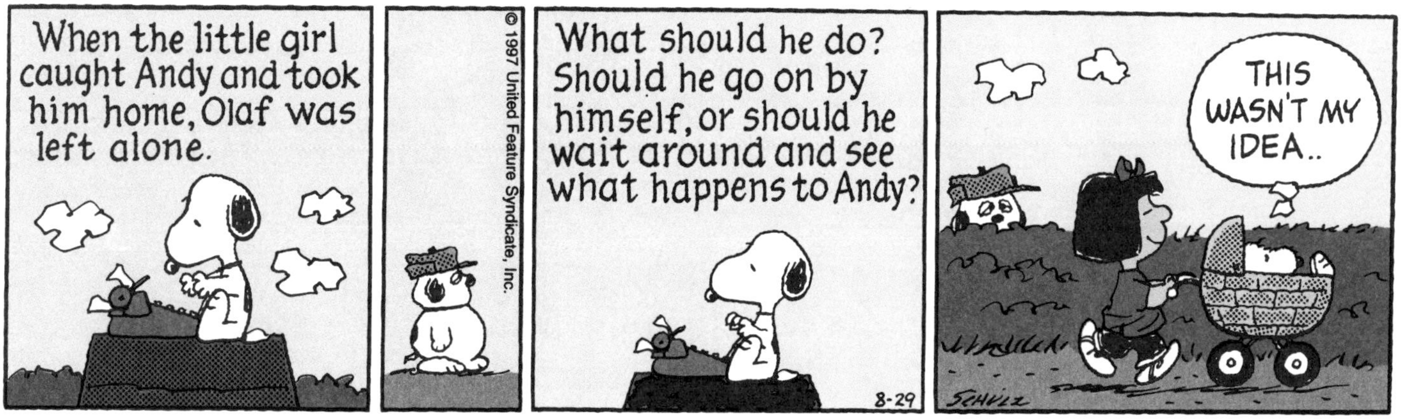
When the little girl caught Andy and took him home, Olaf was left alone.
© 1997 United Feature Syndicate, Inc.
What should he do? Should he go on by himself, or should he wait around and see what happens to Andy?
8-29
THIS WASN'T MY IDEA..
SCHULZ

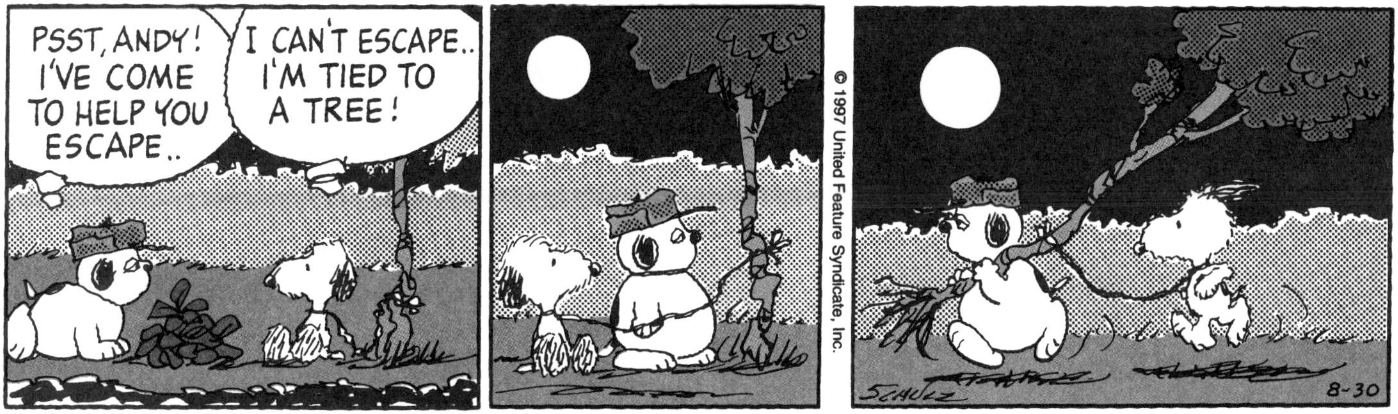
PSST, ANDY! I'VE COME TO HELP YOU ESCAPE..
I CAN'T ESCAPE.. I'M TIED TO A TREE!
© 1997 United Feature Syndicate, Inc.
SCHULZ
8-30

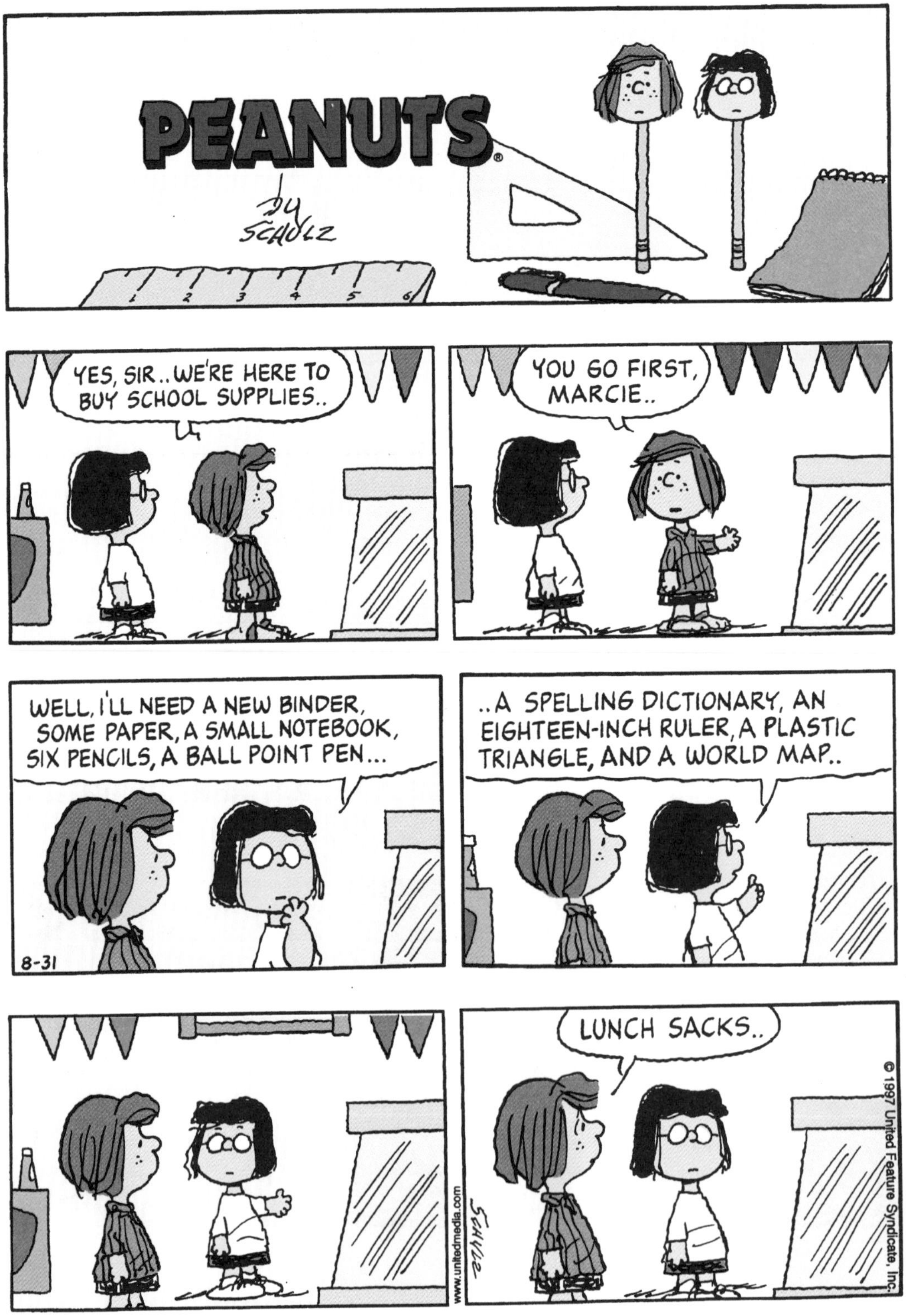
PEANUTS
by SCHULZ
YES, SIR.. WE'RE HERE TO BUY SCHOOL SUPPLIES..
YOU GO FIRST, MARCIE..
WELL, I'LL NEED A NEW BINDER, SOME PAPER, A SMALL NOTEBOOK, SIX PENCILS, A BALL POINT PEN...
8-31
..A SPELLING DICTIONARY, AN EIGHTEEN-INCH RULER, A PLASTIC TRIANGLE, AND A WORLD MAP..
www.unitedmedia.com
SCHULZ
LUNCH SACKS..
© 1997 United Feature Syndicate, Inc.

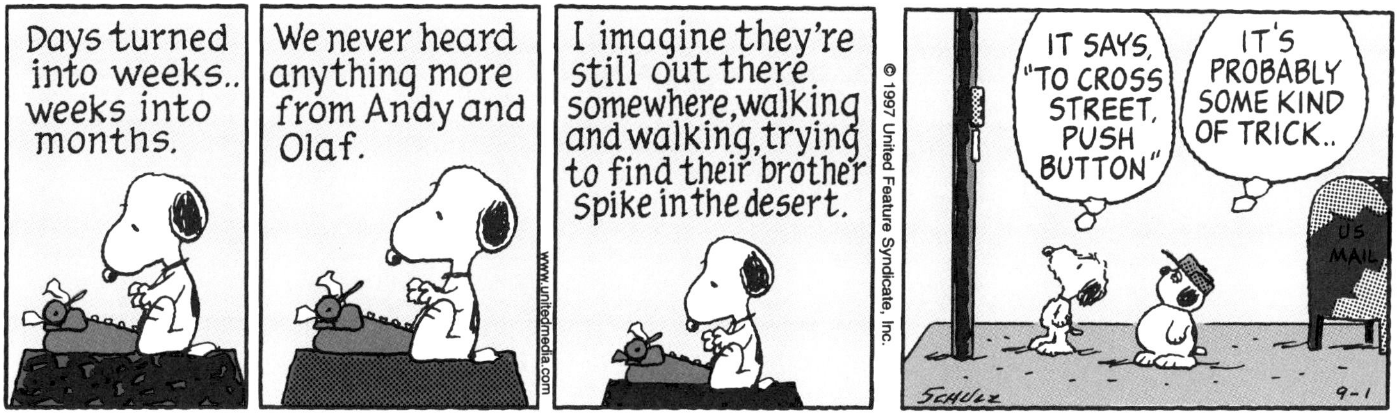
Days turned into weeks.. weeks into months.
We never heard anything more from Andy and Olaf.
I imagine they're still out there somewhere, walking and walking, trying to find their brother Spike in the desert.
IT SAYS, "TO CROSS STREET, PUSH BUTTON"
IT'S PROBABLY SOME KIND OF TRICK..
US MAIL
SCHULZ
9-1
© 1997 United Feature Syndicate, Inc.
www.unitedmedia.com

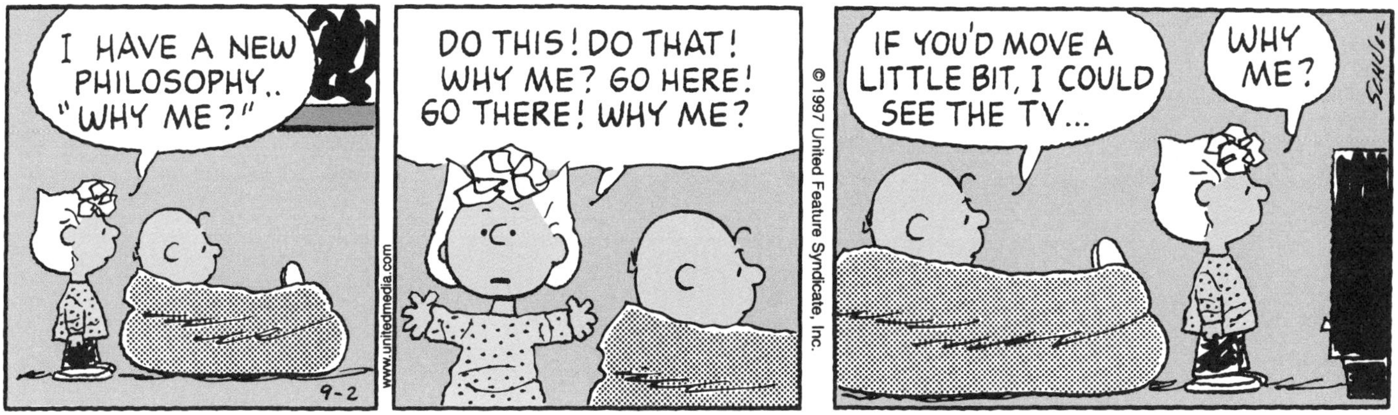
I HAVE A NEW PHILOSOPHY.. "WHY ME?"
DO THIS! DO THAT! WHY ME? GO HERE! GO THERE! WHY ME?
IF YOU'D MOVE A LITTLE BIT, I COULD SEE THE TV...
WHY ME?
SCHULZ
9-2
© 1997 United Feature Syndicate, Inc.
www.unitedmedia.com

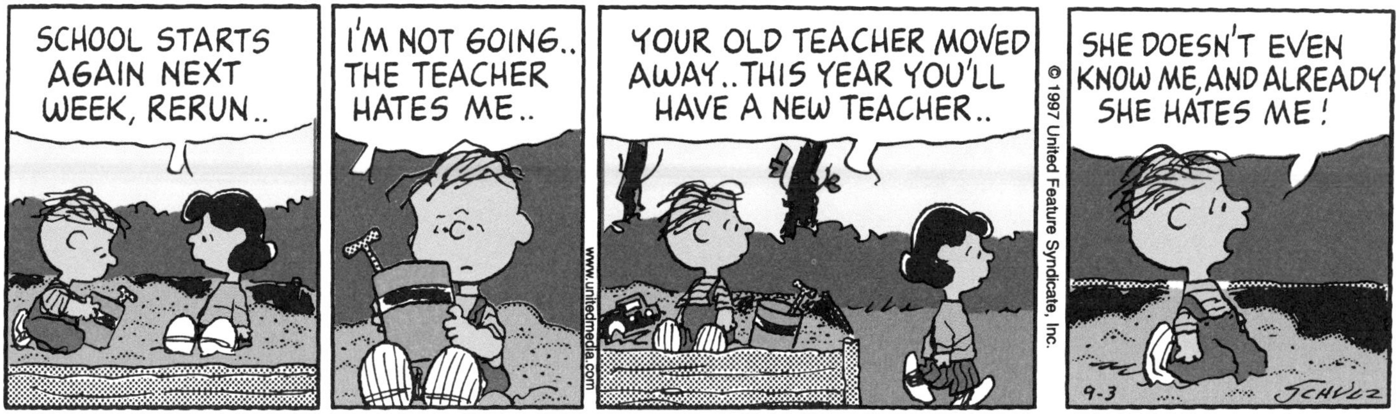
SCHOOL STARTS AGAIN NEXT WEEK, RERUN..
I'M NOT GOING.. THE TEACHER HATES ME..
YOUR OLD TEACHER MOVED AWAY..THIS YEAR YOU'LL HAVE A NEW TEACHER..
SHE DOESN'T EVEN KNOW ME, AND ALREADY SHE HATES ME!
9-3
SCHULZ
© 1997 United Feature Syndicate, Inc.
www.unitedmedia.com

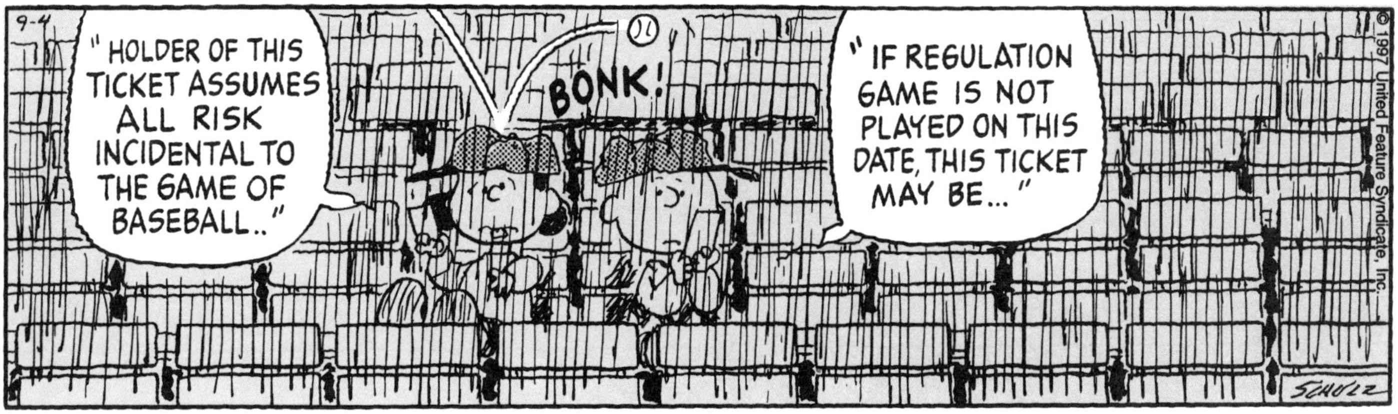
9-4
"HOLDER OF THIS TICKET ASSUMES ALL RISK INCIDENTAL TO THE GAME OF BASEBALL.."
BONK!
"IF REGULATION GAME IS NOT PLAYED ON THIS DATE, THIS TICKET MAY BE..."
© 1997 United Feature Syndicate, Inc.
SCHULZ

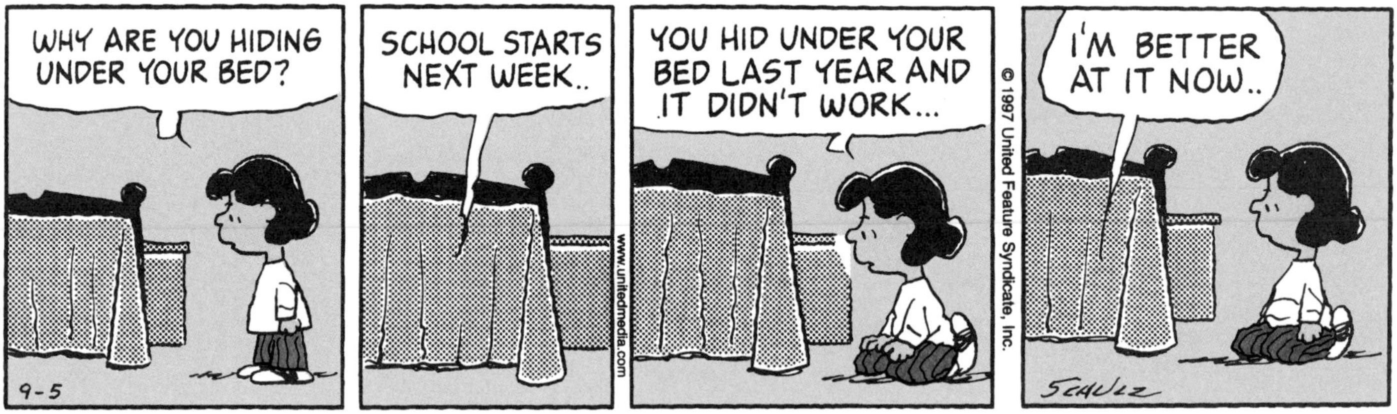
WHY ARE YOU HIDING UNDER YOUR BED?
9-5
SCHOOL STARTS NEXT WEEK..
www.unitedmedia.com
YOU HID UNDER YOUR BED LAST YEAR AND IT DIDN'T WORK...
© 1997 United Feature Syndicate, Inc.
I'M BETTER AT IT NOW..
SCHULZ

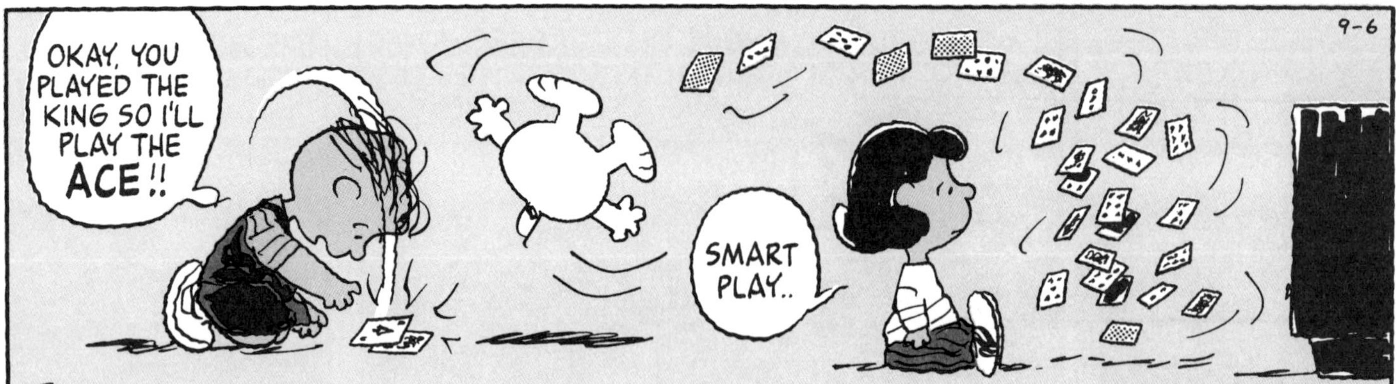
9-6
OKAY, YOU PLAYED THE KING SO I'LL PLAY THE ACE!!
SMART PLAY..
SCHULZ
© 1997 United Feature Syndicate, Inc.

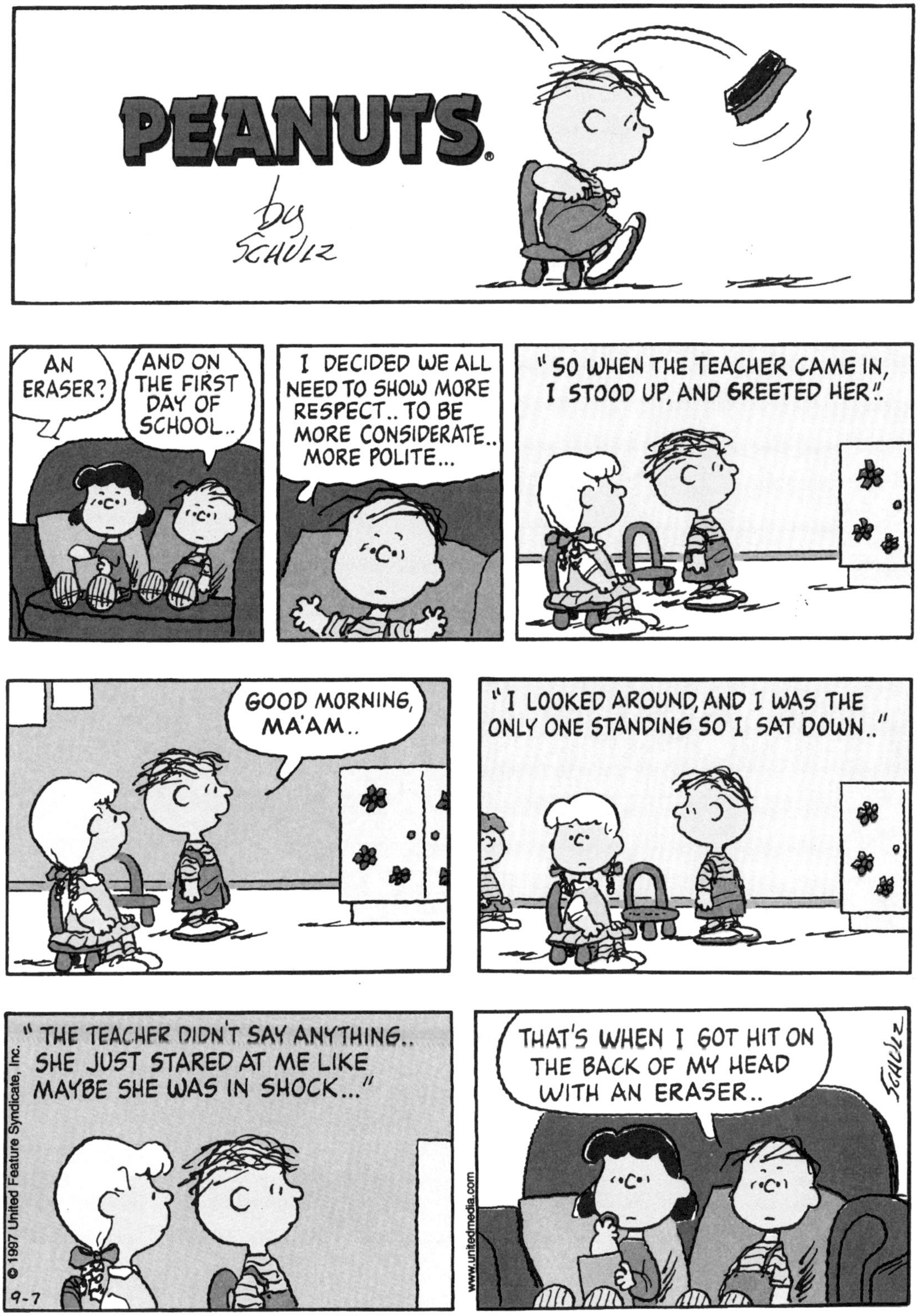
PEANUTS®
by SCHULZ
AN ERASER?
AND ON THE FIRST DAY OF SCHOOL..
I DECIDED WE ALL NEED TO SHOW MORE RESPECT.. TO BE MORE CONSIDERATE.. MORE POLITE...
"SO WHEN THE TEACHER CAME IN, I STOOD UP, AND GREETED HER".
GOOD MORNING, MA'AM..
"I LOOKED AROUND, AND I WAS THE ONLY ONE STANDING SO I SAT DOWN.."
"THE TEACHER DIDN'T SAY ANYTHING.. SHE JUST STARED AT ME LIKE MAYBE SHE WAS IN SHOCK..."
© 1997 United Feature Syndicate, Inc.
9-7
www.unitedmedia.com
THAT'S WHEN I GOT HIT ON THE BACK OF MY HEAD WITH AN ERASER..
SCHULZ

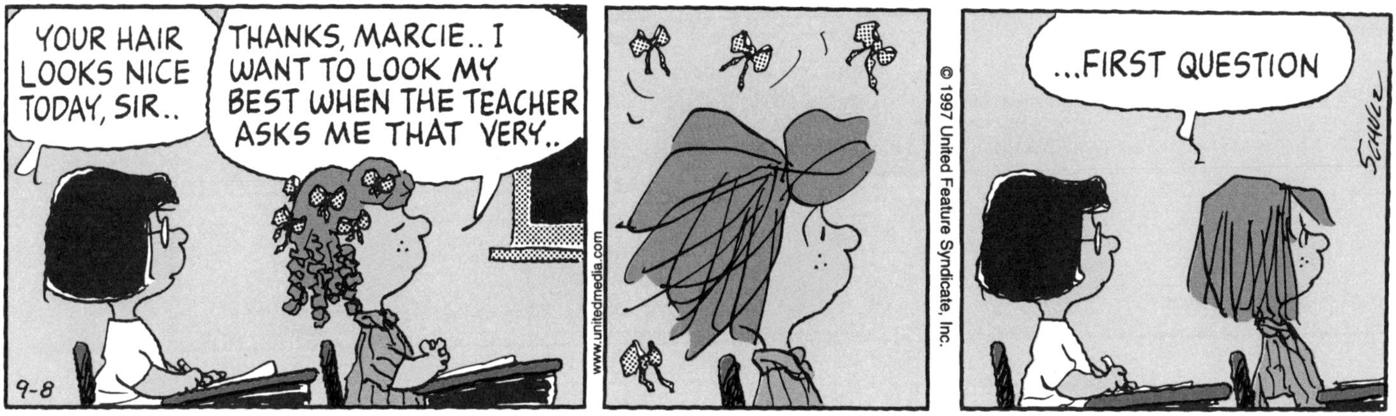
YOUR HAIR LOOKS NICE TODAY, SIR..
THANKS, MARCIE.. I WANT TO LOOK MY BEST WHEN THE TEACHER ASKS ME THAT VERY..
9-8
www.unitedmedia.com
© 1997 United Feature Syndicate, Inc.
...FIRST QUESTION

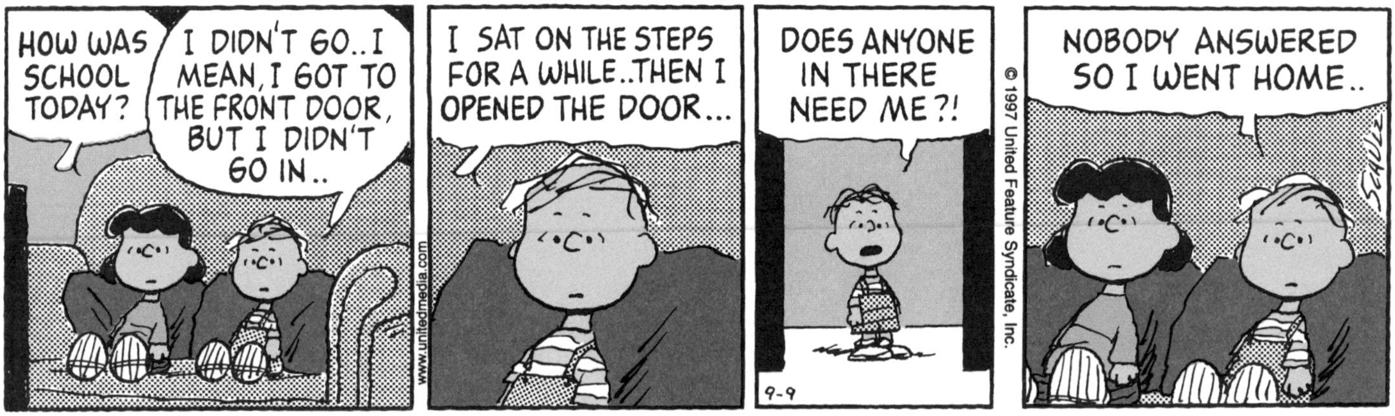
HOW WAS SCHOOL TODAY?
I DIDN'T GO.. I MEAN, I GOT TO THE FRONT DOOR, BUT I DIDN'T GO IN..
www.unitedmedia.com
I SAT ON THE STEPS FOR A WHILE..THEN I OPENED THE DOOR...
DOES ANYONE IN THERE NEED ME?!
9-9
© 1997 United Feature Syndicate, Inc.
NOBODY ANSWERED SO I WENT HOME..

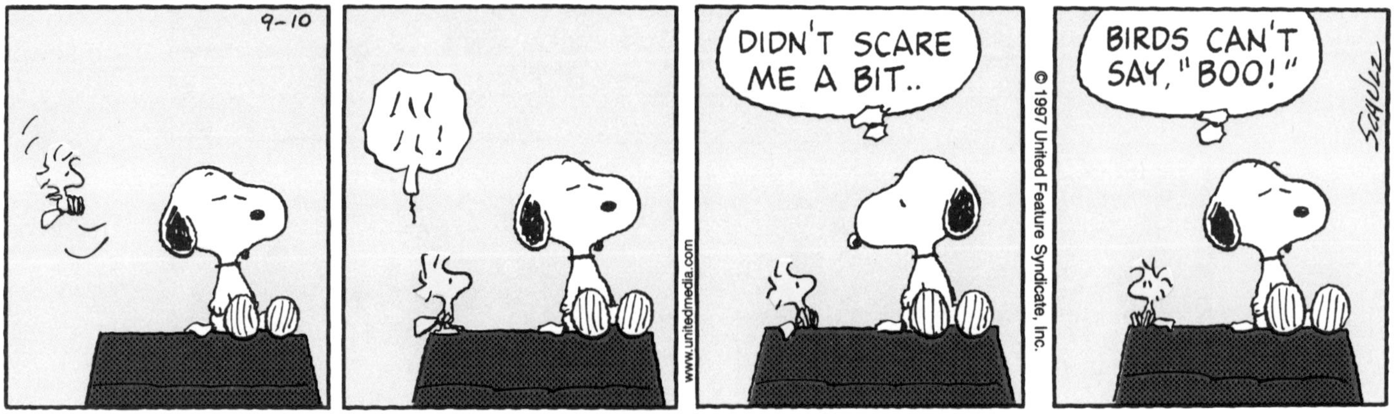
9-10
www.unitedmedia.com
DIDN'T SCARE ME A BIT..
© 1997 United Feature Syndicate, Inc.
BIRDS CAN'T SAY, "BOO!"

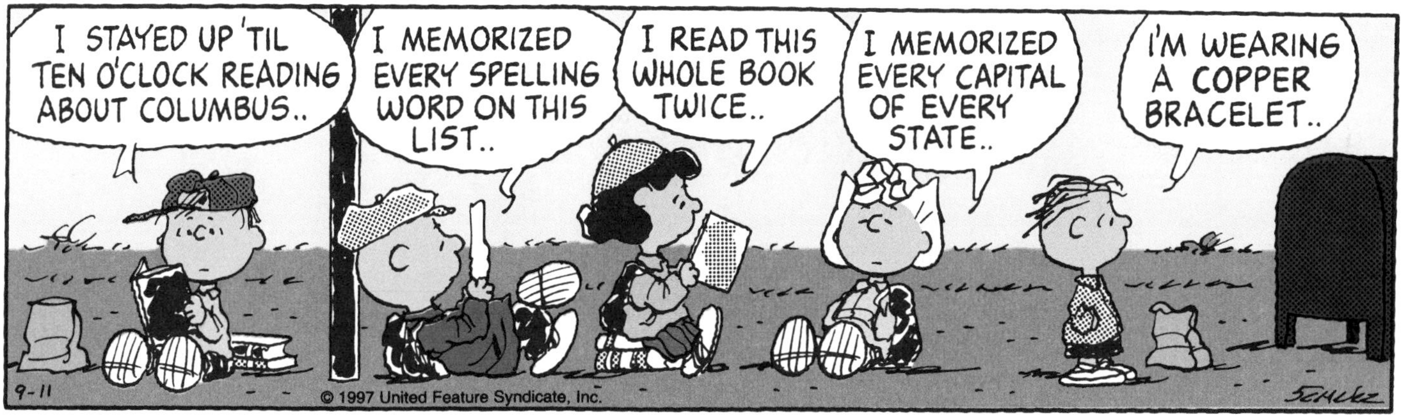
I STAYED UP 'TIL TEN O'CLOCK READING ABOUT COLUMBUS..
I MEMORIZED EVERY SPELLING WORD ON THIS LIST..
I READ THIS WHOLE BOOK TWICE..
I MEMORIZED EVERY CAPITAL OF EVERY STATE..
I'M WEARING A COPPER BRACELET..
9-11
© 1997 United Feature Syndicate, Inc.
SCHULZ

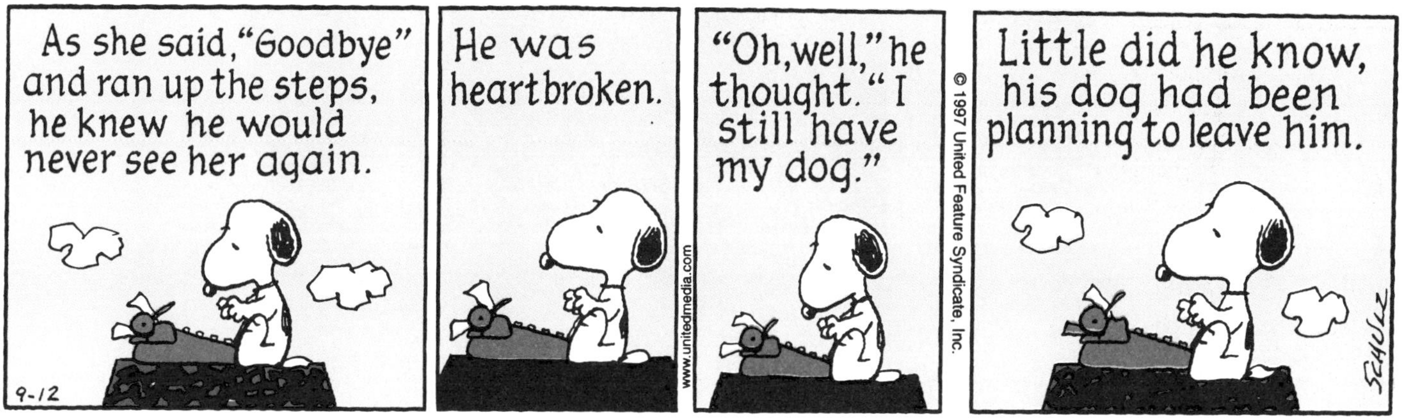
As she said, "Goodbye" and ran up the steps, he knew he would never see her again.
He was heartbroken.
"Oh, well," he thought. "I still have my dog."
Little did he know, his dog had been planning to leave him.
9-12
www.unitedmedia.com
© 1997 United Feature Syndicate, Inc.
SCHULZ

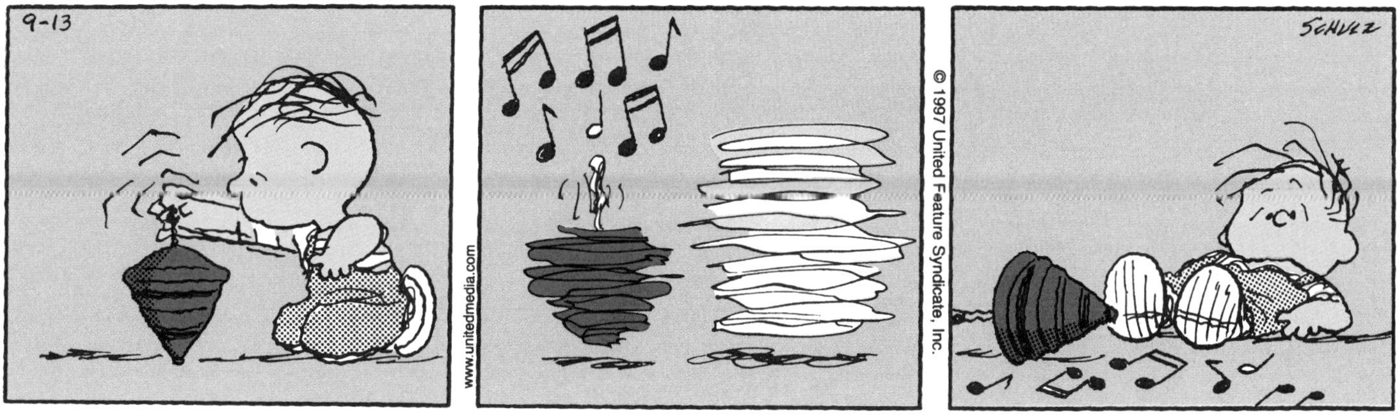
9-13
www.unitedmedia.com
© 1997 United Feature Syndicate, Inc.
SCHULZ

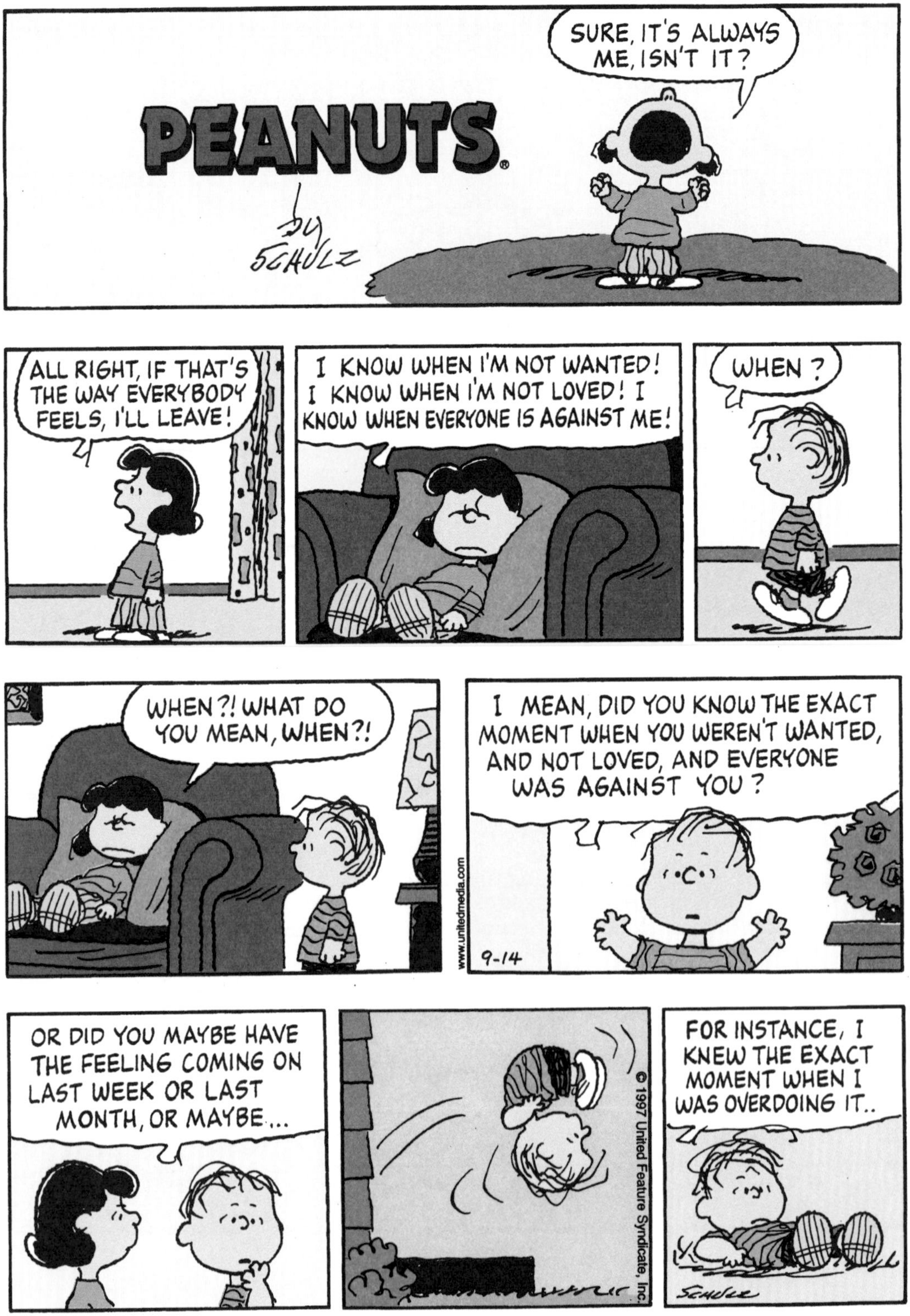
SURE, IT'S ALWAYS ME, ISN'T IT?
PEANUTS
by SCHULZ
ALL RIGHT, IF THAT'S THE WAY EVERYBODY FEELS, I'LL LEAVE!
I KNOW WHEN I'M NOT WANTED! I KNOW WHEN I'M NOT LOVED! I KNOW WHEN EVERYONE IS AGAINST ME!
WHEN?
WHEN?! WHAT DO YOU MEAN, WHEN?!
www.unitedmedia.com
I MEAN, DID YOU KNOW THE EXACT MOMENT WHEN YOU WEREN'T WANTED, AND NOT LOVED, AND EVERYONE WAS AGAINST YOU?
9-14
OR DID YOU MAYBE HAVE THE FEELING COMING ON LAST WEEK OR LAST MONTH, OR MAYBE...
© 1997 United Feature Syndicate, Inc.
FOR INSTANCE, I KNEW THE EXACT MOMENT WHEN I WAS OVERDOING IT..
SCHULZ

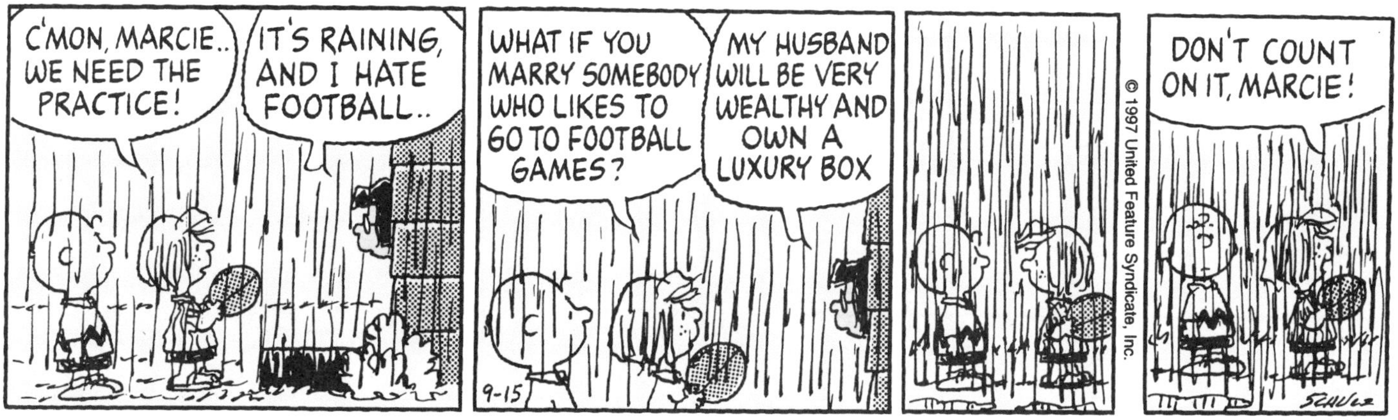
C'MON, MARCIE.. WE NEED THE PRACTICE!
IT'S RAINING, AND I HATE FOOTBALL..
WHAT IF YOU MARRY SOMEBODY WHO LIKES TO GO TO FOOTBALL GAMES?
MY HUSBAND WILL BE VERY WEALTHY AND OWN A LUXURY BOX
© 1997 United Feature Syndicate, Inc.
DON'T COUNT ON IT, MARCIE!

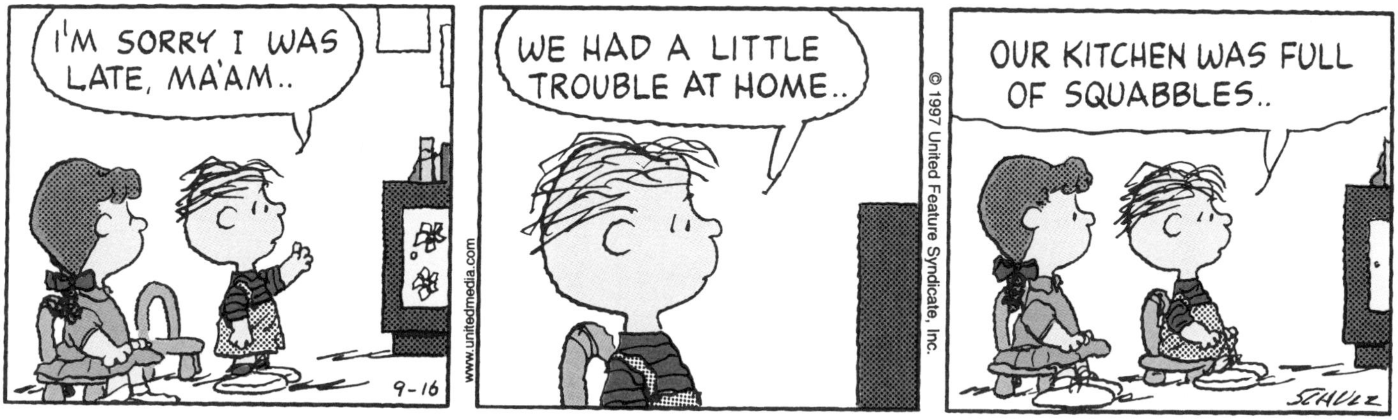
I'M SORRY I WAS LATE, MA'AM..
www.unitedmedia.com
WE HAD A LITTLE TROUBLE AT HOME..
© 1997 United Feature Syndicate, Inc.
OUR KITCHEN WAS FULL OF SQUABBLES..

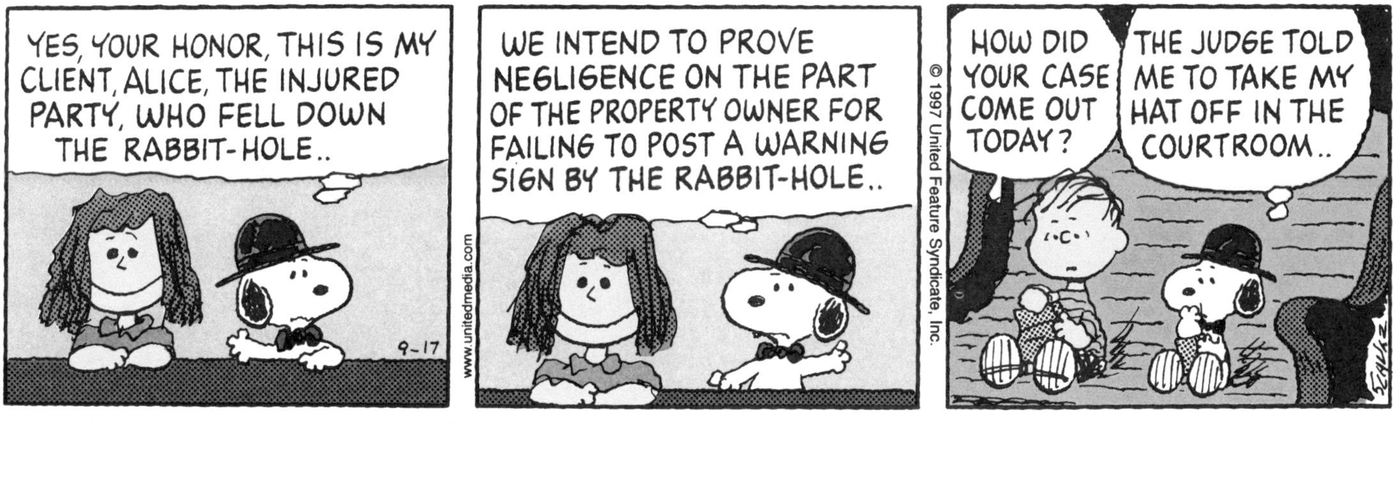
YES, YOUR HONOR, THIS IS MY CLIENT, ALICE, THE INJURED PARTY, WHO FELL DOWN THE RABBIT-HOLE..
www.unitedmedia.com
WE INTEND TO PROVE NEGLIGENCE ON THE PART OF THE PROPERTY OWNER FOR FAILING TO POST A WARNING SIGN BY THE RABBIT-HOLE..
© 1997 United Feature Syndicate, Inc.
HOW DID YOUR CASE COME OUT TODAY?
THE JUDGE TOLD ME TO TAKE MY HAT OFF IN THE COURTROOM..

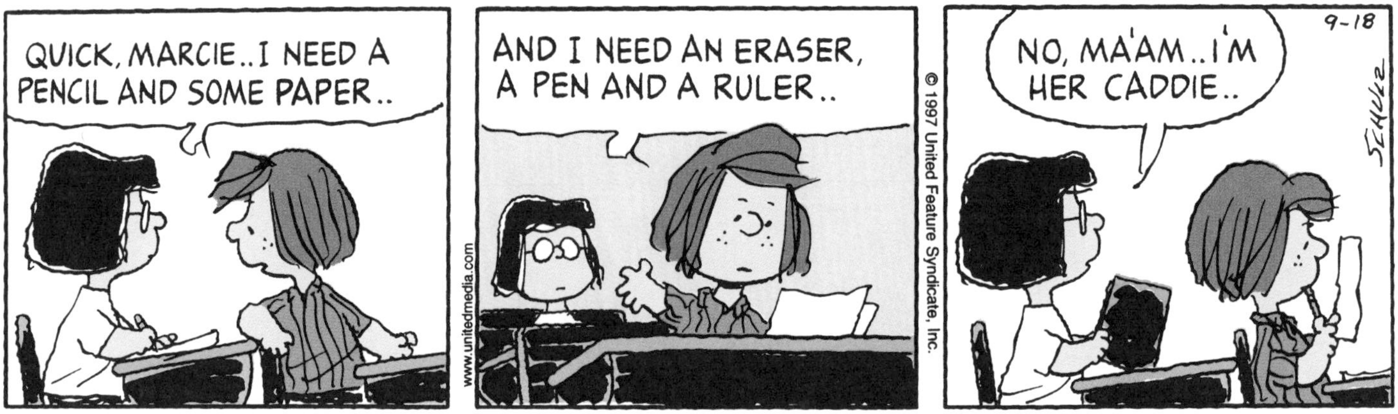
QUICK, MARCIE..I NEED A PENCIL AND SOME PAPER..
AND I NEED AN ERASER, A PEN AND A RULER..
NO, MA'AM..I'M HER CADDIE..
9-18
SCHULZ
www.unitedmedia.com
© 1997 United Feature Syndicate, Inc.

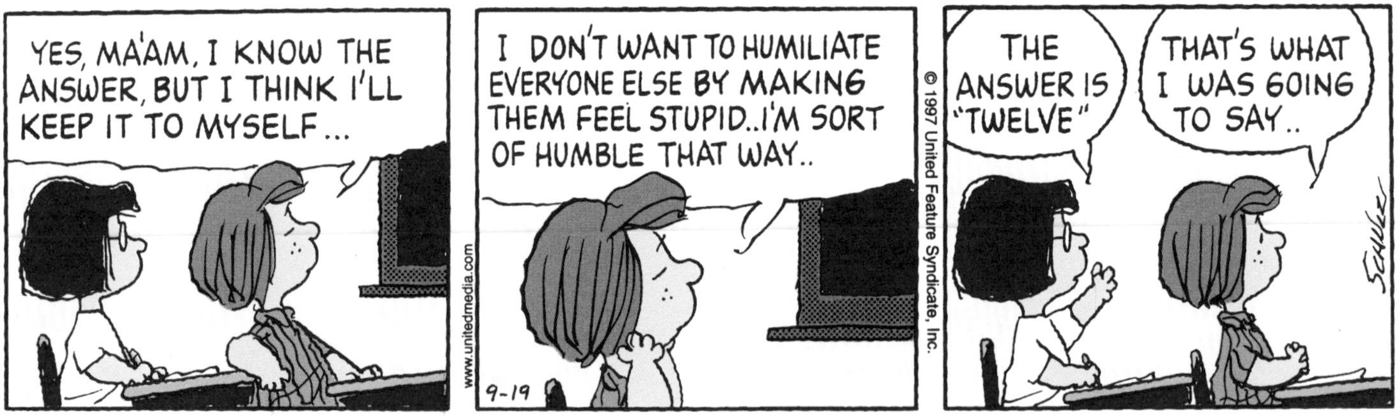
YES, MA'AM, I KNOW THE ANSWER, BUT I THINK I'LL KEEP IT TO MYSELF...
I DON'T WANT TO HUMILIATE EVERYONE ELSE BY MAKING THEM FEEL STUPID..I'M SORT OF HUMBLE THAT WAY..
THE ANSWER IS "TWELVE"
THAT'S WHAT I WAS GOING TO SAY..
9-19
SCHULZ
www.unitedmedia.com
© 1997 United Feature Syndicate, Inc.

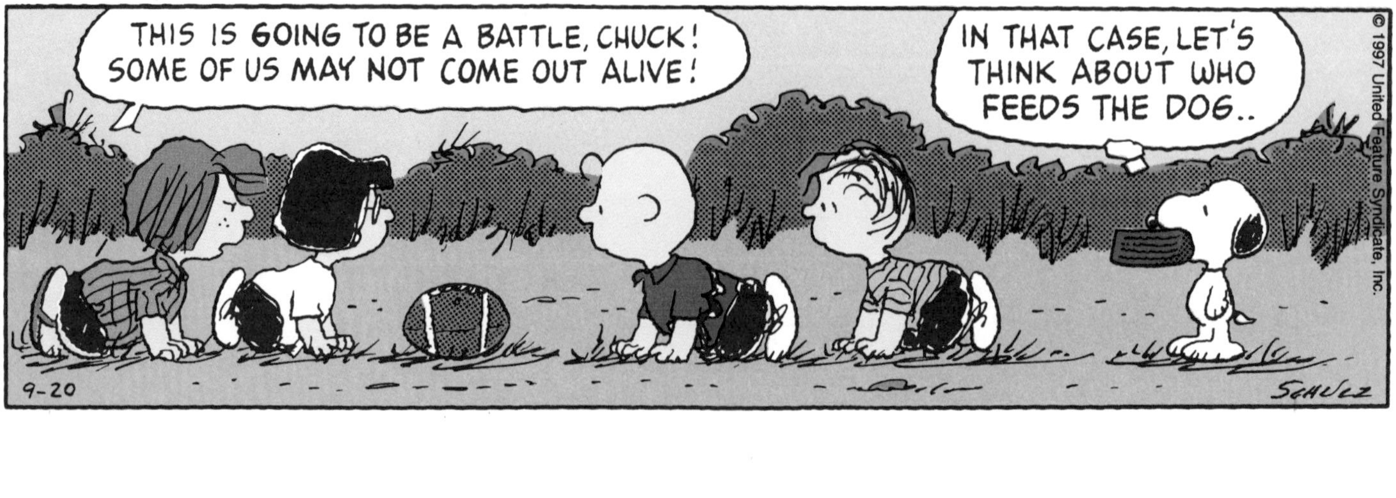
THIS IS GOING TO BE A BATTLE, CHUCK! SOME OF US MAY NOT COME OUT ALIVE!
IN THAT CASE, LET'S THINK ABOUT WHO FEEDS THE DOG..
9-20
SCHULZ
© 1997 United Feature Syndicate, Inc.

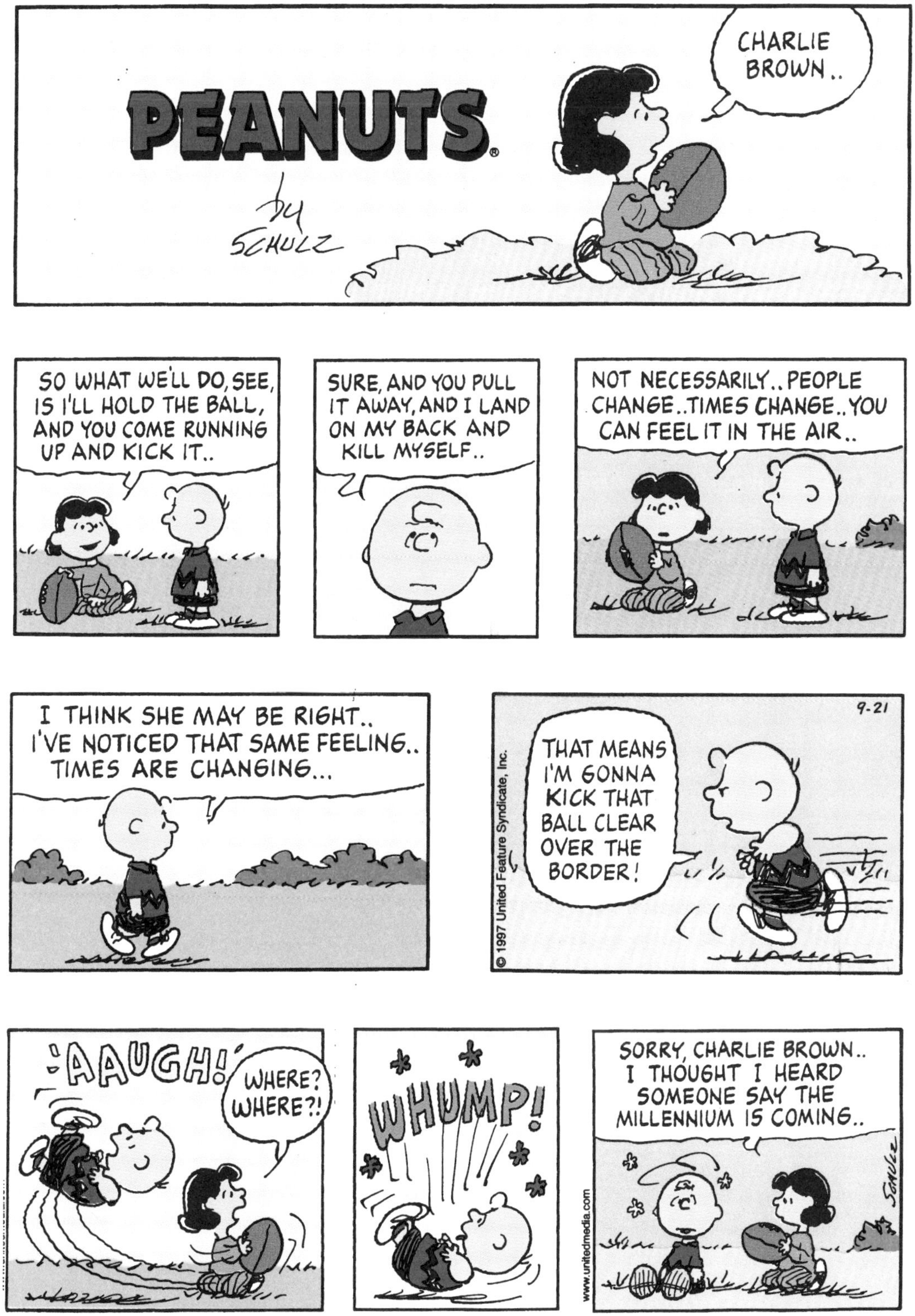
PEANUTS
by SCHULZ
CHARLIE BROWN..
SO WHAT WE'LL DO, SEE, IS I'LL HOLD THE BALL, AND YOU COME RUNNING UP AND KICK IT..
SURE, AND YOU PULL IT AWAY, AND I LAND ON MY BACK AND KILL MYSELF..
NOT NECESSARILY.. PEOPLE CHANGE.. TIMES CHANGE.. YOU CAN FEEL IT IN THE AIR..
I THINK SHE MAY BE RIGHT.. I'VE NOTICED THAT SAME FEELING.. TIMES ARE CHANGING...
9-21
© 1997 United Feature Syndicate, Inc.
THAT MEANS I'M GONNA KICK THAT BALL CLEAR OVER THE BORDER!
AAUGH!
WHERE? WHERE?!
WHUMP!
www.unitedmedia.com
SORRY, CHARLIE BROWN.. I THOUGHT I HEARD SOMEONE SAY THE MILLENNIUM IS COMING..
SCHULZ

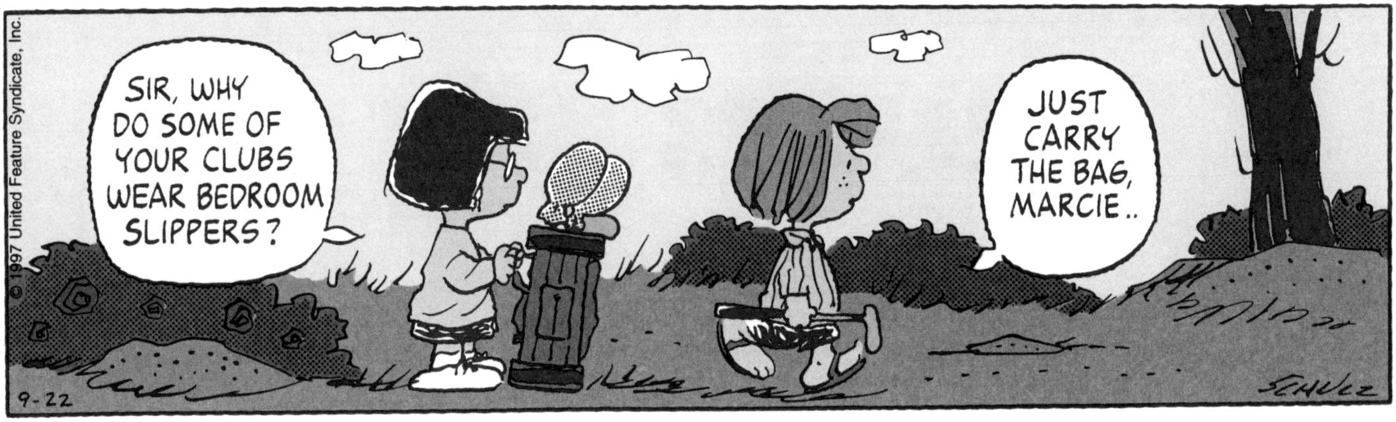
SIR, WHY DO SOME OF YOUR CLUBS WEAR BEDROOM SLIPPERS?
JUST CARRY THE BAG, MARCIE..
© 1997 United Feature Syndicate, Inc.
9-22
SCHULZ

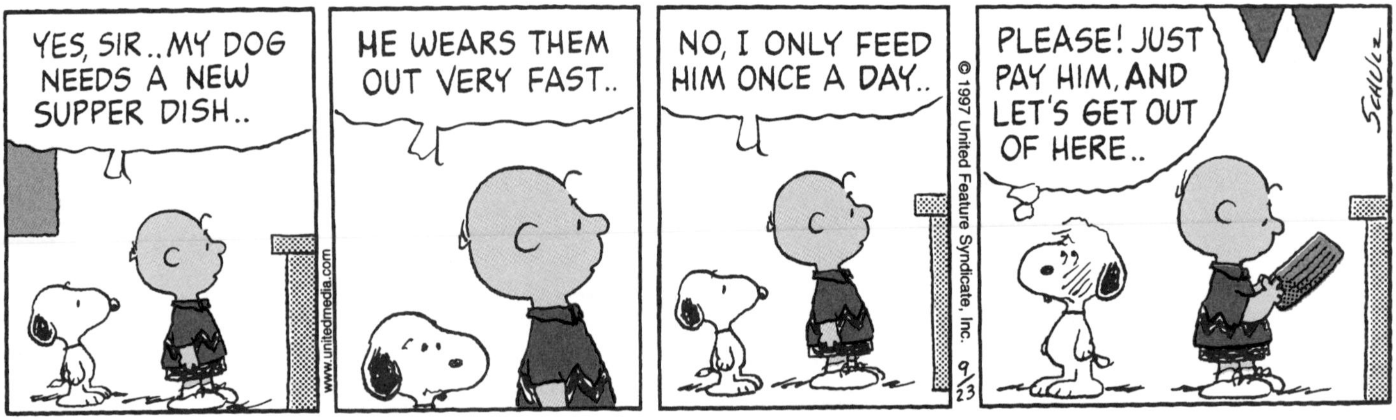
YES, SIR..MY DOG NEEDS A NEW SUPPER DISH..
www.unitedmedia.com
HE WEARS THEM OUT VERY FAST..
NO, I ONLY FEED HIM ONCE A DAY..
© 1997 United Feature Syndicate, Inc.
9/23
PLEASE! JUST PAY HIM, AND LET'S GET OUT OF HERE..
SCHULZ

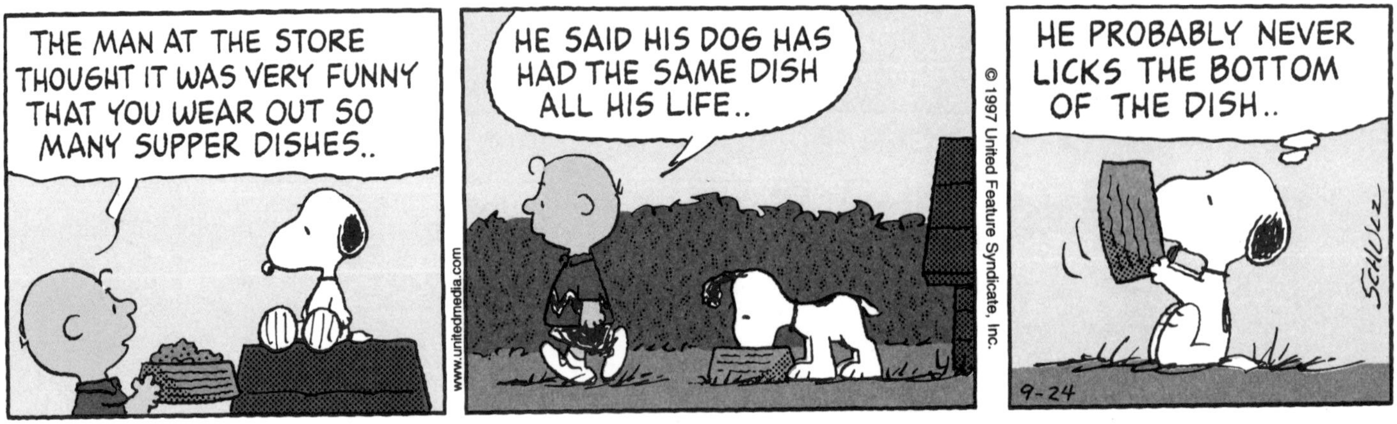
THE MAN AT THE STORE THOUGHT IT WAS VERY FUNNY THAT YOU WEAR OUT SO MANY SUPPER DISHES..
www.unitedmedia.com
HE SAID HIS DOG HAS HAD THE SAME DISH ALL HIS LIFE..
© 1997 United Feature Syndicate, Inc.
HE PROBABLY NEVER LICKS THE BOTTOM OF THE DISH..
SCHULZ
9-24

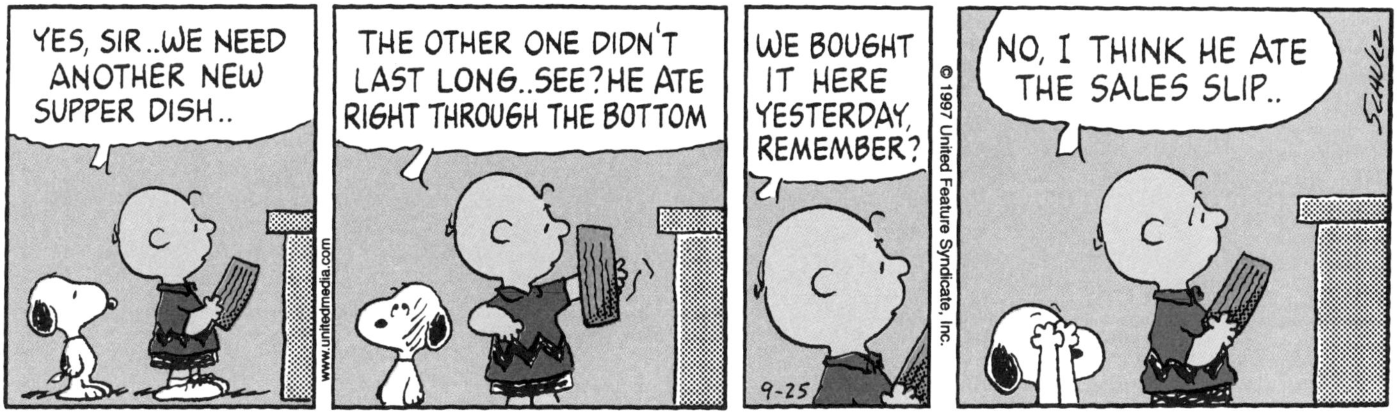
YES, SIR..WE NEED ANOTHER NEW SUPPER DISH..
THE OTHER ONE DIDN'T LAST LONG..SEE? HE ATE RIGHT THROUGH THE BOTTOM
WE BOUGHT IT HERE YESTERDAY, REMEMBER?
NO, I THINK HE ATE THE SALES SLIP..
www.unitedmedia.com
© 1997 United Feature Syndicate, Inc.
9-25
SCHULZ

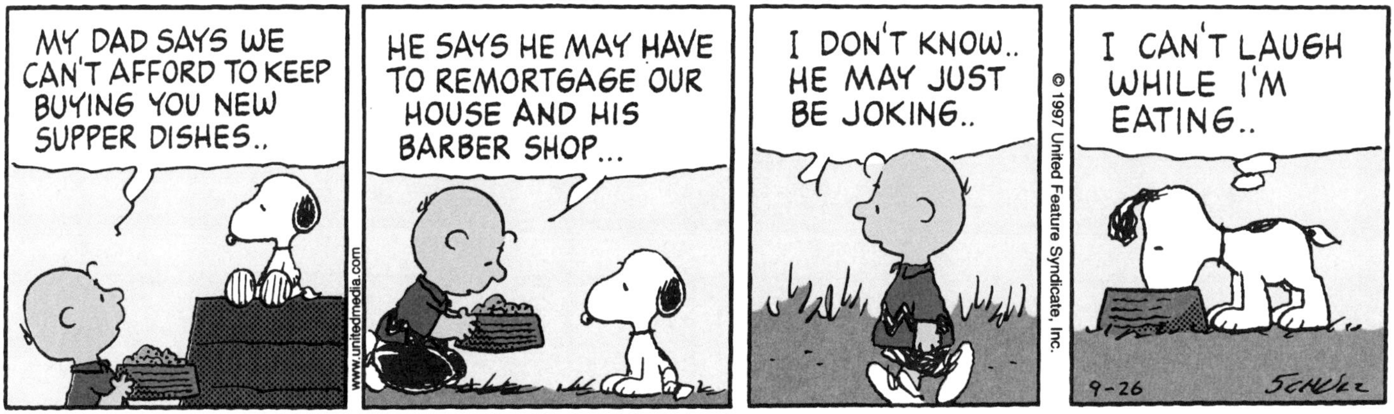
MY DAD SAYS WE CAN'T AFFORD TO KEEP BUYING YOU NEW SUPPER DISHES..
HE SAYS HE MAY HAVE TO REMORTGAGE OUR HOUSE AND HIS BARBER SHOP...
I DON'T KNOW.. HE MAY JUST BE JOKING..
I CAN'T LAUGH WHILE I'M EATING..
www.unitedmedia.com
© 1997 United Feature Syndicate, Inc.
9-26
SCHULZ

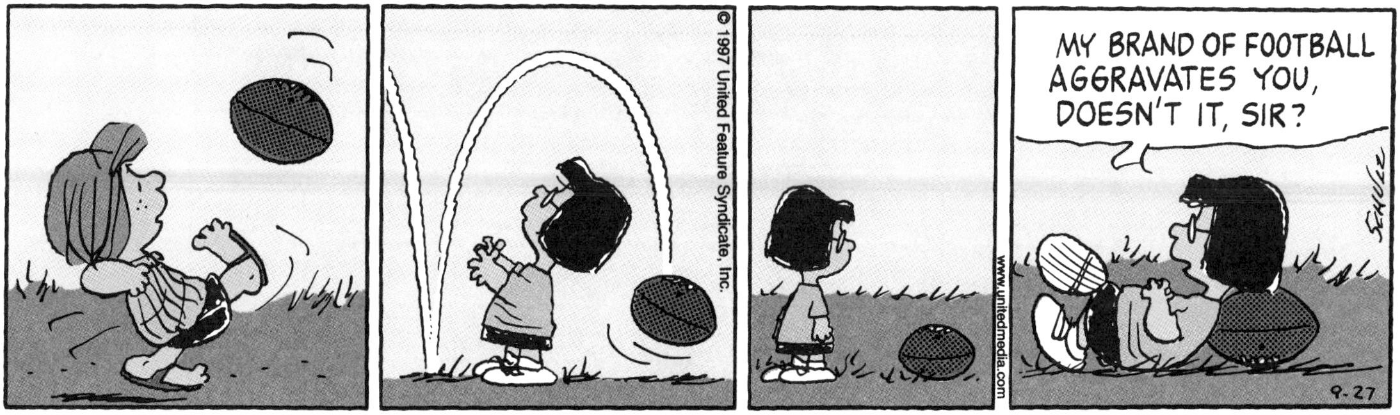
MY BRAND OF FOOTBALL AGGRAVATES YOU, DOESN'T IT, SIR?
© 1997 United Feature Syndicate, Inc.
www.unitedmedia.com
9-27
SCHULZ

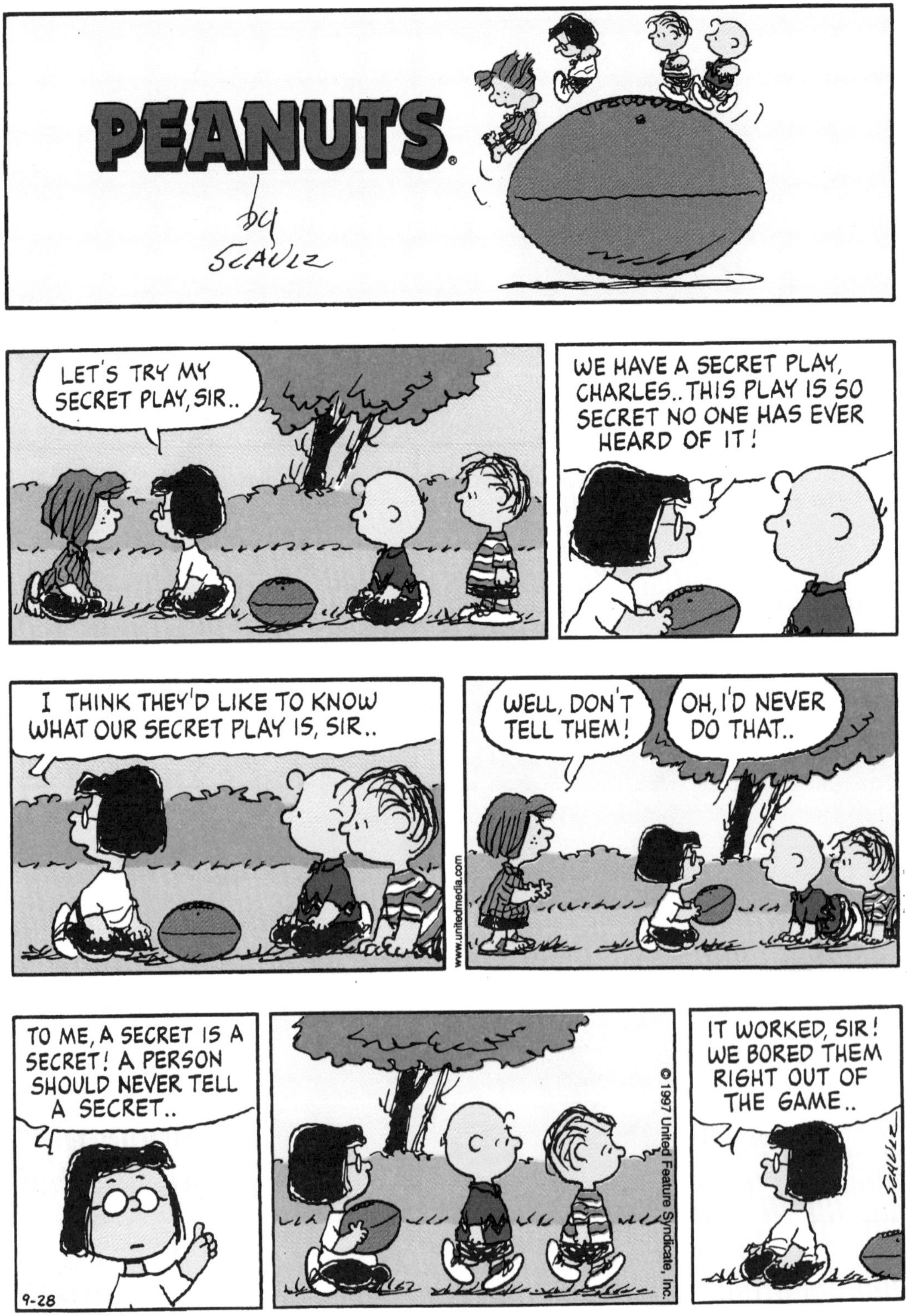
PEANUTS®
by SCHULZ
LET'S TRY MY SECRET PLAY, SIR..
WE HAVE A SECRET PLAY, CHARLES.. THIS PLAY IS SO SECRET NO ONE HAS EVER HEARD OF IT!
I THINK THEY'D LIKE TO KNOW WHAT OUR SECRET PLAY IS, SIR..
www.unitedmedia.com
WELL, DON'T TELL THEM!
OH, I'D NEVER DO THAT..
TO ME, A SECRET IS A SECRET! A PERSON SHOULD NEVER TELL A SECRET..
9-28
© 1997 United Feature Syndicate, Inc.
IT WORKED, SIR! WE BORED THEM RIGHT OUT OF THE GAME..
SCHULZ

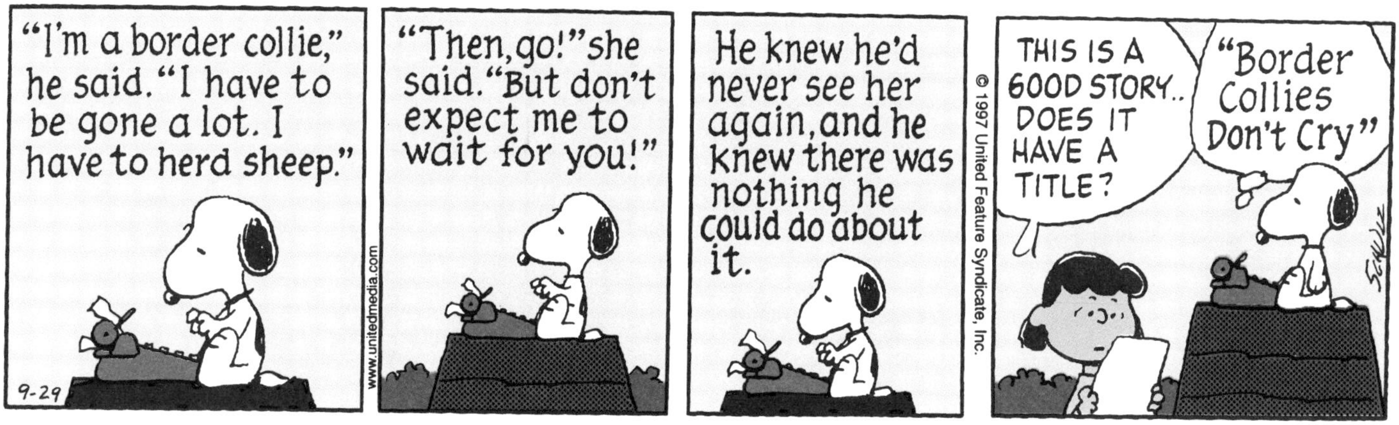
"I'm a border collie," he said. "I have to be gone a lot. I have to herd sheep."
9-29
www.unitedmedia.com
"Then, go!" she said. "But don't expect me to wait for you!"
He knew he'd never see her again, and he knew there was nothing he could do about it.
© 1997 United Feature Syndicate, Inc.
THIS IS A GOOD STORY.. DOES IT HAVE A TITLE?
"Border Collies Don't Cry"
SCHULZ

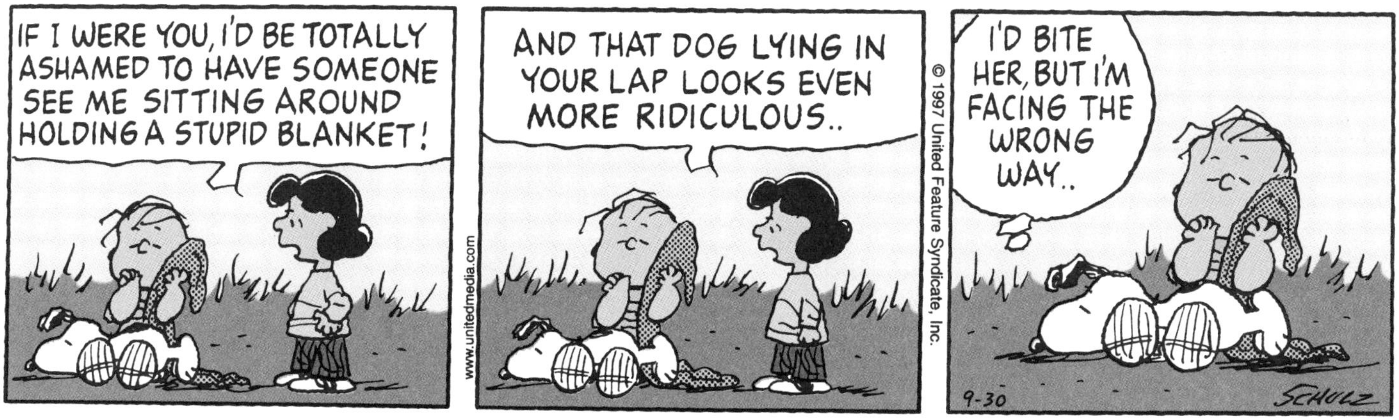
IF I WERE YOU, I'D BE TOTALLY ASHAMED TO HAVE SOMEONE SEE ME SITTING AROUND HOLDING A STUPID BLANKET!
www.unitedmedia.com
AND THAT DOG LYING IN YOUR LAP LOOKS EVEN MORE RIDICULOUS..
© 1997 United Feature Syndicate, Inc.
I'D BITE HER, BUT I'M FACING THE WRONG WAY..
9-30
SCHULZ

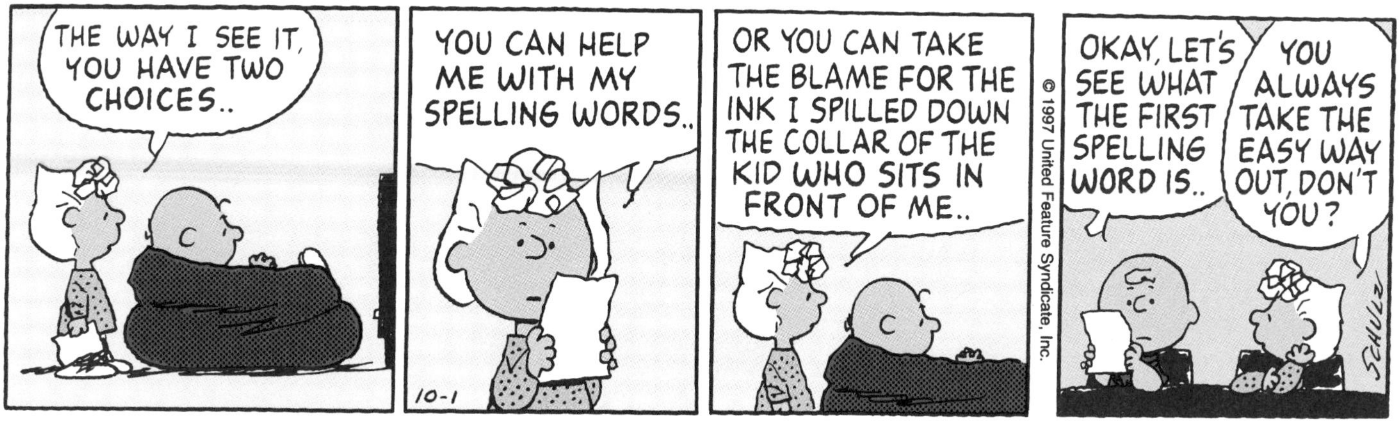
THE WAY I SEE IT, YOU HAVE TWO CHOICES..
YOU CAN HELP ME WITH MY SPELLING WORDS..
10-1
OR YOU CAN TAKE THE BLAME FOR THE INK I SPILLED DOWN THE COLLAR OF THE KID WHO SITS IN FRONT OF ME..
© 1997 United Feature Syndicate, Inc.
OKAY, LET'S SEE WHAT THE FIRST SPELLING WORD IS..
YOU ALWAYS TAKE THE EASY WAY OUT, DON'T YOU?
SCHULZ

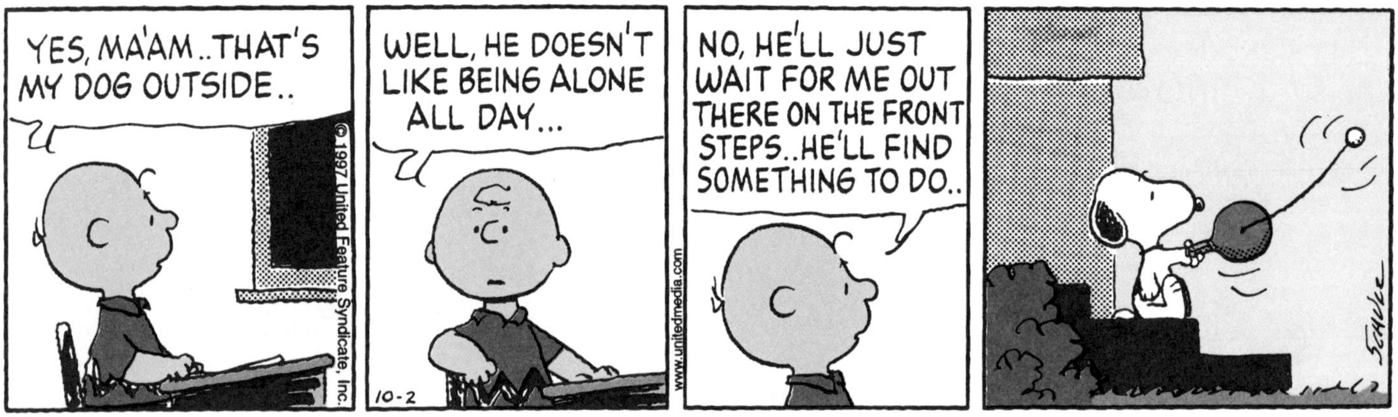
YES, MA'AM..THAT'S MY DOG OUTSIDE..
© 1997 United Feature Syndicate, Inc.
WELL, HE DOESN'T LIKE BEING ALONE ALL DAY...
10-2
www.unitedmedia.com
NO, HE'LL JUST WAIT FOR ME OUT THERE ON THE FRONT STEPS..HE'LL FIND SOMETHING TO DO..
SCHULZ

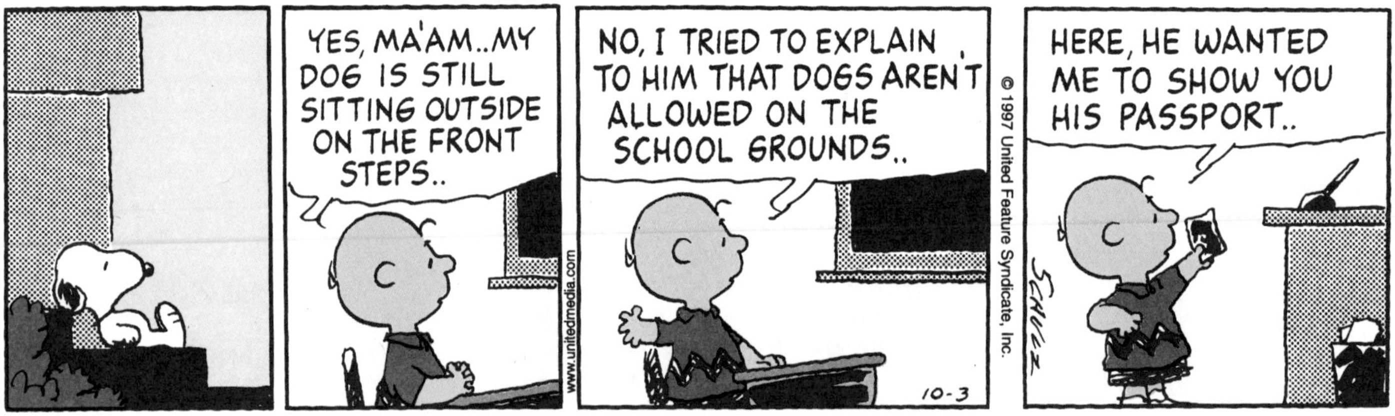
YES, MA'AM..MY DOG IS STILL SITTING OUTSIDE ON THE FRONT STEPS..
www.unitedmedia.com
NO, I TRIED TO EXPLAIN TO HIM THAT DOGS AREN'T ALLOWED ON THE SCHOOL GROUNDS..
10-3
© 1997 United Feature Syndicate, Inc.
SCHULZ
HERE, HE WANTED ME TO SHOW YOU HIS PASSPORT..

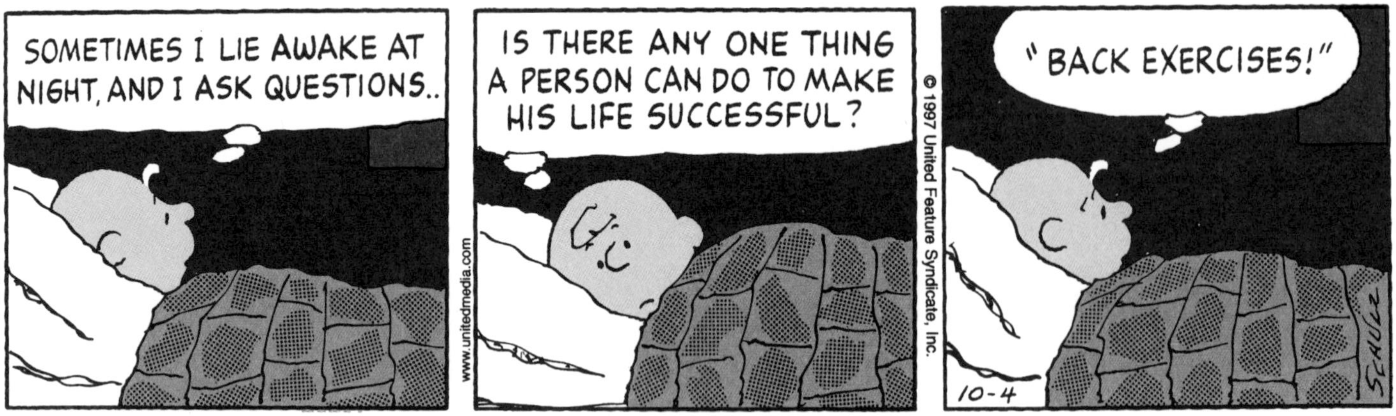
SOMETIMES I LIE AWAKE AT NIGHT, AND I ASK QUESTIONS..
www.unitedmedia.com
IS THERE ANY ONE THING A PERSON CAN DO TO MAKE HIS LIFE SUCCESSFUL?
© 1997 United Feature Syndicate, Inc.
"BACK EXERCISES!"
10-4
SCHULZ

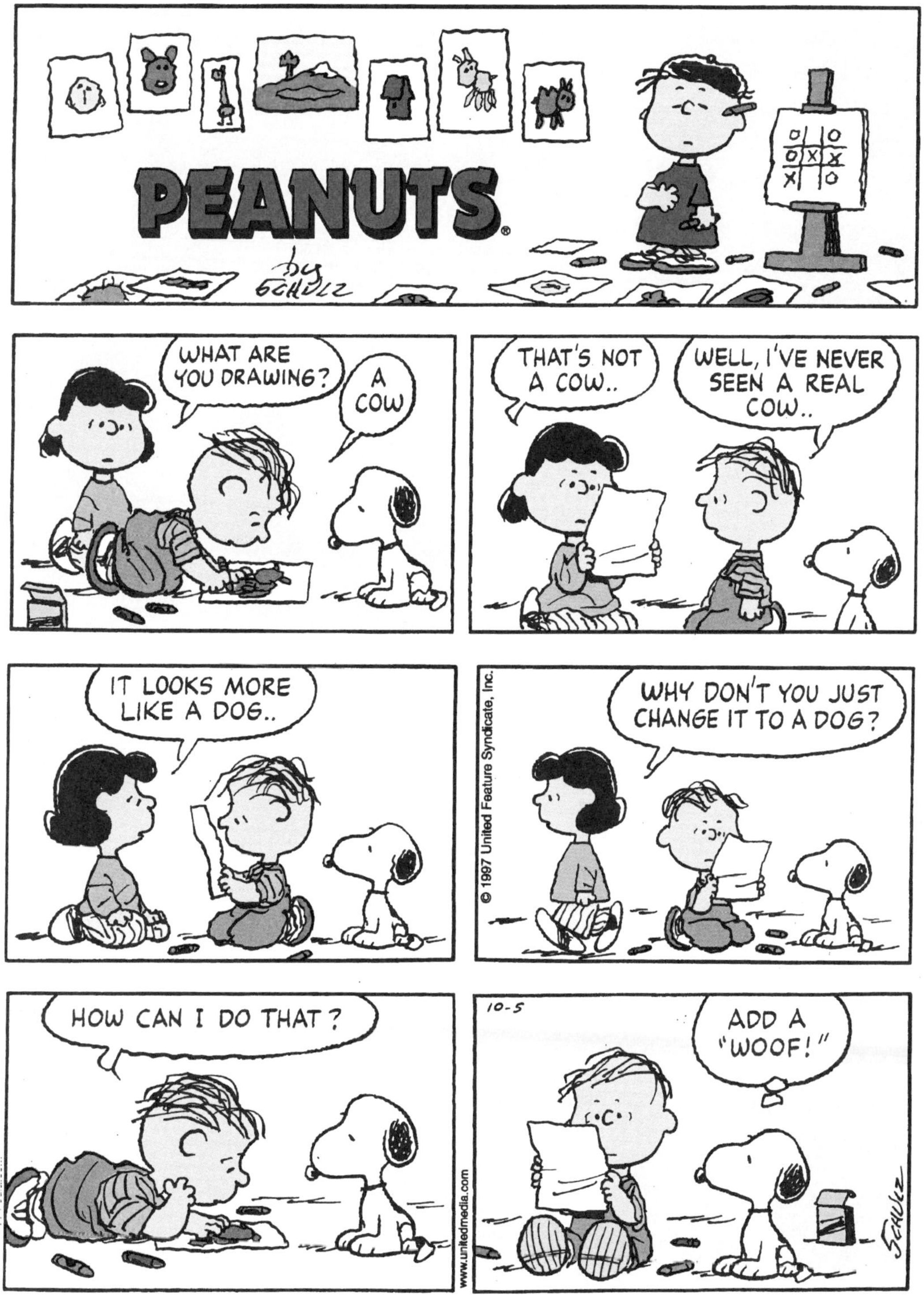
PEANUTS
by SCHULZ
WHAT ARE YOU DRAWING?
A COW
THAT'S NOT A COW..
WELL, I'VE NEVER SEEN A REAL COW..
IT LOOKS MORE LIKE A DOG..
WHY DON'T YOU JUST CHANGE IT TO A DOG?
© 1997 United Feature Syndicate, Inc.
HOW CAN I DO THAT?
www.unitedmedia.com
10-5
ADD A "WOOF!"
SCHULZ

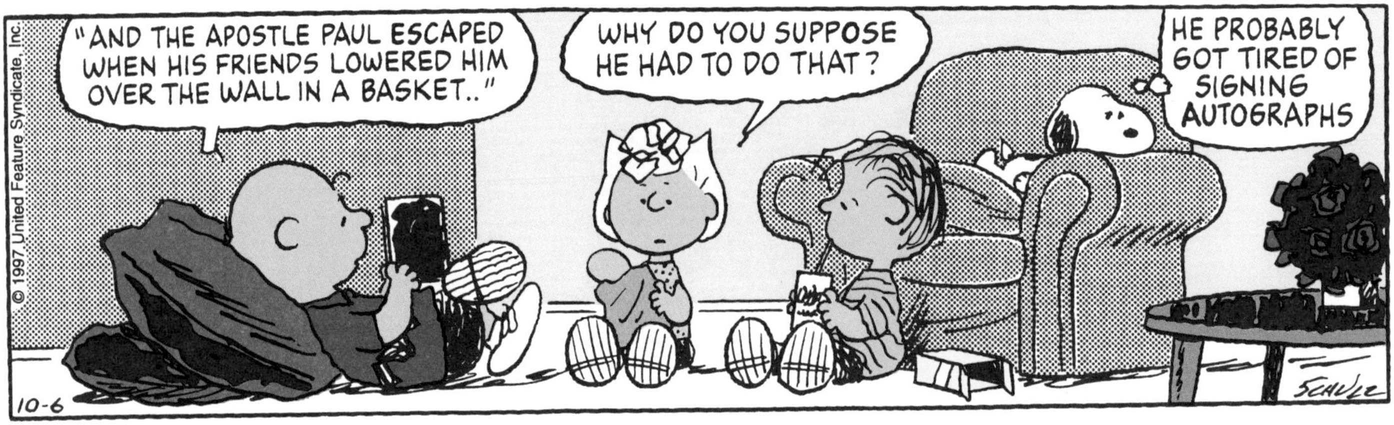
© 1997 United Feature Syndicate, Inc.
"AND THE APOSTLE PAUL ESCAPED WHEN HIS FRIENDS LOWERED HIM OVER THE WALL IN A BASKET.."
WHY DO YOU SUPPOSE HE HAD TO DO THAT?
HE PROBABLY GOT TIRED OF SIGNING AUTOGRAPHS
10-6
SCHULZ

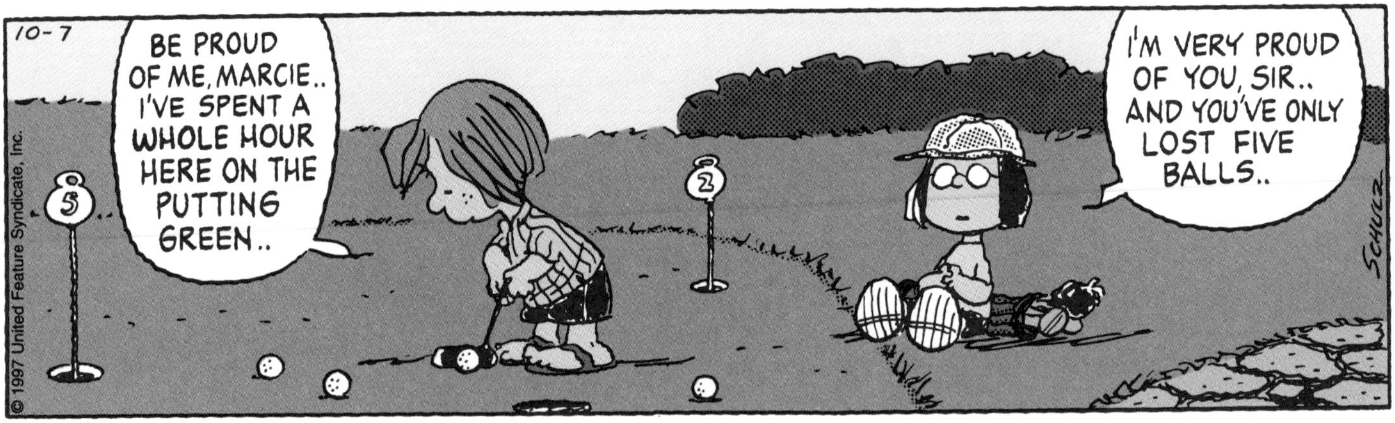
10-7
© 1997 United Feature Syndicate, Inc.
BE PROUD OF ME, MARCIE.. I'VE SPENT A WHOLE HOUR HERE ON THE PUTTING GREEN..
I'M VERY PROUD OF YOU, SIR.. AND YOU'VE ONLY LOST FIVE BALLS..
SCHULZ

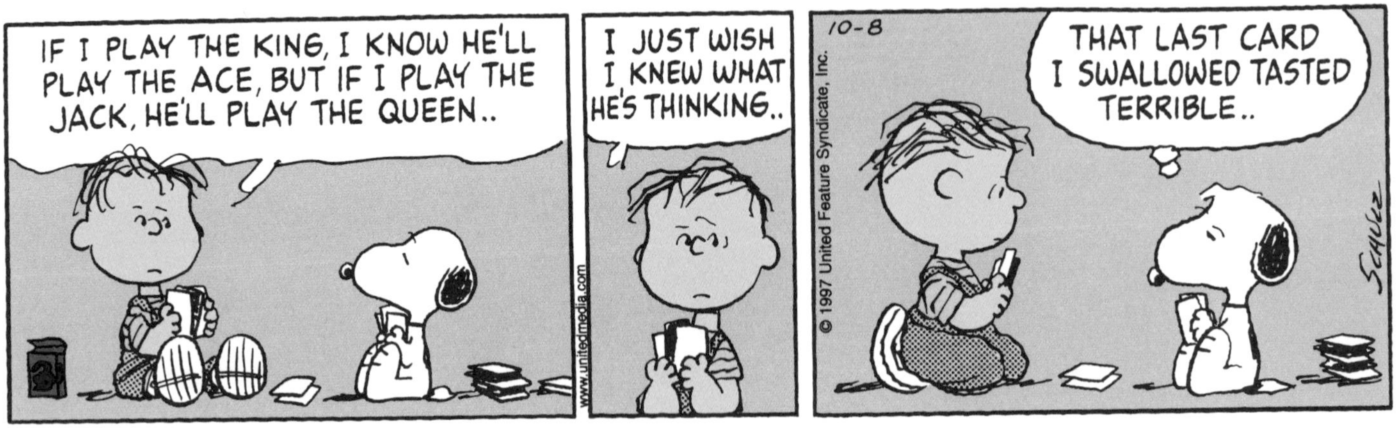
IF I PLAY THE KING, I KNOW HE'LL PLAY THE ACE, BUT IF I PLAY THE JACK, HE'LL PLAY THE QUEEN..
www.unitedmedia.com
I JUST WISH I KNEW WHAT HE'S THINKING..
10-8
© 1997 United Feature Syndicate, Inc.
THAT LAST CARD I SWALLOWED TASTED TERRIBLE..
SCHULZ

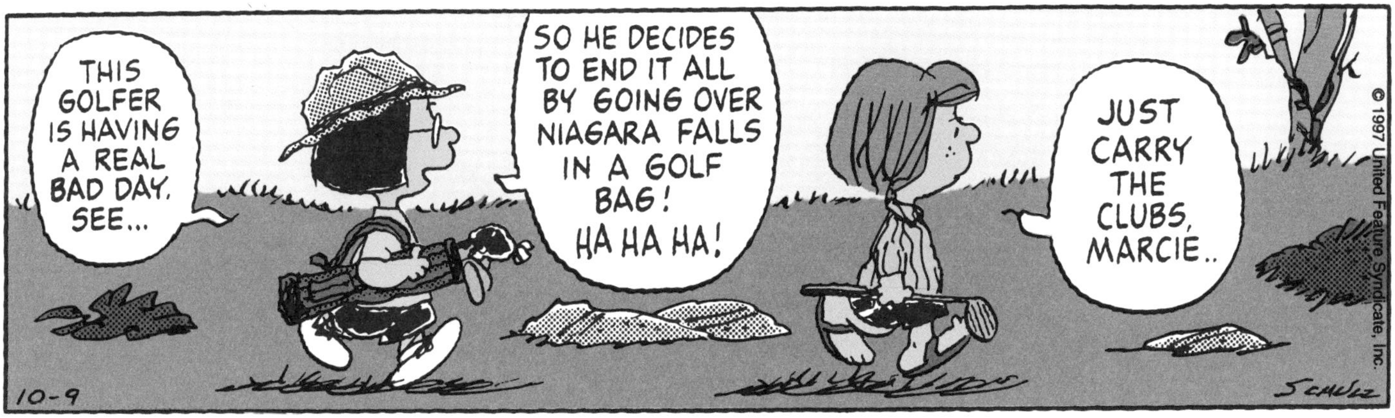
THIS GOLFER IS HAVING A REAL BAD DAY. SEE...
SO HE DECIDES TO END IT ALL BY GOING OVER NIAGARA FALLS IN A GOLF BAG! HA HA HA!
JUST CARRY THE CLUBS, MARCIE..
© 1997 United Feature Syndicate, Inc.
10-9
SCHULZ

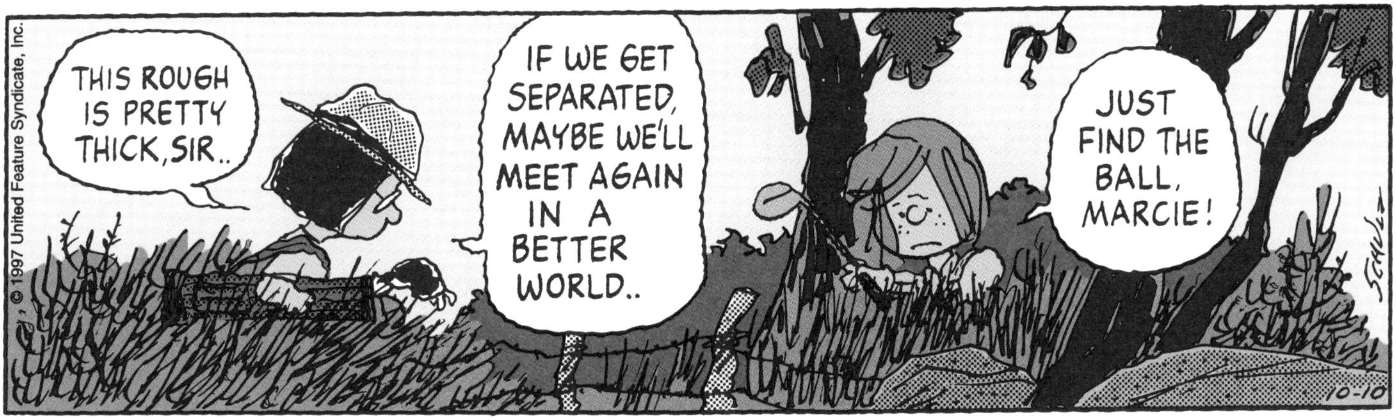
THIS ROUGH IS PRETTY THICK, SIR..
IF WE GET SEPARATED, MAYBE WE'LL MEET AGAIN IN A BETTER WORLD..
JUST FIND THE BALL, MARCIE!
© 1997 United Feature Syndicate, Inc.
SCHULZ
10-10

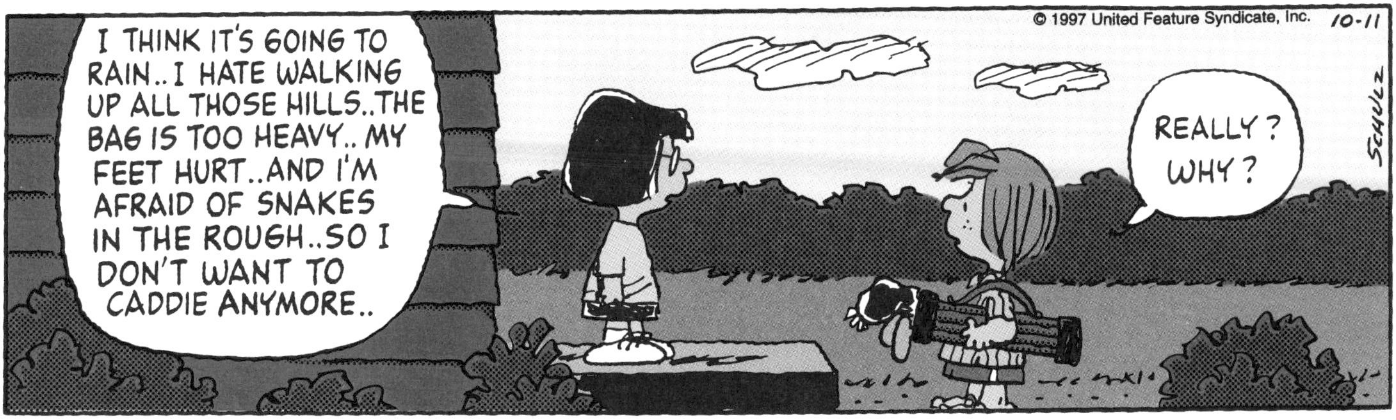
© 1997 United Feature Syndicate, Inc.
10-11
I THINK IT'S GOING TO RAIN.. I HATE WALKING UP ALL THOSE HILLS..THE BAG IS TOO HEAVY.. MY FEET HURT..AND I'M AFRAID OF SNAKES IN THE ROUGH..SO I DON'T WANT TO CADDIE ANYMORE..
REALLY? WHY?
SCHULZ

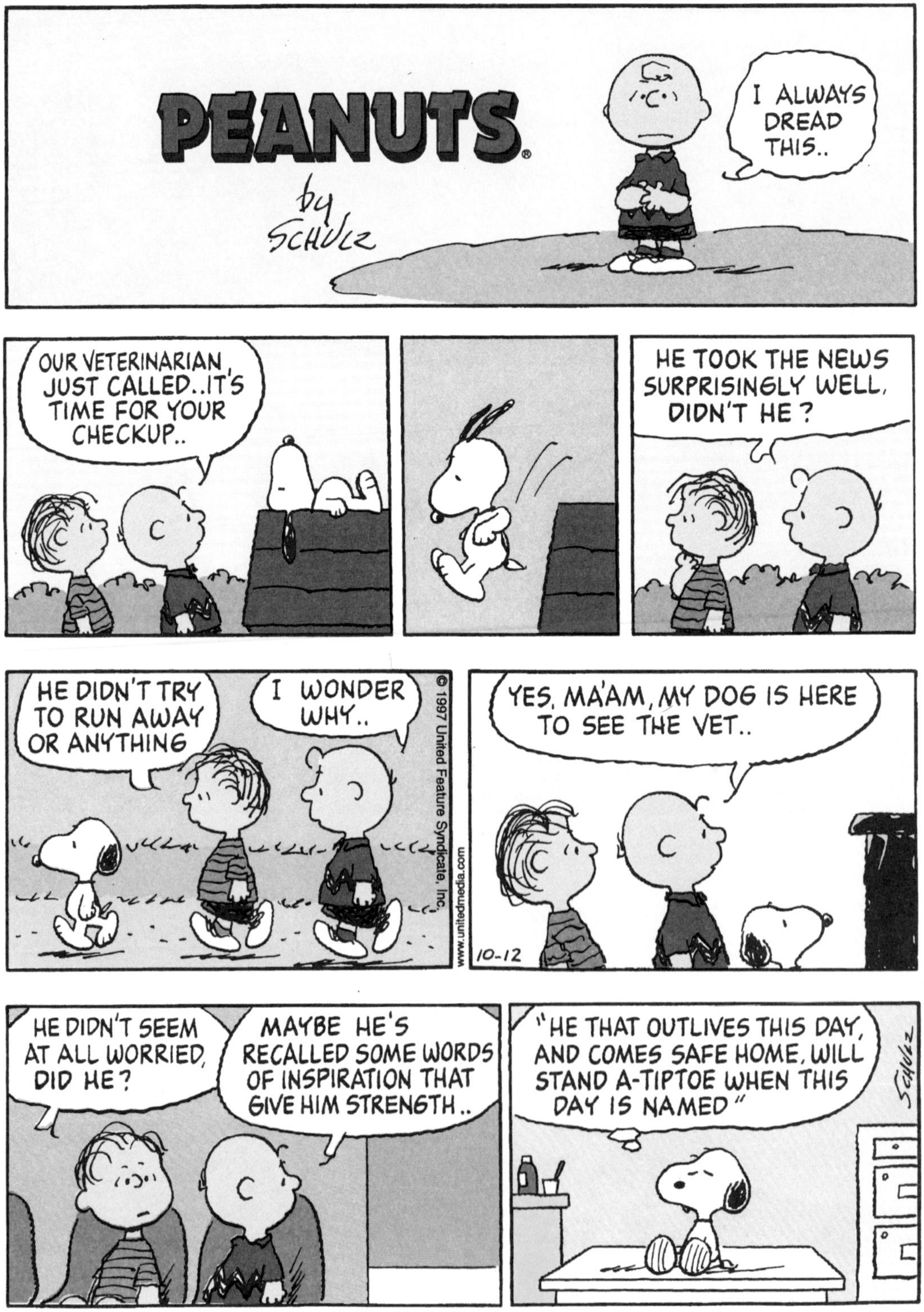
PEANUTS®
by SCHULZ
I ALWAYS DREAD THIS..
OUR VETERINARIAN JUST CALLED..IT'S TIME FOR YOUR CHECKUP..
HE TOOK THE NEWS SURPRISINGLY WELL, DIDN'T HE ?
HE DIDN'T TRY TO RUN AWAY OR ANYTHING
I WONDER WHY..
© 1997 United Feature Syndicate, Inc.
www.unitedmedia.com
YES, MA'AM, MY DOG IS HERE TO SEE THE VET..
10-12
HE DIDN'T SEEM AT ALL WORRIED, DID HE ?
MAYBE HE'S RECALLED SOME WORDS OF INSPIRATION THAT GIVE HIM STRENGTH..
"HE THAT OUTLIVES THIS DAY, AND COMES SAFE HOME, WILL STAND A-TIPTOE WHEN THIS DAY IS NAMED"
SCHULZ

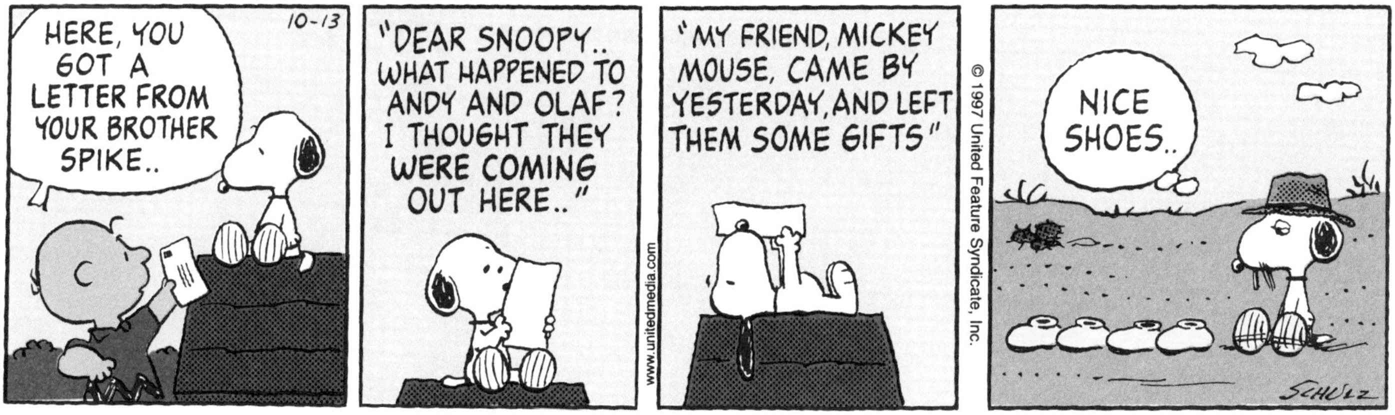
10-13
HERE, YOU GOT A LETTER FROM YOUR BROTHER SPIKE..
"DEAR SNOOPY.. WHAT HAPPENED TO ANDY AND OLAF? I THOUGHT THEY WERE COMING OUT HERE.."
www.unitedmedia.com
"MY FRIEND, MICKEY MOUSE, CAME BY YESTERDAY, AND LEFT THEM SOME GIFTS"
© 1997 United Feature Syndicate, Inc.
NICE SHOES..
SCHULZ

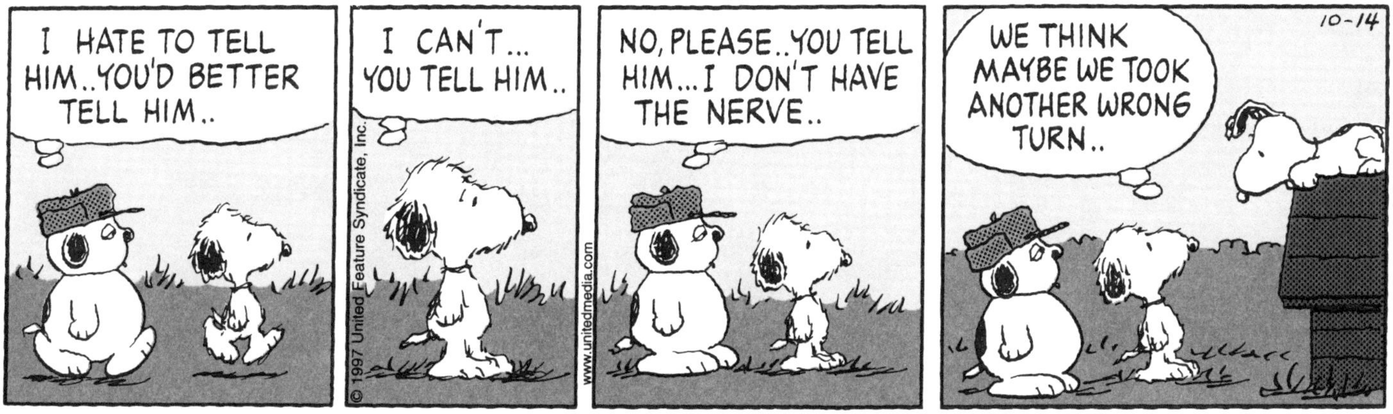
I HATE TO TELL HIM..YOU'D BETTER TELL HIM..
I CAN'T... YOU TELL HIM..
© 1997 United Feature Syndicate, Inc.
NO, PLEASE..YOU TELL HIM...I DON'T HAVE THE NERVE..
www.unitedmedia.com
10-14
WE THINK MAYBE WE TOOK ANOTHER WRONG TURN..

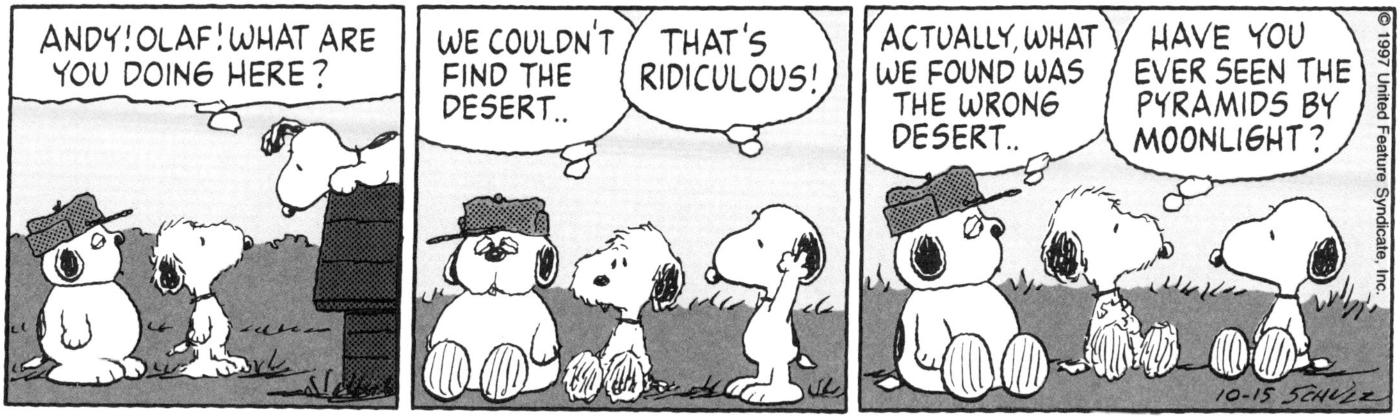
ANDY! OLAF! WHAT ARE YOU DOING HERE?
WE COULDN'T FIND THE DESERT..
THAT'S RIDICULOUS!
ACTUALLY, WHAT WE FOUND WAS THE WRONG DESERT..
HAVE YOU EVER SEEN THE PYRAMIDS BY MOONLIGHT?
© 1997 United Feature Syndicate, Inc.
10-15 SCHULZ

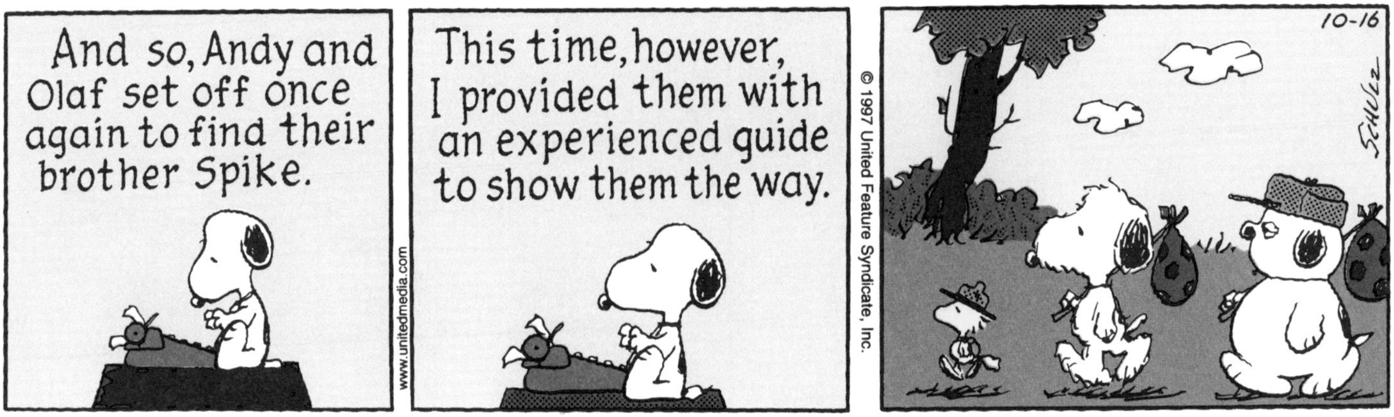
And so, Andy and Olaf set off once again to find their brother Spike.
This time, however, I provided them with an experienced guide to show them the way.
10-16
www.unitedmedia.com
© 1997 United Feature Syndicate, Inc.
SCHULZ

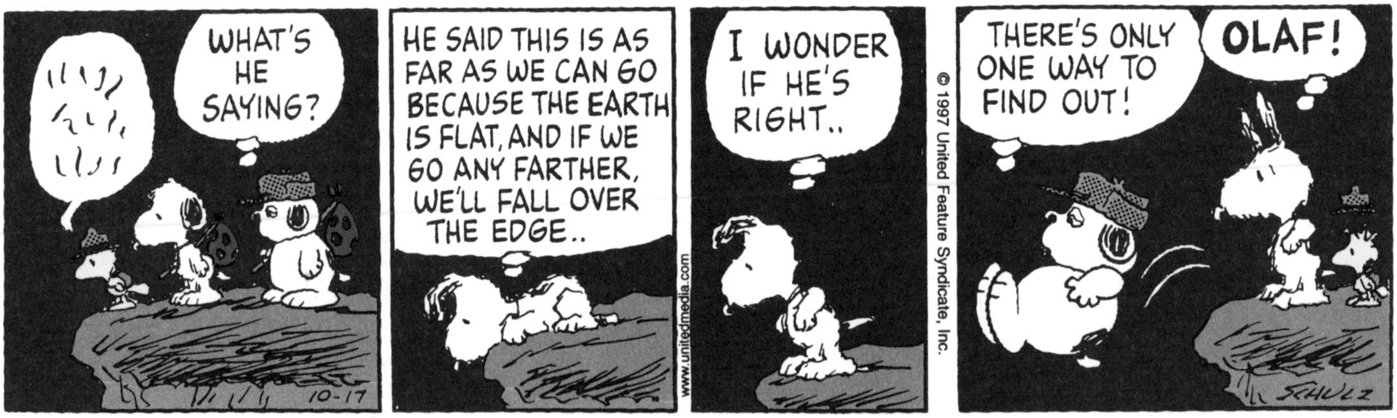
WHAT'S HE SAYING?
10-17
HE SAID THIS IS AS FAR AS WE CAN GO BECAUSE THE EARTH IS FLAT, AND IF WE GO ANY FARTHER, WE'LL FALL OVER THE EDGE..
www.unitedmedia.com
I WONDER IF HE'S RIGHT..
© 1997 United Feature Syndicate, Inc.
THERE'S ONLY ONE WAY TO FIND OUT!
OLAF!
SCHULZ

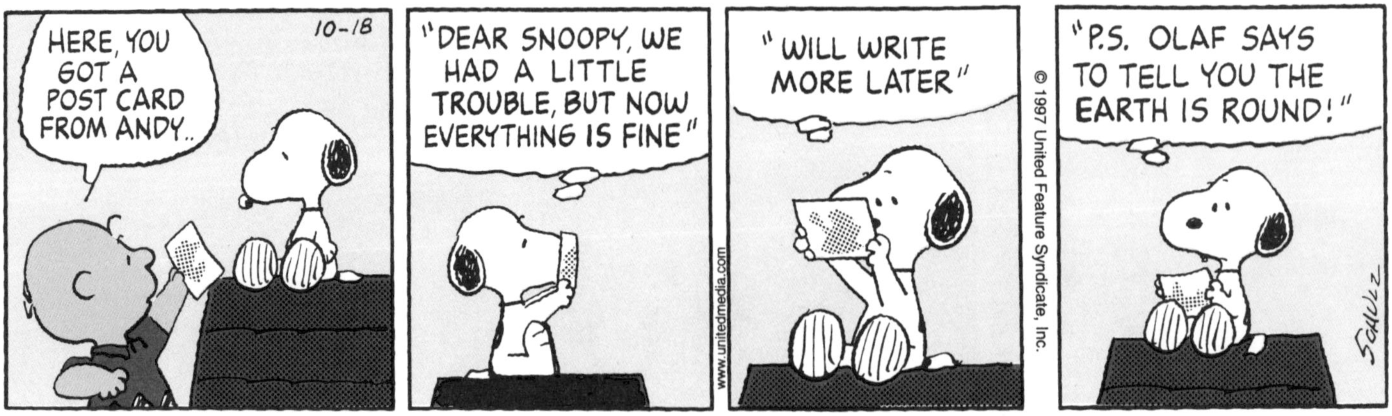
10-18
HERE, YOU GOT A POST CARD FROM ANDY..
"DEAR SNOOPY, WE HAD A LITTLE TROUBLE, BUT NOW EVERYTHING IS FINE"
www.unitedmedia.com
"WILL WRITE MORE LATER"
© 1997 United Feature Syndicate, Inc.
"P.S. OLAF SAYS TO TELL YOU THE EARTH IS ROUND!"
SCHULZ

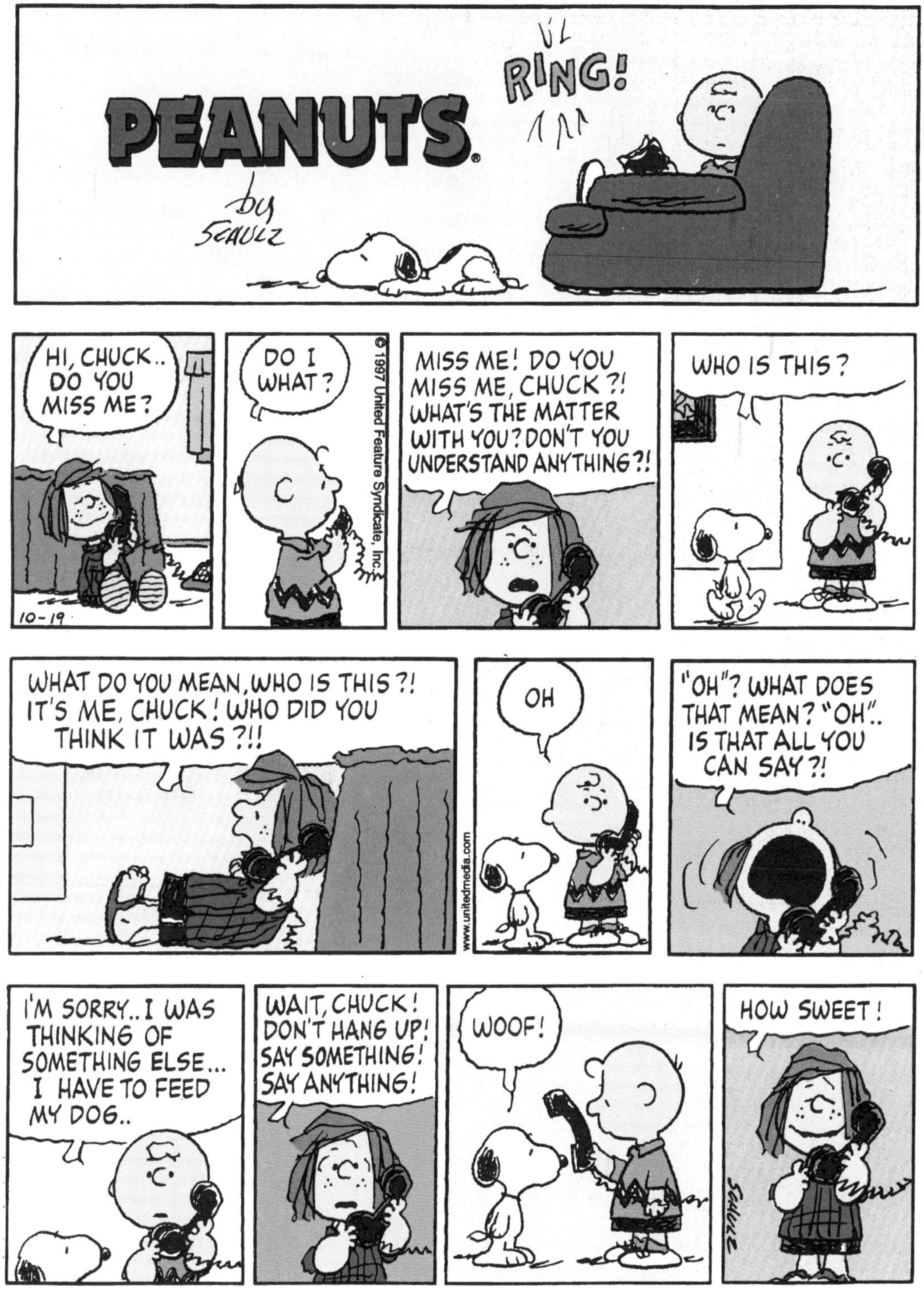
PEANUTS
by SCHULZ
RING!
HI, CHUCK.. DO YOU MISS ME?
DO I WHAT?
© 1997 United Feature Syndicate, Inc.
MISS ME! DO YOU MISS ME, CHUCK?! WHAT'S THE MATTER WITH YOU? DON'T YOU UNDERSTAND ANYTHING?!
WHO IS THIS?
WHAT DO YOU MEAN, WHO IS THIS?! IT'S ME, CHUCK! WHO DID YOU THINK IT WAS?!!
OH
www.unitedmedia.com
"OH"? WHAT DOES THAT MEAN? "OH".. IS THAT ALL YOU CAN SAY?!
I'M SORRY.. I WAS THINKING OF SOMETHING ELSE... I HAVE TO FEED MY DOG..
WAIT, CHUCK! DON'T HANG UP! SAY SOMETHING! SAY ANYTHING!
WOOF!
HOW SWEET!
SCHULZ

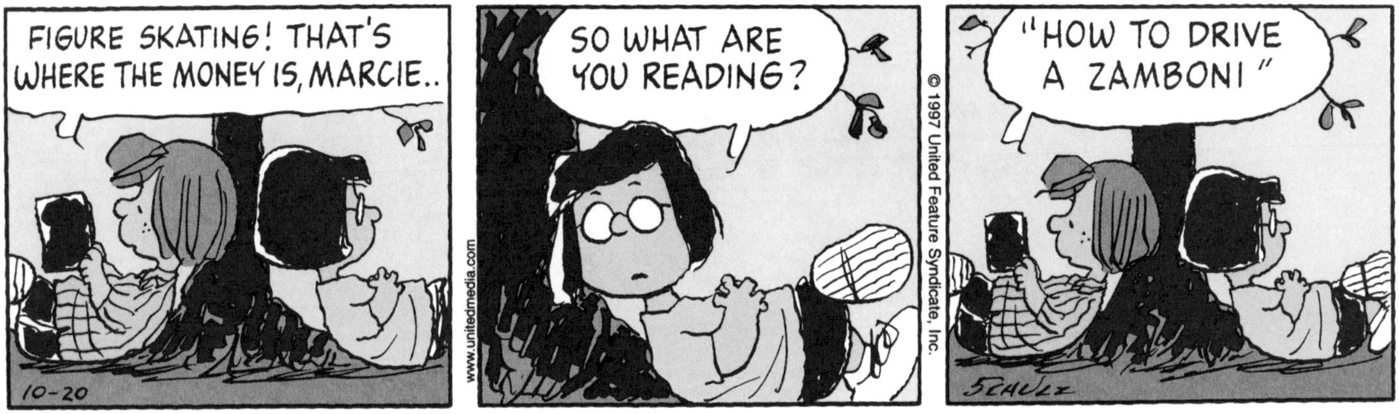
FIGURE SKATING! THAT'S WHERE THE MONEY IS, MARCIE..
SO WHAT ARE YOU READING?
"HOW TO DRIVE A ZAMBONI"
10-20
www.unitedmedia.com
© 1997 United Feature Syndicate, Inc.
SCHULZ

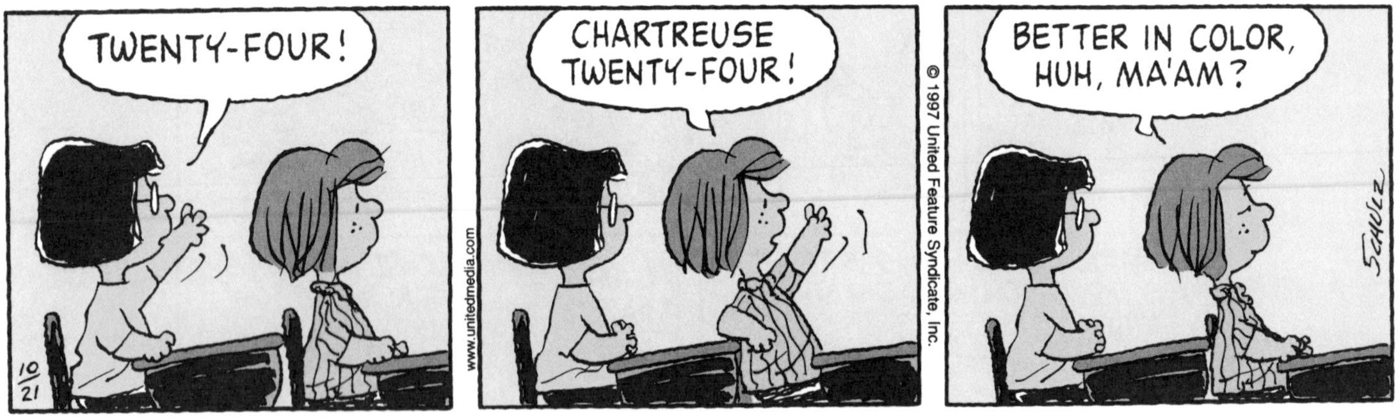
TWENTY-FOUR!
CHARTREUSE TWENTY-FOUR!
BETTER IN COLOR, HUH, MA'AM?
10/21
www.unitedmedia.com
© 1997 United Feature Syndicate, Inc.
SCHULZ

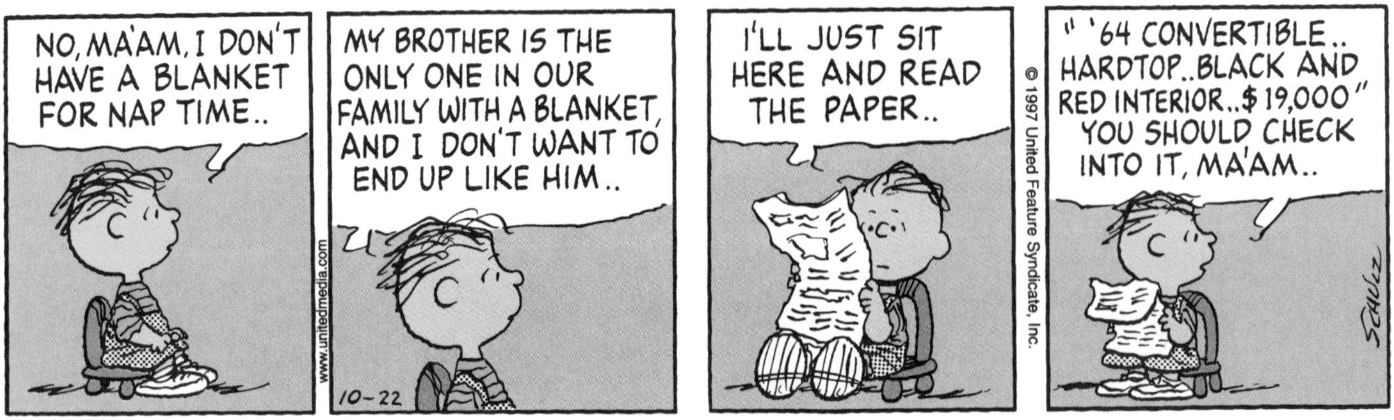
NO, MA'AM, I DON'T HAVE A BLANKET FOR NAP TIME..
MY BROTHER IS THE ONLY ONE IN OUR FAMILY WITH A BLANKET, AND I DON'T WANT TO END UP LIKE HIM..
I'LL JUST SIT HERE AND READ THE PAPER..
"'64 CONVERTIBLE.. HARDTOP..BLACK AND RED INTERIOR..$19,000" YOU SHOULD CHECK INTO IT, MA'AM..
10-22
www.unitedmedia.com
© 1997 United Feature Syndicate, Inc.
SCHULZ

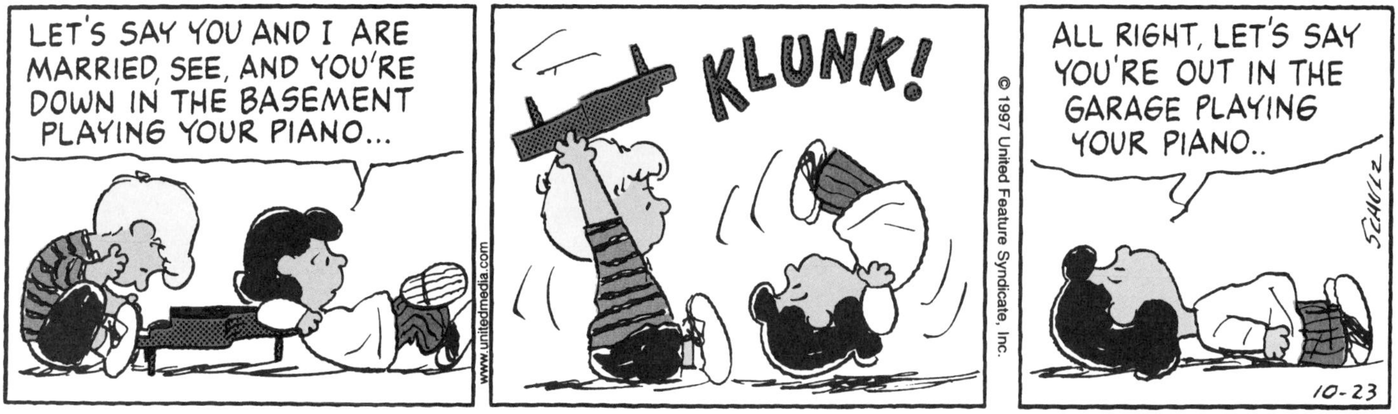
LET'S SAY YOU AND I ARE MARRIED, SEE, AND YOU'RE DOWN IN THE BASEMENT PLAYING YOUR PIANO...
www.unitedmedia.com
KLUNK!
© 1997 United Feature Syndicate, Inc.
ALL RIGHT, LET'S SAY YOU'RE OUT IN THE GARAGE PLAYING YOUR PIANO..
SCHULZ
10-23

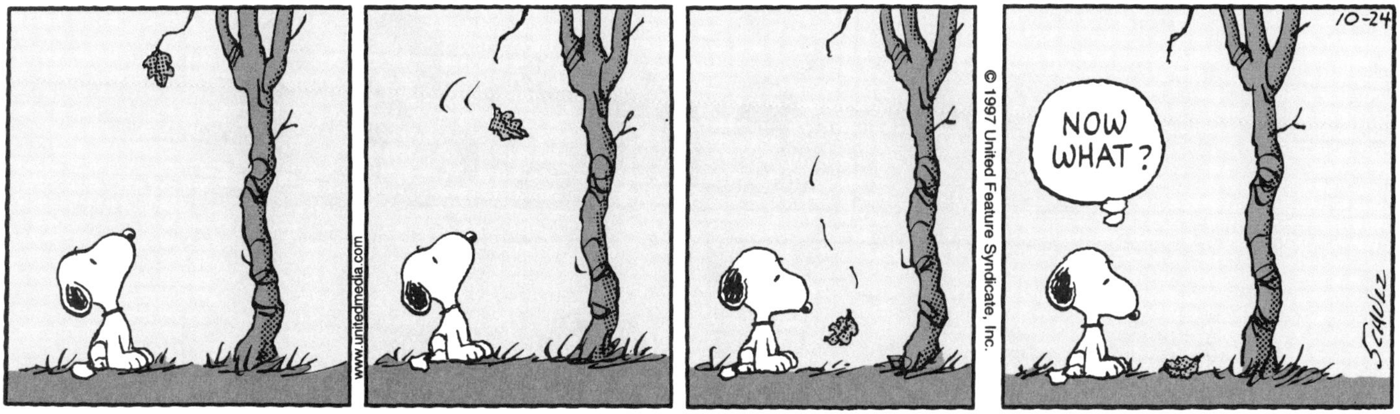
www.unitedmedia.com
© 1997 United Feature Syndicate, Inc.
10-24
NOW WHAT?
SCHULZ

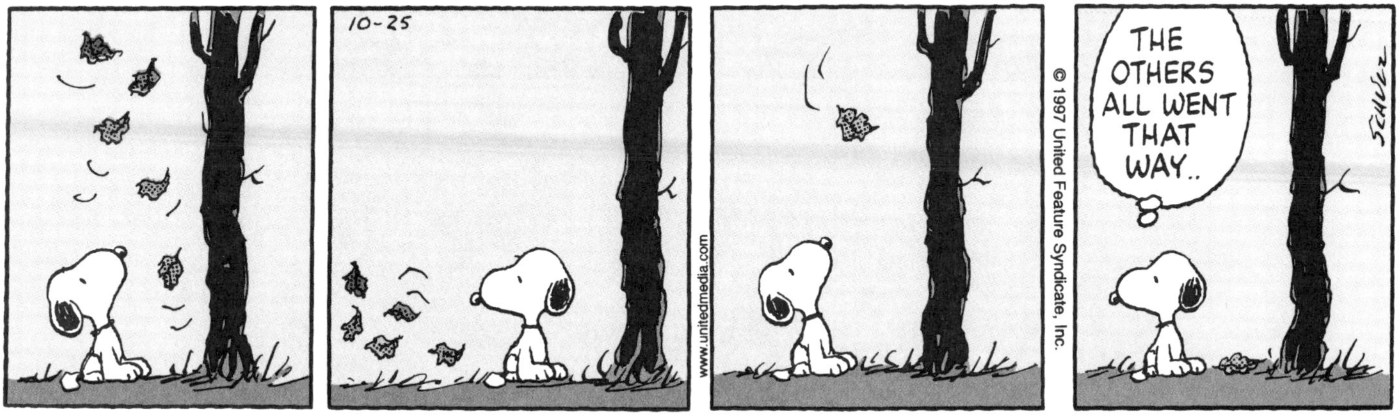
10-25
www.unitedmedia.com
© 1997 United Feature Syndicate, Inc.
THE OTHERS ALL WENT THAT WAY..
SCHULZ

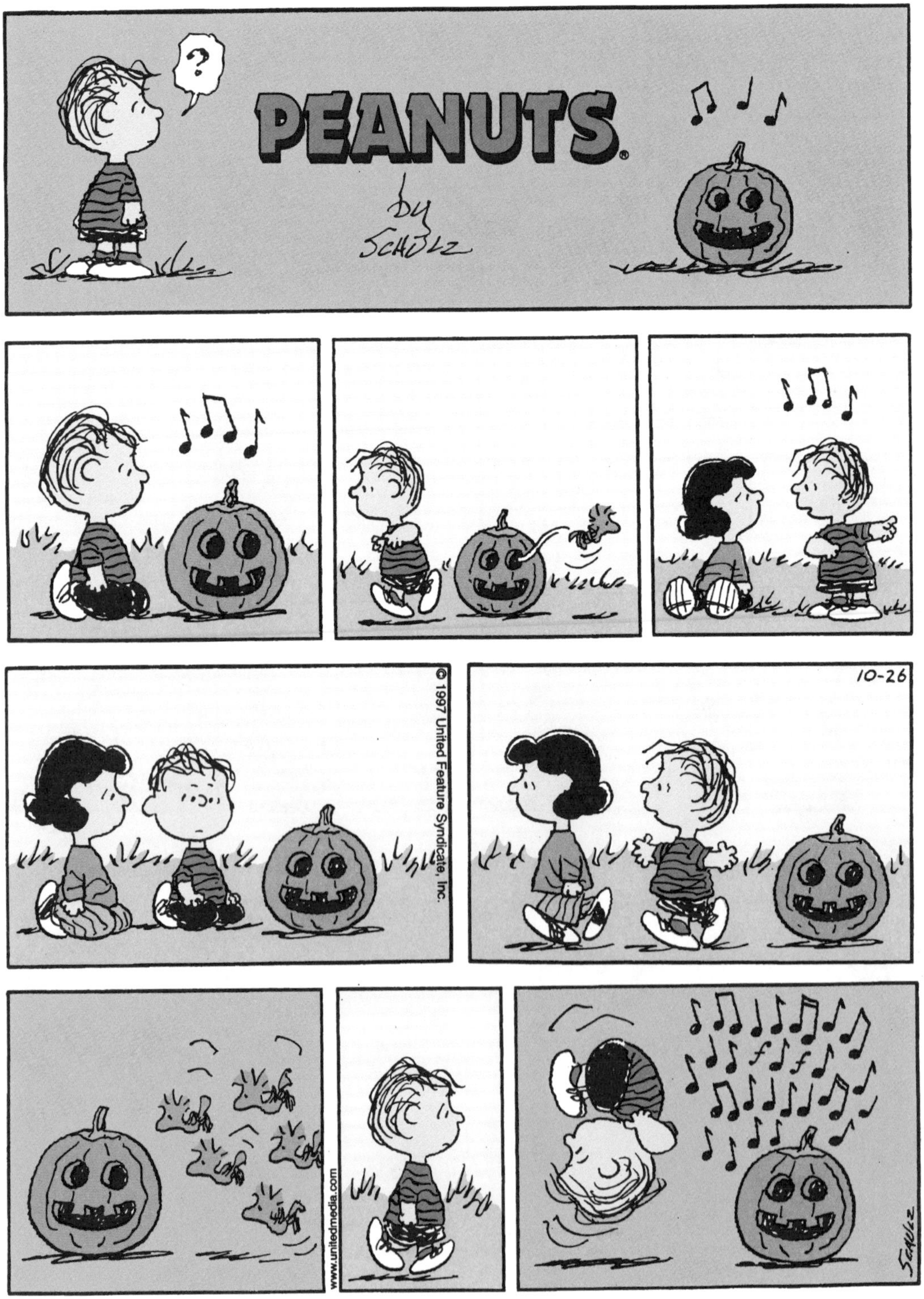
?
PEANUTS
by SCHULZ
10-26
© 1997 United Feature Syndicate, Inc.
www.unitedmedia.com
SCHULZ

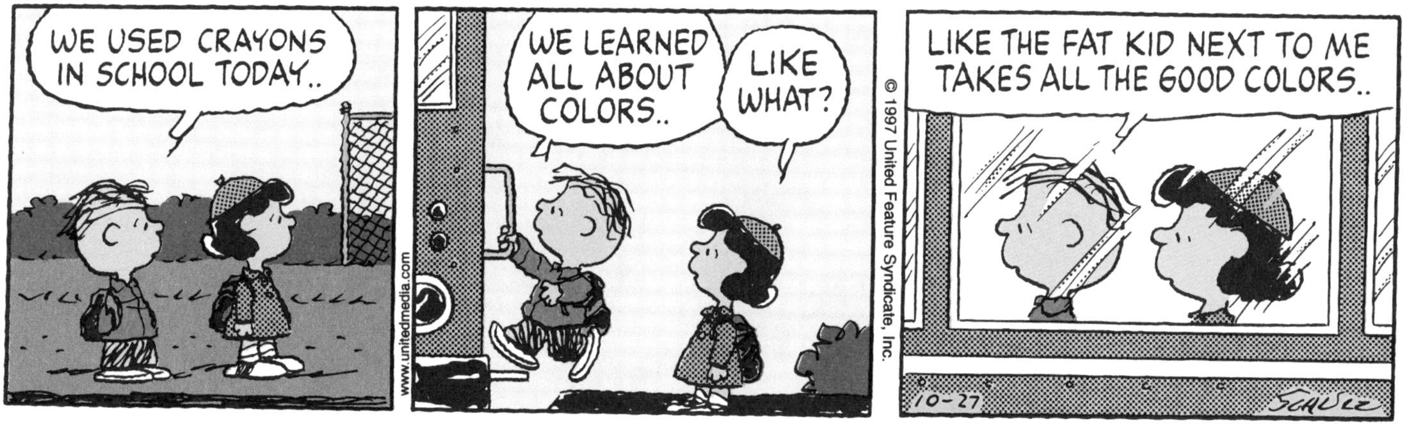
WE USED CRAYONS IN SCHOOL TODAY..
WE LEARNED ALL ABOUT COLORS..
LIKE WHAT?
LIKE THE FAT KID NEXT TO ME TAKES ALL THE GOOD COLORS..
www.unitedmedia.com
© 1997 United Feature Syndicate, Inc.
10-27
SCHULZ

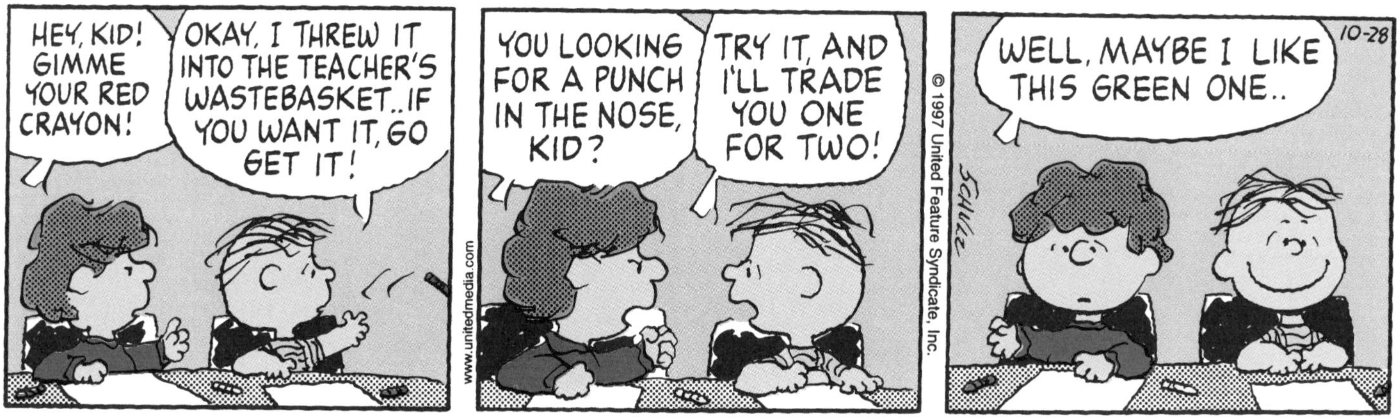
HEY, KID! GIMME YOUR RED CRAYON!
OKAY, I THREW IT INTO THE TEACHER'S WASTEBASKET..IF YOU WANT IT, GO GET IT!
YOU LOOKING FOR A PUNCH IN THE NOSE, KID?
TRY IT, AND I'LL TRADE YOU ONE FOR TWO!
WELL, MAYBE I LIKE THIS GREEN ONE..
www.unitedmedia.com
© 1997 United Feature Syndicate, Inc.
SCHULZ
10-28

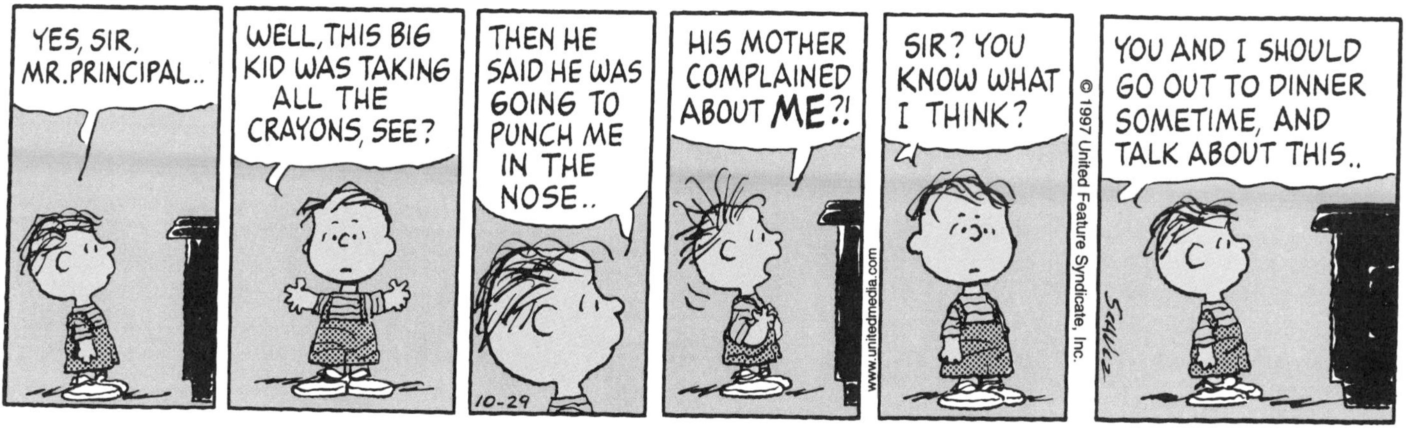
YES, SIR, MR. PRINCIPAL..
WELL, THIS BIG KID WAS TAKING ALL THE CRAYONS, SEE?
THEN HE SAID HE WAS GOING TO PUNCH ME IN THE NOSE..
10-29
HIS MOTHER COMPLAINED ABOUT ME?!
www.unitedmedia.com
SIR? YOU KNOW WHAT I THINK?
© 1997 United Feature Syndicate, Inc.
YOU AND I SHOULD GO OUT TO DINNER SOMETIME, AND TALK ABOUT THIS..
SCHULZ

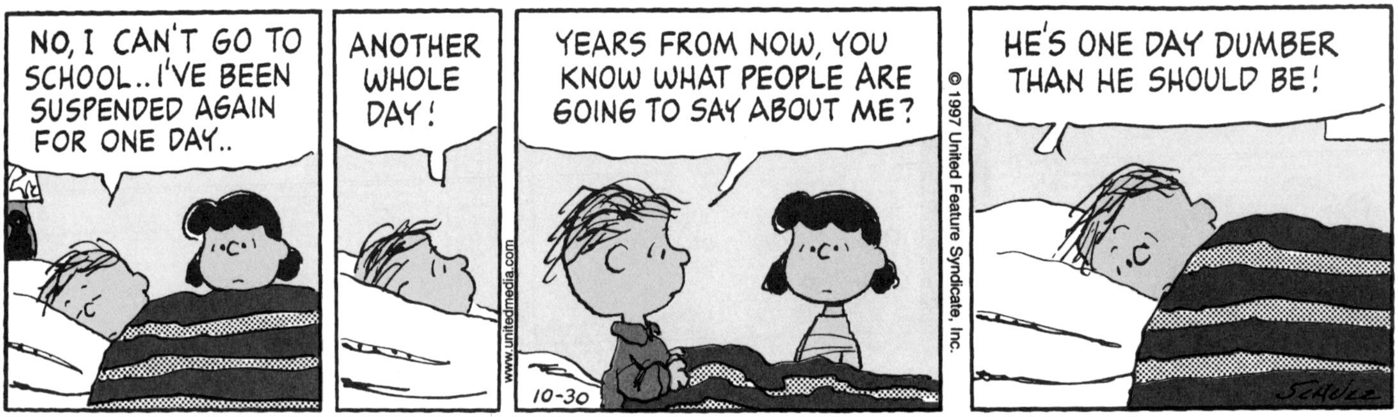
NO, I CAN'T GO TO SCHOOL.. I'VE BEEN SUSPENDED AGAIN FOR ONE DAY..
ANOTHER WHOLE DAY!
YEARS FROM NOW, YOU KNOW WHAT PEOPLE ARE GOING TO SAY ABOUT ME?
HE'S ONE DAY DUMBER THAN HE SHOULD BE!
10-30
www.unitedmedia.com
© 1997 United Feature Syndicate, Inc.
SCHULZ

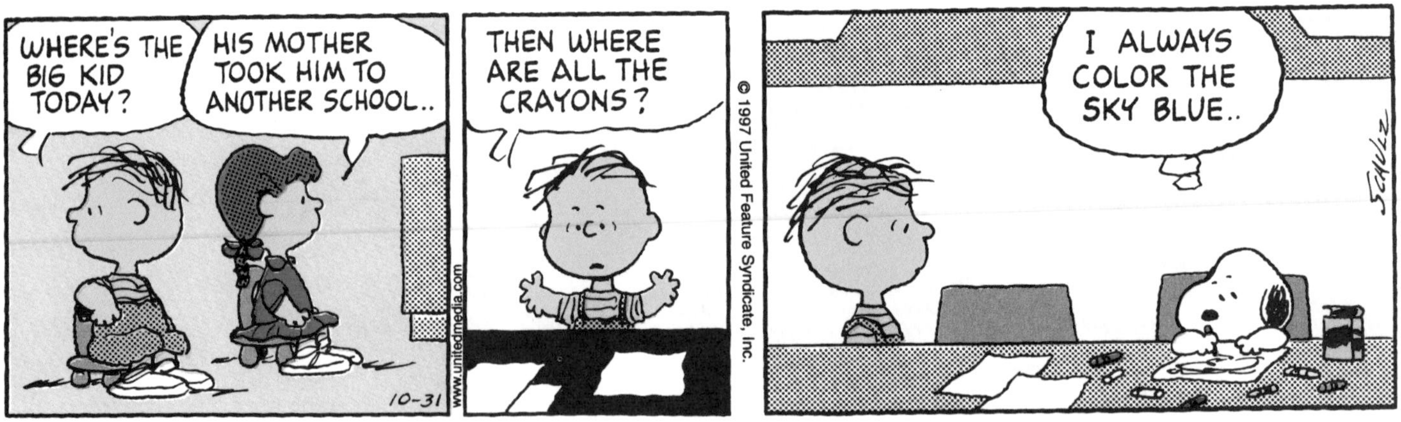
WHERE'S THE BIG KID TODAY?
HIS MOTHER TOOK HIM TO ANOTHER SCHOOL..
THEN WHERE ARE ALL THE CRAYONS?
I ALWAYS COLOR THE SKY BLUE..
10-31
www.unitedmedia.com
© 1997 United Feature Syndicate, Inc.
SCHULZ

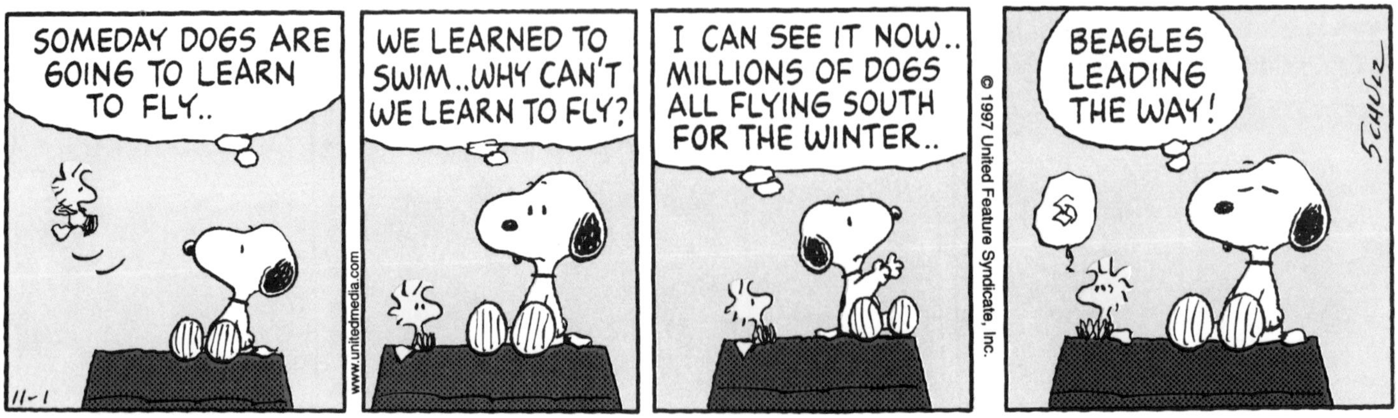
SOMEDAY DOGS ARE GOING TO LEARN TO FLY..
WE LEARNED TO SWIM.. WHY CAN'T WE LEARN TO FLY?
I CAN SEE IT NOW.. MILLIONS OF DOGS ALL FLYING SOUTH FOR THE WINTER..
BEAGLES LEADING THE WAY!
11-1
www.unitedmedia.com
© 1997 United Feature Syndicate, Inc.
SCHULZ

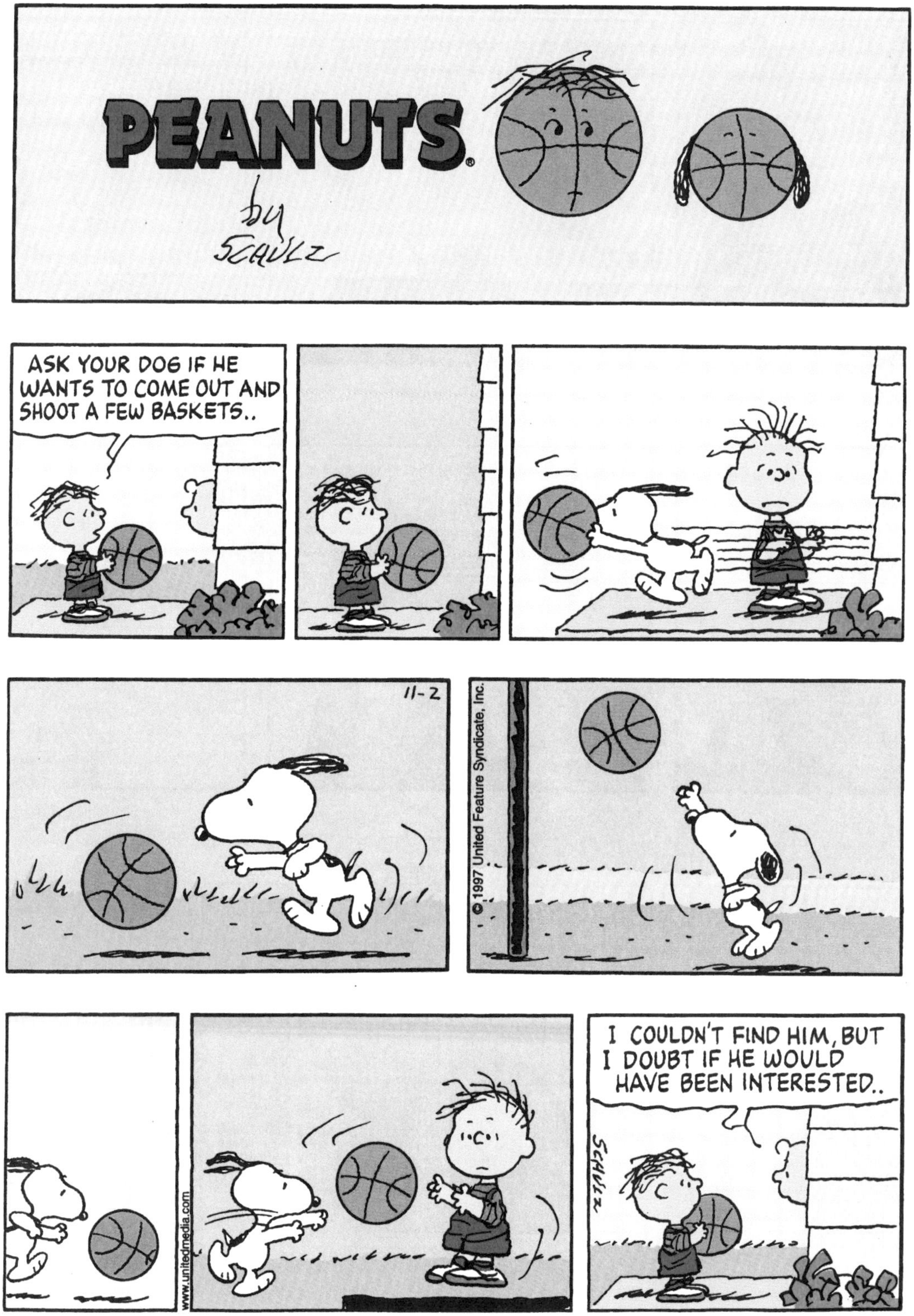
PEANUTS
by SCHULZ
ASK YOUR DOG IF HE WANTS TO COME OUT AND SHOOT A FEW BASKETS..
11-2
© 1997 United Feature Syndicate, Inc.
www.unitedmedia.com
I COULDN'T FIND HIM, BUT I DOUBT IF HE WOULD HAVE BEEN INTERESTED..
SCHULZ

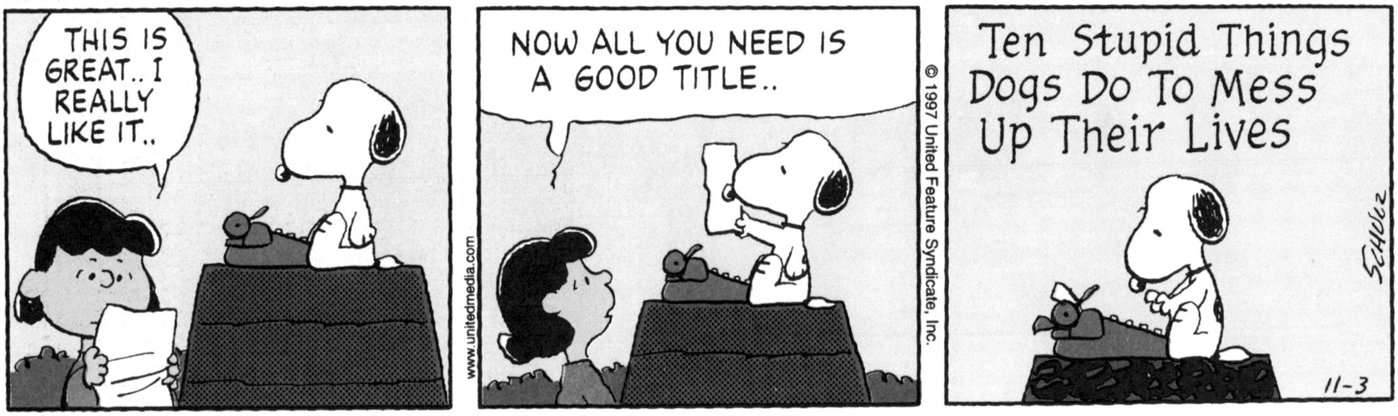
THIS IS GREAT.. I REALLY LIKE IT..
NOW ALL YOU NEED IS A GOOD TITLE..
Ten Stupid Things Dogs Do To Mess Up Their Lives
© 1997 United Feature Syndicate, Inc.
www.unitedmedia.com
11-3

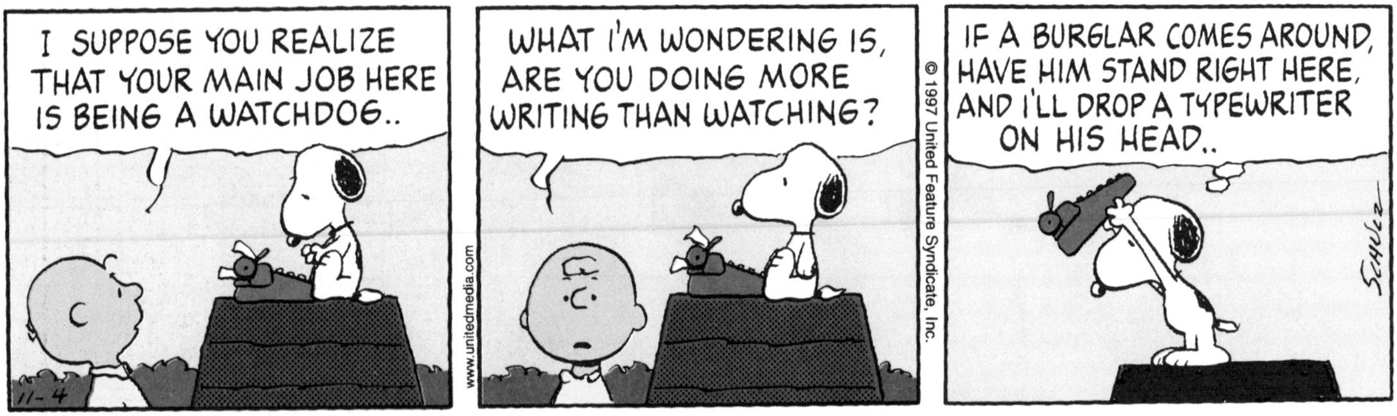
I SUPPOSE YOU REALIZE THAT YOUR MAIN JOB HERE IS BEING A WATCHDOG..
WHAT I'M WONDERING IS, ARE YOU DOING MORE WRITING THAN WATCHING?
IF A BURGLAR COMES AROUND, HAVE HIM STAND RIGHT HERE, AND I'LL DROP A TYPEWRITER ON HIS HEAD..
© 1997 United Feature Syndicate, Inc.
www.unitedmedia.com
11-4

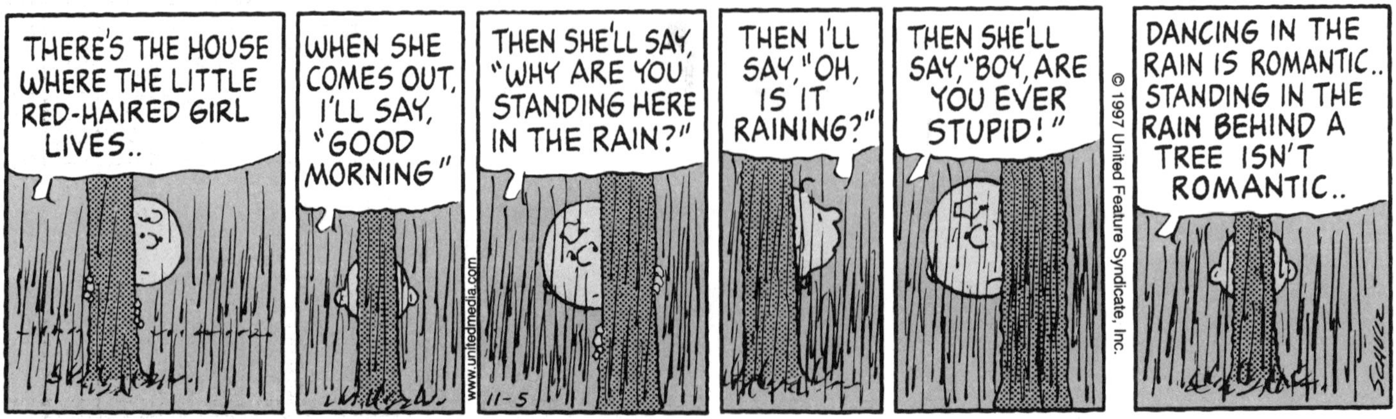
THERE'S THE HOUSE WHERE THE LITTLE RED-HAIRED GIRL LIVES..
WHEN SHE COMES OUT, I'LL SAY, "GOOD MORNING"
THEN SHE'LL SAY, "WHY ARE YOU STANDING HERE IN THE RAIN?"
THEN I'LL SAY, "OH, IS IT RAINING?"
THEN SHE'LL SAY, "BOY, ARE YOU EVER STUPID!"
DANCING IN THE RAIN IS ROMANTIC.. STANDING IN THE RAIN BEHIND A TREE ISN'T ROMANTIC..
© 1997 United Feature Syndicate, Inc.
www.unitedmedia.com
11-5

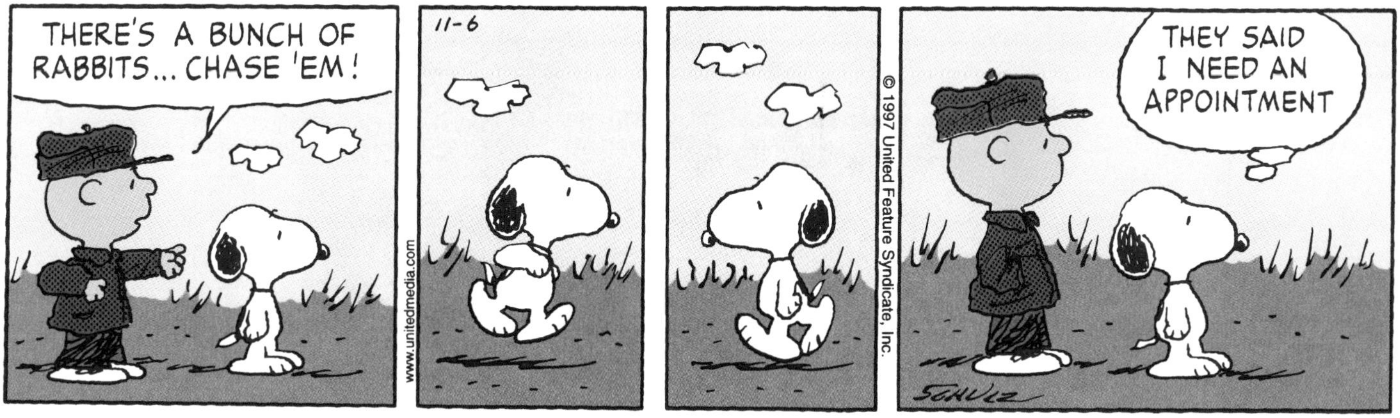
THERE'S A BUNCH OF RABBITS... CHASE 'EM!
www.unitedmedia.com
11-6
© 1997 United Feature Syndicate, Inc.
THEY SAID I NEED AN APPOINTMENT
SCHULZ

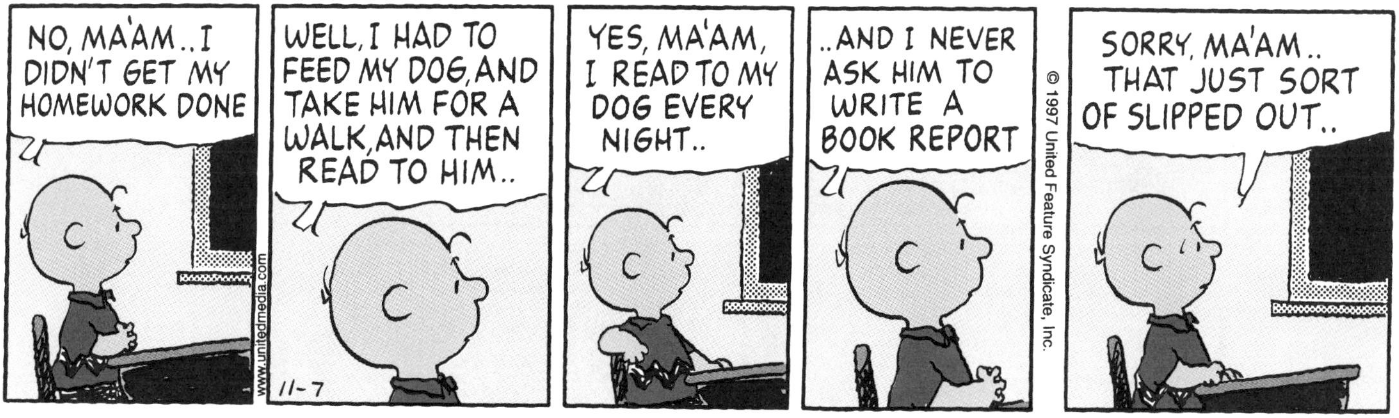
NO, MA'AM.. I DIDN'T GET MY HOMEWORK DONE
www.unitedmedia.com
WELL, I HAD TO FEED MY DOG, AND TAKE HIM FOR A WALK, AND THEN READ TO HIM..
11-7
YES, MA'AM, I READ TO MY DOG EVERY NIGHT..
..AND I NEVER ASK HIM TO WRITE A BOOK REPORT
© 1997 United Feature Syndicate, Inc.
SORRY, MA'AM.. THAT JUST SORT OF SLIPPED OUT..

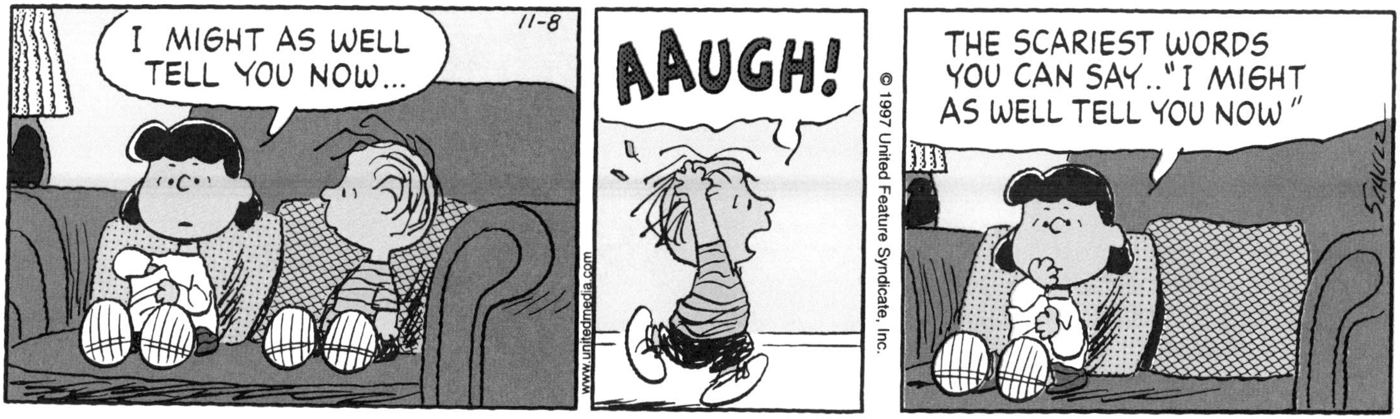
I MIGHT AS WELL TELL YOU NOW...
11-8
www.unitedmedia.com
AAUGH!
© 1997 United Feature Syndicate, Inc.
THE SCARIEST WORDS YOU CAN SAY.."I MIGHT AS WELL TELL YOU NOW"
SCHULZ

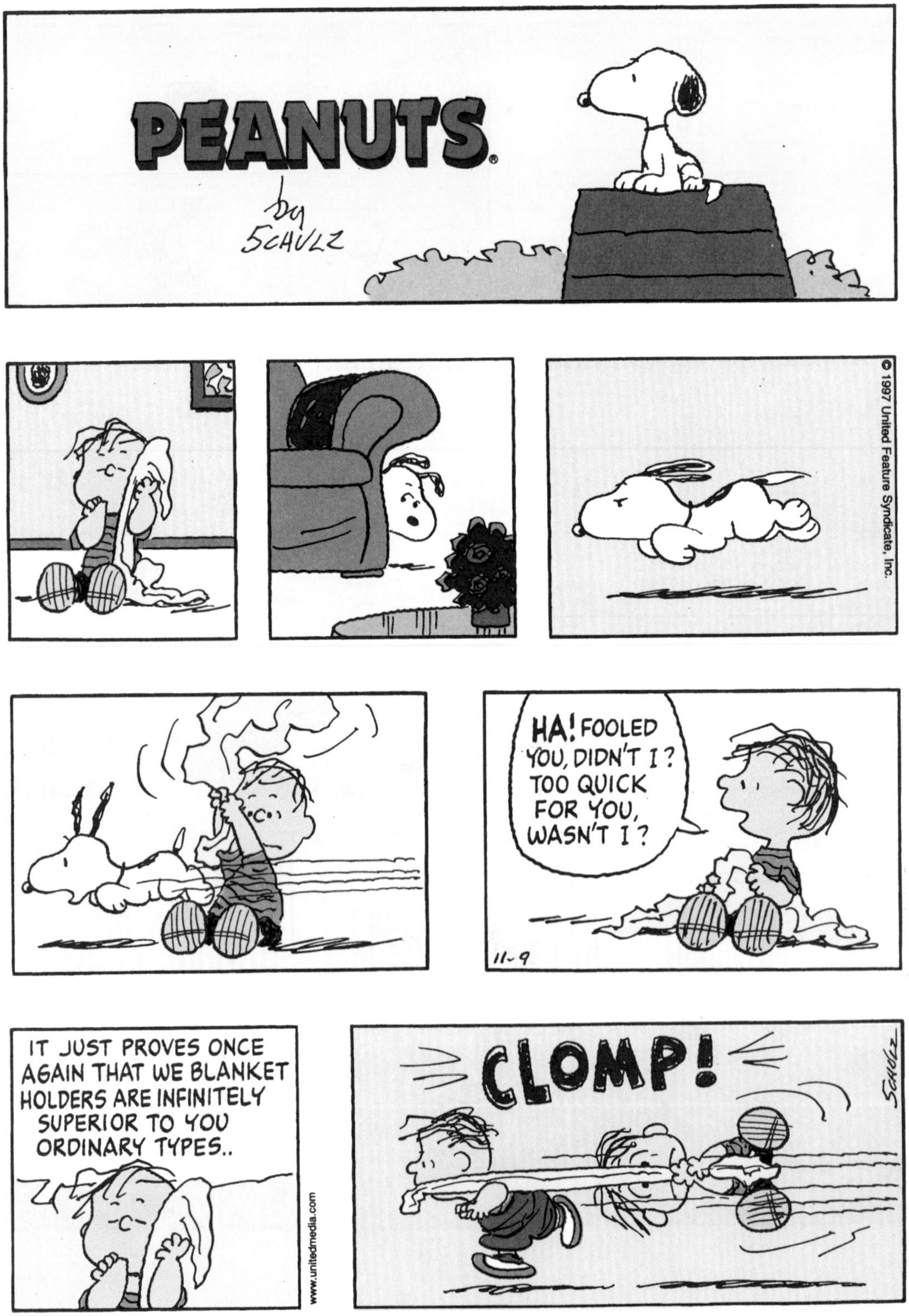
PEANUTS
by SCHULZ
© 1997 United Feature Syndicate, Inc.
HA! FOOLED YOU, DIDN'T I? TOO QUICK FOR YOU, WASN'T I?
11-9
IT JUST PROVES ONCE AGAIN THAT WE BLANKET HOLDERS ARE INFINITELY SUPERIOR TO YOU ORDINARY TYPES..
www.unitedmedia.com
CLOMP!
SCHULZ

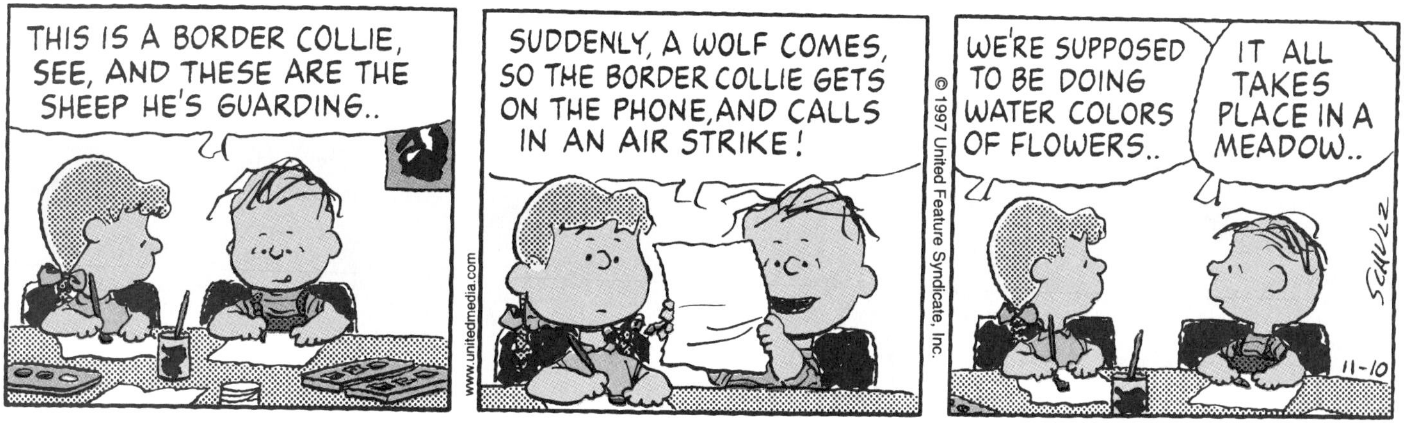
THIS IS A BORDER COLLIE, SEE, AND THESE ARE THE SHEEP HE'S GUARDING..
SUDDENLY, A WOLF COMES, SO THE BORDER COLLIE GETS ON THE PHONE, AND CALLS IN AN AIR STRIKE!
WE'RE SUPPOSED TO BE DOING WATER COLORS OF FLOWERS..
IT ALL TAKES PLACE IN A MEADOW..
www.unitedmedia.com
© 1997 United Feature Syndicate, Inc.
SCHULZ
11-10

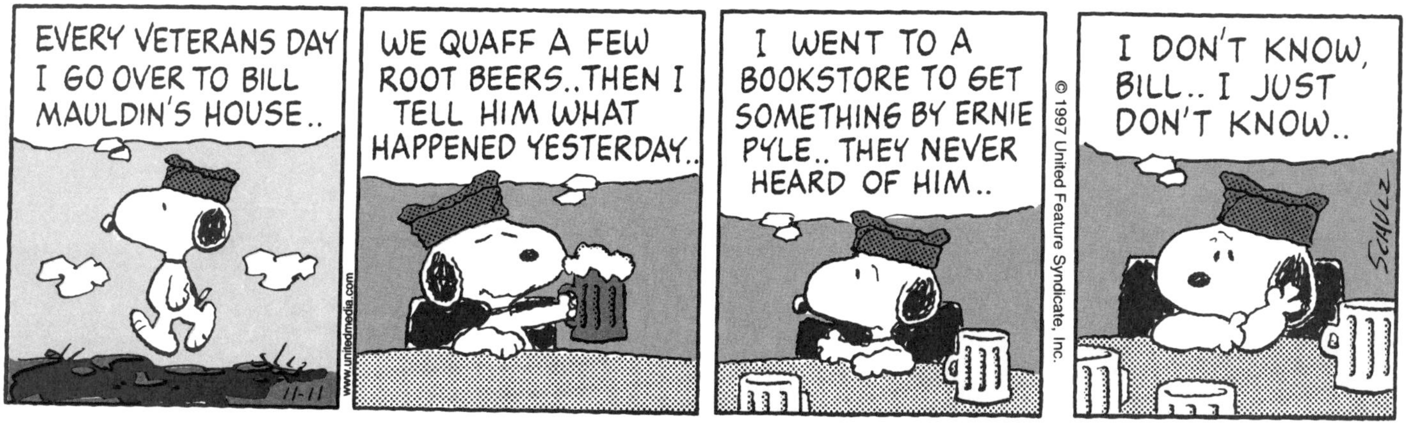
EVERY VETERANS DAY I GO OVER TO BILL MAULDIN'S HOUSE..
WE QUAFF A FEW ROOT BEERS..THEN I TELL HIM WHAT HAPPENED YESTERDAY..
I WENT TO A BOOKSTORE TO GET SOMETHING BY ERNIE PYLE.. THEY NEVER HEARD OF HIM..
I DON'T KNOW, BILL.. I JUST DON'T KNOW..
11-11
www.unitedmedia.com
© 1997 United Feature Syndicate, Inc.
SCHULZ

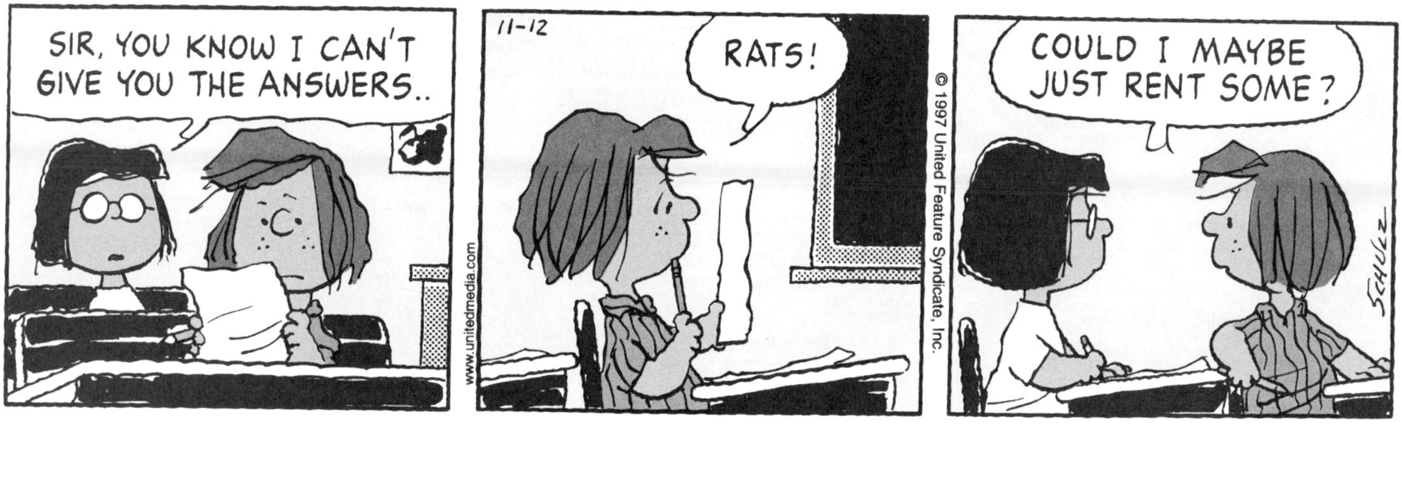
SIR, YOU KNOW I CAN'T GIVE YOU THE ANSWERS..
11-12
RATS!
COULD I MAYBE JUST RENT SOME?
www.unitedmedia.com
© 1997 United Feature Syndicate, Inc.
SCHULZ

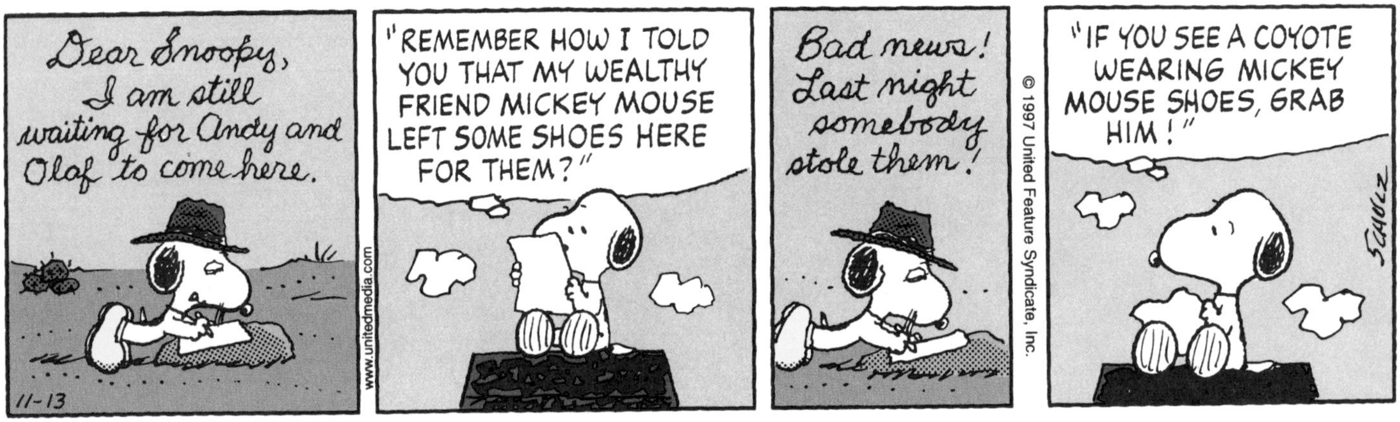
Dear Snoopy, I am still waiting for Andy and Olaf to come here.
"REMEMBER HOW I TOLD YOU THAT MY WEALTHY FRIEND MICKEY MOUSE LEFT SOME SHOES HERE FOR THEM?"
Bad news! Last night somebody stole them!
"IF YOU SEE A COYOTE WEARING MICKEY MOUSE SHOES, GRAB HIM!"
11-13
www.unitedmedia.com
© 1997 United Feature Syndicate, Inc.
SCHULZ

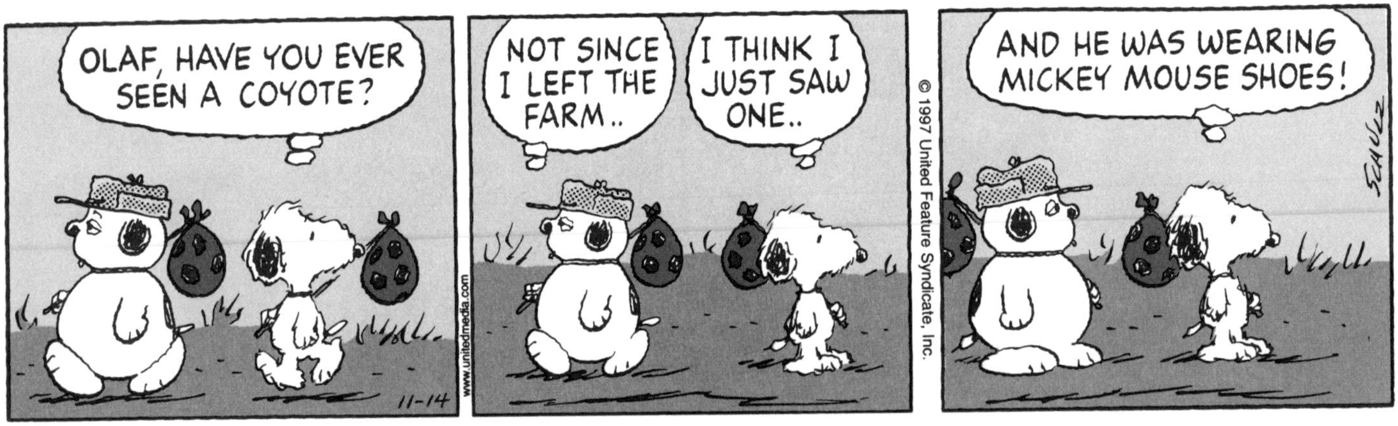
OLAF, HAVE YOU EVER SEEN A COYOTE?
NOT SINCE I LEFT THE FARM..
I THINK I JUST SAW ONE..
AND HE WAS WEARING MICKEY MOUSE SHOES!
11-14
www.unitedmedia.com
© 1997 United Feature Syndicate, Inc.
SCHULZ

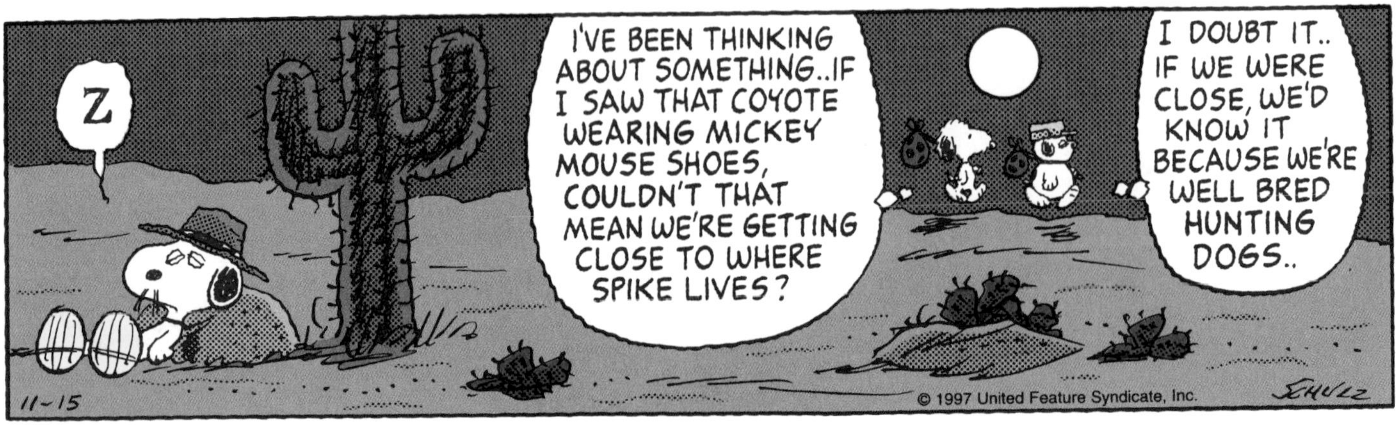
Z
I'VE BEEN THINKING ABOUT SOMETHING..IF I SAW THAT COYOTE WEARING MICKEY MOUSE SHOES, COULDN'T THAT MEAN WE'RE GETTING CLOSE TO WHERE SPIKE LIVES?
I DOUBT IT.. IF WE WERE CLOSE, WE'D KNOW IT BECAUSE WE'RE WELL BRED HUNTING DOGS..
11-15
© 1997 United Feature Syndicate, Inc.
SCHULZ

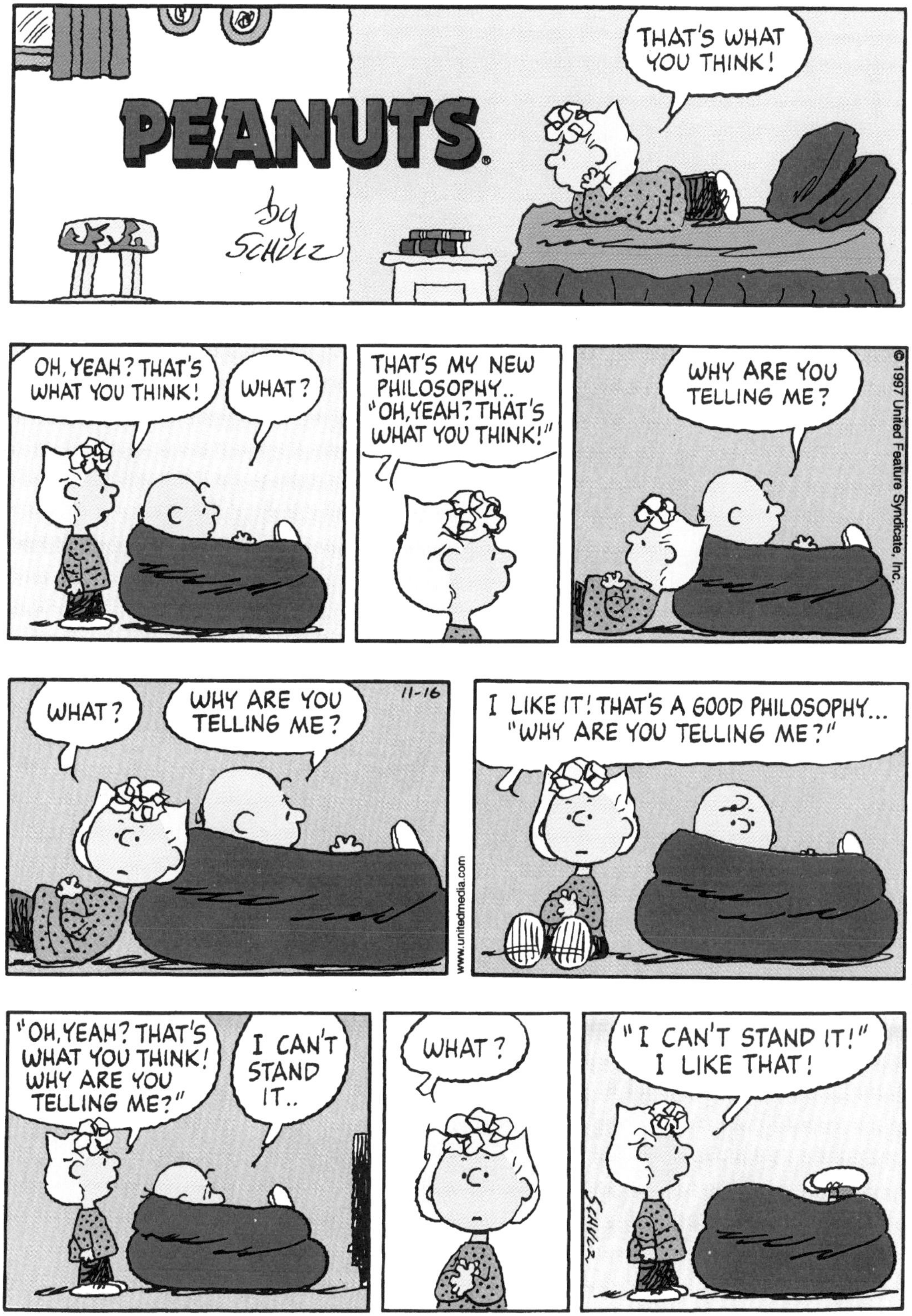
PEANUTS
by SCHULZ
THAT'S WHAT YOU THINK!
OH, YEAH? THAT'S WHAT YOU THINK!
WHAT?
THAT'S MY NEW PHILOSOPHY.. "OH, YEAH? THAT'S WHAT YOU THINK!"
WHY ARE YOU TELLING ME?
© 1997 United Feature Syndicate, Inc.
WHAT?
WHY ARE YOU TELLING ME?
11-16
www.unitedmedia.com
I LIKE IT! THAT'S A GOOD PHILOSOPHY... "WHY ARE YOU TELLING ME?"
"OH, YEAH? THAT'S WHAT YOU THINK! WHY ARE YOU TELLING ME?"
I CAN'T STAND IT..
WHAT?
"I CAN'T STAND IT!" I LIKE THAT!
SCHULZ

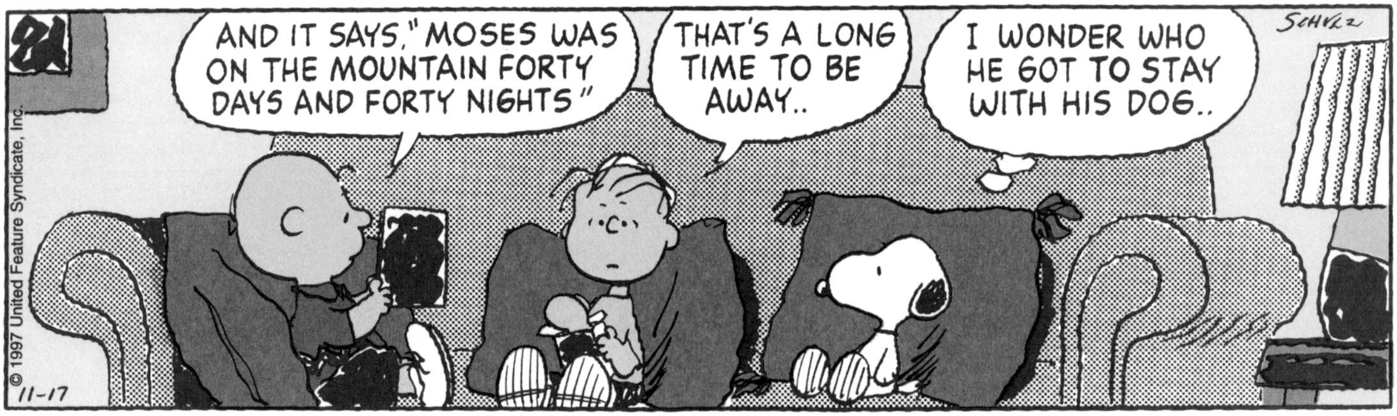
AND IT SAYS, "MOSES WAS ON THE MOUNTAIN FORTY DAYS AND FORTY NIGHTS"
THAT'S A LONG TIME TO BE AWAY..
I WONDER WHO HE GOT TO STAY WITH HIS DOG..
© 1997 United Feature Syndicate, Inc.
11-17
SCHULZ

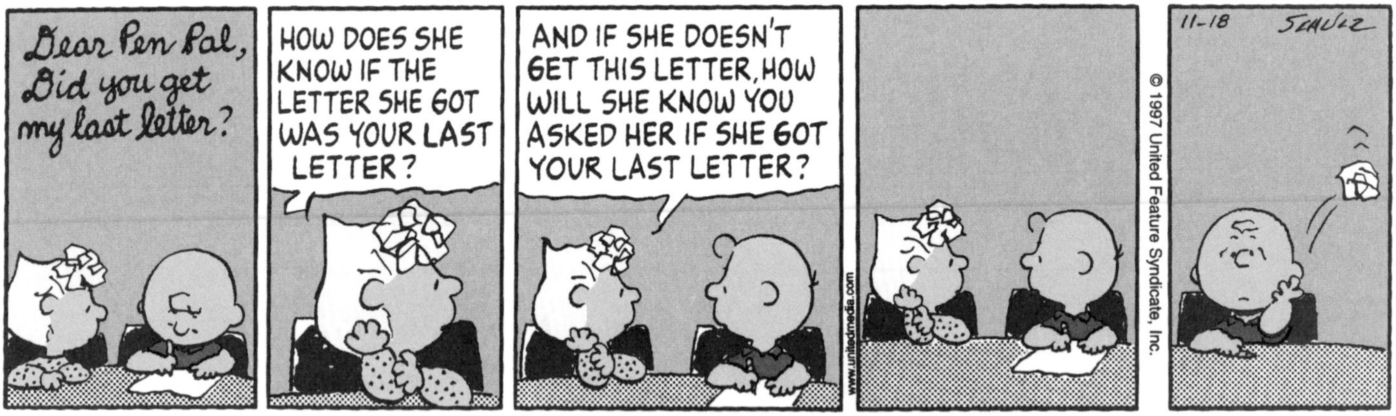
Dear Pen Pal,
Did you get my last letter?
HOW DOES SHE KNOW IF THE LETTER SHE GOT WAS YOUR LAST LETTER?
AND IF SHE DOESN'T GET THIS LETTER, HOW WILL SHE KNOW YOU ASKED HER IF SHE GOT YOUR LAST LETTER?
www.unitedmedia.com
11-18
SCHULZ
© 1997 United Feature Syndicate, Inc.

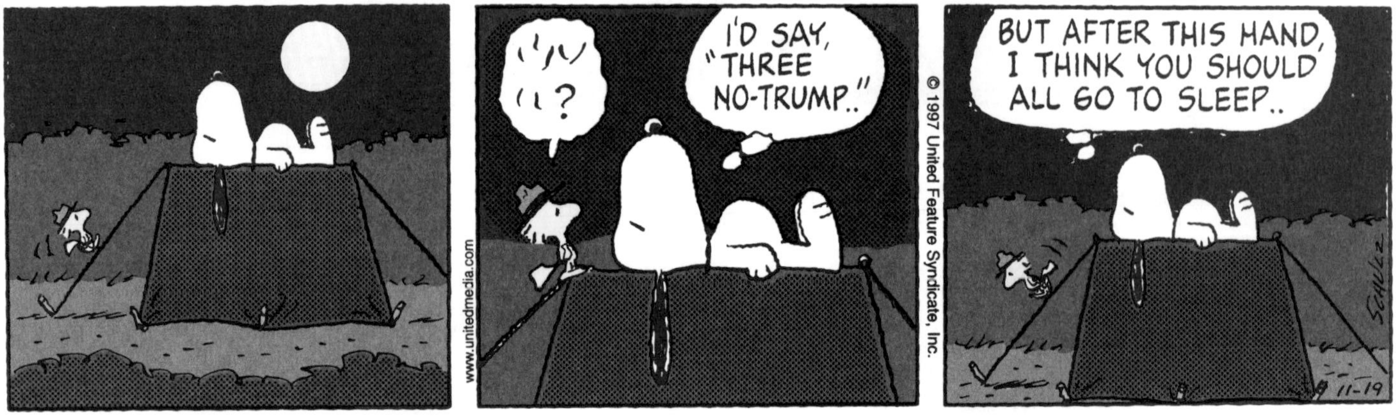
www.unitedmedia.com
I'D SAY, "THREE NO-TRUMP.."
© 1997 United Feature Syndicate, Inc.
BUT AFTER THIS HAND, I THINK YOU SHOULD ALL GO TO SLEEP..
SCHULZ
11-19

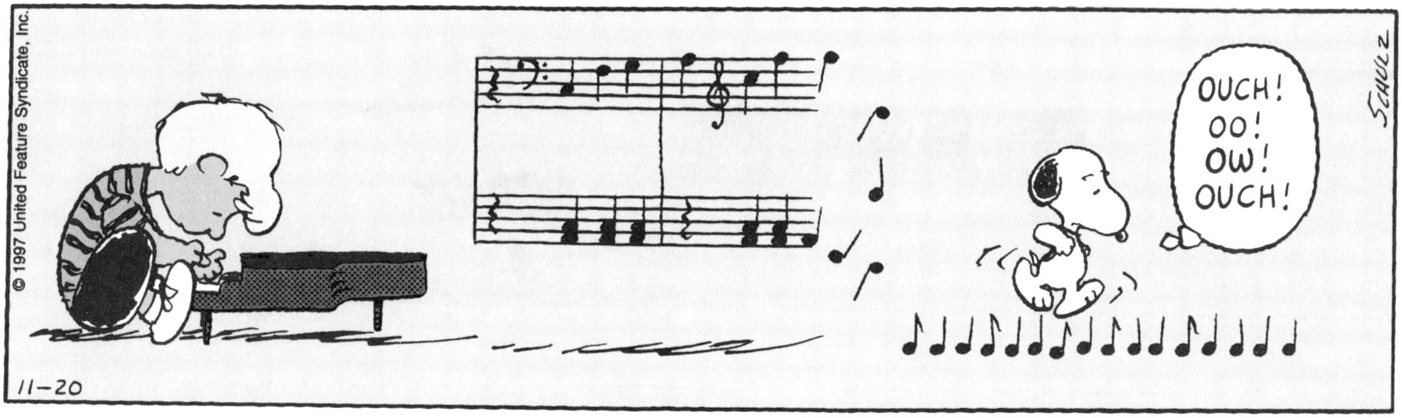
© 1997 United Feature Syndicate, Inc.
OUCH! OO! OW! OUCH!
SCHULZ
11-20

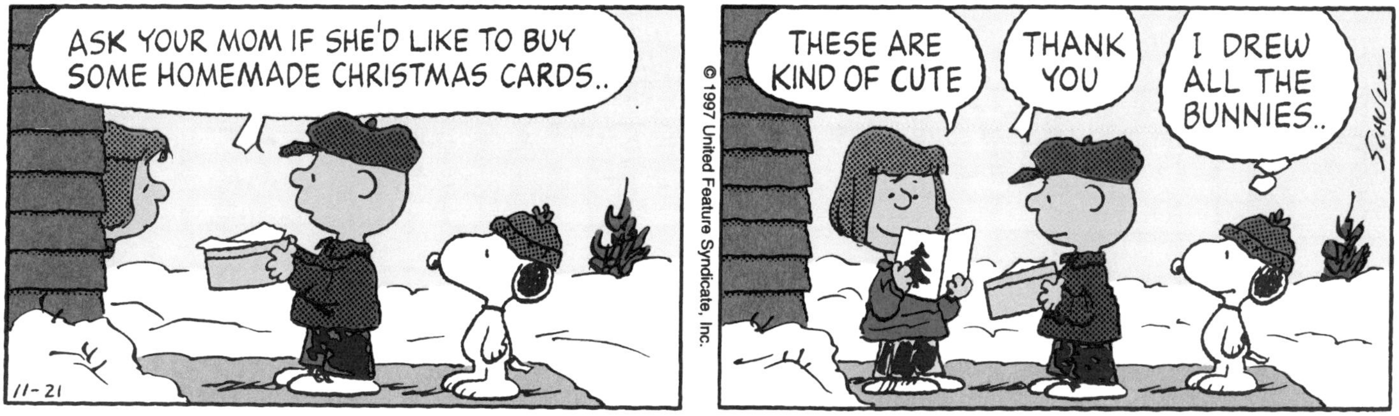
ASK YOUR MOM IF SHE'D LIKE TO BUY SOME HOMEMADE CHRISTMAS CARDS..
11-21
© 1997 United Feature Syndicate, Inc.
THESE ARE KIND OF CUTE
THANK YOU
I DREW ALL THE BUNNIES..
SCHULZ

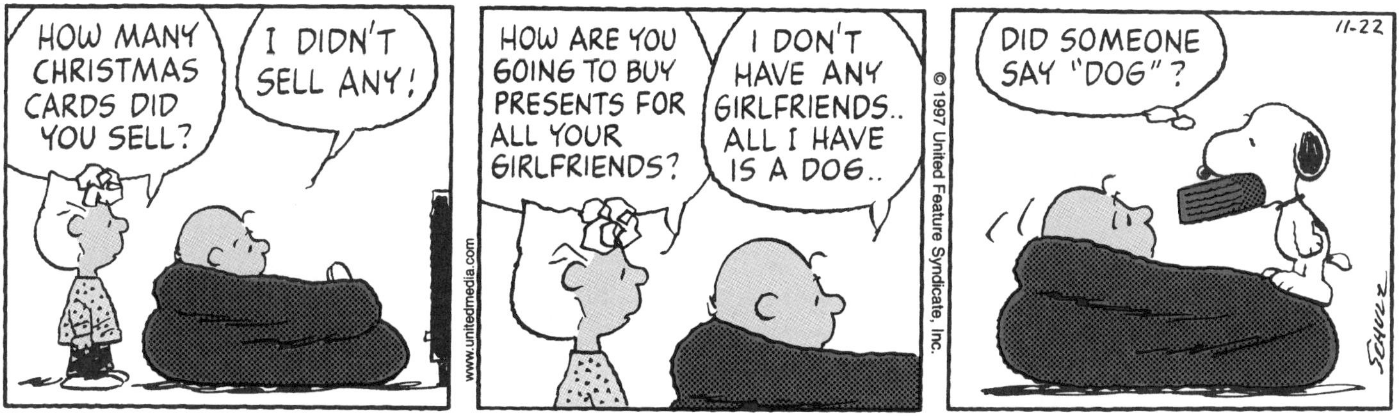
HOW MANY CHRISTMAS CARDS DID YOU SELL?
I DIDN'T SELL ANY!
www.unitedmedia.com
HOW ARE YOU GOING TO BUY PRESENTS FOR ALL YOUR GIRLFRIENDS?
I DON'T HAVE ANY GIRLFRIENDS.. ALL I HAVE IS A DOG..
© 1997 United Feature Syndicate, Inc.
11-22
DID SOMEONE SAY "DOG"?
SCHULZ

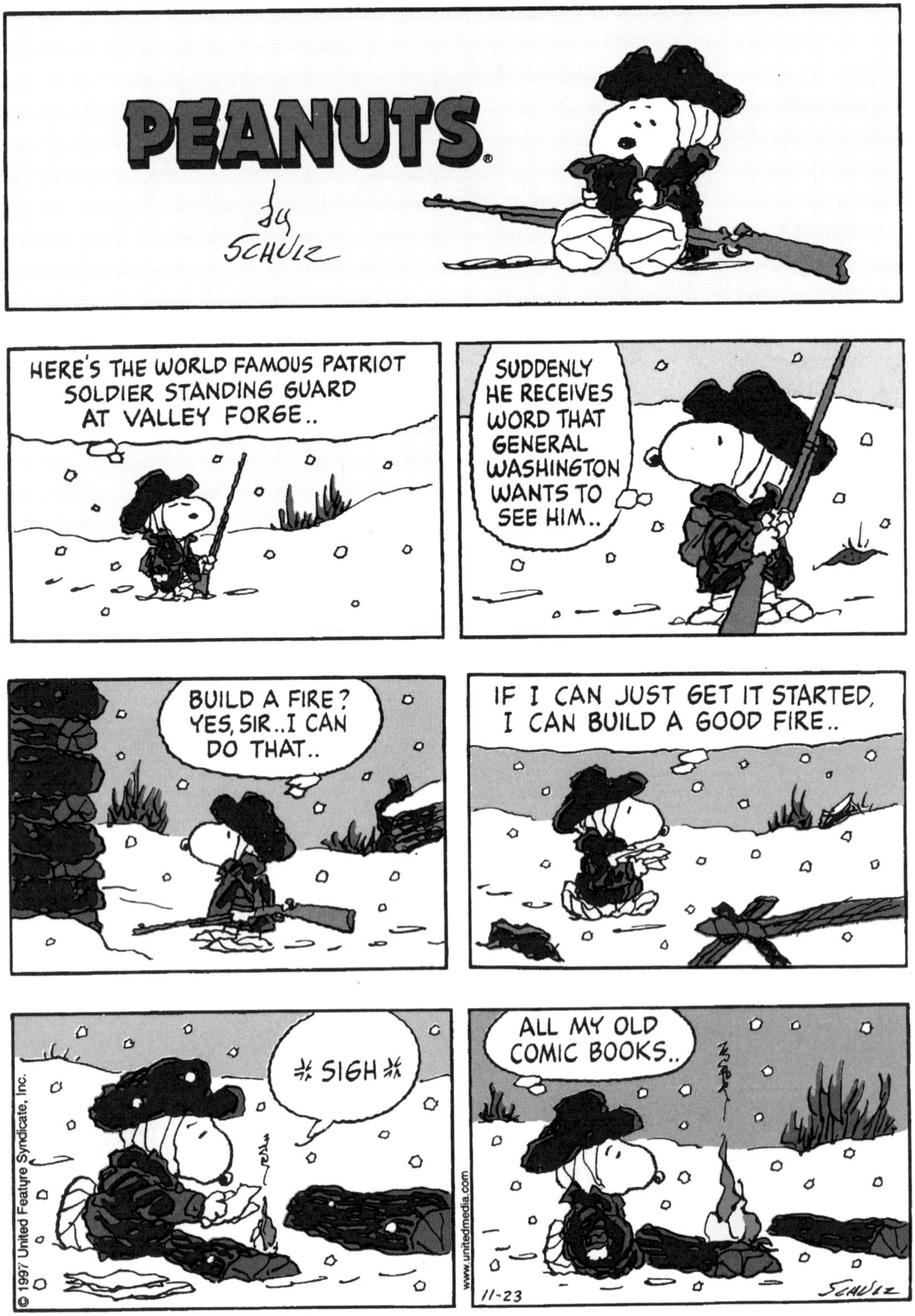
PEANUTS®
by SCHULZ
HERE'S THE WORLD FAMOUS PATRIOT SOLDIER STANDING GUARD AT VALLEY FORGE..
SUDDENLY HE RECEIVES WORD THAT GENERAL WASHINGTON WANTS TO SEE HIM..
BUILD A FIRE? YES, SIR..I CAN DO THAT..
IF I CAN JUST GET IT STARTED, I CAN BUILD A GOOD FIRE..
SIGH
ALL MY OLD COMIC BOOKS..
© 1997 United Feature Syndicate, Inc.
www.unitedmedia.com
11-23
SCHULZ

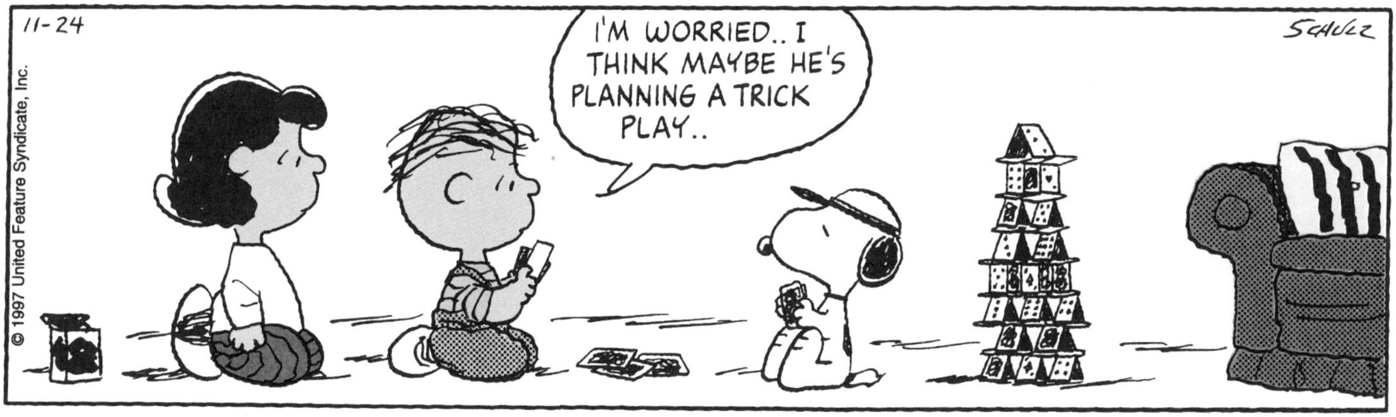
11-24
© 1997 United Feature Syndicate, Inc.
I'M WORRIED.. I THINK MAYBE HE'S PLANNING A TRICK PLAY..
SCHULZ

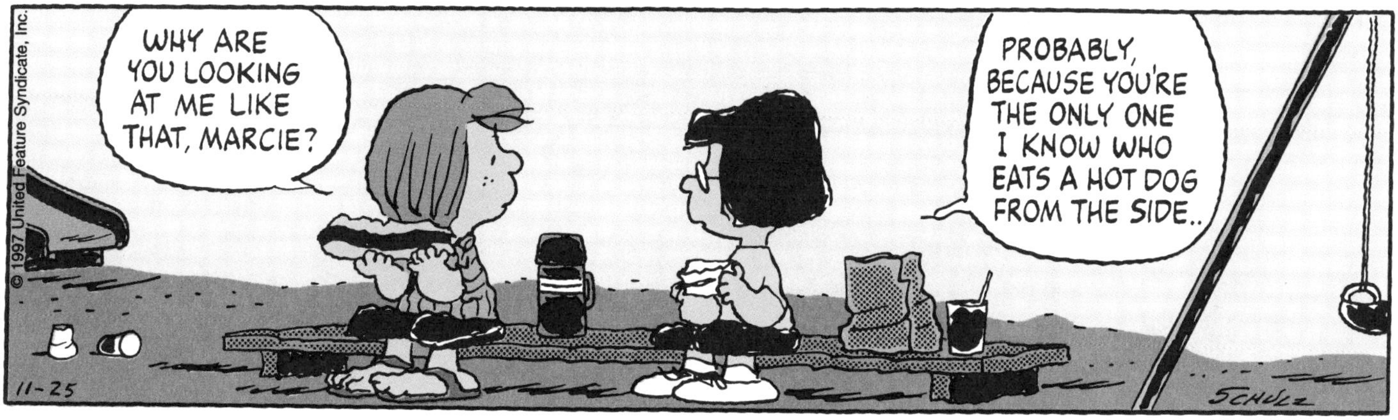
© 1997 United Feature Syndicate, Inc.
WHY ARE YOU LOOKING AT ME LIKE THAT, MARCIE?
PROBABLY, BECAUSE YOU'RE THE ONLY ONE I KNOW WHO EATS A HOT DOG FROM THE SIDE..
11-25
SCHULZ

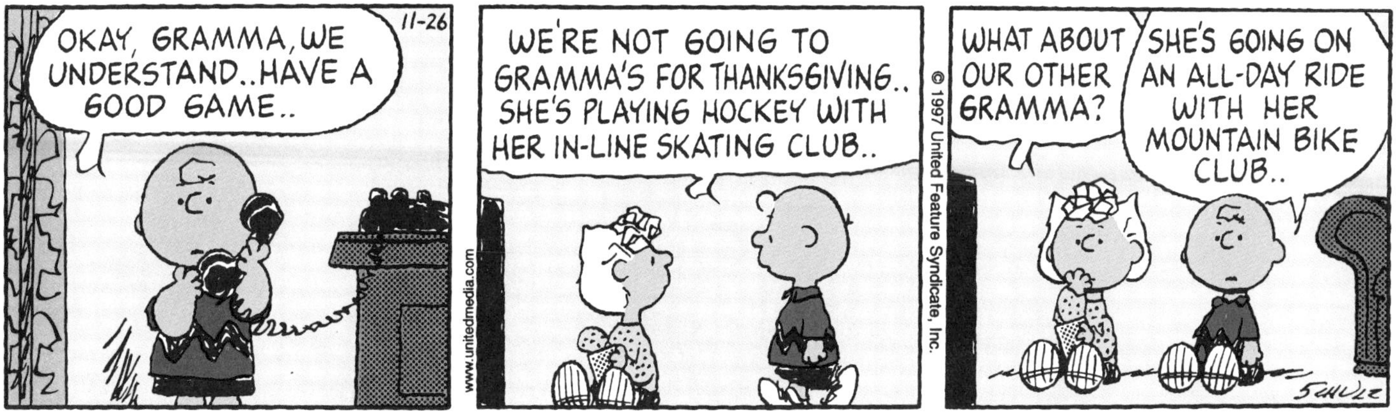
11-26
OKAY, GRAMMA, WE UNDERSTAND..HAVE A GOOD GAME..
WE'RE NOT GOING TO GRAMMA'S FOR THANKSGIVING.. SHE'S PLAYING HOCKEY WITH HER IN-LINE SKATING CLUB..
www.unitedmedia.com
© 1997 United Feature Syndicate, Inc.
WHAT ABOUT OUR OTHER GRAMMA?
SHE'S GOING ON AN ALL-DAY RIDE WITH HER MOUNTAIN BIKE CLUB..
SCHULZ

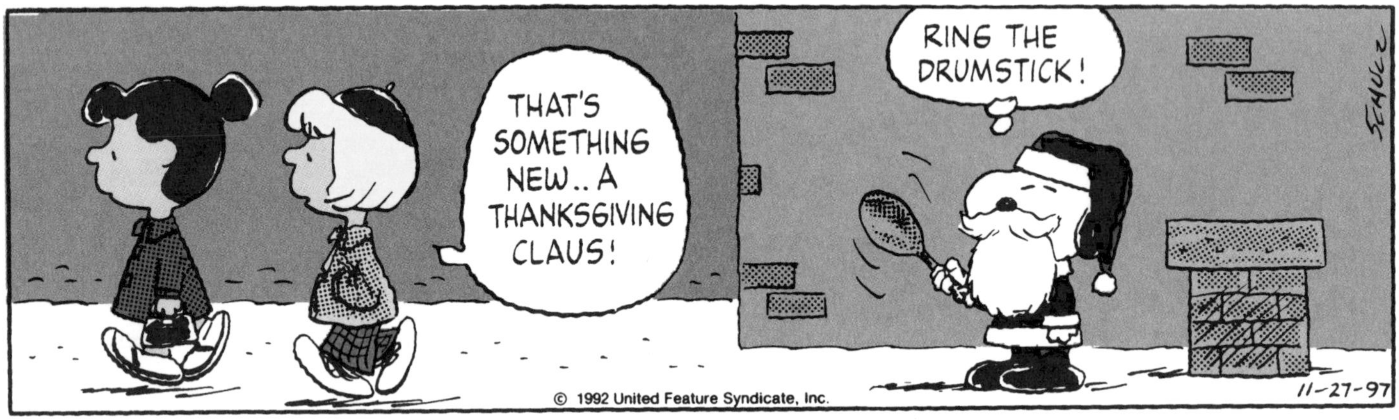
THAT'S SOMETHING NEW.. A THANKSGIVING CLAUS!
RING THE DRUMSTICK!
© 1992 United Feature Syndicate, Inc.
11-27-97

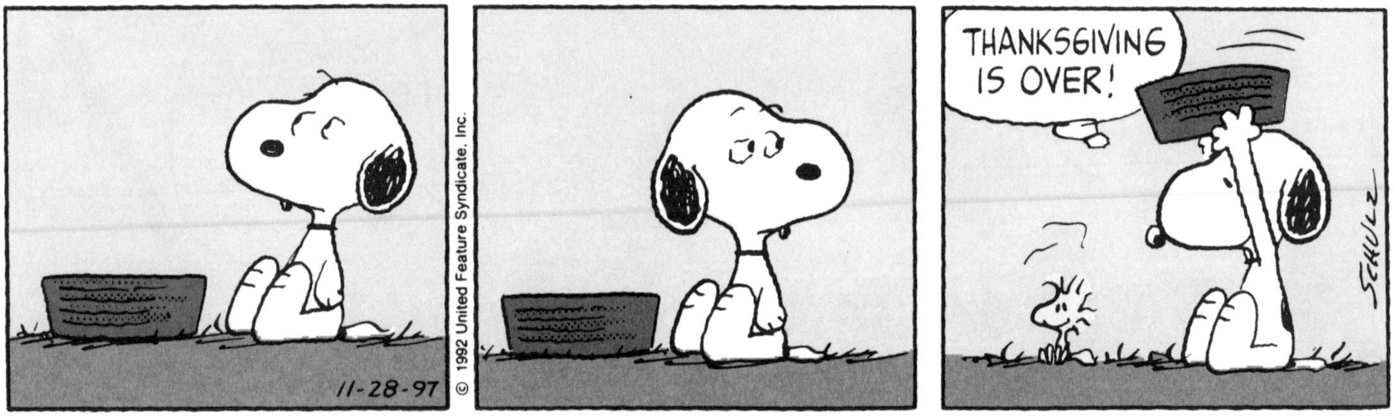
11-28-97
© 1992 United Feature Syndicate, Inc.
THANKSGIVING IS OVER!

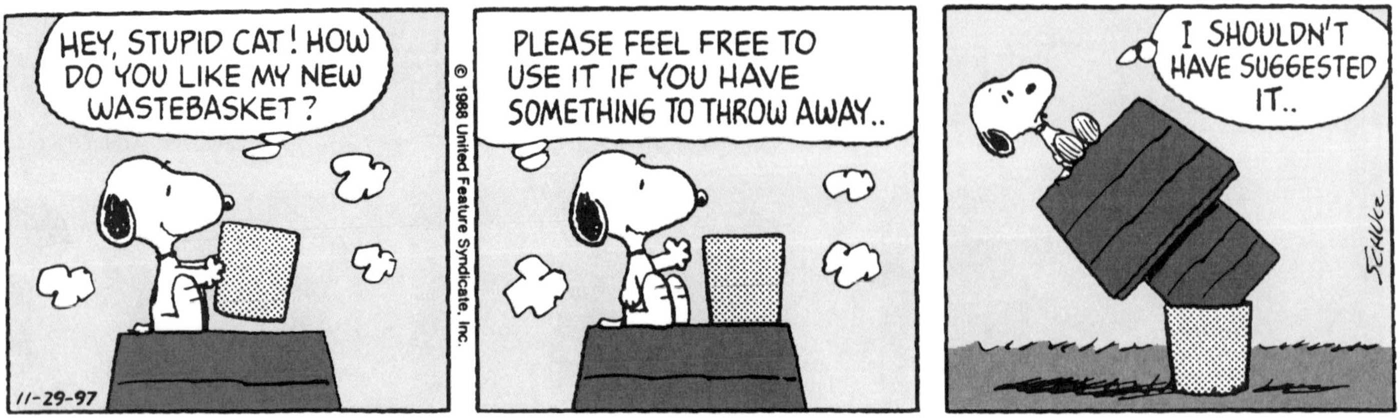
HEY, STUPID CAT! HOW DO YOU LIKE MY NEW WASTEBASKET?
11-29-97
© 1988 United Feature Syndicate, Inc.
PLEASE FEEL FREE TO USE IT IF YOU HAVE SOMETHING TO THROW AWAY..
I SHOULDN'T HAVE SUGGESTED IT..

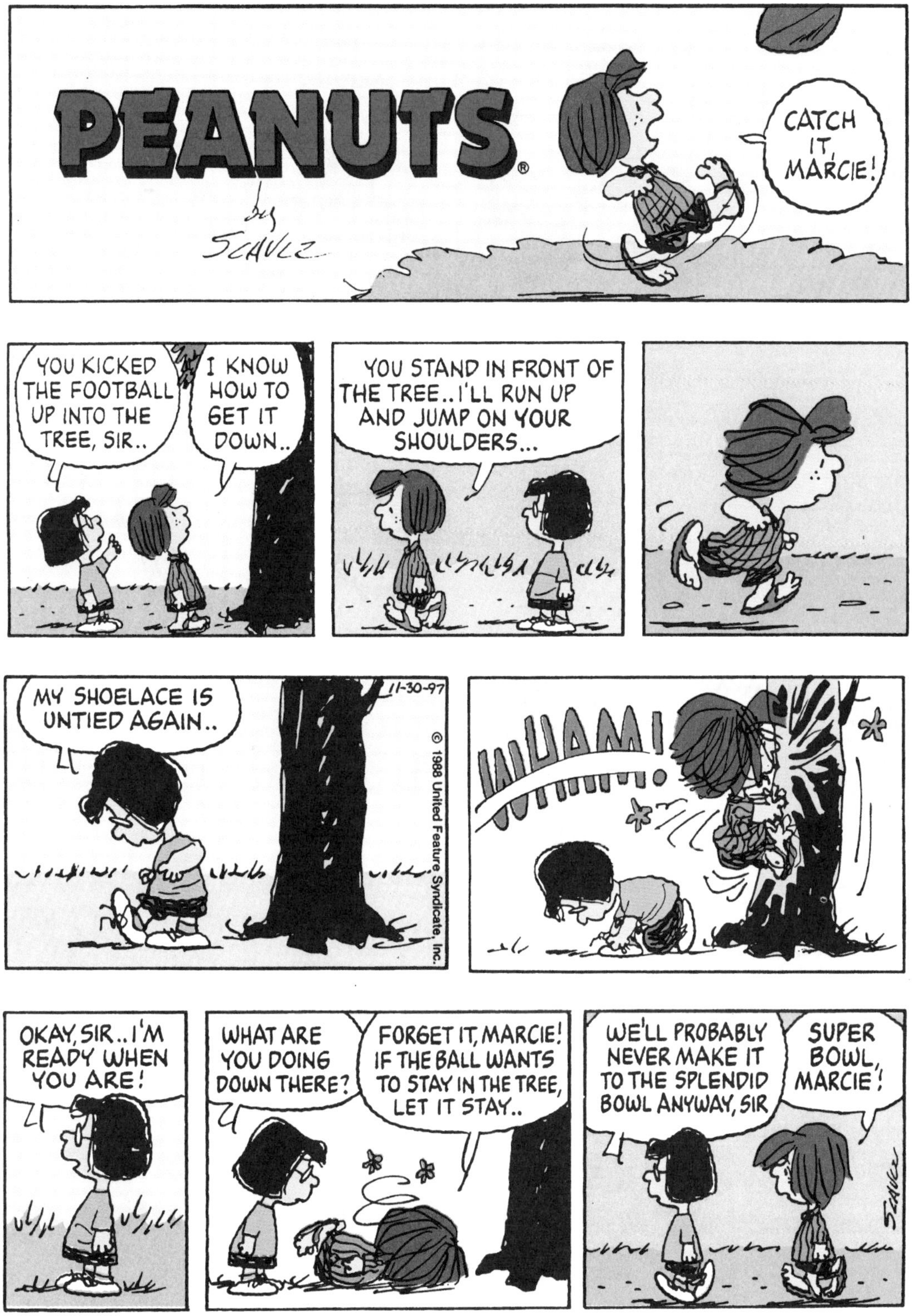
PEANUTS
by SCHULZ
CATCH IT, MARCIE!
YOU KICKED THE FOOTBALL UP INTO THE TREE, SIR..
I KNOW HOW TO GET IT DOWN..
YOU STAND IN FRONT OF THE TREE.. I'LL RUN UP AND JUMP ON YOUR SHOULDERS...
MY SHOELACE IS UNTIED AGAIN..
11-30-97
© 1988 United Feature Syndicate, Inc.
WHAM!
OKAY, SIR.. I'M READY WHEN YOU ARE!
WHAT ARE YOU DOING DOWN THERE?
FORGET IT, MARCIE! IF THE BALL WANTS TO STAY IN THE TREE, LET IT STAY..
WE'LL PROBABLY NEVER MAKE IT TO THE SPLENDID BOWL ANYWAY, SIR
SUPER BOWL, MARCIE!
SCHULZ

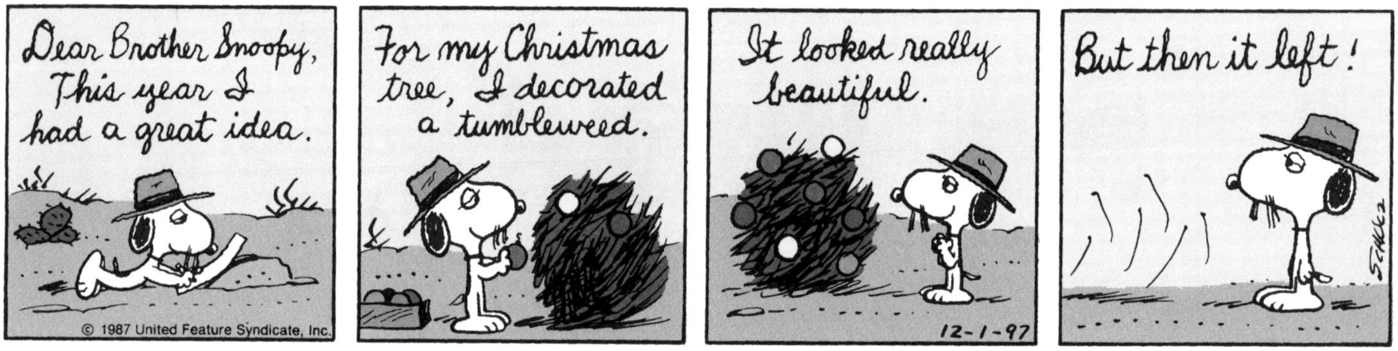
Dear Brother Snoopy, This year I had a great idea.
For my Christmas tree, I decorated a tumbleweed.
It looked really beautiful.
12-1-97
But then it left!
SCHULZ
© 1987 United Feature Syndicate, Inc.

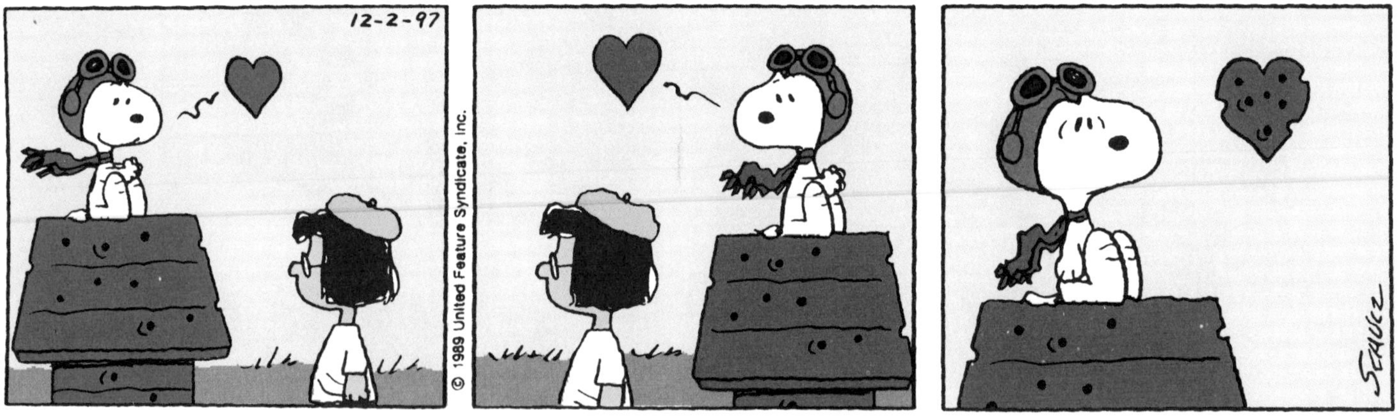
12-2-97
© 1989 United Feature Syndicate, Inc.
SCHULZ

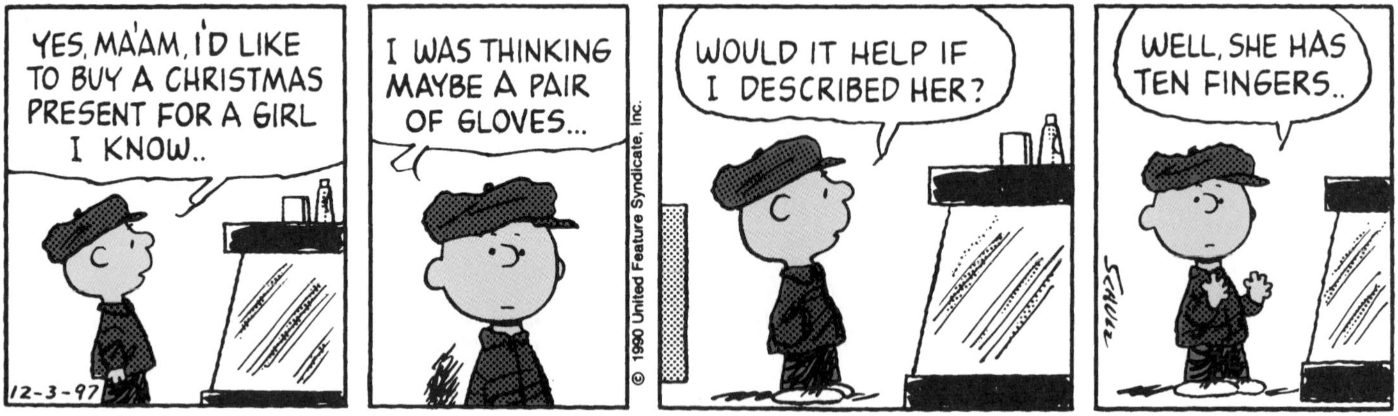
YES, MA'AM, I'D LIKE TO BUY A CHRISTMAS PRESENT FOR A GIRL I KNOW..
12-3-97
I WAS THINKING MAYBE A PAIR OF GLOVES...
© 1990 United Feature Syndicate, Inc.
WOULD IT HELP IF I DESCRIBED HER?
WELL, SHE HAS TEN FINGERS..
SCHULZ

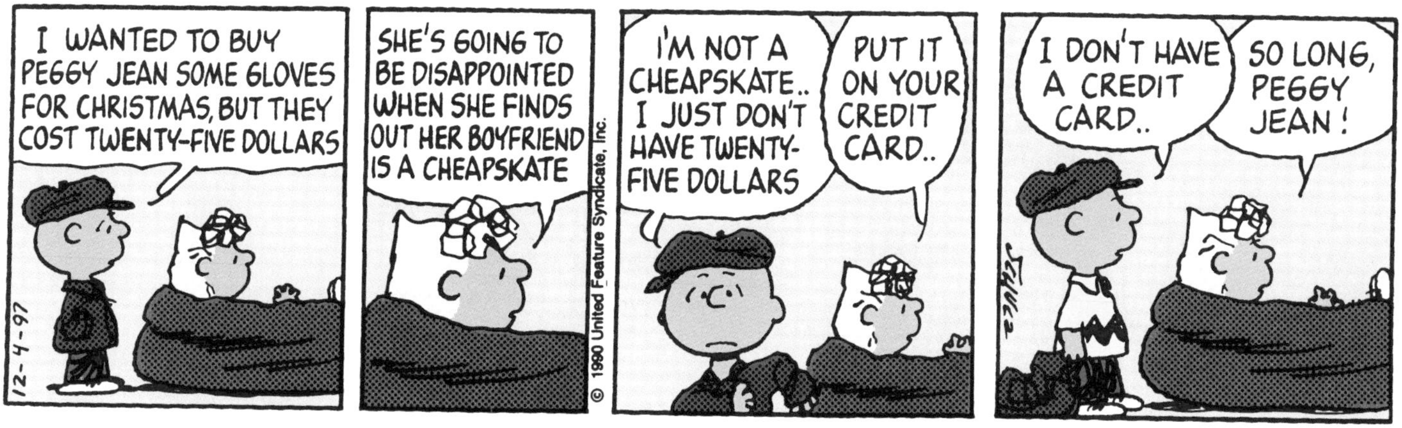
I WANTED TO BUY PEGGY JEAN SOME GLOVES FOR CHRISTMAS, BUT THEY COST TWENTY-FIVE DOLLARS
12-4-97
SHE'S GOING TO BE DISAPPOINTED WHEN SHE FINDS OUT HER BOYFRIEND IS A CHEAPSKATE
© 1990 United Feature Syndicate, Inc.
I'M NOT A CHEAPSKATE.. I JUST DON'T HAVE TWENTY-FIVE DOLLARS
PUT IT ON YOUR CREDIT CARD..
I DON'T HAVE A CREDIT CARD..
SO LONG, PEGGY JEAN!
SCHULZ

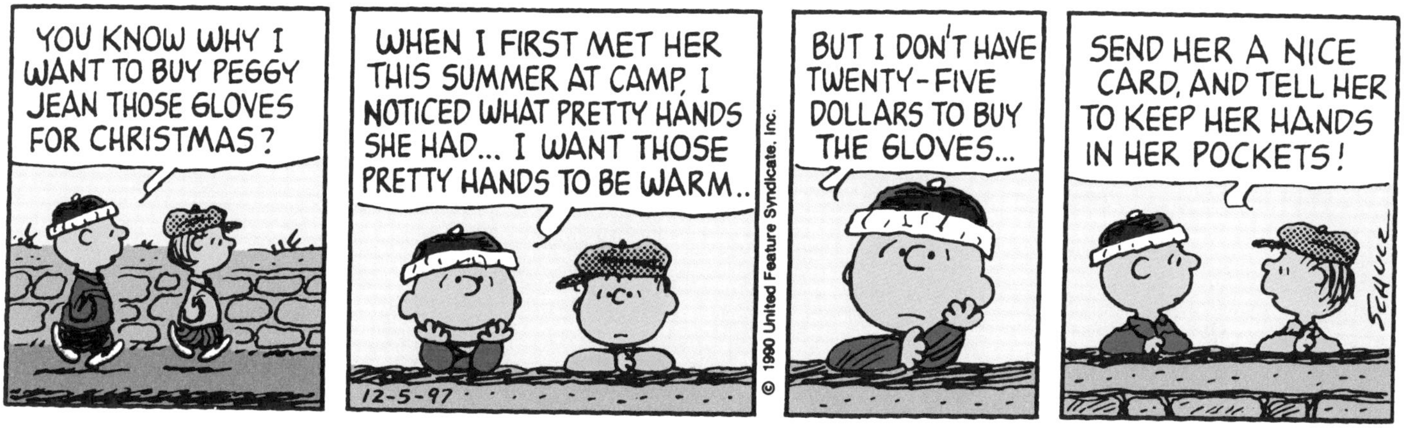
YOU KNOW WHY I WANT TO BUY PEGGY JEAN THOSE GLOVES FOR CHRISTMAS?
WHEN I FIRST MET HER THIS SUMMER AT CAMP, I NOTICED WHAT PRETTY HANDS SHE HAD... I WANT THOSE PRETTY HANDS TO BE WARM..
12-5-97
© 1990 United Feature Syndicate, Inc.
BUT I DON'T HAVE TWENTY-FIVE DOLLARS TO BUY THE GLOVES...
SEND HER A NICE CARD, AND TELL HER TO KEEP HER HANDS IN HER POCKETS!
SCHULZ

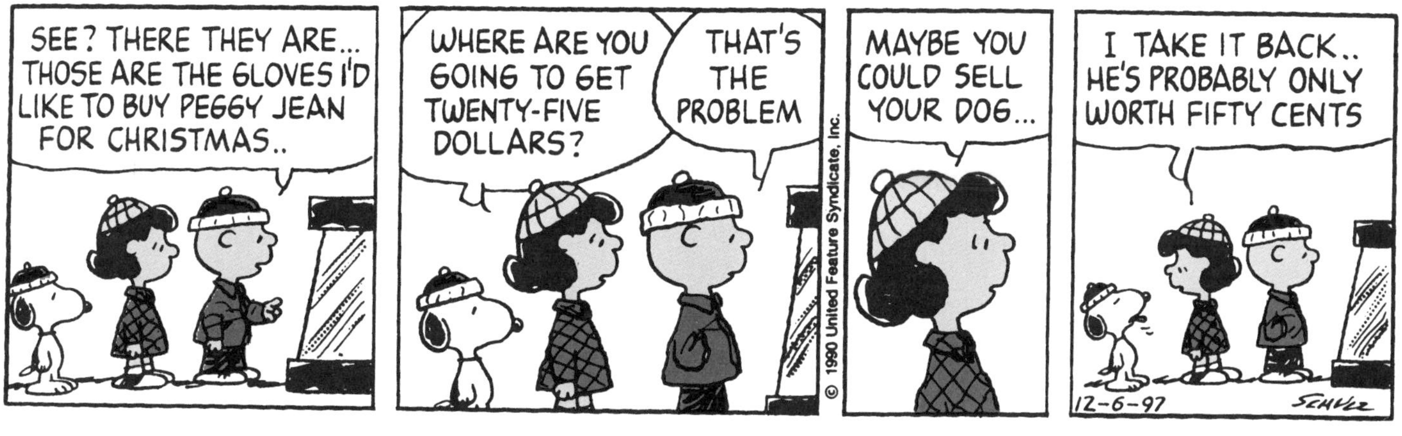
SEE? THERE THEY ARE... THOSE ARE THE GLOVES I'D LIKE TO BUY PEGGY JEAN FOR CHRISTMAS..
WHERE ARE YOU GOING TO GET TWENTY-FIVE DOLLARS?
THAT'S THE PROBLEM
© 1990 United Feature Syndicate, Inc.
MAYBE YOU COULD SELL YOUR DOG...
I TAKE IT BACK.. HE'S PROBABLY ONLY WORTH FIFTY CENTS
12-6-97
SCHULZ

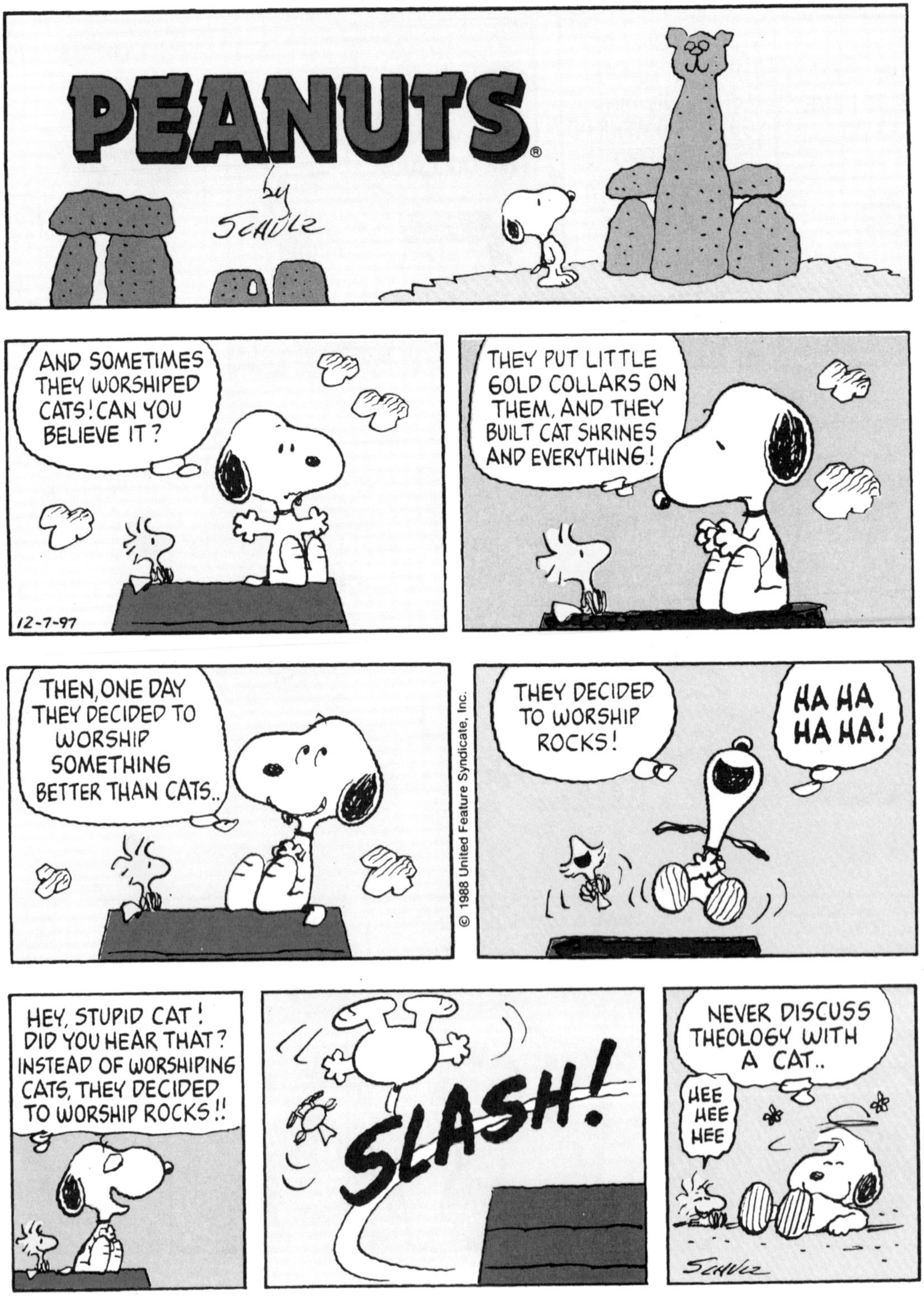
PEANUTS®
by SCHULZ
AND SOMETIMES THEY WORSHIPED CATS! CAN YOU BELIEVE IT?
12-7-97
THEY PUT LITTLE GOLD COLLARS ON THEM, AND THEY BUILT CAT SHRINES AND EVERYTHING!
THEN, ONE DAY THEY DECIDED TO WORSHIP SOMETHING BETTER THAN CATS..
© 1988 United Feature Syndicate, Inc.
THEY DECIDED TO WORSHIP ROCKS!
HA HA HA HA!
HEY, STUPID CAT! DID YOU HEAR THAT? INSTEAD OF WORSHIPING CATS, THEY DECIDED TO WORSHIP ROCKS!!
SLASH!
NEVER DISCUSS THEOLOGY WITH A CAT..
HEE HEE HEE
SCHULZ

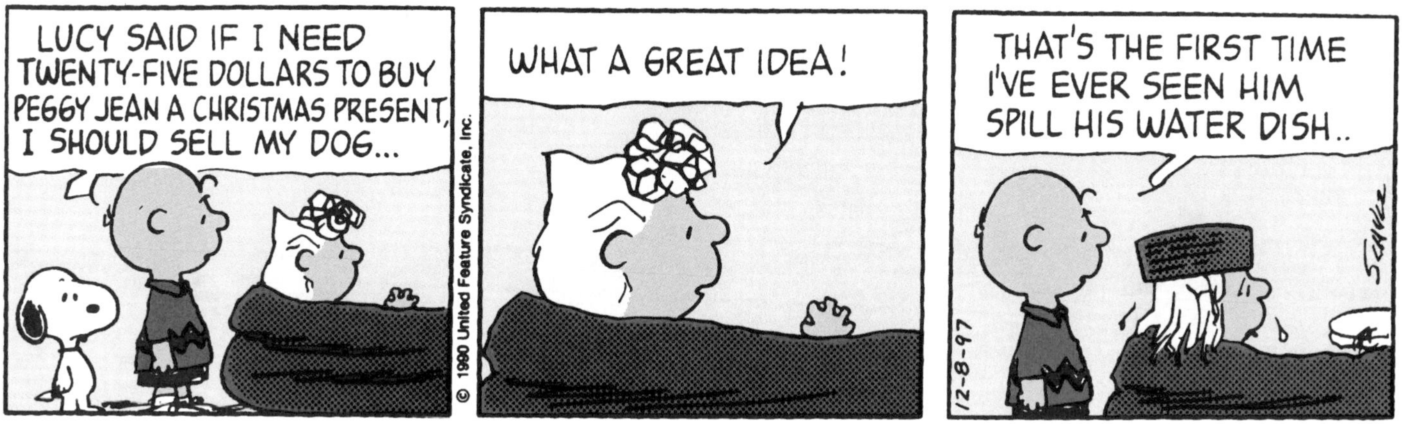
LUCY SAID IF I NEED TWENTY-FIVE DOLLARS TO BUY PEGGY JEAN A CHRISTMAS PRESENT, I SHOULD SELL MY DOG...
© 1990 United Feature Syndicate, Inc.
WHAT A GREAT IDEA!
THAT'S THE FIRST TIME I'VE EVER SEEN HIM SPILL HIS WATER DISH..
12-8-97
SCHULZ

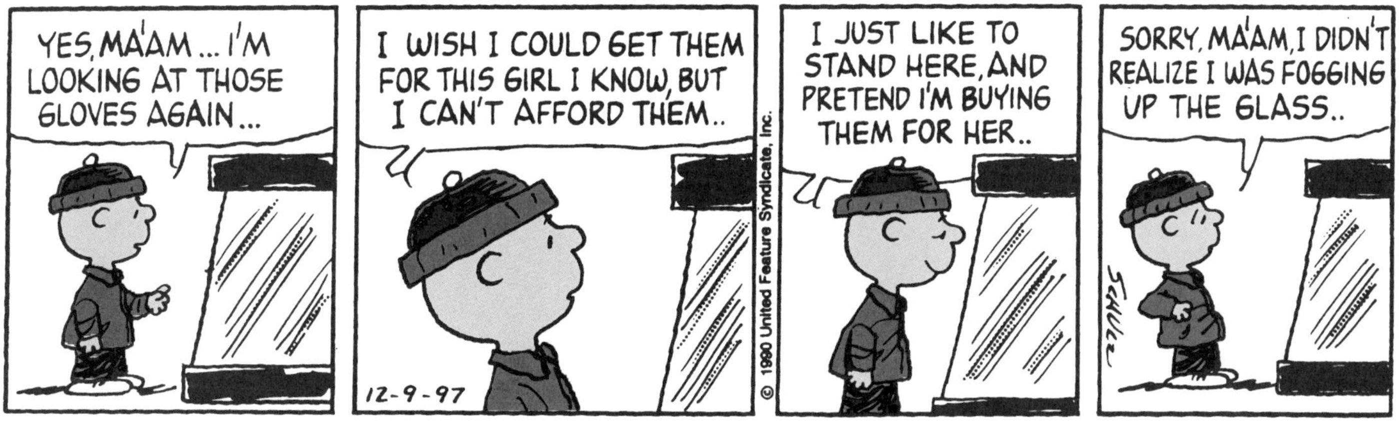
YES, MA'AM ... I'M LOOKING AT THOSE GLOVES AGAIN...
I WISH I COULD GET THEM FOR THIS GIRL I KNOW, BUT I CAN'T AFFORD THEM..
12-9-97
© 1990 United Feature Syndicate, Inc.
I JUST LIKE TO STAND HERE, AND PRETEND I'M BUYING THEM FOR HER..
SORRY, MA'AM, I DIDN'T REALIZE I WAS FOGGING UP THE GLASS..
SCHULZ

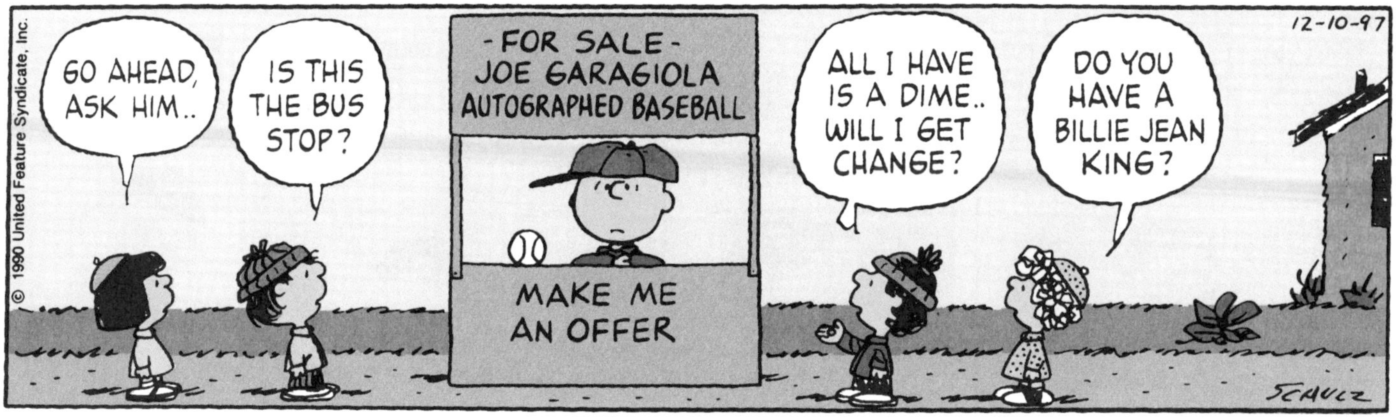
© 1990 United Feature Syndicate, Inc.
GO AHEAD, ASK HIM..
IS THIS THE BUS STOP?
- FOR SALE - JOE GARAGIOLA AUTOGRAPHED BASEBALL
MAKE ME AN OFFER
ALL I HAVE IS A DIME.. WILL I GET CHANGE?
DO YOU HAVE A BILLIE JEAN KING?
12-10-97
SCHULZ

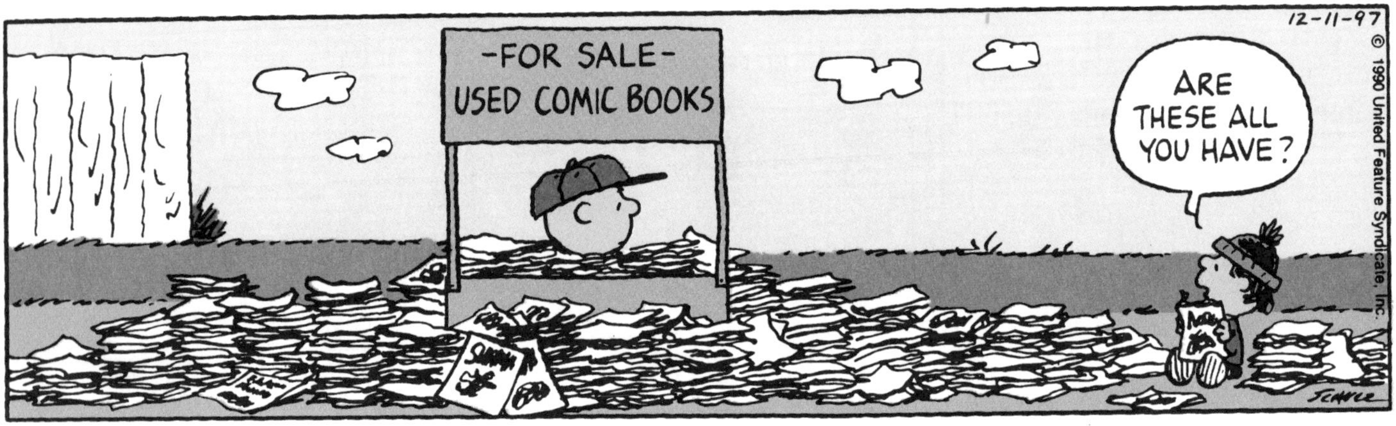
12-11-97
© 1990 United Feature Syndicate, Inc.
-FOR SALE-
USED COMIC BOOKS
ARE THESE ALL YOU HAVE?
SCHULZ

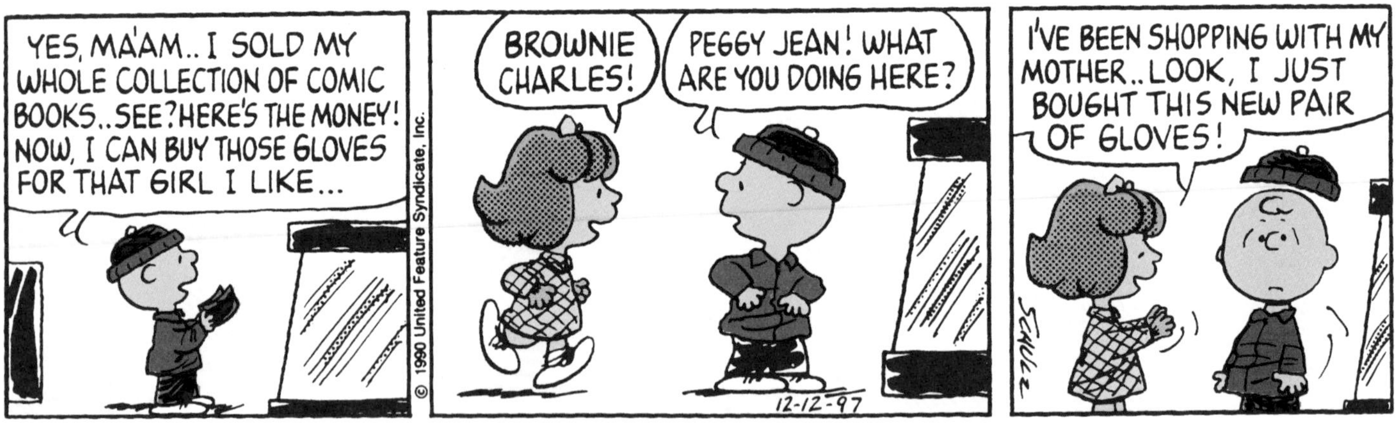
YES, MA'AM.. I SOLD MY WHOLE COLLECTION OF COMIC BOOKS..SEE? HERE'S THE MONEY! NOW, I CAN BUY THOSE GLOVES FOR THAT GIRL I LIKE...
© 1990 United Feature Syndicate, Inc.
BROWNIE CHARLES!
PEGGY JEAN! WHAT ARE YOU DOING HERE?
12-12-97
I'VE BEEN SHOPPING WITH MY MOTHER.. LOOK, I JUST BOUGHT THIS NEW PAIR OF GLOVES!
SCHULZ

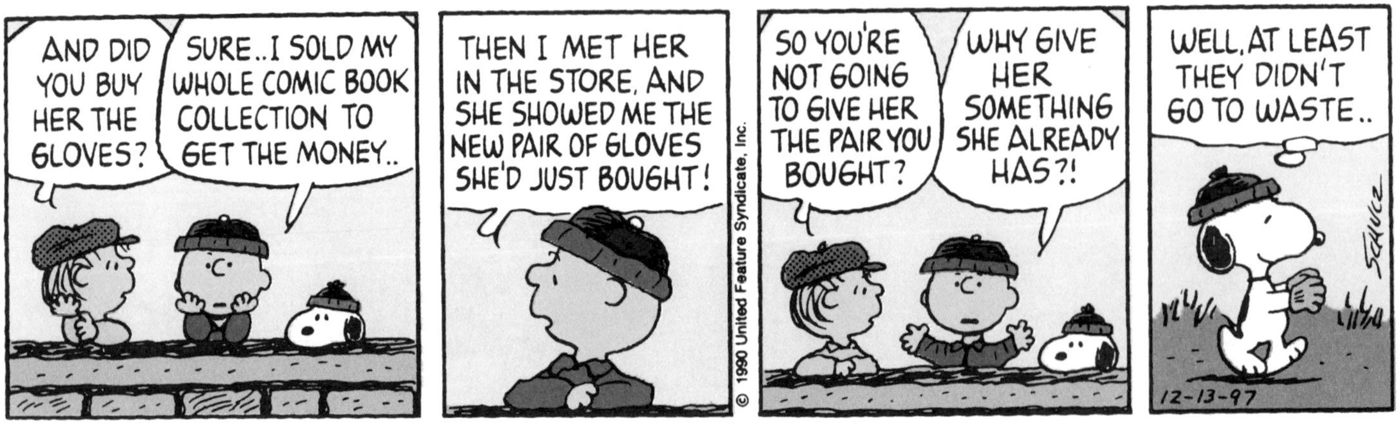
AND DID YOU BUY HER THE GLOVES?
SURE..I SOLD MY WHOLE COMIC BOOK COLLECTION TO GET THE MONEY..
THEN I MET HER IN THE STORE, AND SHE SHOWED ME THE NEW PAIR OF GLOVES SHE'D JUST BOUGHT!
© 1990 United Feature Syndicate, Inc.
SO YOU'RE NOT GOING TO GIVE HER THE PAIR YOU BOUGHT?
WHY GIVE HER SOMETHING SHE ALREADY HAS?!
WELL, AT LEAST THEY DIDN'T GO TO WASTE..
SCHULZ
12-13-97

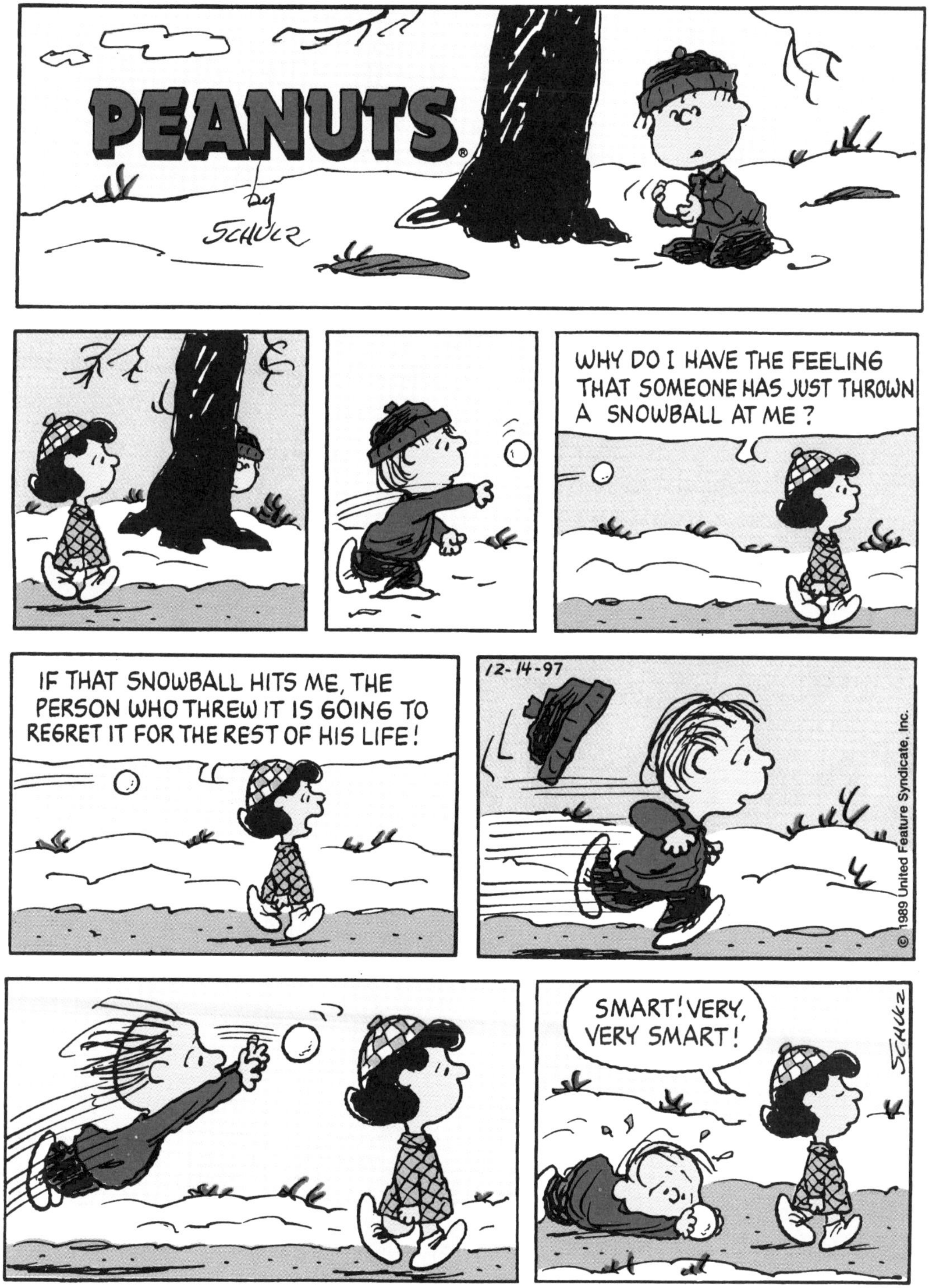
PEANUTS
by SCHULZ
WHY DO I HAVE THE FEELING THAT SOMEONE HAS JUST THROWN A SNOWBALL AT ME ?
IF THAT SNOWBALL HITS ME, THE PERSON WHO THREW IT IS GOING TO REGRET IT FOR THE REST OF HIS LIFE!
12-14-97
© 1989 United Feature Syndicate, Inc.
SMART! VERY, VERY SMART!
SCHULZ

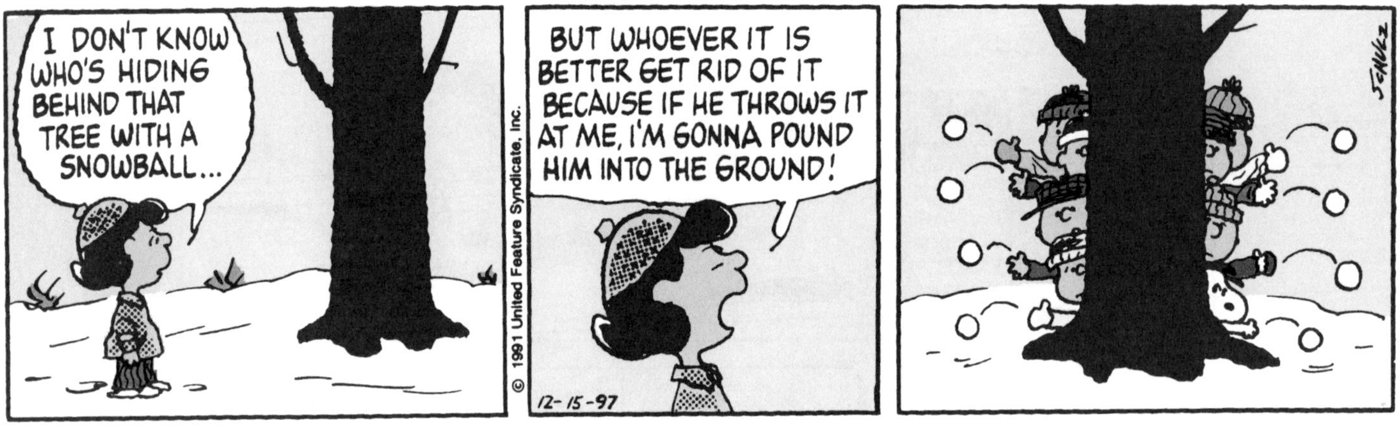
I DON'T KNOW WHO'S HIDING BEHIND THAT TREE WITH A SNOWBALL...
© 1991 United Feature Syndicate, Inc.
BUT WHOEVER IT IS BETTER GET RID OF IT BECAUSE IF HE THROWS IT AT ME, I'M GONNA POUND HIM INTO THE GROUND!
12-15-97
SCHULZ

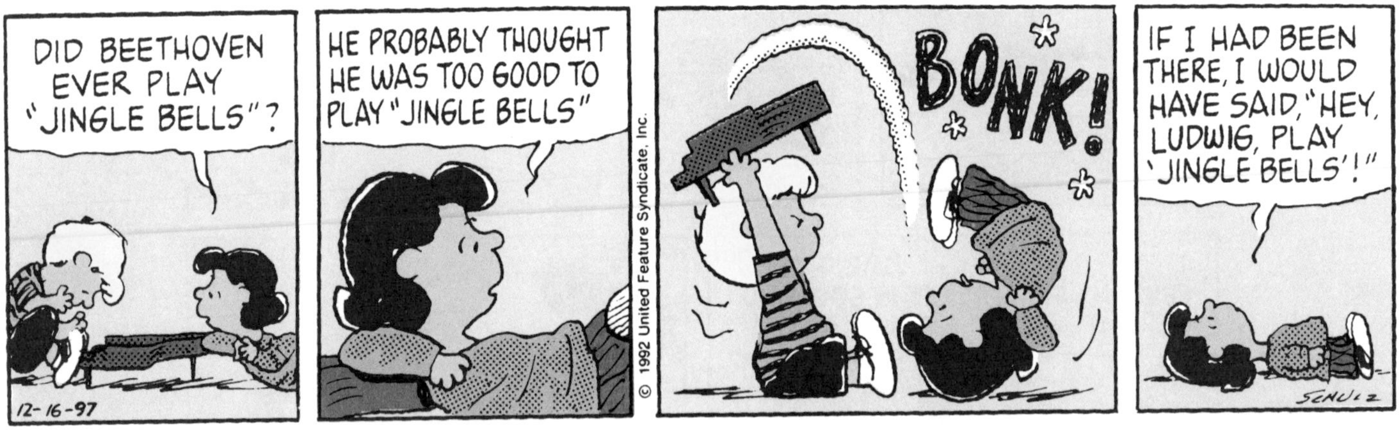
DID BEETHOVEN EVER PLAY "JINGLE BELLS"?
12-16-97
HE PROBABLY THOUGHT HE WAS TOO GOOD TO PLAY "JINGLE BELLS"
© 1992 United Feature Syndicate, Inc.
BONK!
IF I HAD BEEN THERE, I WOULD HAVE SAID, "HEY, LUDWIG, PLAY 'JINGLE BELLS'!"
SCHULZ

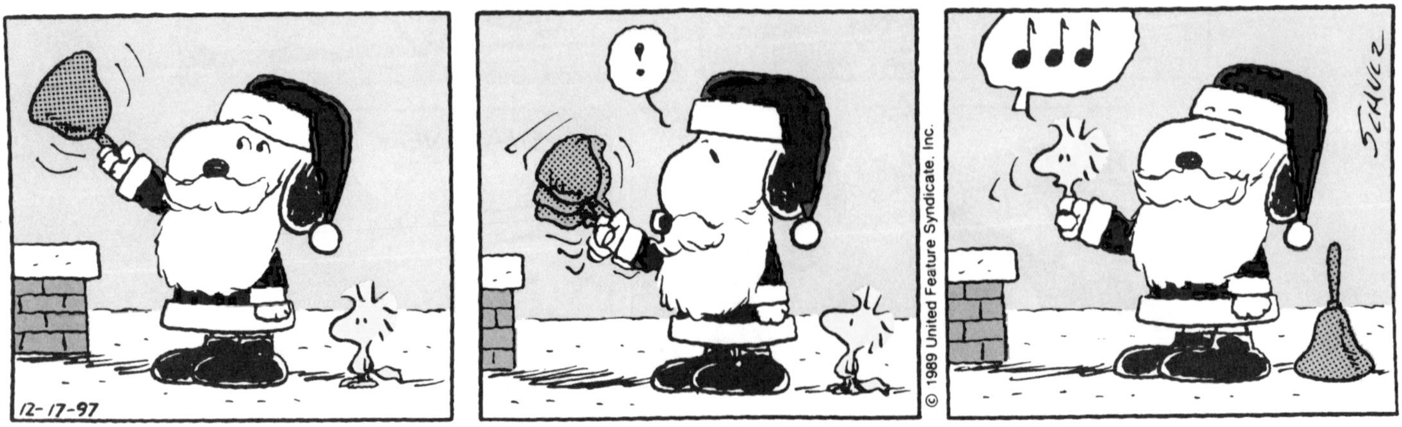
12-17-97
!
© 1989 United Feature Syndicate, Inc.
SCHULZ

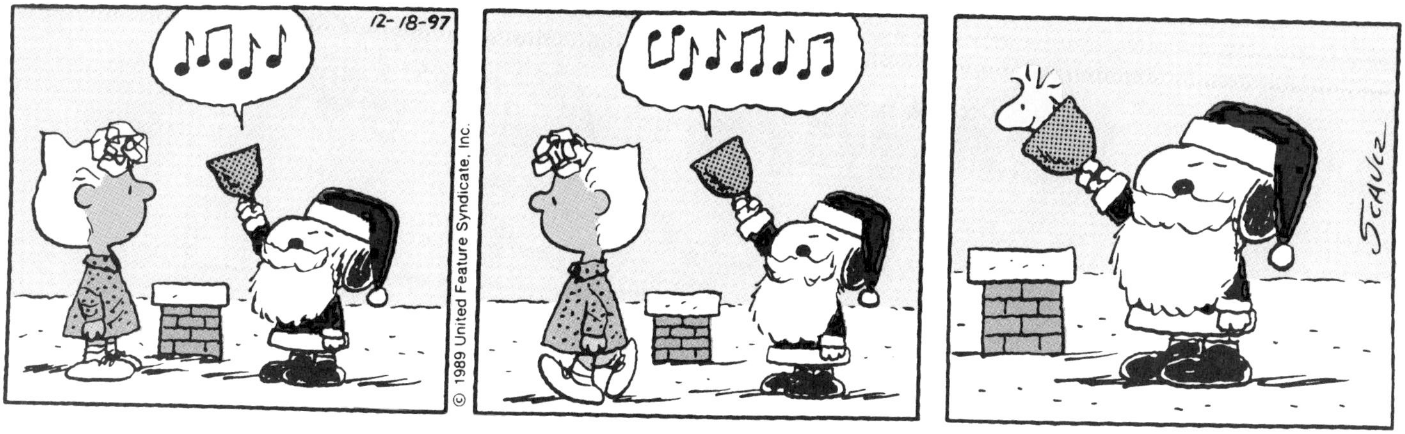
12-18-97
© 1989 United Feature Syndicate, Inc.

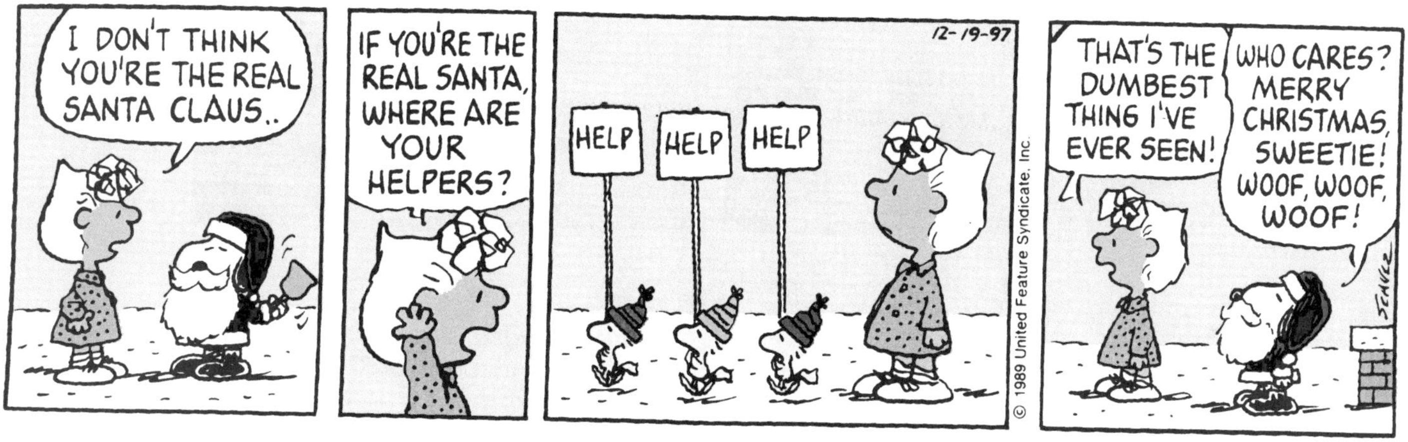
I DON'T THINK YOU'RE THE REAL SANTA CLAUS..
IF YOU'RE THE REAL SANTA, WHERE ARE YOUR HELPERS?
12-19-97
HELP
HELP
HELP
© 1989 United Feature Syndicate, Inc.
THAT'S THE DUMBEST THING I'VE EVER SEEN!
WHO CARES? MERRY CHRISTMAS, SWEETIE! WOOF, WOOF, WOOF!

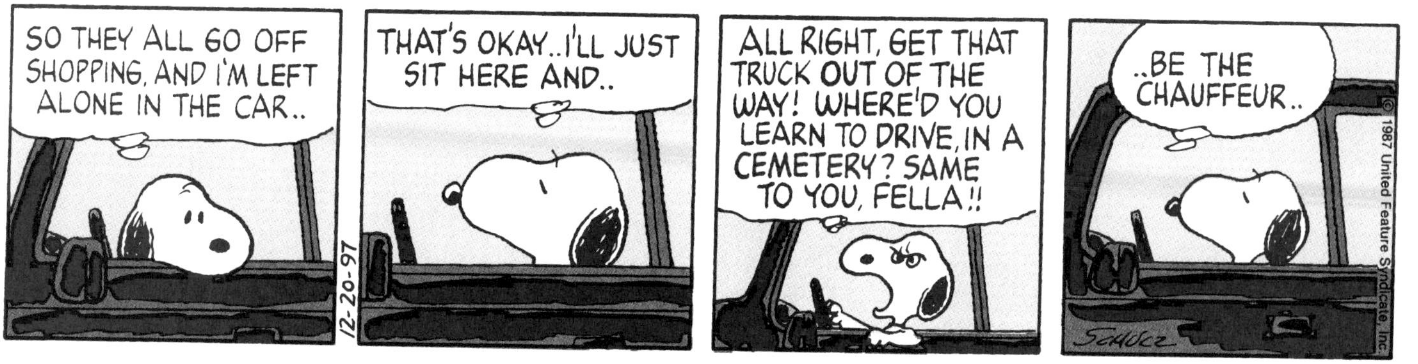
SO THEY ALL GO OFF SHOPPING, AND I'M LEFT ALONE IN THE CAR..
12-20-97
THAT'S OKAY..I'LL JUST SIT HERE AND..
ALL RIGHT, GET THAT TRUCK OUT OF THE WAY! WHERE'D YOU LEARN TO DRIVE, IN A CEMETERY? SAME TO YOU, FELLA!!
..BE THE CHAUFFEUR..
© 1987 United Feature Syndicate, Inc.

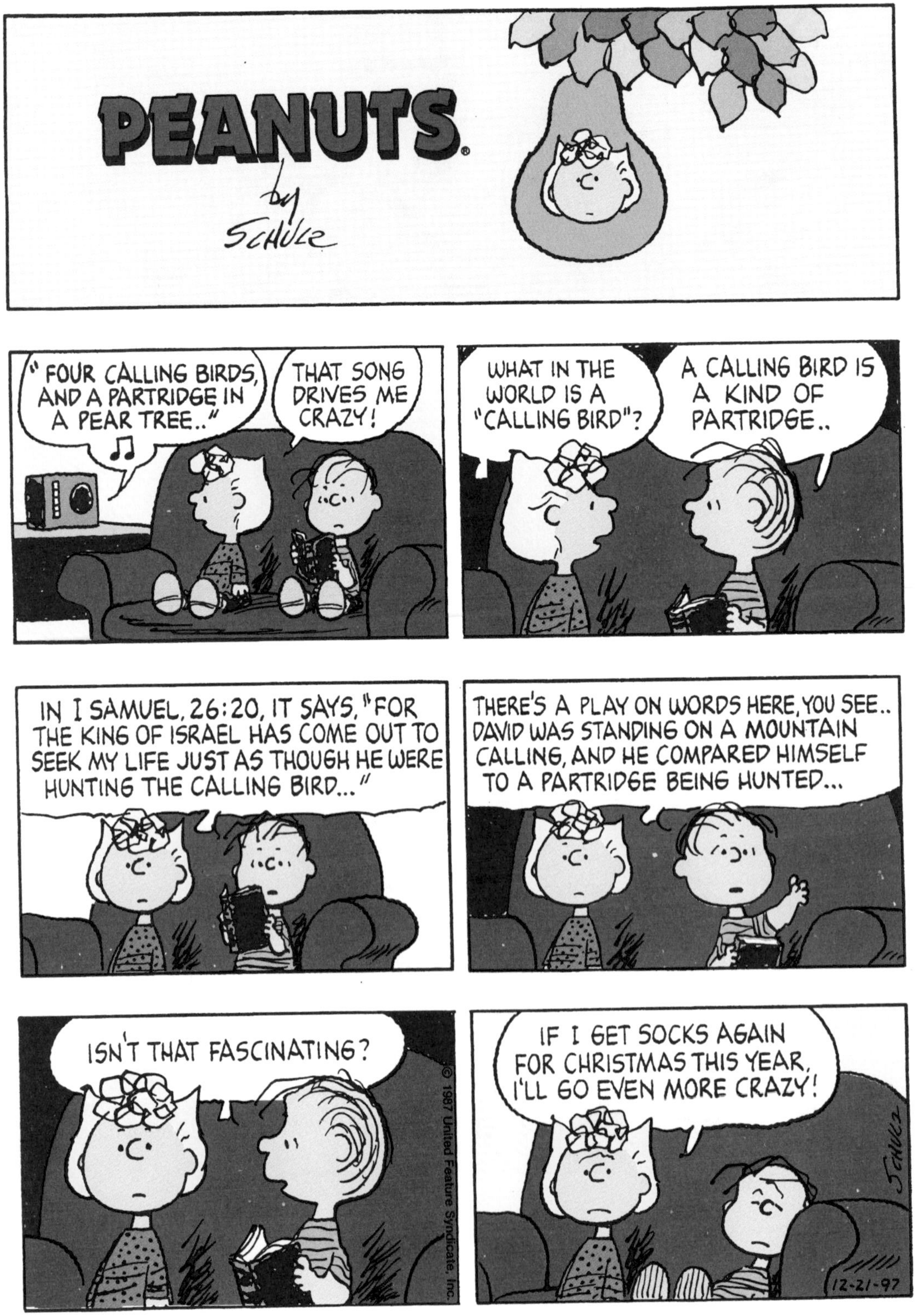
PEANUTS
by Schulz
"FOUR CALLING BIRDS, AND A PARTRIDGE IN A PEAR TREE.."
THAT SONG DRIVES ME CRAZY!
WHAT IN THE WORLD IS A "CALLING BIRD"?
A CALLING BIRD IS A KIND OF PARTRIDGE..
IN I SAMUEL, 26:20, IT SAYS, "FOR THE KING OF ISRAEL HAS COME OUT TO SEEK MY LIFE JUST AS THOUGH HE WERE HUNTING THE CALLING BIRD..."
THERE'S A PLAY ON WORDS HERE, YOU SEE.. DAVID WAS STANDING ON A MOUNTAIN CALLING, AND HE COMPARED HIMSELF TO A PARTRIDGE BEING HUNTED...
ISN'T THAT FASCINATING?
© 1987 United Feature Syndicate, Inc.
IF I GET SOCKS AGAIN FOR CHRISTMAS THIS YEAR, I'LL GO EVEN MORE CRAZY!
SCHULZ
12-21-97

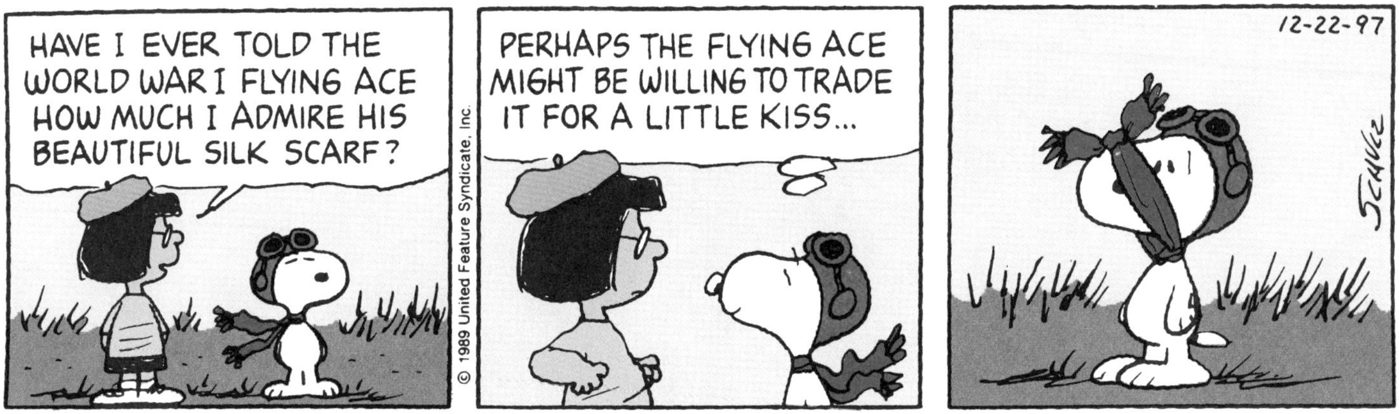
HAVE I EVER TOLD THE WORLD WAR I FLYING ACE HOW MUCH I ADMIRE HIS BEAUTIFUL SILK SCARF?
© 1989 United Feature Syndicate, Inc.
PERHAPS THE FLYING ACE MIGHT BE WILLING TO TRADE IT FOR A LITTLE KISS...
12-22-97
SCHULZ

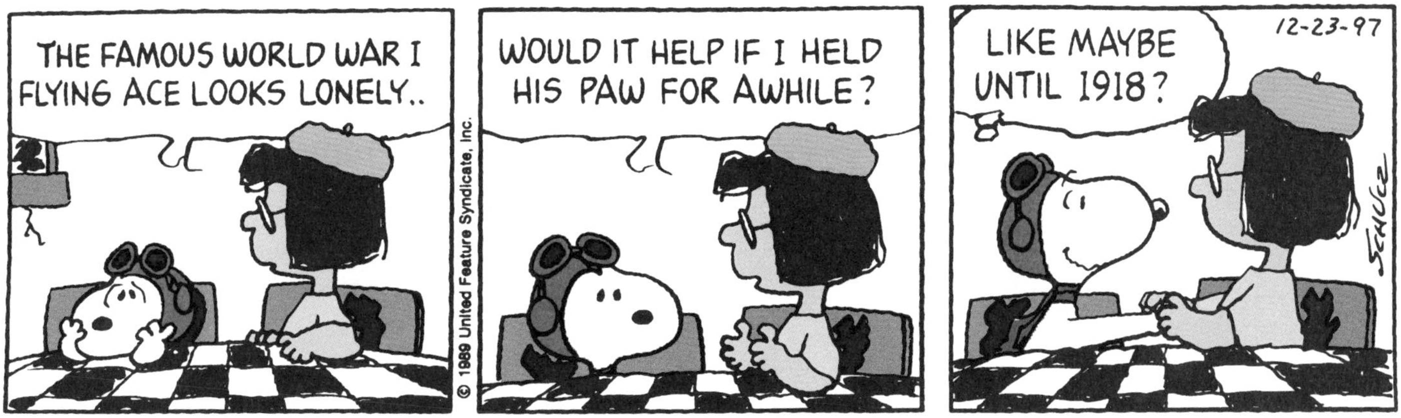
THE FAMOUS WORLD WAR I FLYING ACE LOOKS LONELY..
© 1989 United Feature Syndicate, Inc.
WOULD IT HELP IF I HELD HIS PAW FOR AWHILE?
LIKE MAYBE UNTIL 1918?
12-23-97
SCHULZ

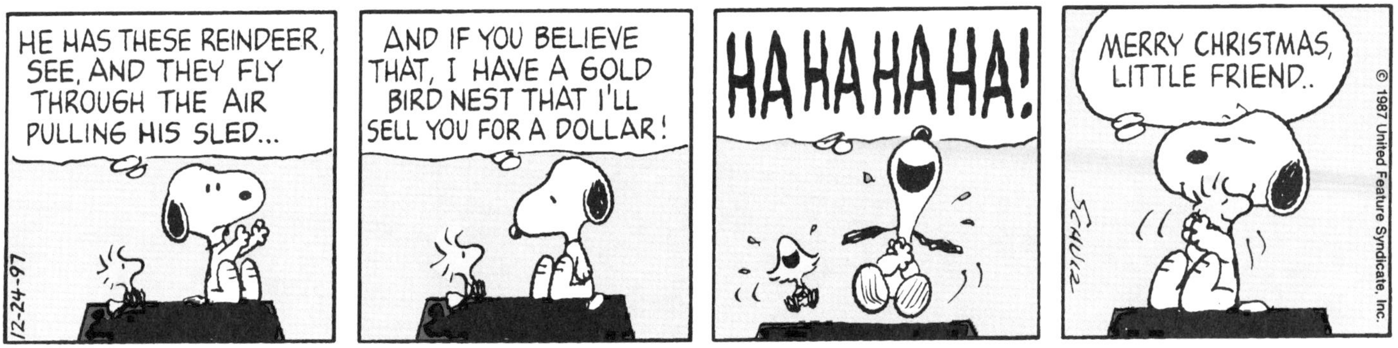
HE HAS THESE REINDEER, SEE, AND THEY FLY THROUGH THE AIR PULLING HIS SLED...
12-24-97
AND IF YOU BELIEVE THAT, I HAVE A GOLD BIRD NEST THAT I'LL SELL YOU FOR A DOLLAR!
HAHAHAHA!
SCHULZ
MERRY CHRISTMAS, LITTLE FRIEND..
© 1987 United Feature Syndicate, Inc.

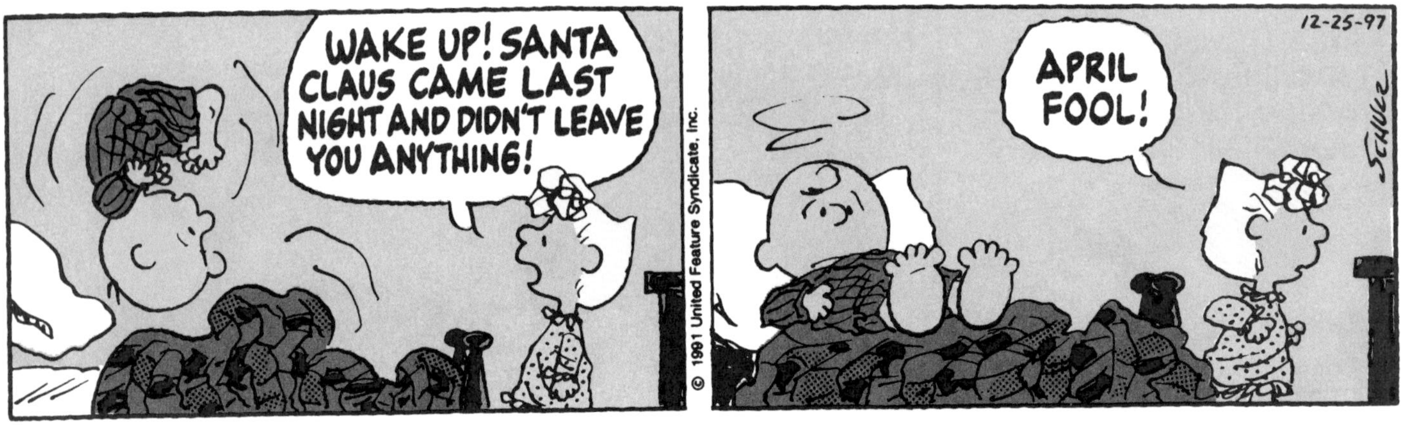
WAKE UP! SANTA CLAUS CAME LAST NIGHT AND DIDN'T LEAVE YOU ANYTHING!
© 1991 United Feature Syndicate, Inc.
12-25-97
APRIL FOOL!
SCHULZ

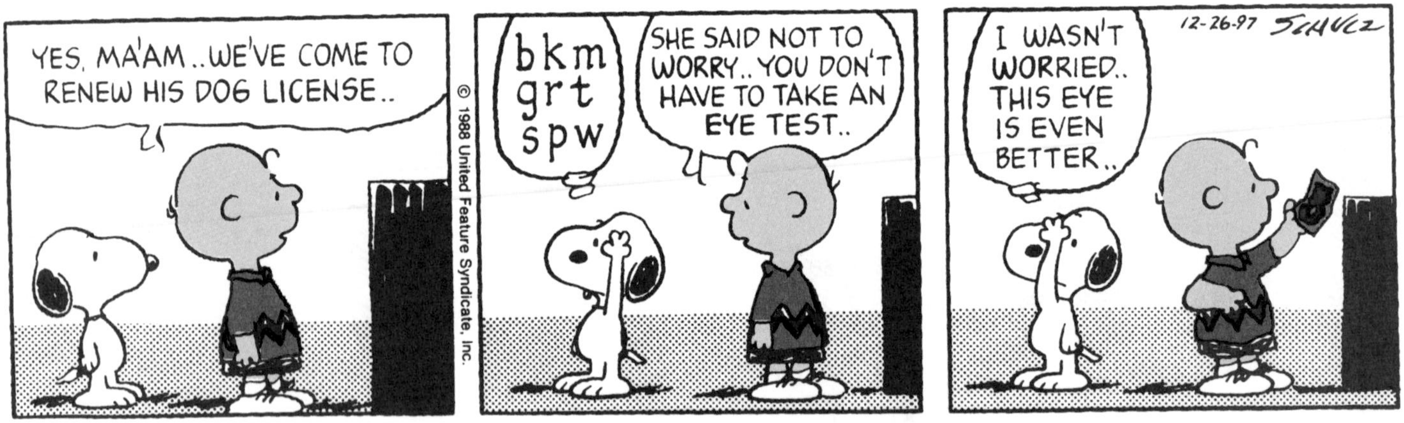
YES, MA'AM..WE'VE COME TO RENEW HIS DOG LICENSE..
© 1988 United Feature Syndicate, Inc.
bkm grt spw
SHE SAID NOT TO WORRY.. YOU DON'T HAVE TO TAKE AN EYE TEST..
12-26-97 SCHULZ
I WASN'T WORRIED.. THIS EYE IS EVEN BETTER..

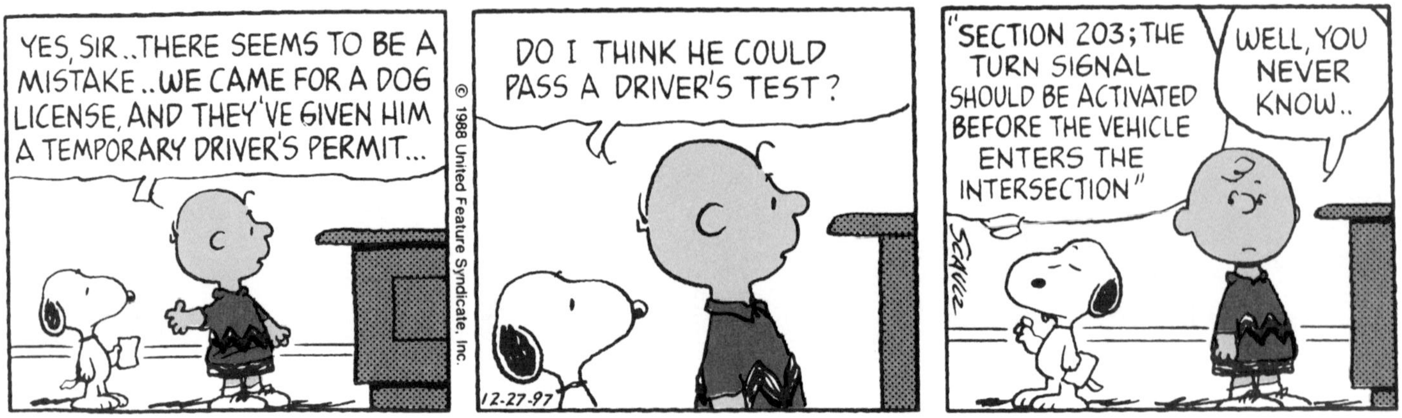
YES, SIR..THERE SEEMS TO BE A MISTAKE..WE CAME FOR A DOG LICENSE, AND THEY'VE GIVEN HIM A TEMPORARY DRIVER'S PERMIT...
© 1988 United Feature Syndicate, Inc.
DO I THINK HE COULD PASS A DRIVER'S TEST?
12-27-97
"SECTION 203; THE TURN SIGNAL SHOULD BE ACTIVATED BEFORE THE VEHICLE ENTERS THE INTERSECTION"
WELL, YOU NEVER KNOW..
SCHULZ

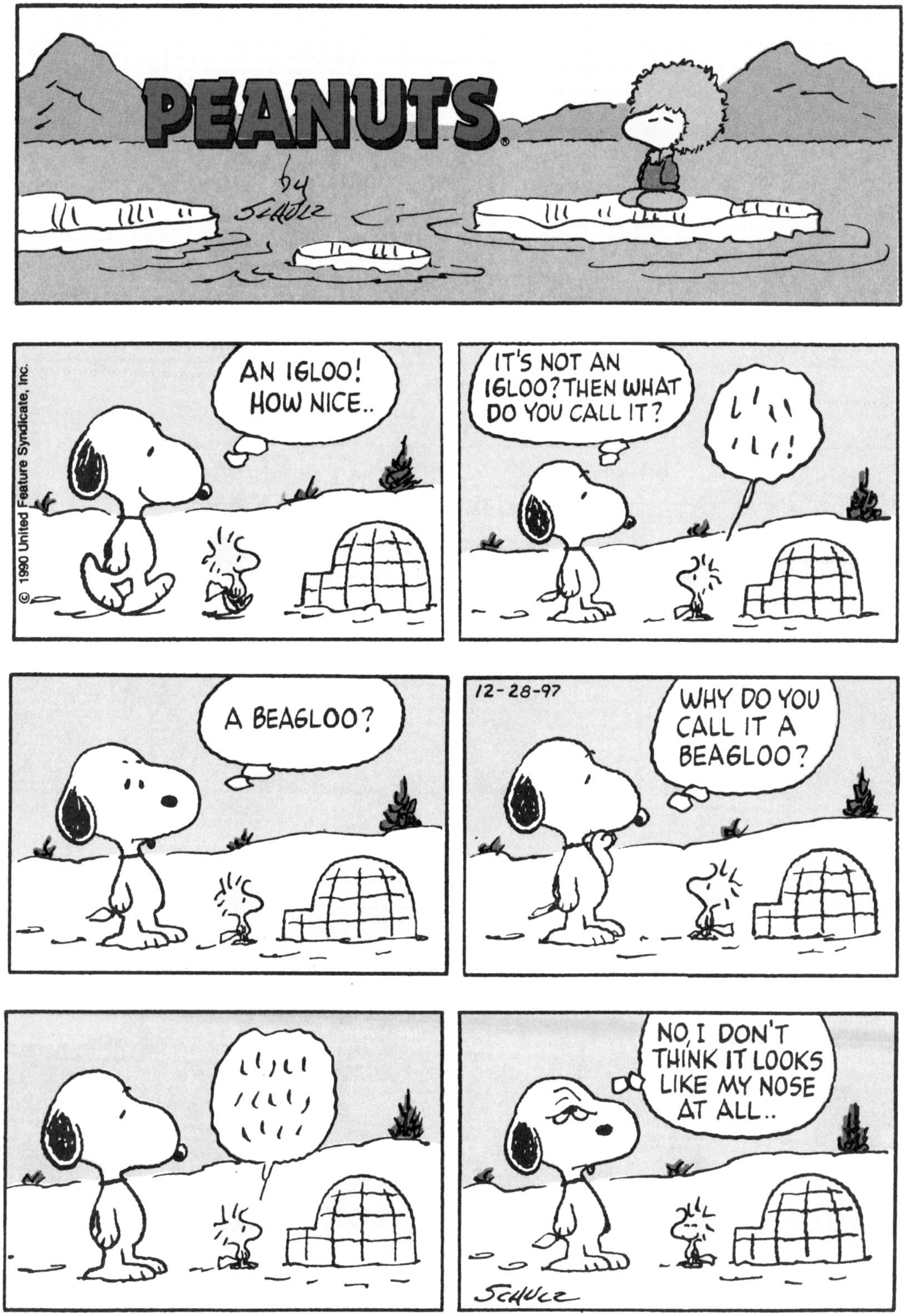
PEANUTS
by SCHULZ
© 1990 United Feature Syndicate, Inc.
AN IGLOO! HOW NICE..
IT'S NOT AN IGLOO? THEN WHAT DO YOU CALL IT?
A BEAGLOO?
12-28-97
WHY DO YOU CALL IT A BEAGLOO?
NO, I DON'T THINK IT LOOKS LIKE MY NOSE AT ALL..
SCHULZ

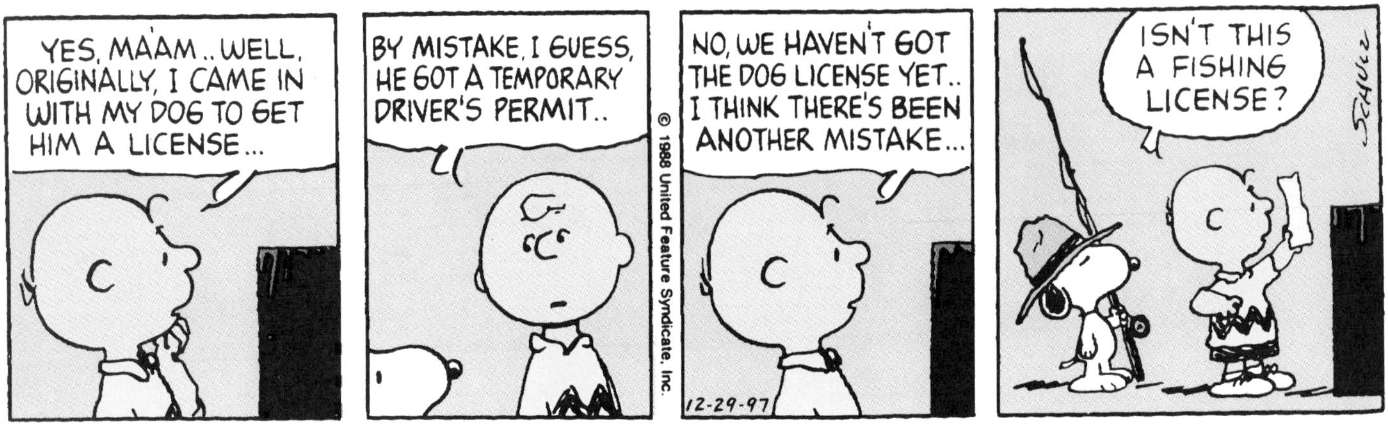
YES, MA'AM.. WELL, ORIGINALLY, I CAME IN WITH MY DOG TO GET HIM A LICENSE...
BY MISTAKE, I GUESS, HE GOT A TEMPORARY DRIVER'S PERMIT..
© 1988 United Feature Syndicate, Inc.
NO, WE HAVEN'T GOT THE DOG LICENSE YET.. I THINK THERE'S BEEN ANOTHER MISTAKE...
12-29-97
ISN'T THIS A FISHING LICENSE?
SCHULZ

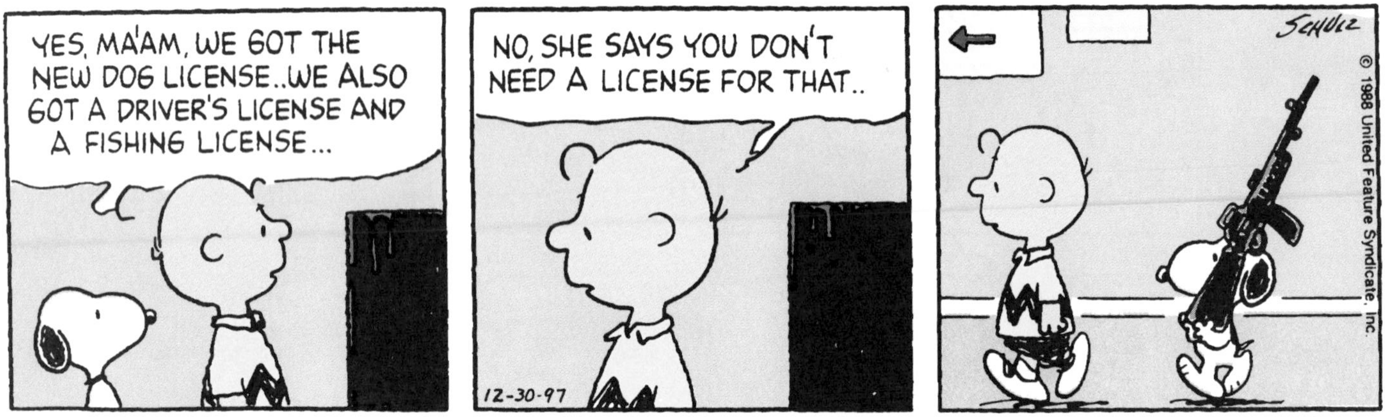
YES, MA'AM, WE GOT THE NEW DOG LICENSE..WE ALSO GOT A DRIVER'S LICENSE AND A FISHING LICENSE...
NO, SHE SAYS YOU DON'T NEED A LICENSE FOR THAT..
12-30-97
SCHULZ
© 1988 United Feature Syndicate, Inc.

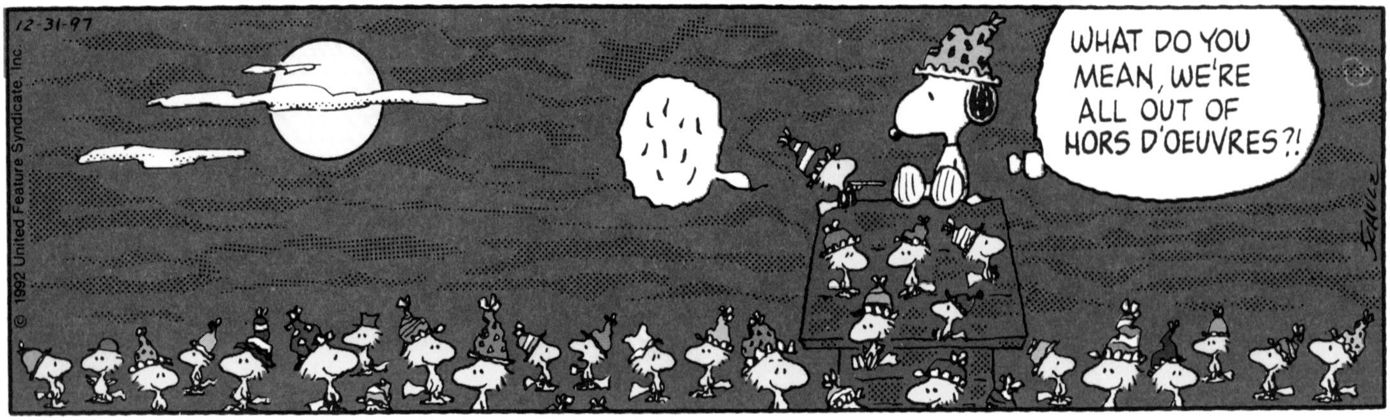
12-31-97
© 1992 United Feature Syndicate, Inc.
WHAT DO YOU MEAN, WE'RE ALL OUT OF HORS D'OEUVRES?!
SCHULZ